The Global Political
Economy of Food

The Global Political Economy of Food

Edited by
Raymond F. Hopkins
and
Donald J. Puchala

58470

The University of Wisconsin Press

The University of Wisconsin Press
Box 1379, Madison, Wisconsin 53701

The University of Wisconsin Press, Ltd.
1 Gower St., London, WC1E 6HA, England

First printing

Printed in the United States of America
ISBN 0-299-07750-0 cloth, 0-299-07754-3 paper
LC 78-65012

The Global Political Economy of Food reproduces the contents of the Summer 1978 issue of
International Organization (Vol. 32, No. 3), sponsored by the World Peace Foundation, edited at
Stanford University, and published by the University of Wisconsin Press, © 1978 by the Regents
of the University of Wisconsin System.

To

Carol

Jeanne

Mark

Susan

Kathryn

Elizabeth

Madeline

Contents

Part IV. Considerations for Future Policy

Preface

This volume was conceived in the aftermath of the international concern about world food shortages in 1973–74. In April, 1975, at a meeting of the Board of Editors of *International Organization,* a special issue was authorized to examine "world food institutions." In August, 1975, work on planning the volume began. From the beginning our understanding of "institutions" and the range of relevant world food concerns has been quite broad.

As world food production has returned to normal and above normal in recent years, food supplies have accumulated and the priority accorded food issues has declined. This shift in public attention away from global food "crises" has encouraged authors to address the chronic problems of the global food system and its institutions. The completed volume takes the shortage period of 1973–74 as a warning, but focuses not merely on potential shortages but also on deficiencies that are inherent in the current system, even when crops are good and overall supplies ample.

Early chapters were prepared for 1976 meetings of the International Studies Association and the American Political Science Association. Papers were circulated for a conference at Airlie House in April, 1977, on Global Food Interdependence. Based on criticisms and suggestions at this conference and on earlier reviews by colleagues, the authors worked together to create a volume with a common intellectual focus—the sources of and possible solutions to problems in global food systems. This focus led us to investigate various principles of the contemporary institutional framework shaping world production and distribution practices, which we refer to as the *global food regime.* Food problems are analyzed in terms of regional and national actors, structural features, diplomatic patterns and policies for change.

This volume was made possible through the financial support of the Rockefeller Foundation and the Office of External Research of the Department of State. In particular, the editors are grateful to John Stremlau and Pio Uliassi, of the Rockefeller Foundation and Department of State respectively, for their advice and assistance in bringing this volume to fruition. Authors and editors benefited from preliminary papers by Steven Green, Ray Goldberg, Raymond Hopkins, Dale Hathaway and Robert Tetro and the comments and suggestions of Hayward Alker, Jr., Larry Krause, and Gene Skolnikoff. The final editorial review committee, appointed by the board of *International Organization* for this volume, further helped us refine and improve the volume. We are indebted to Ernst Haas, Roger Hansen, Peter Katzenstein and Robert Keohane for their efforts in carefully reading and recommending changes in the papers. Robert Keohane, especially, as editor of *International Organization* has been a valuable and hard-working collaborator in helping shape the volume.

The editors have also benefited from suggestions and comments of many others: our colleagues at Columbia and Swarthmore, Joan Spero, Howard Pack and J. Roland Pennock; individuals knowledgeable in dealing with various facets of American or international food concerns, Barnett Baron, Eric Eckholm, John Ferch, Lincoln Gordon, Catherine Gwin, Ronald Herring, Barbara Huddleston, Carol Lancaster, Edwin Martin, Donald Paarlberg, Roger Porter, Fred Sanderson, Tom Saylor, Lyle Schertz, Nevin Schrimshaw, Henry Shue, Larry Witt, Sterling Wortman, Regina Ziegler; and from others who were participants at the Global Food Interdependence Conference. Rapporteurs of the conference—Joseph Gavin, Steven Mink, David Sacks and Jane Staveley—also assisted us in other ways, including compiling the bibliography and glossary for the volume; Ellen Hanak helped in the final revisions of these two volume features. Finally, we are happy to acknowledge the editorial and secretarial services of Betsy Bain from the early stages of the volume and for typing assistance of Helen Di Feliciantonio, Georgia Kanary, Ritva Poom, Mary Sivak and Tricia Whitehurst.

Raymond F. Hopkins and Donald J. Puchala

I. Overview

1

Perspectives on the
International Relations of Food

Raymond F. Hopkins and Donald J. Puchala

The international system of production, distribution and consumption of food is managed by states, corporations and international organizations. International organizations play minor roles in the food regime, principally as arenas for policy coordination among state bureaucracies and as agents for modest multilateral programs. All of these actors work within the framework of a set of norms, rules and practices that constitutes a global food regime. Currently, the regime is undergoing change. Growing demand for food, tighter connections among markets, and greater reliance on technology have increased the importance of international adjustments. American preponderance in shaping regime features and insuring food security through reserves has declined. The dramatic price rises and rationing of international food supplies that occurred during the "crisis" of 1973–74 exposed serious deficiencies in the existing regime. At least five world food problems—potential shortages, instability, insecurity, low productivity and malnutrition—continue as real or potential threats. To solve these problems the norms of the current regime that has existed since World War II are seriously under challenge. Re-evaluation and reform of the major principles characterizing the food regime are needed.

Securing adequate food is one of the oldest problems confronting political institutions.[1] Historically this intimate connection between food and politics has emerged in diverse forms. From the "minimal government" of nomadic herdsmen and hunting-gathering peoples and the complex despotisms found in societies relying on

Raymond F. Hopkins is Professor of Political Science at Swarthmore College. Donald J. Puchala is Professor of Political Science at Columbia University.

[1]This paper is adapted from revised versions of "Global Food Regimes: Overcoming Hunger and Poverty," prepared by Raymond Hopkins for the 1980s Project of the Council on Foreign Relations. The authors wish to thank Edwin Martin, Lyle Schertz, Dale Hathaway, I. M. Destler, Eugene Skolnikoff, Hayward Alker, Lawrence Krause, and a host of other food experts and CFR staff members for their insights and comments offered during various phases of the preparation of this chapter.

irrigation to the elaborate regulations for food growing and marketing in most contemporary states, the procuring of food has been a central factor shaping political patterns and, in most cases, encouraging substantial government intervention.[2] It is small wonder then that as food systems have become increasingly global, with national markets linked together and technology diffusing rapidly, demands for solving food problems have shifted to the international arena. Unfortunately, in recent years the contemporary international system has been unable to deal effectively with global food problems.

This essay will discuss some of the most notable of these inadequacies. In addition, we will introduce a set of concepts for describing and explaining what will be termed the international relations of food. Guided by the conceptual framework designed in this chapter, this volume of analytical essays will explore the international relations of food, with particular emphasis upon the capacities of national and international institutions involved in promoting the production, distribution and consumption of basic foodstuffs among the earth's peoples.

Global food problems

It hardly needs saying that the stimulus to the efforts which produced this volume is the consensus among editors and authors that there are global food problems. Problems, in the sense we use the term, are conditions of production, distribution or consumption that are sufficiently undesirable to at least some actors in the system that they initiate calls for change. It should be noted that there is a lively debate among experts over the dimensions and severity of world food problems. The controversy stems from many sources including differences in analysts' disciplinary training and ideological perspective, as well as from the varying data they call upon, the different forecasting and other methodological techniques they employ, and from crop conditions prevailing at the moment of analysis. In the judgments that follow, our approach has been to consider the literature carefully, to see points of consensus among otherwise contending writers, to evaluate others' conclusions and to frame our own arguments in the light of the best systematic evidence. Our analysis steers a rather unspectacular middle course between the positions of those who unrealistically minimize food problems and those who view them as so severe as to conclude that world-wide starvation will soon be upon us.

We suggest that five important food problems exist. First, we face the threat of *chronic food shortages* in some regions, most notably in South Asia and Africa, and their attendant economic, political and human consequences. Second, current arrangements lead to *undesirable instability in supply* bound up with unreasonable fluctuations in prices, unpredictable markets, and undependable trade flows. Third, certain countries encounter the problem of *security of food imports,* especially

---

[2]Lucy Mair, *Primitive Government* (Baltimore: Penguin, 1962); Karl A. Wittfogel, *Oriental Despotism* (New Haven: Yale University Press, 1957).

where imports represent either important elements in national standards of living, or, more crucially, where they represent hedges against starvation. A fourth problem results from the *low productivity of agriculture* and related poverty in many less developed countries. Such conditions represent a barrier to both food production and general economic development as well as a costly waste of human resources. Fifth, there is *chronic malnutrition,* especially among underprivileged groups and classes in certain countries and regions.

Each of the five problems is significant and hence deserving of extended analysis. For this reason we have asked several of our authors to discuss particular dimensions of the global food problem. Nicholson and Esseks, for example, deal with problems of underproduction and food scarcity in less developed countries. Seevers and Johnson each address the problem of market and price instability. Paarlberg takes up the issue of import security and studies characteristic responses to it. In separate articles, Christensen and Austin analyze problems of rural poverty and malnutrition.

The five global food problems are obviously interrelated. Each is a cause of one or several of the others, and all lead to or follow from fundamental distortions of supply or demand for food. What makes the interrelatedness of global food problems analytically perplexing is that various elements of distributional distortion affect different countries and populations in different ways, sometimes at different times. As a result the universality of the food system tends to be blurred. Several of the essays in this volume are addressed to the interrelatedness of the dimensions of the world food problem. Destler shows how the very multi-dimensionality of world food problems creates a complex and at times contradictory policy process as the United States Government deals with food and agricultural issues. Nau examines how global considerations further complicate food policy making and lead to a multifaceted and multimotivated international diplomacy. Austin explores problems of international institutional proliferation and the consequent problems of coordination that follow as the interrelatedness of food affairs defies attempts to organize internationally.

The truism underlined in this volume is that no single or simple policy, indeed no unilateral one, can solve all of the global problems of food. Nonetheless, as several of the authors individually suggest, and as the anthology as a whole implies, practicable steps toward coordinating national and international action can significantly alleviate the severity of world food problems.

As preview and overview to more detailed analyses in the essays that follow, let us look more closely at each of the problems on the agenda of world food diplomacy.

Food shortages

Food shortages in recent years were responsible for the dramatic increases in the price of grain and other basic foodstuffs in the early 1970s and for heightened domestic and international political interest in food problems. The shortages that developed between 1972 and 1974 were particularly severe due to the convergence of an extraordinary cluster of causal factors. These factors include unfavorable weather conditions in major grain producing regions, shifts in American and Canadian reserve policies, unprecedented Soviet interventions into grain import markets, high fertilizer prices, the world energy crisis, and a failure in the Peruvian anchovy catch. Analysts tend to refer to the years 1973–1974 as a period of "scarcity crisis" for the global food system, and several of the contributors to this volume use these years as a baseline for their analyses. The term *crisis* carries emotional loading and using it too frequently tends to destroy its analytical relevance. Therefore, we do not insist that readers accept that the years 1973–1974 were crisis years in world food affairs. It should be understood, however, that they were years of extreme and rapid change in global food supply and price conditions. Furthermore, they were dangerous years because food supplies had dwindled to the point where major famines would have occurred if conditions had deteriorated further. The gravity of the situation as it developed between 1972 and 1975 is captured rather dramatically in two sets of indices — (1) grain export prices, and (2) reserve stocks of grains. These are reported in Tables 1 and 2.

Note in the tables how prices began their steep rise and total reserves began their deterioration in 1972. Although some American idle land was put into production in 1973 to meet the situation, prices continued to climb and total reserves dwindled. However, the key factor affecting the price at which grains moved internationally in this period is not the total working stocks in the world, but rather the stocks of exporting countries. Many large importing countries maintain working stocks that are practically never available for export and hence not directly a factor in international market prices. Therefore, it is the stocks of the exporting countries that both provide the security backup for world food needs and constitute the major variable affecting prices and control over markets.

Table 1   Average wheat export prices, 1968–1976[1]

Dollars/bushel (60 lbs.) averaged for grades and varieties

Year	United States	Canada[2]	Australia[3]
1968	1.69	1.96	1.42
1969	1.67	1.89	1.38
1970	1.74	1.71	1.33
1971	1.69	1.70	1.40
1972	1.86	1.89	1.54
1973	3.55	4.37	2.77
1974	5.16	6.22	3.72
1975	4.79	5.52	3.11
1976[4]	3.98	4.34	2.96

1. Source: United Nations, *Monthly Bulletin of Statistics,* Vol. XXX, No. 12, (December, 1970), p. 165.
2. Canadian dollars.
3. Australian dollars.
4. Figures are for June, 1976.

Table 2 World food reserves, 1961–67 to 1976

Year	Reserve stocks of grain[1]	Grain equivalent of idled US cropland	Total reserves	Reserves as days of annual grain consumption
	(MILLION METRIC TONS)			
1961–67	151	70	220	89
1968	144	61	205	71
1969	159	73	232	85
1970	188	71	259	89
1971	168	41	209	71
1972	130	78	208	69
1973	148	24	172	55
1974	108	0	108	33
1975	111	0	111	35
1976	116	0	116	43
1977	171	0	171	48[2]

Source: Lester Brown, *The Politics and Responsibility of the North American Breadbasket,* World Watch Paper #2, Worldwatch Institute, October, 1975, p. 8; USDA, *Foreign Agricultural Circular* (September 19, 1977), p. 2.
1. Based on carry-over stocks of grain at beginning of crop year in individual countries for year shown. Stocks include those held by both exporting and importing countries.
2. Authors' estimate.

Comparing Table 3 with Table 1 indicates that the price of wheat mounted in 1973 and 1974 as supplies tightened and, most dramatically, *as the stocks of exporters declined.*

Table 3 Wheat in world trade

WHEAT PAST CARRYOVERS (MILLION METRIC TONS)

Year	Exporting countries beginning stock	Working[1] stocks	Total export use	Beginning stock as % of total use
Av. 60/61– 70/71	42.7	10.4	68.3	.64
71/72	44.4	12.6	75.5	.59
72/73	41.4	12.8	88.3	.47
73/74	22.7	15.0	82.3	.28
74/75	19.8	14.0	80.5	.25
75/76	22.3	13.7	87.1	.26

Source: International Food Policy Research Institute, communication with Barbara Huddleston.
1. Stocks committed to specific future uses and hence unavailable for alternative allocations.

World prices became most extreme in 1974 (the first half of 1974 to be exact)[3] when they peaked at postwar highs, nearly four times above 1968 levels. Although world reserves fell to a two-decade low—where the world held only thirty-three days consumption of grain in storage—actual stock scarcity conditions among exporters became less severe by the end of 1974 and succeeding years. But, as of 1976, world reserves (Table 2) were still critically low. There had been no replacement of importers' reserves and the import-dependent world was still eating largely from month to month. During 1977, with production at or above trend for the second year, surpluses began to build, especially among exporters. But how these will affect the per capita food available globally, currently or in the future, is uncertain.

The years 1972–75, then, are benchmarks in the analysis of global food problems. By hindsight, their greatest significance lies in the fact that they prompted a long overdue and sober analysis of the global food system. It must be borne in mind, however, that regardless of the apparent uniqueness of contributing factors, shortages in 1973 and 1974 fundamentally reflected the global growth in demand for food stimulated by rapidly expanding population. Scarcities in export-import markets in 1973 and 1974 were extraordinary only as regards their unprecedented severity. Improvements in supply conditions since 1975 by no means suggest that food scarcity is on the way to being overcome, either in world trade or in poor countries.

Tables 4 and 5 depict some longer-run developments in the global food system. They dramatically document growing demands upon the stocks of food exporters as

Table 4 The changing pattern of world grain trade, 1934–1938 to 1976[1]

Region	*1934–38*	*1948–52*	*1960*	*1970*	*1972–73*	*1976*[2]
			(MILLION METRIC TONS)			
North America	5	23	39	56	89	94
Latin America	9	1	0	4	−3	−3
Western Europe	−24	−22	−25	−30	−18	−17
E. Europe & USSR	5	—	0	0	−26	−27
Africa	1	0	−2	−5	−1	−10
Asia[3]	2	−6	−17	−37	−38	−47
Australia & N.Z.	3	3	6	12	7	8

Note: Positive numbers indicate net exports; negative numbers indicate net imports.
1. Figures derived from Lester Brown, Table 1.2, p. 11, and *Potential Implications of Trends in World Population, Food Production and Climate,* OPR-401, United States Central Intelligence Agency, Washington, August, 1974, p. 15.
2. Preliminary estimates of fiscal year data.
3. Includes Japan and Asian Communist Countries.

[3]FAO, *FAO Commodity Review and Outlook 1975–76* (FAO: Rome, 1976), pp. 8–9.

Table 5   Net cereal deficits in less developed regions[1]

(MILLION METRIC TONS)

Region	Actual aver. 1969–71	Actual 1974–75	Projected[2] 1990
Asia	8.3	15.1[4]	41.2[4]
N. Africa/Middle East	7.9	12.0	29.7
Sub-Sahara Africa	1.5	2.1	23.9
Latin America	(1.0)[3]	4.2	(8.4)
Total	16.7	33.4	86.4

Source: Based on data presented in, *Meeting Food Needs in the Developing World,* International Food Policy Research Institute, Research Report #1, (Washington: February, 1976), p. 27; and "Food Needs of Developing Countries," Nathan Koffsky, Annex, April, 1977 (mimeo, IFPRI).
1. Figures represent net deficits—i.e., larger gross deficits minus the predicted surpluses of potential exporting countries in the region.
2. Projected on the basis of 1960–1974 production trend in cereals which averaged 2.5% per year; consumption projected on the basis of assumed population growth, income growth and income elasticities of demand for food grain and feed grain. Income assumptions that produced the projections in this table reflect "low growth" variants (between 1.5 and 2%/year); if higher economic growth occurred, the projected demand and the consequent size of the deficits would be even larger (unless *growth* in production increased, growth already higher than in developed countries).
3. Parentheses indicate net surpluses for region. Argentina is projected to remain a net exporter and Brazil will become a net exporter by 1990.
4. Developing market economies only. Excludes Japan and Asian Communist Countries.

(1) an increasing number of countries have had to turn to imports to feed their populations and (2) the degree of external dependence of importing states has also increased during the last two decades.

The period from roughly 1950 to the present has witnessed a dramatic shift toward world dependency (especially Asian) upon North American grain surpluses, and this, hypothetically speaking, is projected to increase even more dramatically over the next ten to fifteen years.[4] We say "hypothetically" because projections of North American output suggest that export supplies will not be available to meet import demands to the end of the next decade, except at higher levels of prices (and correspondingly reduced demand), unless the growth of population and income in less developed countries is reduced and rates of growth in food production in these countries are raised dramatically. Even if high prices should push back demand, such a textbook "equilibrium" adjustment would not signal a solution to the problem of food scarcity. Indeed, it would most likely signal mounting hunger among the poorest people in the poorest countries.

In addition to the food import needs of the less developed world, projected to

[4]See USDA, *The World Food Situation and Prospects to 1985* (Washington: United States Department of Agriculture, 1974), and Lester Brown, "The World Food Prospect," *Science* (Dec. 12, 1975): 1053–59.

be at least 86.4 million tons in 1990 (Table 5), import demand over the next several years will be increased by the growing needs of customers such as Japan, Western Europe and the Soviet Union, unless these countries manage major strides in the direction of self-sufficiency. By a conservative estimate, needs in these areas will climb from 30-40 million tons in 1972–76 to the neighborhood of 45 million tons of food and feed grains in 1985.[5] It should also be noted that the "Asian" figures in Table 4 probably do not properly anticipate Mainland China's possible emergence as a major food importer. The expansion of China's agricultural production is estimated at between 2 and 2.69 percent per annum. While this rate has remained constant for several years and may be keeping pace with population growth, the instability of weather conditions in China would suggest at least some occasional severe shortages.

As noted, the growth of demand for foodstuffs world wide is largely attributable to rapid population growth, especially in Asia and Africa. But heightened demand is also linked to shifts toward higher protein diets in more affluent countries. In food deficit and poor countries population growth remains rapid, ranging from 2.0 to 3.5 percent per year. By contrast food production in these countries as a group has averaged 2.9 percent per year for the past fifteen years, and declined to 1.7 percent in the early 1970s.[6] For Bangladesh to be self-sufficient by 1990 her food production growth rate would need to rise from 1.5 percent to 4.5 percent for the next twelve years. Even if bumper crops produced in South Asia in 1975 and 1976 were to continue, scarcities in that region would be likely to persist. The dramatic 1975–77 rise in grain production in South Asia put the region back near its longer-run trend of yearly increase. But, even at this level, output in the region remains one to three percent below what is needed for meeting domestic economic demand for food. As expanding population threatens food supplies in poorer countries, consumers in industrialized countries, notably in the United States, Japan and Western Europe and recently in the Soviet Union, are buying more meat, thus inflating global demands for feed grains. As economic development progresses in parts of the Third World there is good reason to believe that further shifts to meat diets will occur, at least among the more privileged classes.

Given projected uncertainties in export supplies over the next decade, estimates of the capacities of deficit countries to increase domestic production become important and revealing. Unfortunately, many of these assessments are rather pessimistic for a variety of reasons. Some analysts, for example, cite the rising ecological problems that will accompany the use of more land for crops, and more intensive use of fertilizers and other agro-chemicals.[7] Others point out that diminishing returns from land-saving technologies are already being encountered, that marginal

---

[5]International Food Policy Research Institute, *Meeting Food Needs in the Developing World,* Research Report #1 (Washington: IFPRI, February 1976).

[6]Ibid., p. 13.

[7]Eric Eckholm, *Losing Ground: Environmental Stress and World Food Prospects* (New York: Norton, 1976).

land brought into production is frequently ruined by erosion or desertification in short order, and that rising relative prices for energy and other basic input resources point to a tightening supply situation (current oversupply notwithstanding). In addition, there has been a marked secular decline in funding of basic agronomic research in the United States and elsewhere, and some experts at least, suggest that this may have ushered in a levelling in the growth of output that is irreversible in the short run.[8] Recent initiatives in funding for agricultural development are encouraging, but their impact will be felt only over the longer run.

Despite the notable pessimism, however, it is fair to say that the preponderance of those who have looked into production problems in agriculture can identify adequate capacity in the years ahead to meet growing demands, including demands based on a desire for better diets. Notably, the capacity in question is the capacity of less developed countries to increase *domestic* production. But this will only be realized if research and technology gains are acted upon, if requisite investments are made, and if all other varieties of output-enhancing opportunity are grasped. For several less developed countries, including those discussed by Nicholson and Esseks, this means stemming declining rates of growth of domestic food production. For others it means pushing agricultural growth rates toward four or five or six percent per year. Even if such optimistic production potentials were approached, instability and occasional acute shortages are likely as long as sizable, readily distributable reserves do not exist.

Instability

Instability marked by extreme and erratic fluctuations in commodity prices has come to characterize and confuse international agricultural markets in recent years. Price instability tends to skew rewards from market participation toward those participants who can best afford to speculate. Conversely, it imposes penalities from market dependence on those who can least easily and least quickly adjust to fluctuation, namely lower income countries in general and lower income consumers in particular. Beyond adjustment effects, fluctuating world food prices also tend to wreak havoc with public and private economic planning, again, most notably in less developed countries where planners must estimate food costs in their national development plans.

One can look at the global food problem in terms of conditions of increasing scarcity, as we did in the previous section. But, in addition, one can also view the problem in terms of fluctuations or deviations around the basic trend lines. From the latter perspective what we observe is that global supplies of foodstuffs fluctuate markedly and erratically from year to year due mainly to changing weather conditions, variations in farmers' planting strategies, and government-promoted incen-

---

[8]James G. Horsfall and Charles R. Frink, ''Perspective on Agriculture's Future: Rising Costs — Rising Doubts'' (unpublished paper presented at Symposium on Limits to Growth, University of Connecticut, October 21, 1975).

Figure 1. Wheat area and production in the United States, Canada, Australia, and Argentinia

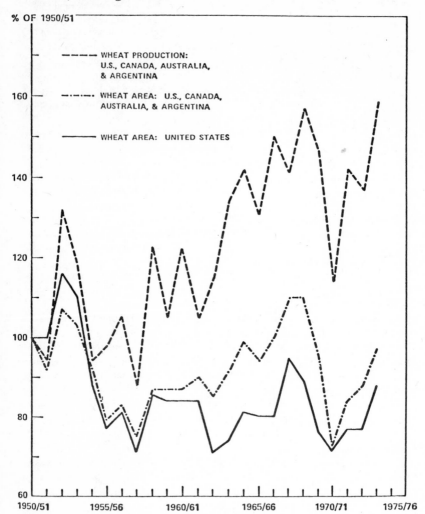

Source: USDA, *The World Food Situation and Prospects to 1985*, p. 23.

tives and disincentives. But until very recently, major fluctuations in production have prompted only minor changes in price due to the fact that during the 1950s and 1960s the United States and Canada accumulated large reserves in periods of surplus and were able to release them in periods of shortage, thus buffering price shifts. They acted in a duopolistic manner to manage international grain markets. But large public reserves no longer exist, and North American policies no longer encourage their accumulation. Therefore, unless policies and capacities change, we have a situation wherein even mild shifts (less than 2 percent) in world supply can and do bring about abrupt and extreme fluctuations in price. Figures 1 and 2, charting conditions in the wheat market, illustrate our points concerning changing relationships between shifts in supply and fluctuations in price. Observe in Figure 1 how outputs of wheat in the major exporting countries have varied in the past two decades (due in large measure to changes in planting related to variations in government support policies). By contrast, note in Figure 2 how prices remained relatively (indeed remarkably) stable through the 1950s and 1960s, despite the varying supply conditions, and then how they moved rapidly upward in the early 1970s. The price rise is accounted for by the elimination of publicly held reserves, aggravated by the onset of worldwide inflation and the tightening of international supplies discussed in the previous section. As already shown in Table 1, prices continued to fluctuate erratically from 1972/73 onward (jumping approximately 300 percent on the average between 1973 and 1974, when world production dropped by roughly 4 percent from trend, and then later dropping by approximately 20 percent

Figure 2. World Export Unit Values for Wheat, 1948–1976

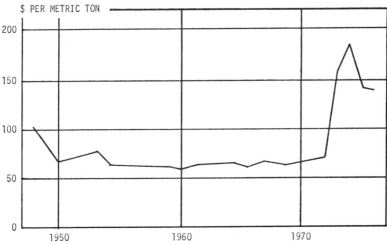

Source: USDA, *The World Food Situation and Prospects to 1985*, p. 25, for years 1948–1972; FAO, *FAO Commodity Review and Outlook, 1975–76*, Figure 1, p. 10, for years 1973–1976, estimated yearly average U.S. No. 2, for years 1973–1975, projected yearly average for 1976.

between 1975 and 1976, when world production increased by roughly 9 percent.[9] This, of course, is in great contrast to the 1950s and 1960s, in which increases or decreases in production of up to 35 percent in a country resulted in price changes of only two to three percent.

Price instability in international food markets exacerbates hunger in a number of ways. For one thing instability created by shortages can lead to "windfall" profits for those who control supplies, especially when prices rise far above levels needed to stimulate additional production. In such cases the extraordinary profits constitute largely a tax on consumers by producers. Within some states these excess gains are captured by grain dealers (private or public), credit agencies and other intermediaries rather than by farmers. When supplies are in excess, producers suffer as prices plummet. Marginal producers facing such market forces can be wiped out; supplies, moreover, may drop more than needed to adjust to the market and a new cycle of instability follows.

Second, and equally important, excessive fluctutations in commodity prices undermine planning, both for individual farmers and for import-dependent states. In selecting the most profitable (and efficient) crop or mix of crops a farmer must estimate the prices he is likely to receive. When these fluctuate widely, rational decisions about planting are impossible. Similarly, development planners in most developing countries can see their efforts rendered useless when food prices fluctuate widely, drawing off funds for development to pay for expensive imports or, when their countries are producers, excessively rewarding or punishing their rural sector. Government marketing boards and controls on agricultural prices through tariffs and domestic price supports are common buffers used in Europe and many developing countries to alleviate price instability by insulating producers, consumers or both from market extremities. Seevers, in his essay below, discusses such practices under the rubric "market separation." When such devices work well, they transfer the costs of adjusting to price fluctuations onto national treasuries, directly or ultimately at the expense of public policy goals or taxpayers' pocketbooks. In addition, evidence from less developed countries suggests that market intervention programs are poorly or corruptly managed. As a result, they do not stabilize income, they seldom stabilize prices of agricultural inputs such as fertilizers (which also fluctuate widely and particularly at times of food price fluctuation), they often act as revenue-raising or income subsidizing rather than stabilizing devices, and they tend to keep acting after necessities for intervention have eased. The problematic record of market separation notwithstanding, public authorities can be expected to continue such practices, not only in the expectation that wide and erratic price fluctuations will continue in international food markets, but also because they are intimately linked to domestic politics.[10]

[9]FAO, p. 23 for production figures for 1973–74 and estimates for 1975–76.
[10]Peter Katzenstein, "International Interdependence: Some Long-Term Trends and Recent Changes," International Organization, Vol. 29, No. 4 (Autumn 1975): 1021–34.

In developed food exporting countries large fluctuations in prices and export demands stimulate political discontent among farmers, as currently in the United States and recurrently in several Common Market countries. On the other hand, in food importing developed countries, fluctuating prices tend to raise fears about availability of supply and to provoke political problems accordingly. Although as Johnson argues below some price instability may be beneficial as it signals changing supply conditions and often prompts market-adjusting behavior, recent price instability seems to have exceeded what might theoretically be beneficial to the matching of international supply and demand.[11]

Security of food imports

Food imports in many poor countries have become a chronically recurring "crisis." Food is transferred internationally via two channels: trade and aid. Both of these channels have become less reliable sources of supply. Price inflation in foodstuffs and competing demand from industrialized importing countries such as Japan and the Soviet Union limits LDC access to the international commercial system. Industrial countries' willingness to extend aid, which has fluctuated more according to both domestic and international political expediencies than to needs for food, similarly constrains LDC access to the international concessional system. What periodically changes this import problem into an import crisis is that many of the most populous less developed countries, notably India and Bangladesh, possess extremely limited capacities to adjust to internal shortfalls. Periodically, internal crop failures and the absence of internal reserves leave imports as the only difference between meager diets and starvation. If such imports are not obtainable at crucial times, famine or near famine conditions ensue with their attendant national and international political disruptions. In Africa, for example, successful coups in Niger and Ethiopia were directly related to drought and famine, and the whole Sahelian region suffered turmoil with international dimensions. Needless to say, even the threat that imports will not be available when needed breeds tension and insecurity, as illustrated by the role of food in Japanese-American diplomacy.

For reasons already discussed imports of food cannot be the solution, at least not alone, to longer term scarcity problems of food deficit LDCs. Clearly, if the supply and demand projections discussed earlier are at all reliable, it is unlikely that adequate supplies will be available on future world markets. There simply will not be enough food to meet importers' demand even if exporters increase production to predicted maximums! Least of all, under these conditions, will very much food be available on concessional terms. In addition, it has been argued with some merit that food imports, and especially those that came gratis or on concessional terms, have aggravated poorer countries' development problems. They add to long-term debt,

[11]Odin Knudsen and Andrew Parnes, *Trade Instability and Economic Development: An Emprical Study* (Lexington Mass.: Lexington Books, 1975). These authors point out that export instability, on balance, encourages economic development and that some degree of instability is probably desirable.

they often encourage the continuation of policies emphasizing urban industrialization that were responsible for inadequate food production in the first place, and they tend to encourage tastes and food consumption preferences that lead to continuing dependency upon imports. Nevertheless, regardless of the second best solution that concessional imports represent, some guarantee of food supplies or food aid will certainly be needed by deficit states in the foreseeable future.[12] Otherwise supply crises will recur, and, at the very least, these will cloud and confuse rational efforts toward internal development.

Low productivity and poverty

Low productivity and poverty plague millions of the world's populace engaged in agriculture, a point made both forcefully and compassionately in Cheryl Christensen's contribution to this volume. The rural populations of the less developed countries, constituting 60 to 90 percent of these nations' peoples, account for more than half of the world's population. As a rural labor force they are a key potential resource for greater food production. In addition, of course, these poor people are in most need of more and better food. Their low productivity is at the heart of the supply side of the world food problem.

We cannot explore the problems of rural underdevelopment in any depth; they are beyond the scope and intent of this volume. To say the least, the problems are immense, their manifestations are almost as varied as the peoples and institutions of the Third World, the literature on these problems is voluminous, and prescriptions for their solution are numberless.[13] In the most general way, it could be said that low productivities in peasant agriculture in Asia, Africa and Latin America follow basically from the underemployment of land and labor. Technologies that would heighten the productivities of these factors are often not available. But, more fundamentally what are lacking are educational facilities and sources of credit that would enable farmers to use more productive technologies and markets that would offer inducements to technological innovation.

Still, to look at problems of rural underdevelopment simply in terms of standard economic categories is to treat them superficially. Broader and deeper questions have to do with why backwardness often perpetuates itself when knowledge, and sometimes even capital, are available to overcome it. The search for answers to such questions leads one to explore the social, economic and political factors inside underproducing countries, and the international context within which these factors

---

[12]All USDA and FAO projections tend to agree on this point.

[13]Bruce F. Johnston and Peter Kilby, *Agriculture and Structural Transformation* (New York: Oxford University Press, 1975); Guy Hunter, *Modernizing Peasant Societies* (New York and London: Oxford University Press, 1969); Yujiro Hayami and Vernon Ruttan, *Agricultural Development: An International Perspective* (Baltimore: Johns Hopkins Press, 1971); Herman Southworth and Bruce Johnston, eds., *Agricultural Development and Economic Growth* (Ithaca: Cornell University Press, 1967); Keith Griffin, *Underdevelopment in Spanish America* (Cambridge: M.I.T. Press, 1969); Keith Griffin, *The Political Economy of Agrarian Change* (Cambridge: Harvard University Press, 1974).

exist. One needs to ask rather sensitive questions about who benefits from things as they are and who would stand to gain or lose economically, politically or otherwise if agricultural modernization were actually to come about. Although it is dangerous to generalize, politically powerful traditional elements in less developed countries who oppose land reform or other rationalizations of holdings are often major obstacles to rural development. There are other obstacles. For instance, modernizing elite factions usually prefer urban industrialization to investing scarce capital in agriculture; credit institutions (indigenous and international) balk at the high risks and uncertain outcomes in rural sector investments; and private and public agencies in developed countries see their interests challenged by the emergence of food processing industries in LDCs which would help to bring peasant agriculture into the cash economy. One could go on to cite even more unsavory obstacles to rural development such as programmatic racism and ethnic repression. At its crux, the problem is usually political, and the sad commentary is that peasants tend to be politically powerless.

Some forces do push vigorously for rural modernization and increased productivity in LDCs, and on balance the situation is not totally discouraging. The contribution by Nicholson and Esseks below offers a rather positive assessment of some LDC efforts at agricultural modernization. In addition, as Austin and others point out, international institutions such as the World Bank, the Organization for Economic Cooperation and Development (OECD) and the European Communities (EC) have lately begun encouraging greater attention to agricultural modernization and attempting to gear their aid strategies accordingly. The United States Agency for International Development (USAID) also has been involved in this task for many years with comparatively increased efforts in the 1970s. Still, given the decline in per capita real aid flows over the last decade, progress toward heightened peasant productivity is likely to be slow and halting in years ahead, perhaps too slow and too halting to meet scarcity crises projected for the 1980s. Ironically too, given the meager diets of rural populations in less developed countries, most of these people constitute an enormous latent demand for food. Should they achieve increased productivity, increased demand would accompany it. For this reason, expanding output of such poor farmers is not an important threat to developed country export interests in agriculture.

Malnutrition

Malnutrition is both the most general and the most basic world food problem. By shifting attention from production and aggregate distribution problems to the actual consumption of food, the most intractable elements of world food problems are revealed. These are dramatized by Austin's contribution to this volume. Malnutrition, estimated to afflict between one half and one billion people, is substantially a product of poverty.[14] People generally suffer from protein and/or caloric deficien-

---

[14]Overconsumption is also a form of malnutrition. It is not, however, a concern of this volume.

cies because they or their families cannot afford more or better food. The inequality of income that determines undernourishment is an international problem, as illustrated by low daily calorie intakes in Africa, Asia and Latin America. For instance, the average calorie intake of Brazilians in 1964–66 was adequate in aggregate statistical terms, but 44 percent of the Brazilian population was probably malnourished.[15] Malnutrition deserves special attention not only because it is so widespread, but because different targets and different institutions are required to solve it than rather simply to raise productivity. Poor farmers and poor urban workers are debilitated by the effects of malnutrition. High underemployment and unemployment in poor countries may reflect the weakened health and low energy levels of undernourished people, and, to close a vicious circle, undernourished people are naturally the products of under- and unemployment. Even with successful steps to increase the aggregate amount of food available in the world and in each food deficit country, chronic malnutrition with its long-run debilitation of human capacities may continue largely unabated.[16]

Global nutrition problems have been the subject of concrete efforts by national and international groups, including church groups, foundations, development banks, ministries responsible for overseas aid and foreign trade, and US agencies. Political pressure for even greater efforts has been generated by numerous voluntary associations in developed states and by Third-World lobbying for the New International Economic Order, as at the 1977 FAO Conference. But so far, pressure has been diffusely targeted at a problem with no self-evident solution and has had little real impact on actually reducing malnutrition.

Food systems and food regimes

While the nature and severity of world food problems provide the context for the analyses contained in this volume, the focus of our collective effort is upon the international relations of food. There is presently, and has been for some time, an active international diplomacy of food affairs—communication among governments about food and agricultural issues, proliferating international organizations and bureaucracies concerned with food questions, countless international meetings and conferences, a good deal of official buying and selling, and all manner of bargaining with regard to commodities, money and technology. Paralleling these public activities are broad ranges of private venturings into international food affairs, from marketing to investing, to education and lobbying, to humanitarian projects of impressive scope. But, what exactly has been the impact of all this? Are peoples

[15]See FAO, *Assessment of The World Food Situation,* (Rome: FAO, 1974), pp. 49–50, and Shlomo Reutlinger and Marcelo Selowsky, *Undernourishment and Poverty,* International Bank for Reconstruction and Development, Bank Staff Working Paper no. 202 (Washington: IBRD, April, 1975).

[16]For a general review of malnutrition, see, James Austin, "Attacking the Malnutrition Problem," (unpublished paper presented at the Conference of the Institute for the Study of Human Development, Madrid, Spain, September, 1975). See also Austin's contribution to this volume.

better fed because of it? Might they be better fed without it? Or, do we have here a case of the proverbial "sound and fury," signifying very little?

Our volume is designed to explore the effects of the contemporary international relations of food upon human welfare, most notably nutritional well-being. We are not agronomists, hydrologists, biologists or other technical specialists in the agricultural sciences, and we therefore do not claim insights or aspire to new knowledge in matters of making things grow better, faster and in greater quantity. Here, we can but acknowledge the findings of colleagues in other disciplines and their implications. As social scientists, we begin from the assumption that food systems are social systems as much as they are biological ones, and food problems are political and institutional as much as they are agricultural. Food production, distribution and consumption are purposeful acts, following implicitly or explicitly from calculated decisions taken within the contexts of formal or informal social institutions. Understanding such decisions within such contexts is essential to understanding food systems and their impact upon human welfare. Much of the work contained in the essays to follow was informed, and guided, by these assumptions; much was also based on a common set of analytical concepts which it will be useful to make explicit.

First, throughout the volume the concept "global food system" is rather narrowly defined. It has been necessary to specify carefully this concept because it embodies many of our dependent variables, i.e., the outcomes we are trying to understand. Therefore, regardless of what the term "global food system" might mean in other contexts, here it refers to *three interconnected functions—production, distribution and consumption—and to their means of interconnectedness via public and private transactions.* By "transactions" we mean bargains or other manners of agreement that initiate flows of commodities, capital, information, technology or personnel. Such flows, of course, link production to distribution to consumption. Structurally, the global food system is composed of centers of production, centers of consumption and channels of distribution (and exchange). Typical centers are countries and regions and, as noted below, channels are commercial and concessional, public and private. It should be understood that most of the transactions that constitute characteristic patterns in the production, distribution and consumption of food at given times are not international transactions (as most food is produced with local inputs and consumed domestically) but some important ones are. These international transactions are of prime analytical interest to the contributors to this volume, both as important characteristics of the global food system and as factors affecting non-international patterns. Food aid, for example, has been frequently cited as an important factor depressing production in recipient countries.[17]

Of central importance to our collective study is the assumption that conditions prevailing in the global food system occur neither haphazardly nor entirely in

---

[17]Theodore W. Schultz, "Value of U.S. Farm Surpluses to Underdeveloped Countries," *Journal of Farm Economics,* Vol. 42 (December 1960): 1028–9, and Clifford R. Kern, "Looking a Gift Horse in the Mouth: The Economics of Food Aid Programs," *Political Science Quarterly,* Vol. 8 (March 1968): 59–75.

response to agronomic or economic imperatives. Rather, they occur because people make decisions about production, distribution and consumption that accord with commonly accepted and widely prevailing norms which lend legitimacy to certain practices and declare others illegitimate. Sets of such guiding norms prevailing at given times constitute *regimes*. We find the concepts "regime" and "global food regime" particularly useful analytically and use them consistently throughout the volume. A regime is *a set of rules, norms or institutional expectations that govern a social system. Govern,* in the sense we use it, means to *control, regulate or otherwise lend order, continuity or predictability.* We assume that there is a global food regime that governs the global food system, and we shall attempt to demonstrate in this volume that a specifiable regime has governed international aspects of the food system for some time. Furthermore, we believe that it can be shown that the food regime governs the food system because regime norms influence the transactions which determine the system. That is, the international relations of food affairs are by and large conducted within normative parameters which prescribe certain kinds of transactions and proscribe others. Some norms are formal rules or laws, others exist as informal but institutionalized expectations. Together they influence practices which in turn shape the general behavior of the system as adjustments occur among various parts of the food system to particular actions fostered or tolerated by the regime. Empirically speaking, the existence and nature of the regime is observable in such events as (1) the intensities and directions of flows of food-related transactions among regime participants; (2) the agendas, manifest and latent, of forums where food issues are discussed; (3) the patterns of allocation of public and private resources for solving food problems; (4) the patterns of outcome, recommendation, institutionalization and practice reflected in the results of public and private food diplomacy; and (5) the rhetoric, both supportive and critical, of participants.

The usefulness of the "regime" concept is as much in the kinds of questions it raises as in the order it lends to analysis. For example, if indeed there is such a thing as a global food regime which consists of hundreds of specific rules and norms that guide international decisions about food transactions, what in fact are these rules and norms? What are their principal features and what principles seem to underlie them? Furthermore, where, when and how do they originate? How and by whom or what are they maintained or enforced? To what extent are they consistent, coherent and valued (and hence likely to be heavily institutionalized)? When, why and how do they change? Most significant, perhaps, what kind of global food system do regime norms create? In this last respect it is important to ask and answer questions about the ways in which the global food regime affects participants in the global food system, i.e., those individuals, organizations and populations that either produce, consume and distribute food or directly affect these processes. The regime could affect participants in the system by affecting the values they derive from participation. These might include wealth, power, autonomy, community, nutritional well-being, aesthetic satisfaction in eating and sometimes physical survival. Since any regime conditions the distribution of such values among participants, usually in some skewed fashion, it is important to inquire into the ways that particular regimes condition particular distributions. A good deal of the analysis in this volume pursues such issues.

Readers moving progressively from chapter to chapter will observe the emergence of a comprehensive picture of the global food system. The system appears decentralized into national subsystems where most production, consumption and exchange take place, though still heavily affected by international transactions. In its international aspects the global food system is bifurcated along two dimensions. First, it is clearly divided into surplus and deficit producing countries, that is, exporters and importers, and the dependence of the latter upon the former is apparently increasing (which is not to deny that there are elements of reciprocal dependence in the relationship). Moreover, as Table 6 shows, exporting developed countries are also much heavier grain consumers than are developing country importers, because they consume a large share of grain through feed for animals.

Table 6   Annual grain consumption by main uses, 1970–1990

	ACTUAL CONSUMPTION		PROJECTED DEMAND[1]	
	1970	*1980*	*1985*	*1990*
Developed Countries		(Million Tons)		
Food	160.9	163.1	164.1	164.6
Feed	371.5	467.9	522.7	565.7
Other Uses	84.9	100.6	109.5	116.4
Total	617.3	731.6	796.3	846.7
		(Kilograms)		
Per Capita	576	623	649	663
Developing Market Economies		(Million Tons)		
Food	303.7	409.3	474.5	547.2
Feed	35.6	60.9	78.6	101.9
Other Uses	46.4	64.1	75.4	88.5
Total	385.7	534.3	628.5	737.6
		(Kilograms)		
Per Capita	220	233	240	246
Developing Centrally Planned Economies		(Million Tons)		
Food	164.1	200.5	215.2	225.3
Feed	15.3	38.7	48.7	61.4
Other Uses	24.6	32.6	36.0	39.1
Total	204.0	271.8	299.9	325.8
		(Kilograms)		
Per Capita	257	290	298	304

1. FAO projections based on "trend" GDP growth and U.S. "medium" population projections.
Source: In *Overseas Development Council (1977) The United States and World Development Agenda* (New York: Praeger Publishers), p. 184; adapted by the ODC from: *Food and Agriculture Organization of the US (1975) Population, Food Supply and Agricultural Development* (Rome: FAO), p. 28.

Second, two networks of transactions link producing countries to consuming countries: a commercial network of sellers and buyers and a concessional network of donors and recipients. Commercial channels carry the bulk of food through the food system, as well as the inputs for growing it, and these channels primarily link North America to Europe, Japan, Korea and Taiwan, and recently the USSR and China. Concessional channnels run mainly in North-South directions and remain crucial to less developed countries which lack the financial resources to meet all their needs in commercial exchanges. Production, distribution and consumption patterns in the global food system are markedly skewed; the populations in wealthy industrialized countries and the wealthy in some less developed countries are distinctly privileged. The global food system, overall, is inadequate to the needs and aspirations of many of its participants, and these multiple inadequacies, as explained above, are the causes of "world food problems."

Both the nature and the inadequacies of the global food system are influenced but not fully determined by the contemporary global food regime. This regime, as regards the international relations of food, has been American centered and prescribed, and based principally upon national government actions. To some extent it has relied upon multinational enterprises, private interest groups, and formal international organizations to enforce its rules and norms. The regime was fairly stable and institutionalized from the late 1940s until the early 1970s, during which time participants had complementary, congruent, and usually accurate expectations about relationships between their transactions and systemic outcomes.

Norms that guided (and constrained) the international relations of food from the late forties to the early seventies can be grouped into at least eight sets of principles.

1. *Respect for the free market.* Most major participants in the international diplomacy of food between 1948 and 1972 adhered to the belief that a properly functioning free market would be the most efficient allocator of globally traded food commodities and agricultural inputs. They therefore advocated such a market, aspired towards it, at least in rhetoric, and assessed food affairs in terms of free market models. Actual practice deviated rather markedly from free trade ideals.

In fact, cynics might want to suggest that the principle under discussion here could better be labelled, "talk about free trade, but practice mercantilism." Canada and the U.S. have been described as alternate price leaders in a North American duopoly during the 1960s. Yet, whatever the practice, free trade, anti-monopoly ideals remained so strong that deviators were continually compelled to explain and justify their behavior, and such inquiry and defense provided the making for endless debate within international institutions such as the Food and Agriculture Organization (FAO) and the International Wheat Council.[18] Allowing for the impact of the social-political factors that render international market reality different from the ideal of economic theory, a case can be made that food flows through the interna-

[18]Robert C. Tetro, "The International Organization of Food Affairs" (unpublished paper circulated at the Airlie House Conference on Global Food Interdependence, April 7, 1977).

tional commercial system did in fact reflect norms maintaining free market aspirations during the postwar era. Seevers' analysis below fits such an interpretation and advances the widely held argument that "perfecting" markets would have a benign impact upon the global food system. Christensen accepts the realities of "market" norms but criticizes their impact on the food system.

2. *National absorption of adjustments imposed by international markets.* As indicated, relative price stability in international food markets obtained during much of the postwar era and can be accounted for in large measure by American (and to a lesser extent Canadian) willingness to accumulate reserves in times of market surplus and to release these, commercially and concessionally, in times of tightness. Such North American behavior made the international market a much more predictable and acceptable food allocator than it might otherwise have been, and as a result free market norms of access and information were fortified. Still, it must be underlined that it was a rule of the food regime that North America would adjust domestically in the interest of domestic and international price stability and stable market shares, and that it would do this over and over again. Further, both American and Canadian participants in global food affairs carried out adjustments that served these *de facto* norms of market stability without much dissent from overseas or at home.

3. *Qualified acceptance of extra-market channels of food distribution.* Food aid on a continuing basis and as an instrument both of national policy and international program became an accepted part of the postwar food regime in the years following 1954. Heated debates took place over the price-cutting and surplus-dumping practices that followed the adoption of Public Law 480 (later the Food for Peace Program) in 1954. Eventually, multilateral concessional food transfers were legitimized by the United Nations World Food Program in 1961. Bilateral concessional flows were accepted under terms of the Food Aid Conventions that accompanied the international wheat agreements of 1967. Previously, acceptance of this practice had been limited to food emergencies such as those in Europe following both World War I and II. Otherwise exporters condemned food concessions as dumping and recipients occasionally sought side-payments for accepting such food. In a system of free-trade-oriented participants, acquiescence in extra-market distribution could be obtained only upon the stipulation that market distribution was to take precedence over extra-market distribution. More simply, it was acceptable to American and foreign producer/exporters to give food away as long as this did not reduce income or distort market shares. While this qualification implies consistency between the commercial and concessional norms of the food regime, in practice there has been a good deal of tension, even within the United States, and energetic efforts were made to use concessional transactions to create commercial markets.

4. *Avoidance of starvation.* The obligation to prevent starvation as an international norm was not novel to the postwar period; it derives from more remote times (although the international community's capacity actually to muster meaningful relief is recent). There has been and remains a prevailing consensus that famine situations are extraordinary and that they should be met by extraordinary means. To

fail to do would be gross immorality according to world-wide standards. Ironically, the attention to and strength of this norm may be increasing currently, at the very time that food reserves available for famine relief remain near their thirty-year low point.

5. *Free flow of scientific information.* There is some question about the analytical usefulness of labelling "free information" a norm of the global food regime because there has been great deviation from it in practice. Whereas most of the other norms discussed here emerged and prevailed during the postwar era largely because of American advocacy and practice, "free information" emerged in spite of American misgivings. "Freedom of information" about the results of agricultural research was a principle nurtured by the United Nations Food and Agricultural Organization and welcomed by those seeking modern technologies for agricultural development. In these ways this principle upheld norms for disclosure for the global food regime. On the other hand, American commercial practice, both public and private, was to protect certain information for market advantage. As long as the United States adhered to these practices the global flow of scientific information about agriculture was impaired. Many recent developments suggest, however, that American attitudes and practices with regard to disseminating scientific information have changed. However, many countries, notably the Soviet Union, have never accepted the principle of free information, at least with respect to "timely" (for them strategic) information.

6. *Low priority for national food self-reliance.* Partly because the global food system of the past thirty years was perceived by most participants as one of relative abundance, and partly because of international divisions of labor implicit in free trade philosophies, autarky was not accepted as a norm of the global food regime. Quite the contrary was in fact the case. External sources of supply were accepted as dependable. Markets were accepted as stable. Aid was available both to those who would exchange political allegiance for food, and to those who threatened political deviation if food was withheld. There were, in general, low perceived risks in dependence. Most Communist countries, of course, rejected this principle of "agricultural dependence" in favor of agricultural development and internal adjustments. But the majority of other participants in the global food system acquiesced.

7. *Lack of concern for chronic hunger.* That international transactions in food should be addressed to alleviating hunger and malnutrition, or that these concerns should take priority over other goals, such as profit maximization, market stability or political gains, were notions somewhat alien to the global food regime of the postwar era. This is not to say that some individuals and organizations were not at work combatting malnutrition. But, in general, it was simply not a rule of international food diplomacy that hunger questions should be given high priority, or even that they should be raised if there were dangers of insulting friendly governments by doing so. As a result, relatively few resources were devoted to alleviating chronic malnutrition globally, and little concerted action was undertaken. Austin argues pointedly below that the result of this has been a continuing deterioration of nutri-

tional conditions among the world's poor in spite of small gains in per capita production.

8. *National sovereignty and the illegitimacy of external penetration.* It need hardly be pointed out that the global food system of the last thirty years functioned within the confines of the international political system, so that the norms governing the latter necessarily conditioned those of the food regime. Important among these was the general acceptance of the principle of national sovereignty; among the norms this supported was a tendency to define problems as those *between* states and a consequent proscription against international interference by one state in "domestic" affairs of another. In practice with regard to food this meant that production, distribution and consumption within the confines of national frontiers remained largely beyond the "legitimate" reach of the international community, even under famine conditions, as long as national governments chose to exclude the outside world, as Ethiopia did in 1973.[19] In practice, this meant that many of the poorest and hungriest people of the world could not be reached via the distributive processes of the global food system. The world acquiesced because sovereignty was the norm, and hence the malnourishment of millions was not seen as a collective responsibility in any strong sense.

Some effects of the prevailing food regime upon the global food system during the postwar era are easily discernable. In setting and enforcing regime norms for commercial transactions, the U.S. worked out trading rules through bargaining and formal policy coordination with key importers and other exporters. Communist countries remained peripheral participants with their own rules within Comecon (when the Soviets were exporters), although they occasionally interacted with "western" food traders, playing by the rules when they did. World trade in foodstuffs attained unprecedented absolute levels, and North Americans became grain merchants to the world to unprecedented degrees. Through concessional transactions the major problems of oversupply and instability in the commercial markets were resolved. Surpluses were disposed of in ways that probably enhanced the prospects of subsequent commercial growth for major food suppliers. Especially with respect to grain trading, adherence to regime norms enhanced the wealth and power (i.e., market share and control) of major exporters, most notably farmers and trading firms in the United States. Also enhanced were the nutritional well-being and general standard of living of fairly broad cross-sections of populations within major commercial grain-importing countries. Adhering to regime norms, however, also encouraged interdependencies among exporters and importers which, over time, impeded the international autonomy and flexibility of both.

With regard to concessional food flows regime norms facilitated global humanitarianism and enhanced survival during shortfalls and famines, as in the Indian food shortage of 1965–67. But the norms contributed to huge gaps in living standards between richer countries and poorer ones, they helped to perpetuate large

[19]Jack Shepherd, *The Politics of Starvation* (New York: The Carnegie Endowment for International Peace, 1975).

gaps between the rich and poor within countries, and they failed to affect chronic nutritional inadequacies of poor people worldwide. By promoting transfers of certain types of production technology as well as foodstuffs, regime norms also contributed to diffusing more capital intensive farming, specialized rather than self-reliant crop choices, and a sharp rise in productivity (India, for example, doubled her production growth rate after 1950 compared to the historic trend in the first half of this century). One result has been cultural; expectations of people everywhere include a growing demand for "high income" food commodities, as for example wheat and meat, and a growing reliance upon high technology, high energy inputs. Over all, the food regime reflected, and probably reinforced, the global political-economic *status quo* that prevailed from the late 1940s to the early 1970s.

Later chapters of this volume suggest that the global food regime may be changing. For one thing many of the norms seem to be in question at present, either because they are unacceptable to increasingly powerful Third-World countries and coalitions, or because they are no longer acceptable to the United States. Free trade philosophies, for example, are under assault by exponents of the New International Economic Order. International market stability and open market access provided by domestic adjustments and practices in the United States are no longer guaranteed by the support of substantial political interests in this country. Other norms, such as the primacy of market development over economic assistance goals, are in question because participants widely recognize that adhering to them would exacerbate the whole range of world food problems. To take a case in point, almost no one any longer is discouraging national agricultural developments that enhance self-reliance in grain crops, and almost no one any longer is withholding scientific information or technical assistance that could further such agricultural development. Moreover, capital intensive technology is out of vogue; labor intensive techniques to provide rural populations with work are encouraged. To be sure, elements of carryover and continuity from the postwar regime persist, and rather intense international debate surrounds the wisdom of changing norms. Unfortunately, as we write (1978), the most accurate conclusion concerning the global food regime is a rather unsatisfactory one. The normative content of the regime is in flux. Any number of indices suggest that the postwar global food regime has probably passed into history. Yet its successor has failed to emerge clearly. The 1970s are unlikely to be years that produce global consensus on almost anything. For policy makers these years of regime flux are likely to prove extraordinarily difficult.

Participants: key food actors and institutions

The norms guiding the international relations of food emerge in the decentralized world polity. They arise from the actions and interactions of states and other organizations. They are bargained rules, for the most part, though bargaining capacity tends to be asymmetric and closely linked to participants' command over the resources required to make transactions. More simply put, big buyers and sellers, producers and consumers in commercial networks and big donors in concessional ones have major (though not exclusive) influence over food regime norms. At times ''global norms'' have entailed little more than universal acceptance of a major participant's unilateral policies.

The United States and the global food regime

Because of the United States' position as the leading food exporter, and a huge consumer, especially on a per capita basis, the decisions of public and private officials in this country have weighed heavily, often decisively, in setting and enforcing norms of the global food regime. This is especially true with regard to the setting of patterns and prices in the international grain trade, and volumes and directions of international food aid. In some instances, the American ability to produce and export huge yearly surpluses placed this country in the position of supplier of first, last, and just about only resort for food-deficit populations overseas. Such quantitative dominance has doubtlessly amplified American influence over the global food regime. As a US official responsible for the daily operation of the export monitoring system, set up in 1974, remarked: ''We come very close to being one market; world grain prices, for instance are set in Chicago — it is the Chicago price plus transportation anywhere.'' Previously, the US domestic price, less subsidies set by Congress or the Secretary of Agriculture, largely determined world wheat prices, and, except for rice where Thailand's influence is important, North American policies determined the international prices at which most grains would flow both commercially and concessionally.

The preponderance of the United States is declining in some areas (for instance, US food aid provided 90 percent of the total in the 1960s but only 60 percent in 1975) and in other areas its dominance is precarious. The U.S., for example, was the leading rice exporter for the decade 1965–1975, while producing less than two percent of the world's rice. But this position is regularly challenged by Thailand. More recently, Brazil has been challenging the US in the soybean market; likewise, competition in beef is stiffening. Meanwhile, Western European agricultural scientists have been working with strains and breeds to lower the EC's dependence on imported North American feedgrains. Agricultural trade as a proportion of world trade is also declining, from 33 percent in 1950–1955 to 17 percent in 1971–1975. Still, the US *share* of world agricultural trade has remained stable, averaging 12 to 15 percent in the period 1950–1977, though rising to 16 percent during the ''crisis'' period of 1973–1974.

American preponderance in the global food system, and US influence over the food regime, are less challengeable in other respects. The United States Department of Agriculture (USDA) has a central role in the global intelligence network which informs production, consumption and trade worldwide. USDA monitoring and research activities with regard to world crops (plus complementary work by the Central Intelligence Agency with special attention to the Soviet and Chinese situations) are looked upon as highly authoritative. Published intelligence from US sources is used by many other governments, as well as by farmers and multinational agribusiness firms. The contribution of these data-gathering and processing activities to the functioning of the global food system should not be underestimated. Nor should we underestimate the global systemic impacts of American public and private agronomic research, which remains the most extensive in the world. Greater openness and attention to more diverse problems in recent years has heightened further the global impacts of American agricultural research.

All of this suggests that American behavior in international food affairs, and above all American public policy decisions with regard to agriculture, have a great deal to do with the functioning of the global food system and the setting and enforcement of the norms that govern it. Understanding the principles and forces that shape US agricultural policy therefore is crucial to understanding the global system. Extended discussion of American policy and policy making is beyond the scope of this essay, but these issues are analyzed in detail by I. M. Destler in this volume.

In general, agricultural policy in this country, both in its domestic and foreign aspects, emerges from public policy processes characteristic of American government generally. Pressures from farm organizations, the agribusiness community, consumers' associations, church and international relief agencies and a great many other factions play a part. Members of Congress, their constituents, committees, debates and election campaigns are important. Various inter- and intradepartmental interests within the administration intervene, including Agriculture, Treasury, State Department and the Office of Management and Budget. Foreign delegations and governments also attempt to influence the domestic political process. Because of the way the process works, United States agricultural policy predominantly serves domestic interests. Yet these interests are often in conflict; this frequently undermines the consistency of policy, even with respect to national goals. Destler discusses these policy issues at length below.

The role of international organizations

National policy decisions (or non-decisions) reverberate through a network of international organizations with food-related missions. Eighty-nine such intergovernmental bodies were recently listed in a report on American participation in world food politics prepared by the United States Senate.[20] If one were to go on to also count private associations, organizations involved in global food affairs would number in the thousands. It would require research and analysis well beyond the scope of this volume even to begin to map the full structure of the international organizational arena for food. Nonetheless, some mapping is required to help sort out the maze of acronyms and relatively obscure formal organizations that exist. Figure 3 provides such an overview map.

[20]U.S. Congress, Senate, Select Committee on Nutrition and Human Needs, *The United States, FAO and World Food Politics: U.S. Relations With An International Food Organization,* Staff Report 94th Congress, 2nd Session, (Washington: U.S. Government Printing Office, June, 1976), pp. 11–13.

Figure 3. The United Nations food network

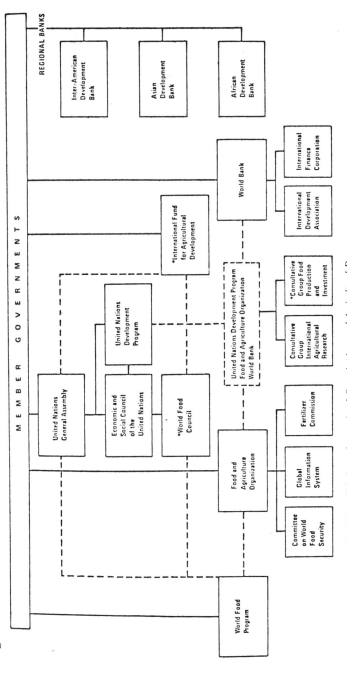

Source: Based upon Figure 3 in Martin Kriesberg, *International Organizations and Agricultural Development*, Economic Research Service, Foreign Agricultural Economic Report No. 131 (Washington: USDA, May, 1977), p. 19.

*Existed from 1975 to 1978 only.

What in the diagram is called the "United Nations Food Network" is a set of functionally interrelated institutions, individually and collectively mandated to respond to problems in the global food system as defined by their member-governments and international staffs. The Food and Agriculture Organization (FAO) is a specialized agency of the United Nations operating under a 1945 agreement between the FAO Conference and the General Assembly. It is an autonomous association, responsible only to its members (currently 136 national governments) and financed by them for its "regular" budget which largely pays for staff operations. The charter mandate of the FAO calls on it (1) to collect, analyze and disseminate information relating to food and agriculture, (2) to provide an international forum for the consideration of food problems, and (3) to provide technical assistance to member countries.[21]

Most closely bound to the FAO (or vice versa) within the UN network is the United Nations Development Program (UNDP). The main source of technical assistance in the UN, UNDP was founded in 1966 through a merging of the Expanded Program of Technical Assistance and the United Nations Special Fund. FAO currently serves as the executing agency for most projects in food and agricultural development financed by UNDP, and UNDP reimbursements yearly constitute the single largest category of the FAO's total receipts—about double that of the regular budget of 106 million (for 1978).

Less intimately associated with FAO, but still importantly linked, are the World Bank Group, the three regional development banks, the World Food Program and other "cooperative" programs. Through an IBRD/FAO Cooperative Program, FAO assists the Bank in identifying and evaluating projects for possible funding, and it aids prospective loan recipients in preparing applications. Less directly, linkages also exist between FAO's Industry Cooperative Program, its Investment Center and the Bank's International Finance Corporation, where liaison and exchanged information guide private-sector investments in food processing and agricultural development. By way of their capital-raising activities, and via intra-professional communication, the World Bank Group is connected to the Inter-American Development Bank (IDB), the Asian Development Bank (ADB) and the African Development Bank (AFDB), all of which finance agricultural development.

The World Food Program (WFP), created in 1966, is essentially an international food-for-work operation that finances development projects with payment in kind pledged by members. WFP also intermittently functions as a disaster and famine relief agency. Organizationally, it is linked to FAO via appointments to its governing body, and via joint field operations. Cooperative programs also link FAO to various other parts of the UN system; these include a program with the World Health Organization (WHO) on food standards — the Codex Alimentarius Commission — a program with the United Nations Children's Fund (UNICEF) directed toward improving nutrition among children, and a program in education about

---

[21]United States Government, FAO Interagency Staff Committee, "United States Objectives in FAO," (Washington, May, 1976).

global hunger and food needs, the Freedom From Hunger Campaign (FFHC).

Several new organs were created by the World Food Conference in November, 1974, and these are now operating in the UN food network.[22] Resolutions approved first by the Conference and later by the UN General Assembly established a World Food Council (WFC) as the "highest" institution on world food problems in the UN system. Meeting at the ministerial level, the WFC is composed of 36 countries, nominated by the Economic and Social Council (ECOSOC) and responsible to it. Its composition represents a world fragmented into an industrialized North, an under-developed South, a capitalist West and a socialist East. For broad policy issues, the WFC was intended to be the hub of the UN Food Network. Whether it will achieve this status remains to be seen. Until its third annual meeting in Manila, in June 1977, disagreements over its authority and staffing blocked significant action. At Manila, a number of resolutions were passed on food aid, reserves, and policy coordination under multinational aegis. These were supported by the Soviet Union as well as Western and Third World governments. However, these resolutions were essentially hortatory, a point the Soviet government made in explaining its support.

Also authorized at Rome in November, 1974, were the International Fund for Agricultural Development (IFAD) and the Consultative Group on Food Production and Investment (CGFPI). The former, after an initial capitalization of just over $1 billion for agricultural development was raised, began operations in 1977 with the special aim of helping the poorest of the less developed countries. It reports to but is not under the authority of the Secretary General of the UN, and its operations are overseen by a governing board composed of representatives of three categories of countries — developed-donor, developing-donor (e.g., OPEC) and developing-recipient. The CGFPI, which began operations in 1975, was called into being to encourage larger flows of resources into food production in less developed countries and to coordinate the activities of various international donors. Patterned after the Consultative Group on International Agricultural Research (CGIAR), the group on production and investment was sponsored by the World Bank, the FAO and the UNDP and hosted meetings of representatives of UN donor agencies, the development banks, foundations, donor governments, and recipient countries. With the successful launching of IFAD, the CGFPI's functions have been absorbed by the Rome-based Fund, which now is responsible for collating information and recommending ways to increase private and public investment.

In addition to organs already described, there are several UN bodies which regularly consider food questions as aspects of their broader programs. Significant among these is the United Nations Conference on Trade and Development (UN-CTAD), where intense debate on North-South trade issues, many having to do with the terms of trade for agricultural commodities, has occurred over the years.[23] In many ways, UNCTAD has become as salient a forum for North-South agricultural

[22]Thomas G. Weiss and Robert S. Jordan, *The World Food Conference and Global Problem Solving* (New York: Praeger, 1976), pp. 155–166.

[23]B. Gosovic, *UNCTAD, Conflict and Compromise: The Third World's Quest for an Equitable World Order Through the United Nations* (Leiden: Sijthoff, 1975), pp. 93–114 and *passim.*; J. C. Nagle, *Agricultural Trade Policies* (Lexington, Mass.: D. C. Heath, 1976), pp. 70–97.

issues as has the General Agreement on Tariffs and Trade (GATT) for developed western states bargaining on agricultural issues (although there has been little "success" within GATT in lowering trade barriers in the agricultural area!).

Some words of caution are in order before we move from mapping into analysis and evaluation. First, organizations depicted in Figure 3 and briefly highlighted here are by no means the only international food bodies, not even as regards the UN network. For one thing, there are various coordinating committees and ad hoc food groups interlaced among the major institutions such as the Committee on Surplus Disposal of the FAO which monitors concessional sales for possible violations of anti-dumping norms. For another, many of the major organizations noted, the FAO in particular, contain any number of quasi-autonomous, differentially responsible organs within them. Second, the operational world of the groups and associations of the UN network is nowhere nearly as orderly, well-organized or separate as Figure 3 indicates or as the discussion suggests. In reality, redundancy (for good or ill) is rampant, complementarity is often unrecognized or at least unexploited, responsibility and accountability are poorly defined, coordination is difficult, and political and bureaucratic competition further complicates the network. Third, let us caution readers against mistaking activity for impact or accomplishment. There is a good deal of activity surrounding the international organization of food affairs, but budgets are modest, authority limited, support from member-states is uncertain at best, and, for myriad political and bureaucratic reasons, organizations tend to be restrained from accomplishing their mandated tasks.[24]

Yet international institutions should not be evaluated in terms of unrealistic criteria. Many global food problems could be more effectively addressed if international organizations were more authoritative, more efficient and more able to command resources in pursuit of global objectives. Contributing authors make this clear in their discussions, and we return to elaborate this point in our concluding chapter. Rather than dwell upon functions international organizations do not (and perhaps cannot) perform given the environment in which they operate, we should note the functions they can and do perform in relation to the global food regime. International organizations in the food area affect, modify and occasionally enforce regime norms in at least four ways: (1) by prodding governments through public and private channels, such as speeches, reports and multilateral conferences, to confront issues that national bureaucrats might otherwise choose to ignore, (2) by collecting information, fostering inter-elite communication and sponsoring research that governments by themselves might take little interest in, (3) by providing international services that governments could not perform for political reasons, and (4) by legitimating unilateral policies or bilateral deals by lending them multilateral imprimatur.

With regard to our point about prodding or stimulating governments, the con-

---

[24]For a discussion of budgetary resources, see, United States Department of Agriculture, Economic Research Service, "Multilateral Assistance for Agricultural Development" (Washington: USDA, 1977). For commentaries on national support and political and bureaucratic problems, see, United States Senate, Select Committee on Nutrition and Human Needs, pp. 25–68.

tinuing debate concerning international grain reserves is particularly illustrative. The latest impetus for the idea of a global grain reserve came from a 1973 proposal by former FAO Secretary-General Boerma. The scheme contradicted American (and Canadian) policies at the time it was articulated, but it did receive collateral support from the number of independent studies by business and academic organizations in the United States and elsewhere. In this way Boerma's initiative became an issue in US policy making and, as Destler shows, it was hotly debated in Washington during preparations for the World Food Conference of 1974. Ultimately, the State Department's positive position toward grain reserves carried the debate and Secretary Kissinger was authorized to announce US acceptance of the reserve principle and to pledge cooperation towards its realization. He did this at the Rome Conference.

At this point the national debate about principle became an international debate about practice. The United States initially offered a plan for a reserve program of 60 million tons — considerably larger than that suggested by Boerma. Washington then retreated from this position and fell back upon a scheme for a more limited reserve, nationally held and coordinated. But this by no means settled the question. Eighteen months after the initial pledge at Rome the reserve discussion was centered at the International Wheat Council (IWC) in London, where debate among potential participants in the reserve turned on questions about the total size of stocks, the size of each country's contribution, the method of holding the reserves, the distribution of costs, the conditions for accumulating and releasing stocks, the relation between food reserves and food aid, and the role of international organizations in the reserve undertaking.

By the autumn of 1976 the "food reserve" question was re-injected into American domestic politics as a campaign issue, as candidate Carter became an advocate of international stocks. Shortly after the installation of the Carter administration, Agriculture Secretary Bergland publicly proposed to build a modest US reserve of about 8 million tons,[25] and renewed efforts at the IWC to attain international support and cost sharing for a broader reserve undertaking. The issue remains unresolved in 1978. The International Wheat Agreement has been extended a year, till 1979. The final outcome will be either a successful incorporation of new multilateral rules for managing international reserves or a failure and a return to relatively uncoordinated national measures. In the latter case, the United States will return (though less dependably) to its *de facto* role of principal reserve holder for the world.

While the food reserve story is not yet concluded, our point is made. International organization prompting injected a significant issue into national policymaking that many officials within relevant national governments would have preferred to avoid. When the issue was projected back into the international arena it took the form of a proposal for global collective action, which, if ultimately accepted, could become a new norm of the global food regime.

---

[25]Under current legislation (1977), a U.S. domestic reserve of 35 million tons of grain may be accumulated and held.

In areas of information, research and communication, the FAO is both central and significant. As the principal intergovernmental organization for food affairs, FAO participates in or reviews nearly all intergovernmental and transnational activities in the field. FAO's budgets for research and publication are small compared to amounts spent by governments for nationally focused research programs. Yet, the organization's output is substantial: its periodicals, yearbooks and country analyses are frequently cited, and its projections frequently guide national planning and policy making.[26] Its studies in agricultural adjustment have aimed to lower barriers to trade. Its research on fisheries helped to establish fishing area councils in which countries could address mutual problems; and through "indicative planning" reports it reviews the investments and activities of countries and MNCs on a global scale with the purpose of mobilizing resources of individual states to address foreseeable problems.

The network of institutions involved in international agricultural research is centered in the FAO, but it extends beyond to include national research and development agencies such as the United States Agency for International Development and Canada's International Development Agency. It also includes a number of quasi-public bodies such as the Consultative Group on Food Production and Investment noted earlier, and the ten international research centers coordinated by the Consultative Group on International Agricultural Research. Widespread international communication about agricultural research is newer still. While a full assessment of the institutions in this area is premature, it is fair to credit cooperative international research ventures during the 1960s with producing the "miracle seeds" for high yielding dwarf varieties of wheat and rice that led to what some proclaimed as a "Green Revolution" in food production.

In addition to disseminating information and coordinating the creation of new knowledge, international organizations have become increasingly involved in field operations in rural modernization and agricultural development. Most of these efforts, naturally, are targeted toward Third-World countries. Some of the development services of the multilateral agencies are discussed by Austin, while Nicholson and Esseks cover the problems that poor countries face. Though still modest, the budget allocations for such interventionist field programs have expanded rapidly since the early 1960s, and it has sometimes been the case that multilateral undertakings have reached countries and peoples denied bilateral assistance for political reasons.

Fourth, international organizations have influenced the global food regime by legitimating practices and patterns of behavior, thereby turning them into norms. It is not surprising that most practices legitimated by international organizations are often simply multilateralized versions of the policies and preferences of powerful member-states. Yet, there is still something to be said for member-states' seeking international endorsement, especially if it creates a barrier to actions that would be detrimental to other states. Furthermore, multilateral debate, such as at the IWC or

---

[26]Joseph M. Jones, *The United Nations at Work: Developing Land, Forests, Oceans and People* (Oxford, England: Pergamon Press, 1965), p. 118.

the Rome World Food Conference, has provided reconsiderations and modifications in national policies that multilateral acceptance often requires. Contributors to this volume report on a number of efforts of multilateral legitimation of norms, including those for maintaining a concessional system of food distribution, those shaping "development" as an international responsibility to be fostered by the UN and FAO, those maintained by GATT for strengthening the free trade principles of the commercial system, and those that foster and direct the international research network, including the principle of free flows of information.

Despite (or possibly because of) their impact, support for international food organizations, most notably the FAO, has declined among industrialized states in recent years. This has coincided with the increased activity of the poorest states in the United Nations, where the various agencies charged with international welfare tasks have become primary arenas of debate between advocates of a New International Economic Order and their critics. As the global food regime of the postwar era has become subject to increasing challenge, stress and deviation, political leaders in the United States and other industrialized countries have sought to protect their states' very large stakes in the traditional status quo. Part of their strategy has been to deflate universal multilateral bodies, and hence to dampen "populist" pressures by circumventing forums controlled by Third World majorities. Alternatively, these countries' spokespersons have sought to create new specialized institutions with built-in veto opportunities, weighted voting, limited membership or limited authority, and to propose bilateral alternatives to multilateral programs where one-on-one rather than one-against-many bargaining conditions would prevail.

Agribusiness and the global food regime

Multinational agribusiness corporations, the largest and most numerous of which are American, must be included in any discussion of the global food system and regime. As managers of global food transfers, promoters of large-scale production and facilitators of technological diffusion, the MNCs are often links between governments' intended policies and their actual accomplishments. This is especially the case with United States foreign agricultural policy, since the realization of official intentions in trade, aid, and development investment has depended consistently upon the compliance and cooperation of the agribusinesses which actually handle the flows of foodstuffs, capital and technology. The major grain companies, Cargill and Continental, for example, are the effective managers of international sales of wheat, corn, rye and other grains to Europe, Japan, the Soviet Union and other major customers. Similarly, US concessional sales, although approved officially, are actually negotiated between private companies and recipient countries.

Multinational firms also affect global food production and agricultural productivity through their investment decisions. Producer firms such as Esmark, Dole, Kraftco and Nestlé affect poorer countries by promoting technological diffusion, altering patterns of land use and impacting upon local patterns of income distribution. Cultural diffusion, also promoted by MNCs, has led to the introduction of western food marketing techniques, from supermarkets to McDonald's "golden arches" throughout the world, and such activities, for better or worse, have also promoted changes in dietary and nutritional habits in many countries.

More analysis and appraisal of the effects of large corporations is included in chapters by Seevers and Christensen. Let it suffice to say here that while intergovernmental organizations operating in the food area can be criticized for their limited impact on the global food system, the contrary is probably true with regard to the MNCs. The large firms have been both aggressive and effective, but their largely profit-motivated activities have had mixed effects. Their contributions in disseminating technology have been impressive. But a goodly proportion of their investments in the Third World have been in cash crops which actually compete with food crops, and in food crops that are exported to richer countries rather than eaten in poorer ones.[27] Similarly, their marketing activities, their occasional oligopolistic influence over prices and the secrecy of their transactions have had unsettling effects upon the food system. These were clearly in evidence in the case of the Soviet grain purchases of 1972, where market management by the large firms, and the secrecy that cloaked it, hindered timely adjustment to the magnitude of the Russian intervention. Both Paarlberg and Destler analyze aspects of this Soviet grain deal in their respective chapters below.

As regards the relationship between the MNCs and the global food regime, our judgment is that the large firms had little to do with the setting of the norms that have prevailed in the postwar era (except perhaps via their influence over US policies).[28] On the other hand, the regime as a whole has been benign by and large toward the interests of the big producers and traders.[29] The companies have profited in the environment that the regime created. The regime's emphasis upon commercial dealings, its ethos of more trade and freer trade, its direction of concessional flows through private transactional networks, its encouragement of research in more productive technologies (notably a boon to fertilizer producers), and its relative underemphasis (until the 1970s) on small farmers in poor countries, who are of little use to MNCs one way or the other, all created an environment which, in no small measure helped produce multinational agribusinesses and sustain their growth.

Food system and regime in perspective

For all its complexity of structure and functioning, the global food system, especially since 1972, has not been functioning very satisfactorily if we impose

---

[27]See Michael Lofchie, "Political and Economic Origins of African Hunger," *Journal of Modern African Studies* (December 1975): 551–567, and Susan George, *How the Other Half Dies* (London: Penguin, 1976).

[28]Similarly, most poor countries have had little influence on the regime, except as their needs became so apparent as to be impossible to ignore.

[29]It might also be considered to have been largely benign toward the interests of poor countries, though not necessarily poor people in these countries, except where these interests conflicted with those of the major participants in the commercial system.

standards such as the stemming of scarcity, provision of security or the maintenance of price stability. Nor, for that matter has it worked very well to overcome low productivities in farming in less developed countries or to improve the basic nutrition of the world's poor.

At the heart of the system's incapacity to respond adequately and equitably to world hunger is the basic principle that underlies the norm-setting process of the regime.

The rules of the regime originate as *national policies which are internationally bargained and coordinated,* by purpose or default, by multilateral agreement or unilateral dictate. This would be satisfactory if national policies (or at least the policies of those national actors that most influence the regime) gave high priority to meeting global needs. In fact, as suggested, the case is exactly the opposite: national foreign policies in agriculture, because of the political imperatives behind them, have tended to serve domestic ends ahead of international ones. This last point, incidentally, tends to be as true for less developed countries as it is for the industrialized states. The outcome of this "nationally decided, internationally coordinated" principle has been a continuing pattern of food flows conditioned primarily by market forces (from those who can sell, to those who can buy) unbuffered in recent years by reserves, and by and large undersupplied in aid. It might be argued that such a system is about the most that we can expect in a world of separate, sovereign and unequally endowed states. A number of authors contributing to this volume, however, are unwilling to accept this.

The political forces shaping norms of the food regime are largely divorced from the majority of people most severely affected by problems in the global food system. These are the rural poor of the Third World. Food trade and aid, investment and information do not affect these people significantly since they are simply not part of the modern interdependent world. The poorest peasants of Asia, Africa and Latin America participate little if at all in cash economies and hence are neither stimulated nor distracted by price changes or other supply and demand fluctuations, international, national or otherwise. They are often unreached, even by their own governments' policies. Certain theorists, of course, argue rather persuasively that such isolation in poverty for the peasantry reflects not their isolation from the world system but their centrality in it. They are its victims, and their continued victimization is crucial to its national and international functioning. Only a revolutionary overturning, it is argued, can break them out of their poverty. Only one of the authors below, Christensen, makes the case for revolution. Whether at the center or the periphery of effects from the international food system, such peasants, once involved in the causal links of the system, are both the most vulnerable and least potent group affected, at least compared to the minor extent of their involvement. Hence sober reflection upon the norms of the global food regime, as we perceive them, does drive one to the conclusion that the rules of the system have focused neither sufficient transactions nor attention upon the plight of the world's rural poor. By legitimizing ongoing concessional dealings, the regime might be said to point in this direction, but the residual role these have played as ways to "dump" have lessened their effectiveness. Further, intentions over who should benefit from foreign donations have tended to shift markedly at the national borders of recipient countries, and the norm of sovereignty has muzzled international concerns with internal affairs, often to the detriment of poor people in the countryside.

Finally, in addition to the broad and endemic inadequacies of the current food system, which will be difficult to rectify, other more specific shortcomings can be singled out that are perhaps easier to deal with. For example, there is currently a lack of productive resources and relevant technology available to countries needing to expand their food supply. Furthermore, in many poor countries public policies actually inject net disincentives to expanded food production.[30] Added to this are inadequacies in financial and administrative infrastructure which further hamper food production. Globally, there is no real control over grain production, no systematic stockpiling and no controls over trade and price. National policies in nearly every country, developed and underdeveloped alike, are still deficient with respect to nutrition and health. Population policies are rare and largely ineffectual. While many of these problems could be alleviated by changes within countries, in many cases the success of what is done will depend partly upon what is done in other countries, and partly, too, upon international norms. Global food interdependence requires collaborative policy efforts to establish rules for a new global food regime. Without such new norms, and appropriately compliant behavior, it is likely that the expansion of food production will occur haphazardly, and too slowly, with little attention to chronic hunger, little heed of environmental side effects, and little concern for distributive justice.

[30]Abdullah A. Saleh, "Disincentives to Agricultural Production in Developing Countries: A Policy Survey," *Foreign Agricultural Supplement* (Washington: GAO, March, 1975), p. 1.

II. Food Policies of Important Countries

2

United States Food Policy 1972-1976: Reconciling Domestic and International Objectives

I. M. Destler

US food policy is a product of four legitimate but competing concerns: (1) *farm policy;* (2) *domestic economic policy;* (3) *foreign policy;* and (4) *global welfare and development policy.* Five major policy episodes in 1972–76 illustrate their interplay: the Soviet grain sales of 1972; the soybean embargo of 1973; the food aid debate of 1974; the food reserves proposal of 1975; and the Soviet grain sales of 1974 and 1975. Competing policy concerns were more explicitly and effectively balanced in 1974 and 1975 than in 1972 and 1973, and policy tended to shift toward protecting domestic food prices in 1973, and meeting world food needs in 1974. But it shifted too late to salvage important policy concerns. The 1972–75 experience suggests that the State Department cannot be the lead international food policy agency because domestic farm and economic concerns are too deeply engaged. But interagency committees based in the Executive Office of the President (EOP) lost their effectiveness as crises waned and their members' attention turned to other things. The best organizational strategy for food would therefore be to accept the day-to-day predominance of the Department of Agriculture and seek to broaden the orientation of the secretary and his staff. Reciprocal State sensitivity to non-foreign policy concerns can help protect international economic and political interests; so can monitoring and intermittent intervention by EOP staffs.

The agricultural policies of the United States have had a prominent role in shaping the global food regime for a number of years. While this is certainly not to say that American preferences became international norms, it nevertheless has been the case that Washington's position almost always had to be taken into account in food diplomacy. The world influence of the United States in agricultural affairs followed

I. M. Destler is Director of the Project on Executive-Congressional Relations in Foreign Policy, Carnegie Endowment for International Peace. He is the author of *Presidents, Bureaucrats, and Foreign Policy* (1972 and 1974) and co-author of *Managing an Alliance: The Politics of U.S. Japanese Relations* (1976). This article is a product of a Brookings Institution study of United States foreign economic policy making, supported in part by the external research program of the Department of State. The author is grateful to Linda Freyer, Raymond Hopkins, Lawrence Krause, Edwin Martin, Henry Nau, Donald Puchala, Fred Sanderson, Gary Seevers and Philip Trezise for their helpful critical comments on earlier drafts.

41

from this country's ascent to predominance as the world's grain trader, from early American initiation of food aid programs, and from Washington's general power and leadership after 1945.

This article reviews key policy episodes of 1972–76 to develop a broader analysis of US food decision making. Its central theme is that food policy often appears contradictory and incoherent because it reflects a variety of conflicting, but entirely legitimate, values held by participants who have differing stakes in the government's response to food and agricultural problems. Policy making inevitably involves trade-offs among these values. *Food policy,* therefore, is not a relatively autonomous policy area, manageable largely on its own terms, but an area where many interests and values converge and often compete.

Four competing concerns

Interests and values relevant to food policy can be grouped into four broad areas of government activity, two of them "domestic" and two "international." Each affects, and in turn is affected by, food policy. The first is *farm policy:* what the government does to influence the production and marketing of US agricultural commodities. The primary goal of postwar farm policy has been protecting and increasing farm income. This goal has been pursued through commodity programs which strengthen prices and seek to limit production to anticipated demand, and through export promotion to increase that demand.

But the supply-demand balance for farm commodities has significant impact on the overall US economy, especially when tight markets drive prices upward. Hence food policy is important to *domestic economic policy,* the primary postwar aims of which have been full employment and price stability. Food policy is also influenced by other goals of frequent but varying importance to economic policy makers: balance in international payments, economic growth, resource mobility, moderate income redistribution, and cost-effectiveness in federal expenditures.

The third concern affecting food policy is *foreign policy,* whose primary general goals are to increase other governments' responsiveness to US interests and foster a world environment in which those interests can prosper. Since access to US food supplies on favorable terms is a goal sought by many other governments, food is to US foreign policy makers a potential source of leverage over these governments.[1] An important instrument for favoring or disfavoring particular food-importing countries is government-subsidized credit, either for largely commercial transactions (that provided Russia in 1972) or through food aid (Public Law 480), whose main recipients are less developed countries.

The fourth concern is *global welfare and development policy.* US food policy affects whether hungry people around the world can eat and whether Third World

---

[1]For an extended discussion of food as leverage, see Nau's essay in this volume.

countries can increase their own food production. This has been the weakest of the four policy concerns in its political support and its base within the federal government. Nevertheless, responding to other peoples' food problems retains a gut appeal, a legitimacy, that other foreign assistance efforts lack. Immediate food needs can be met by PL 480 donation and subsidized sales programs (and by broader policies which keep world prices from rising too high). Longer term production problems are addressed by bilateral and multilateral programs of technical and capital assistance.

Each of these concerns is represented by a community of individuals inside and outside the government who give it priority. Each has institutional voices in the US executive branch — the Department of Agriculture (USDA), the Council of Economic Advisers (CEA), the Department of State, the Agency for International Development (AID). Each has advocates on Capitol Hill. Members of one policy community frequently combat members of another because their goals compete. This does not mean, however, that those who give priority to the same area of concern necessarily agree with one another on what specific actions government should take. Farm interests differ sharply, for example, about how much government should "manage" their marketplace; economists debate how best to combat inflation.

Prologue to 1972: farm policy predominance

To delineate these four concerns is not to argue that they have been of equal importance in US food policy making. In fact, farm policy concerns predominated until 1972. Food policy making was USDA centered; its effects on other policy concerns were largely byproducts of actions taken to strengthen farm income and bring the domestic "farm problem" under control. This farm policy predominance was politically predictable. It was the farm policy community which was most directly and deeply affected by food policy decisions—its lobbyists weighed in to affect these decisions, and farm voters watched farm conditions and voted accordingly. This predominance was acceptable to other policy communities because, under market conditions existing until 1972, the policies which resulted also contributed to their goals.

The prevailing market condition was, of course, chronic surpluses and depressed prices; the "farm problem" was seen as one of overproduction. By the early 1960s the US Commodity Credit Corporation (CCC) had accumulated huge grain stocks as a result of policies which supported prices at well above market-clearing levels. The Kennedy and Johnson Administrations sought to draw down these stocks by reducing production and increasing demand — particularly export demand. Support prices were sharply lowered, and farm income was supported instead by direct payments conditioned on participation in acreage limitation programs managed by the Agriculture Department. Since US market prices were now at or near world prices, export subsidies could be eliminated or reduced. Lower feedgrain prices encouraged domestic livestock production, and facilitated exports to meet the needs of growing livestock industries overseas. Finally, government commodity programs could be altered from year to year (under authority granted by Congress to the Secretary of Agriculture) to ease or tighten acreage limitation according to whether more or less grain production was deemed desirable. This practice became known as "supply adjustment."

These policies met *farm policy* needs because they supported farm income and gave officials a handle on the supply problem. For *foreign policy* interests, grain remained available for PL 480 food aid to "friendly" governments. PL 480 served *global welfare and development policy* also by relieving hunger, supplying capital for LDC governments, and alleviating *their* food price inflation (though too much PL 480 could dampen incentives for LDC producers). For *domestic economic policy*, a major (if unappreciated) byproduct of postwar food policy was stability in the food price index, at least in relation to non-food prices.[2] Moreover, it brought this stability more or less automatically, without requiring economic policy officials to join actively in day-to-day food issues.

If commercial agriculture did thus dominate US food policy prior to 1973, its political base was both weakening and changing. Most important was the rapid decline in the farm population: from 25 percent of the American total in the early thirties (when farm commodity programs were inaugurated), to 15 percent in 1950, 9 percent in 1960, and below 5 percent in the seventies. Fewer farmers and congressional redistricting meant reduced congressional support for farm commodity programs, particularly in the House of Representatives.[3] More and more representatives began to debate not simply the level and organization of farm subsidies, but their very existence. Particularly vulnerable were the large direct payments which went to the biggest commercial farm operators under supply adjustment programs for feedgrains and wheat and above all for cotton (where large production units were concentrated). In addition, as the overall political power of farm interests declined, divisions within the farm community increased.[4] Moreover, US agriculture became more linked to the non-agricultural economy, on which it depended for capital, agricultural chemicals, and markets.[5]

Though ideologically inclined toward a free market and minimum gov-

---

[2]Using 1967 = 1.00 as a base, the ratio between the Consumer Price Index for food and the CPI for all other items was between 1.01 and 1.04 in 1955–58. It was 1.00 or below in every year from then until 1973 (except for 1966, when it was 1.02). Dale E. Hathaway, "Food Prices and Inflation," *Brookings Papers on Economic Activity 1974:* 1, p. 65.

[3]"Rural districts comprised 83 percent of an absolute majority in the House in 1966; the percentage dropped to 71 in 1969, and to 60 by 1973." Weldon V. Barton, "Coalition-Building in the United States House of Representatives: Agricultural Legislation in 1973," in James E. Anderson, ed., *Cases in Public Policy-Making* (New York: Praeger, 1976) p. 144.

[4]See Willard Cochrane, *The City Man's Guide to the Farm Problem* (Minneapolis: University of Minnesota Press, 1965), pp. 139–54.

[5]See "A New U.S. Farm Policy for Changing World Food Needs," A Statement by the Research and Policy Committee of the Committee for Economic Development, October 1974, pp. 29–37.

ernmental management, the Nixon Administration made only limited changes in the Kennedy-Johnson farm policies in 1969–72. The domestic food stamp program was expanded greatly; the Agricultural Act of 1970 gave farmers more flexibility to shift from one crop to another. But commodity programs and supply adjustment were maintained. And to most farm policy actors it appeared that the tendencies toward overproduction and surplus stocks were reasserting themselves strongly in the years after the food crisis of 1965–67.

In retrospect, it is clear that food supplies in the early 1970s were not so ample as they seemed. The package of policies so acceptable to the four major communities concerned with international food policy had one glaring limitation. Stock reduction in the United States, paralleled as it was by similar policies in other major grain exporting countries, had reduced American and world insurance against major downturn in global food production. Wheat stocks held by the US and Canada had been 100 percent of average annual domestic and export demand in 1963, before the last world food crisis. In 1972, they stood at 70 percent.[6] In absolute numbers, and this was how officials tended to look at them, US stocks were relatively high in mid-1972. Carryover stocks of wheat stood at 863 million bushels; they had not been significantly higher since 1964.[7] The US 1972 crop was a good one, though weather was not so favorable in other major producing countries, a fact partly evident in July which would become more evident thereafter. As for feedgrains, carryover stocks stood at 43.9 million tons, close to their high-point since 1965, and well above the low 30 million tons a year earlier.[8] And another good US crop was on the way. These conditions of relative plenty existed despite record acreage diversion totalling 56.7 million acres for grain in 1972.[9] Then, too, 1972 was an election year and the Nixon Administration was not the first to see that the best route to the farmer's vote was through his pocketbook. It was hardly surprising that farm officials would push ongoing policies aimed at raising farmer income with particular force, combining export promotion with maximum acreage diversion. On the first objective, moreover, they were fully in step with President Nixon and National Security Assistant Henry Kissinger, who were moving to utilize food sales to Russia as an instrument in the *foreign* policy which would be labeled "détente." They could not have known that the sales would inaugurate a period of unparalleled prosperity for American farmers and unparalleled food price inflation for American consumers. The latter would be exacerbated because US farm policies were not adjusted in time.

[6]Sanderson, "The Great Food Fumble," Brookings Reprint No. 303 (Washington, D.C.: Brookings Institution, 1975) pp. 505–506. See also Philip H. Trezise, *Rebuilding Grain Reserves: Toward an International System* (Washington, D.C.: Brookings Institution, 1976), p. 1.

[7]U.S. Department of Agriculture, *Agricultural Statistics 1975,* p. 4.

[8]Hathaway, "Food Prices and Inflation," p. 87.

[9]USDA, *Agricultural Statistics 1975,* p. 518.

Grain sales to the Soviet Union and domestic inflation: 1972 [10]

Background

In the year preceding the record sales of American grain to the Soviet Union, the Nixon Administration undertook a series of actions to encourage and facilitate such trade. On June 10, 1971, the White House announced that the President had "decided to terminate the need to obtain Department of Commerce permission for the export of wheat, flour, and other grains, to China, Eastern Europe, and the Soviet Union," and to suspend the requirement that 50 percent of grain sold to these countries be carried in US ships. [11] This freed grain companies to deal directly with Soviet trade representatives, without specific US government clearance, and substantial feedgrain sales were contracted that fall—the first to Russia since 1963. In the first six months of 1972, the Administration worked to encourage further sales through a Commodity Credit Corporation financing agreement. This effort was successful and Nixon announced, on July 8, an agreement that the CCC would supply credit and the Soviet Union would purchase a minimum of $750 million in grain over the next three years.

Agriculture Department officials—including Secretary Earl Butz—were convinced the Russians' main interest was feedgrains for their livestock program. So it was hardly inconsistent for them to announce, one week after completing the credit agreement, a program to reduce US wheat production for the coming year by "setting aside" 25 million acres, compared to 20 million in 1972. In fact, however, three days before the credit announcement, Soviet Exportkhleb representatives had quietly contracted with the Continental Grain Company to supply them 4 million tons (147 million bushels) of wheat as well as 4.5 million tons (177 million bushels) of corn. And they made this purchase not on credit but for cash. Information about this record sale leaked out gradually over the next month, during which the Soviets purchased an additional 7.8 million tons (286 million bushels) of wheat from Continental and five other grain companies. They also purchased about 2 million additional tons of feedgrains and 1 million tons of soybeans.

These amounts were several times what anyone had expected. The 433 million bushel total wheat purchase, for example, amounted to about half of US carryover stocks of July 1, 1972, and a bit over one quarter of 1972 production. The bulk of it

---

[10]This section draws upon interviews with officials and a wide range of public sources, particularly Hathaway, "Food Prices and Inflation"; John H. Schnittker, "The 1972–73 Food Price Spiral," in Arthur M. Okun and George L. Perry, eds., *Brookings Papers on Economic Activity 2: 1973*, pp. 498–507; James Trager, *The Great Grain Robbery*, (New York: Ballantine Books, 1975); House Committee on Agriculture, Subcommittee on Livestock and Grains, "Sale of Wheat to Russia," Hearings, September 1972; and Senate Committee on Governmental Operations, Permanent Subcommittee on Investigations, "Russian Grain Transactions," Hearings and Report, 1973 and 1974.

[11]"Trade with the People's Republic of China," Presidential Announcement of June 10, 1971, in *Weekly Compilation of Presidential Documents*, June 14, 1971, p. 891.

would be shipped before the 1973 crop was in. The Soviets also made substantial purchases from Canada, and poor crops in other major exporting countries meant that little additional wheat was available there. By sometime in August evidence was overwhelming that the world wheat situation had been transformed from a buyers' to a sellers' market; wheat export prices jumped from $1.68 per bushel on July 3 to over $2.00 in early August to $2.40 in late September.

But US policies were slow to adjust. The Nixon Administration officials in 1972 acted in ways that seemed calculated to generate the food price inflation of 1973. Officials were apparently slow in learning about the magnitude of the sales, and slower in grasping their market significance. Even after it became evident that the sales were driving prices up, US export subsidies were maintained. Most important of all, US officials failed to take the obvious step with which everyone should have agreed—encouraging maximum US wheat (and feedgrain) production for 1973. In sum, they ended up stabilizing the Russian food economy while destabilizing their own.

Analysis

US actions on grain sales to Russia in 1972 resulted from a convergence of farm and foreign policy interests. To a longstanding interest in expanding farm exports—one intensified by the grain glut of late 1971 and early 1972—was joined a major foreign policy thrust. In 1971 and more so in 1972, Richard Nixon and Henry Kissinger turned to a policy of increased trade as a major instrument for building a new US-Soviet relationship. Sales to Russia seemed particularly good business—good grain business, good foreign policy business. So they have remained in many respects. The problem was not that grain sales were promoted or that sales of that magnitude were consummated. Rather, the problem lay in the failure to adjust to the new world food situation which the sales had helped to transform.

Subsidizing wheat sales and diverting wheat acreage from production made sense given what officials knew in July 1972, though they might have learned more, sooner, from the grain companies had they really tried. But, by August it was clear that wheat was no longer a drug on the market, and US officials who were closely monitoring the international situation were well aware of this. Within a month, their wheat export projections rose from 650 to 1,100 million bushels. Why then didn't US policies adjust? Why were export subsidies maintained for weeks after it seemed obvious that the US was dominating the world market? More important, why was the restrictive wheat program maintained for months, keeping millions of acres out of production for the 1973 crop year?[12]

---

[12]If one simply multiplied the acreage to be diverted, 25 million, by the average 1972 yield, 32.7 bushels per acre, one would conclude that bringing all the acres back would have led to about 800 million extra bushels of wheat being produced. However, it was known that these were among the less productive wheat acres — it was unlikely that all would be brought back into production on such short notice,

In part, the failure to adjust was due to intellectual lag and resultant institutional lag. US policy makers were not immediately aware of the magnitude of sales to the Soviet Union and there were no established procedures for ensuring such awareness. As Deputy Assistant Secretary of Agriculture Richard Bell told a Senate subcommittee a year later, USDA had "not had a system for keeping track of weekly sales of exports because, basically, we were the grainery of the world and we always had large carryovers and large supplies available for export."[13] Nor had the Russians ever imported on this scale in previous short crop years.

Just as USDA was slow in learning of the magnitude of sales because it had never required current information on export contracts, it unnecessarily prolonged the wheat export subsidy because it did not anticipate the turnaround in conditions that would render it absurd. The subsidy was calculated by subtracting from the current US price an export "target price," which was "based on the price of competing Canadian wheat adjusted for quality and freight differentials."[14] It was thus supposed to *reflect* the world market. But once the target price was set by USDA, it *influenced* world market prices as well, since US exports were a substantial portion of the world wheat trade. And in mid-1972, as in previous years, officials in USDA's Export Marketing Service wanted to keep world prices down. They realized that the world wheat market was changing, at least temporarily, into a "sellers' market" dominated by the United States, since other major exporters had little additional wheat available in 1972. But the US still had a lot to sell. Moreover, higher world prices would, they feared, "bring about increased world wheat production, with a resultant glut and future lower prices."[15] Years of stagnant wheat markets had convinced them that higher prices were not sustainable. Thus they held an export target price around $1.63 even as the purchases by the grain companies to meet their Soviet commitments were driving US prices up and therefore *increasing* the per bushel subsidy—from 5 cents in early July to 38 cents by late August.

The "world price" the subsidies were supposed to permit grain exporters to meet no longer had any economic basis. The subsidy in practice became totally perverse, limiting US returns from the sales, and costing the US Treasury over $300 million (compared to the $67 million budgeted for the FY 1973 wheat subsidy program). To the degree that the low subsidized prices increased the volume of Russian purchases, this increased the inflationary impact in the United States. Yet USDA officials, having assured the grain companies that the subsidy would be maintained, resisted efforts to reverse that policy.

---

and those that were would yield substantially less than the nationwide average. Ultimately the program was changed for spring wheat plantings, and only 7.4 million wheat acres were actually diverted. But if changing the program had increased winter wheat acres by 5 million, and if the average yield for these acres was 25 bushels, this would have meant 125 million badly-needed bushels to cushion the even sharper price rise that would come in the summer of 1973.

[13]U.S. Congress, Senate, Senate Committee on Agriculture and Forestry, "Export Control Policy," Hearings, (Washington: GPO, July 11, 1973), p. 49.

[14]US General Accounting Office, "Russian Wheat Sales and Weaknesses in Agriculture's Management of Wheat Export Subsidy Programs," July 9, 1973, p. 17.

[15]Ibid., p. 23.

But as this example shows, the lag in understanding the new situation and adjusting to it was not just intellectual—it was also a function of USDA's interests. For the costs of failing to adjust did not accrue mainly to farm policy officials. Earl Butz saw his mandate as moving farm prices up and expanding exports. The sales were a godsend in terms of these goals—the more the better. They also served Henry Kissinger's foreign policy purposes admirably, demonstrating a mutual interest in large-scale trade which could only reinforce what he and President Nixon saw as *the* key international political relationship for their "structure of peace." The damage was to economic policy—spurring inflation through grain price increases—and development policy—raising the price of food to countries least able to afford it. And neither of these policy concerns had strong advocates in August 1972 food policy making efforts.

Why was this the case? The weakness of development interests on issues in 1972 was to be expected. But this was hardly true of economic policy interests. The Nixon Administration may have neglected economic policy in 1969 and 1970, but it had been operating a major anti-inflation program ever since the wage-price freeze of August 15, 1971 and the "Phase II" price control program inaugurated in November. Where were the economic policy advisers and institutions now?

On the question of the subsidy, they did join the fray once its escalating costs became evident. The Office of Management and Budget took the lead in calling a series of interagency meetings with representatives of the Council of Economic Advisers and the Council on International Economic Policy as well as USDA. Within sixteen days, a decision was reached to phase out the subsidy of September 25 (by which time the delivered price of wheat to US ports would rise to $2.40). The grain companies were, however, given a grace period so they could register for whatever further subsidies they required to meet their export contracts. By this time, the subsidy rate had reached 47 cents.[16]

But the subsidy question engaged OMB in its area of prime responsibility, budget costs. It posed a clear, immediate problem—a large, rapid, unexpected outlay of funds which needed to be stanched. Economic policy officials were not so centrally responsible for expanding wheat supplies, nor was the impact of inaction on their policy concerns so immediate. Thus while the Nixon Administration Cost of Living Council officials (including its chairman, Secretary of the Treasury George Shultz) did urge Butz to shift to a supply-expanding policy, they did not, by available evidence, make anywhere near an all-out effort. And that would certainly have been required as Butz in 1972 was sticking hard and fast to the narrow goal of moving grain prices up.[17]

[16]US Congress, Senate, Senate Government Operations Committee, "Russian Grain Transactions," cited, pp. 31–32; GAO, "Russian Wheat Sales," pp. 16, 26.

[17]As Treasury Secretary George Shultz described it later, the Cost of Living Council argued in 1972 "that we should expand the supplies of our agricultural products . . . the Secretary of Agriculture *came to accept that point of view,* and became an advocate of it." (Interview in *The Washington Post,* April 14, 1974. Emphasis added.) Butz would later, of course, become a vocal advocate of full production.

Moreover, economic policy officials seeking wheat acreage expansion faced the additional obstacle of having to reverse a program decision already made. Until a program is put into final form and announced, it is current business and subject to new argument and evidence from those with access to the process—OMB and CEA as well as USDA officials in this case. But to change the wheat program after July 17 required reopening the matter, reestablishing it on the decision-making agenda—a considerably more difficult task. The implementing agency is in a strong position to resist such a reopening, especially when it generates the data upon which such a review would depend. It can also argue that, programmatically, there are equity reasons for sticking to declared guidelines. Farmers make purchases and investments on the basis of these guidelines. Changing a program in mid-stream puts them at a disadvantage—it particularly disadvantages those with relatively early planting dates.

The needed action was the very sort of anti-inflation move—i.e., increasing available supplies—that economists, liberal and conservative alike, can applaud. But the economic policy community in 1972 did not push it with the force it merited and would have required. It was paying the price for years of neglect of agricultural issues—it was simply not alert to its stakes in reasonable grain stocks as a foundation for stable food prices. Moreover, the main costs were in the future (therefore subject to dispute), as was the impact of wheat acreage expansion.

But in early January 1973, they became present costs. The economy was burned and the economists felt the heat. Just as the President was preparing to jettison his Phase II price control program and replace it (on Shultz' urging) with a far looser monitoring regime, the news came that the wholesale price index for food products had jumped by six percent—from 125.3 to 132.6—in the single month of December![18] The need to do something was suddenly clear, and action was taken. The Council of Economic Advisers produced, in a matter of hours, a memo listing steps to be taken to ease the food price situation. They were discussed and agreed to in a meeting which the President held with his senior economic advisers but without the Secretary of Agriculture. Presented with a fait accompli, Butz went along with only very minor reservations. On January 10, one day before Nixon announced the abandonment of Phase II, Agriculture announced a number of production-expanding steps, including a decision to bring nearly 15 million wheat acres back into production. It was too late to expand the winter wheat crop, but the shift was made in time to affect spring wheat plantings. Later that month the restrictive feedgrains program announced in December 1972 was amended also to expand acreage.[19]

The virulent wave of food price inflation that began that month should not, of course, be blamed solely on the Soviet wheat purchases of 1972. Russian production shortfalls were part of a global downturn in grain production in 1972. Export demand from other sources, for feedgrains and soybeans as well as wheat, was to

---

[18]*Economic Report of the President,* January 1973, p. 248.

[19]*New York Times,* January 11, 1973, p. 32; Schnittker, "1972–73 Food Price Spiral," p. 503.

increase markedly in the years immediately ahead. Still, the Soviet purchases appear to have been the major destabilizing influence in the world grain trade during 1972–73.[20] And even if other causes deserve more prominence than they have been given here, it is clear that the failure to reverse the 1973 wheat program was a particularly serious policy mistake.

The mistakes of 1972 contributed to the most dramatic food policy decision of 1973, the temporary embargo on soybean exports in June. This action also involved conflicts among policy objectives, but the reason they were resolved as they were is more complicated. An administration which had stressed farm and foreign policy in 1972 would now take an action very damaging to both, and so contrary to its "free market" economic principles that the President's economic "czar" felt moved to offer his resignation.

The 1973 soybean embargo[21]

Background

The food price inflation which had exploded in December 1972 continued through most of 1973. The US wholesale price index for farm products shot up from 132.5 in December 1972 to 184.5 the following August, before settling back to 168.0 in December 1973. The consumer price rise was only slightly less spectacular. Food prices jumped from 126.3 at the close of 1972 to 148.5 in August and 151.5 in December 1973.[22] Moreover, the export demand largely responsible for this inflation rose further in 1973–74, with increased purchases by China, Japan, Western Europe, and the developing countries more than offsetting an 18 million ton decline in total imports by the Soviet Union and Eastern Europe.[23]

The market for oilseeds and protein meals was particularly tight due to a combination of increased world demand and reduced supply from other countries. Foreign buyers turned to soybeans to make up for deficits elsewhere. And the US dominated the world soybean market, producing over 70 percent of the total world crop and supplying the bulk of world exports.[24] For some countries dependence on

[20]Fred H. Sanderson, "The Great Food Fumble," p. 504. For an interpretation giving greater emphasis to other factors, see Hathaway, "Food Prices and Inflation."

[21]The subsequent account draws on contemporary accounts and interviews, and on two secondary sources: Edward F. Graziano, "Commodity Export Controls: The Soybean Case (1973)," pp. 18–32 in Edward K. Hamilton et al., *Cases on a Decade of U.S. Foreign Economic Policy: 1965–74,* Report of the Commission on the Organization of the Government for the Conduct of Foreign Policy (Washington: GPO, 1976) Appendix H; and General Accounting Office, "U.S. Action Needed to Cope with Commodity Shortages," Report to the Congress, April 29, 1974.

[22]*Economic Report of the President,* February 1974, pp. 300, 305.

[23]Sanderson, "Great Food Fumble," p. 504; U.S. Department of Agriculture, Economic Research Service, "The World Food Situation and Prospects to 1985," Foreign Agriculture Economic Report No. 98, December 1974, pp. 3-4.

[24]USDA, *Agricultural Statistics 1975,* p. 133.

the United States was almost total. Japan relied on imports for 97 percent of its considerable use of soybeans for food and feed; 92 percent of these imports came from the United States.[25]

Soybeans had become the postwar "miracle crop" for US farmers, who had responded to the steady increase in domestic and world demand by quadrupling soybean output in twenty years. But soybean carryover stocks, which had always been low compared to those for wheat, had been declining. As exports moved toward a record 479 million bushels in 1972–73, US livestock producers saw their soybean meal prices triple within a year.[26] Meat prices were high and rising, and housewives were organizing meat boycotts amid vehement concern about skyrocketing food prices.

For President Nixon, who had dramatically lifted most price controls in January, food price inflation was a policy crisis and major political embarrassment. So it was also for his chief economic policy adviser, George Shultz, who had strongly favored the easing of controls. Pressure for action mounted on Capitol Hill. In April the Senate narrowly defeated a bill providing an across-the-board price freeze, and on June 4 the Senate Democratic Caucus called for a 90-day freeze on prices, wages, and profits.[27] But prices of raw agricultural commodities were particularly resistant to controls, and if prices of meat at retail were to be frozen, something needed to be done to prevent foreign buyers from bidding up feed prices to a point where it squeezed US livestock producers out of business. So when Nixon responded to the economic crisis (and to his larger, Watergate-generated political crisis) by ordering on June 13 a 60-day freeze on all prices except those of raw agricultural products, economic logic dictated some action against the danger that export demand would continue to bid up the prices of these products and squeeze US livestock producers. The president declared therefore that "a new system for export controls" was needed to hold down "the price of animal feedstuffs and other grains in the American market."[28] Two weeks later, Secretary of Commerce Frederick Dent declared a complete, temporary embargo on US exports of soybeans, cottonseeds, and products thereof.

This was, according to press reports, the first time the United States had imposed such an embargo except in war or threat of war. And though it proved short-lived, it had serious negative impact on farm and foreign policy. It called into question the dependability of the US as a supplier of farm products and raised serious doubts among Europeans and Japanese about whether American economic policy would take account of their urgent needs when crises arose. In Tokyo in particular, the "soybean shock" of 1973 took its place alongside the "Nixon shocks" of 1971.

[25]Testimony of Nelson A. Stitt, Director, United States-Japan Trade Council, in Senate Committee on Agriculture and Forestry, "Export Control Policy," Hearings, July 11, 1973, p. 224.
[26]*Agricultural Statistics 1975*, p. 129; USDA Crop Reporting Board, *Agricultural Prices: 1974*, p. 149.
[27]*Congressional Quarterly*, June 16, 1973, p. 1484.
[28]For the Presidential speech of June 13, see *Weekly Compilation of Presidential Documents*, June 18, 1973, pp. 765–69.

The crowning irony was that subsequent evidence made export controls appear totally unnecessary. Once the embargo was imposed, it became clear that much of the apparent export demand was speculative. By August 1 the Commerce Department announced that it would license the export of up to 100 percent of soybean contracts entered into before June 13, though tighter restrictions were retained for oilcake and meal. The following month controls were effectively lifted, and harvest of the record US 1973 soybean crop began. Major importers ended up getting the soybeans they needed, and US exports from the 1973 crop would top the record set for 1972. And the domestic supply crisis receded.

Analysis

In 1972 the food and foreign policy officials had dominated policy; in 1973 it was the economic officials' turn. It was their crisis, and the most dramatic policy decision—the soybean embargo—gave short shrift to agriculture export needs and international diplomacy just as incipient inflation was neglected the summer before. Yet 1973 was not a mirror image of 1972. Kissinger and Butz saw the Russian grain sales as a major policy achievement, but the embargo was to economic advisers at best an embarrassment, at worst a disaster. In an editorial of July 2, 1973, *The Washington Post* labeled it "a staggering confession of incompetence," since after the Russian experience, "a reasonably foresighted administration would have required, last fall, that traders publicly register all foreign sales." Yet Deputy Assistant Secretary of Agriculture Richard Bell could tell a Senate subcommittee in the summer of 1973 only that USDA had "been working on a voluntary reporting system on export sales" which they "were moving to put . . . into effect" in mid-June.[29]

There were several reasons why administration officials were reluctant to monitor export contracts closely. It is costly to do so. It requires the gathering of information that exporters prefer to keep secret for competitive reasons, and it smacks of interference with the "free market." There is also, for those reluctant to employ controls, the danger that information gathering will help precipitate them by triggering precautionary buying in the marketplace and fueling concern within government. Thus as prices skyrocketed and other signals of an exceptionally tight market accumulated (including "intense pressure" from soybean processors[30]), Agriculture and CEA officials resisted information-gathering steps proposed by Cost of Living Council Director John Dunlop because they saw them as steps toward controls. But pressure was mounting throughout the first half of 1973 for some strong anti-inflation action. For whatever the economic logic of the January 11 termination of Phase II, it proved politically disastrous. In an effort to recoup some of his losses, Nixon imposed price ceilings on beef, lamb, and pork on March 29,

---

[29]US Congress, Senate, Committee on Agriculture and Forestry, Subcommittee on Foreign Agricultural Policy, "Export Control Policy," Hearing, July 11, 1973, p. 49.
[30]GAO, "Commodity Shortages," p. 29.

while his economic advisers resisted pressures inside and outside the executive to move toward a broader freeze. But as inflation continued into early May, Dunlop succeeded in having staff work initiated on a possible retail food price freeze and related issues. Concurrently, an interagency working group was formed under the CEA's Gary Seevers to explore specifically the ramifications of export controls. The State Department was not represented in this group.

Members of the Seevers group were generally opposed to export controls. However, their economic analysis concluded that controlling feed exports would be effective in dampening feed prices. This dampening effect might prove essential to avoid driving many US livestock producers out of business if existing meat price ceilings were maintained or new ones imposed. But the existing export control authority required that the commodity in question be demonstrably in short domestic supply and under serious inflationary pressure due to abnormal foreign demand. So the Seevers group reported that export monitoring was required, and Shultz recommended an export monitoring system to President Nixon.

But Nixon was also getting advice for stronger action, which Shultz opposed. Dunlop was deeply concerned about food price rises, which were particularly likely to generate increased union wage demands and thus fuel further inflation. He saw food retail price controls and agricultural commodity export controls as mutually reinforcing means of combatting them. As Dunlop was making the economic case in administration councils, Nixon was being pushed by political advisers like Melvin Laird, John Connally, and Bryce Harlow to take strong action for political reasons. The President had just suffered through the worse spring of his political life— Watergate disclosures had transformed his standing from that of ascendant president with a near-record electoral mandate to a besieged president struggling to hold onto what remained of his personal credibility and capacity for leadership. The thought cannot have escaped him that he might recoup politically, and rekindle faith in himself as a strong president, if he executed another dramatic policy shift.

Thus, over Shultz's opposition, Nixon decreed a 60-day freeze on prices in a dramatic television address to the nation on June 13, 1973. To support this freeze he called for ''a new system of export controls on food products . . . designed to hold down the price of animal feedstuffs and other grains in the American market,'' so that consumers could get ''meat and eggs and milk at prices you can afford.'' ''In allocating the products of American farms between marketings abroad and those in the United States, we must put the American consumer first,'' he said.[31] Thus notwithstanding the opposition of Shultz and others, it was a *domestic economic policy* decision. Farm policy concerns about keeping overseas markets and foreign policy concerns about political relationships were not prominently raised in the intra-governmental forums where the issues were debated and the staff work was completed. Nor did anyone press these concerns upon the President.

Now that the President had committed the United States to control exports, if necessary, to protect American consumers and meat producers, data were needed to

[31]*Weekly Compilation of Presidential Documents,* June 18, 1973, pp. 765–77.

determine the necessity and provide legal justification if action were to be taken. Since the government had failed to gather information earlier, it was forced now to gather it hastily, which meant the data were likely to prove unreliable. The reporting system quickly instituted on June 13 had not been pre-tested. Its technical weaknesses were exacerbated by the fact that it was the Secretary of Commerce who was legally responsible for imposing export controls (albeit with the Agriculture Secretary's concurrence on farm products). Therefore, Commerce sent out the questionnaire, after amending the Agriculture draft to conform more closely to the format used recently for export reporting on non-agricultural commodities such as ferrous scrap. In the eyes of Agriculture officials, this made it even less likely to produce reliable findings.

But as the data were being collected and as follow up policy consideration of export controls proceeded under Schultz' direction, a far more restricted, emergency process was apparently proceeding involving mainly the CLC and the CEA. One internal CEA memo of June 25 reached an alarming conclusion:

> The combination of high feed prices and the freeze, if continued for 3 or 4 months until new crops are harvested, will force the livestock, dairy and poultry industries through a major contraction during which their capital base (breeding flocks and stock) will be eroded. If this happens, it will be mid-1975 before we get out of the food price problem.

And though its author had formerly opposed export controls, he now concluded that it would be necessary to "act this week to control exports of soybeans, soybean meal and perhaps corn." There was "no other way of avoiding the contraction in the livestock-poultry sector unless we abandon the freeze."[32]

It was in this foreboding frame of mind that officials received, apparently on Monday, June 25, the first results of the Commerce Department survey. Scheduled exports were reported by Commerce at 92 million bushels for July 15 to August 30. This number was later reduced to 66 million bushels after review and elimination of double-counting, but this was still double the estimated 33 million bushels that were believed to be "available for export after fulfillment of domestic requirements."[33] The reaction, as described by more than one participant, was "panic." Officials felt themselves in a bind: they were skeptical of the validity of the data, but had no good way of checking it before they needed to take action. Agriculture Department officials especially were very skeptical of these findings, believing (correctly) that they sharply overestimated actual export demand. But their reputation as experts had sunk very low in the government by mid-1973. Agriculture officials had clearly misread world commodity markets in 1972. By the spring of 1973, USDA assurances that food price inflation was ebbing had become a standing joke among economic policy officials. So the credibility of the "expert" agency had evaporated

---

[32]Stein and Seevers discussed these alternatives publicly on June 25, but without the strong prescriptive tone of the internal memo. (*New York Times,* June 26, 1973, p. 20.)

[33]GAO, "Commodity Shortages," p. 187; Lazarus in Senate Agriculture Committee, "Export Control Policy," p. 56.

just at the point when such expertise was most important as a check on the alarming, but misleading, data the government had just gathered.

Dunlop now pushed very hard for quick action. His earlier warnings about exports wreaking domestic havoc seemed vindicated. No one felt on solid enough ground to resist him effectively. The new statistics were—in effect—the only statistics in town. Notably, no international consultations were undertaken. The State Department, included after mid-June in the general group reviewing the issue, was excluded from the heated, emergency soybean deliberations. The National Security Council staff was included, but its representative—an economist who was personally skeptical about the data—was new to his position and to the specific issues involved. Thus, foreign policy concerns again went largely unvoiced. The actual embargo decision was made by Shultz, with Nixon's concurrence.

As things turned out, the data and assumptions supporting the embargo proved wildly inaccurate. The export contract data grossly exaggerated actual export demand. Many contracts were apparently of a speculative or precautionary nature, as they did not result in applications for export license. Domestically, the soybean crushers did not operate at capacity or anywhere near it. Soybean prices continued to fluctuate erratically, but the general trend was down from the early June peak. By September, all export restrictions were effectively lifted, though monitoring was retained.

In retrospect, the effect of the controls seems to have been the opposite of that desired. They were employed as a short-term measure to tide the US over a difficult period, but their impact on summer 1973 soybean exports was apparently quite limited. The fact and form of their imposition, however, sent a more enduring message to major US markets. It would be harder for the US to argue credibly that the European Economic Community should plan on importing more food from the US and rely less on subsidized domestic production; it would be easier for a Japanese minister of agriculture and forestry to urge steps toward greater production at home, and diversification of overseas sources of soybean supply.

The tight food situation in 1973 also put a major squeeze on the PL 480 program, reducing quantities programmed to a fraction of former levels and heightening conflict over what countries should receive concessional shipments.

Food aid and the World Food Conference: 1974 [34]

Background

Summer 1973 saw an easing of soybean prices and record US harvests of wheat, corn, and soybeans. But the broader farm and food price trend remained

---

[34]This section draws particularly on interviews; two *National Journal* articles by Daniel J. Balz; and Leslie H. Gelb and Anthony Lake, "Washington Dateline: Less Food, More Politics," *Foreign Policy* (Winter 1974–75): 176–89.

sharply upward, particularly for grains, and the world food situation had become precariously tight. The plight of the poorest food-importing countries grew particularly severe, especially after the OPEC nations quadrupled the price of petroleum in late 1973 and early 1974, thus increasing the drain on importers' foreign exchange.

But just as the need in the Third World had grown, the US food aid program had shrunk. The program had been declining in importance, financing 33 percent of agricultural exports in 1957 but only 13 percent in 1972. By 1974, this figure was down to four percent. For wheat, long the major food aid commodity, PL 480 shipments had at least equalled commercial sales for most pre-1972 years. But by 1974 food aid had shrunk to about one-twentieth of commercial sales (i.e., 57 million bushels in aid; 1,092 in sales). Funds for the program dropped below $1 billion in 1974, the lowest level since PL 480's initial year.[35]

Moreover, the allocation of what food aid was provided had been sharply altered. In every year from 1957 through 1971, India had been the largest PL 480 recipient. But in 1972 India had declared it no longer needed subsidized American grain, and subsidized food aid sales to the hungriest nations had virtually disappeared.[36] Priority was given instead to other US political purposes. In FY 1973, South Vietnam and South Korea alone received almost half of all Title I food aid. In FY 1974 South Vietnam and Cambodia alone received 69 percent.[37]

The conditions which had produced these changes continued through 1974. Commodity markets continued tight; pressures for their "political" allocation remained strong. Yet the US government gradually altered its policies both to increase the amounts of PL 480 commodities programmed and to allocate a greater share to the countries most in need. In his April 1974 speech to the Sixth Special Session of the United Nations, Kissinger promised a "major effort to increase the quantity of food aid over the level we provided last year."[38] Addressing the UN General Assembly the following September, in the wake of the worst drought in the US corn belt in twenty years, President Gerald R. Ford promised the US would increase "the amount it spends for food shipments . . . this year."[39] And finally, in early February 1975, Secretary Butz announced a food aid target of $1.6 billion for the fiscal year

---

[35]USDA, Foreign Agricultural Trade of the United States (*FATUS*), December 1975, p. 16; USDA, *Agricultural Statistics 1975,* p. 4.

[36]PL 480 food moves under two titles. Under Title I, food is sold to recipient governments on subsidized credit; the food is then usually sold to people within the recipient country, at prevailing market prices or through low-price government stores. Under Title II, US food is donated — bilaterally, through the UN/FAO World Food Program, through voluntary private relief agencies like CARE — and distributed directly to recipients in school feeding, relief, food-for-work programs, etc.

In recent years, Title I sales have totalled about 70 percent of all PL 480, and it was these sales around which the allocation dispute was centered. In this article, however, "food aid" figures generally include both Title I and II, as well as a modest amount of subsidized sales under other foreign assistance legislation.

[37]*FATUS,* December 1975, pp. 40–43; Daniel J. Balz, "Agriculture Report: Politics of Food Aid Presents US with Policy Dilemma," *National Journal* (November 23, 1974): 1764.

[38]*Department of State Bulletin,* May 6, 1974, p. 480.

[39]*Weekly Compilation of Presidential Documents,* September 20, 1974, p. 1168.

already more than half completed. The amount actually spent was somewhat smaller, a bit over $1.2 billion; but there were increases in the quantities of wheat and rice shipped, and Bangladesh and India headed the list of recipients.[40]

Analysis

In April 1974, Lyle P. Schertz wrote in *Foreign Affairs* that "No major political force in the United States is embracing the food needs of most of the lower-income countries for whatever reason—charity, security, or economic self-interest."[41] Yet before the year was out, the global welfare and development policy community had won at least a limited PL 480 victory, notwithstanding the very unpromising situation as the year began.

Certainly there were few signs of such a victory in the summer of 1973. The adverse impact of US food policy decisions on food-importing poor countries had been largely ignored in both Soviet sales and soybean embargo cases, and the pressures in 1973 were overwhelmingly toward restricting PL 480 to minimal amounts. They underscored a built-in contradiction in the structure and politics of PL 480, i.e., when countries needed it the most, it tended to provide the least.

For food-short developing countries, a ton of grain had become more costly to import; hence their need for concessionary finance had increased. Yet PL 480 funds were budgeted in dollars, so the money allocated for PL 480 bought much less. For example, $655 million bought about 9.1 million tons of PL 480 grain in FY 1971; $727 million bought only 3.4 million tons in 1974.[42] But more important than budgetary ceilings were constraints on commodity availabilities. PL 480 was established as a "surplus-disposal" program. While the law had been amended in 1966 to remove the requirement that a commodity be in surplus in order to be provided, it substituted a provision that aid be limited to commodities determined (by the Secretary of Agriculture) to be "available" after domestic and overseas commercial needs had been met. PL 480 was therefore by law just a residual claimant on American food resources. There were no absolute rules for determining exactly how much wheat or corn was "available"; decisions rested on a balancing of values. But whereas the economic policy community had strong interest in limiting food outflows in that inflationary period, PL 480 had lost its main supporting constituency, the farm policy community. Secretary Butz dramatized this new situation by sending his proposed Agriculture Department budget over to OMB with a zero figure for PL 480. When officials there expressed surprise, he replied that with commercial exports booming he didn't need the program any more. "If Henry needs it, let the money come out of his budget!"

---

[40]*New York Times,* February 4, 1975; *FATUS,* December 1975, pp. 12–13, 17, 31.

[41]"World Food: Prices and the Poor," p. 534.

[42]Totals calculated for wheat and products, feedgrains and products, and rice from USDA/ERS, "US Agricultural Exports under Public Law 480," ERS-Foreign 395, October 1974, pp. 7–8 and 16–18; and *FATUS,* December 1975, p. 17.

"Henry" did need it, because Congress was cutting back other foreign aid funding—particularly for Indochina—and for food-importing countries PL 480 was, up to a point, substitutable for other forms of financial support. Moreover, PL 480 was a flexible program, with far less congressional control over either amounts spent or intended recipients than had developed for the general foreign assistance program. Thus the foreign policy community, led by Henry Kissinger, had become PL 480's prime constituency, and the minimum levels to which food aid was reduced (beginning in mid-1973) were set with these foreign policy purposes preeminent. The development policy community was a weak internal voice; Agriculture had little stake in humanitarian food aid in a tight commodity situation.

But Kissinger also took a step in 1973 which would highlight the humanitarian side of food aid. He proposed, in his first major address as Secretary of State, "that a World Food Conference be convened under United Nations auspices in 1974."[43] The forum was the UN General Assembly; and the apparent source of the idea was Senator Hubert Humphrey, who had urged it in Kissinger's nomination hearings.[44] Kissinger was receptive: he was awakening to the foreign policy importance of food issues and looking for ways to involve himself more in economic issues as he assumed his new post. But, Agriculture Department leadership was reluctant, fearing (correctly) that such a conference would increase unwanted international pressures on US food policies.

As November 1974 approached, the scheduled World Food Conference exerted continuing pressure on the US to expand its food aid. It also tended to increase State Department influence, for while Butz was designated chief of the US delegation, Kissinger was to give the major American speech, and Ambassador Edwin Martin was appointed, at NSC staff initiative, as State-based coordinator of US participation in the conference. Still, through the fall and winter, policy on PL 480 remained to minimize it. New agreements were sharply limited except with "essential" recipients, mainly Cambodia and Vietnam. Holding down shipments took somewhat greater time, but they too dropped rapidly.[45]

[43]Address to the UN General Assembly, September 24, 1973, in *State Department Bulletin*, October 15, 1973, p. 472.
[44]US Congress, Senate, Foreign Relations Committee, "Nomination of Henry A. Kissinger," Part 1, September 1973, p. 148.
[45]The following figures for shipments of Title I PL 480 commodities are illustrative. (Figures are for total shipments, thousands of metric tons.)

July-December	1972	3,020
January-June	1973	1,966
July-December	1973	1,016
January-June	1974	786
July-December	1974	472
January-June	1975	3,103

(USDA/FAS, "Title I, Public Law 480: Total Amounts Shipped Through June 30, 1975, By Country and Commodity," p. 169.)

Though constrained by the tight supply situation, Kissinger nonetheless began to address food issues more aggressively in public forums. One reason was that he wanted to dramatize US responsiveness to world concerns on food as part of the campaign to get OPEC to make *its* commodity available at less burdensome price levels. Moreover, by the time of his April 1974 speech to the UN, grain prices had begun to drop from their early 1974 peaks. They were expected to drop further with all US grain acreage restraints now removed. Thus Kissinger, overcoming resistance from economic policy officials on a matter over which he had maximum leverage (the wording of his speech), promised "a major effort to increase the quantity of food aid over the level we provided last year."[46] But this did not mean a decision to increase the administration's FY 1975 budget for PL 480, though State pressed for one. Rather, the anticipated further declines in US grain prices were expected to make it possible to ship more commodities for the same amount of money.

But then came the summer drought in the midwest corn belt, the worst in twenty years, and unfavorable weather for wheat as well. USDA crop estimates declined sharply as the drought made itself felt: from 6.5 to below 5 billion bushels for corn. Due mainly to the drop in US crops, world grain production for 1974–75 declined about 5 percent from the previous year.[47] So instead of leveling off as expected, US "retail food prices advanced at a 13.4 percent annual rate between June and December 1974."[48] Within an administration already burned by food price inflation, and burned also by the export control fiasco of 1973, this created a particularly severe set of cross-pressures. Export controls were to be avoided, but domestic inflation was to be minimized. These constraints clearly pointed toward minimum food aid. Yet, at the same time, with the World Food Conference approaching and the food situation worsening in areas like South Asia, a world hunger coalition of private church groups and voluntary agencies was pushing to expand food aid, and the Senate unanimously passed a resolution introduced by Hubert Humphrey calling for an increase.[49]

In wrestling with these difficult trade-offs, the US government operated in at least three separate, though related, organizational frameworks. Under the President's Committee on Food, established in June 1974 to review and coordinate domestic and international food policy activities, was the Food Deputies Group chaired by CEA member Gary Seevers. This group worked very actively that summer and fall to develop an overall strategy for coping with the crisis. A separate, OMB-chaired working group was responsible for coordinating PL 480 allocations and decisions on program levels. These two groups, each operating at the assistant secretary level, were dominated by a CEA-OMB-Treasury economic policy alliance

---

[46]One official involved in drafting remembers a careful effort to word this section so that it could mean an increase over either the calendar or the fiscal year, which ever proved easier to accomplish.

[47]*Economic Report of the President*, February 1975, p. 163. World production in 1974/75 was still slightly above that of 1971/72, because of a large increase in production in 1973/74.

[48]*Economic Report of the President*, February 1975, p. 160.

[49]*New York Times*, September 22, 1974.

which sought to constrain both USDA (on commercial exports) and State (on PL 480). These economic agencies were willing to consider increases in PL 480 if the market crisis eased, but they strongly opposed announcing an increase publicly, for fear that would drive commodity prices up further.

The third policy-making framework was US planning for the food conference led by Ambassador Martin in State. Secretary Kissinger wanted a forthcoming US declaratory policy on food aid, an open commitment to do more. This set the stage for a sharp six month battle over the size and visibility of the food aid budget and the commodity amounts to be programmed. The first action-forcing event was Gerald Ford's scheduled speech to the UN General Assembly, his first major presidential foreign policy address. At Kissinger's urging, Ford agreed to promise (over OMB and CEA resistance) that "the United States will not only maintain the amount it spends for food shipments to nations in need but it will increase this amount this year." But reflecting the strong concerns of domestic economic officials staring at bad crop reports and rising grain prices, and his own commitment to a Whip Inflation Now (WIN) program geared to hold down public expenditures, he gave no dollar figure. So the US position as of April—greater tonnage but not necessarily more money—was turned on its head. For Ford was silent on the quantity of food the US would provide—though Kissinger had pressed for a commitment to increased volume.

But the Secretary of State soon renewed his effort to put the United States on record for increasing the quantity of food aid. The action event this time was his conference speech scheduled for November 5, in which he sought to strike a posture of maximum US leadership. His tactics were similar to those he employed on other occasions. His speech was prepared quietly, by a limited group within State, working directly with the President for clearance and sharing the draft with Cabinet colleagues only at the eleventh hour. This created problems for delegation chairman Butz, who had difficulty planning for his role when he did not know what, exactly, the authoritative statement of the US position was going to contain. Kissinger wanted to promise an increase in quantity above the 4.6 million ton figure originally linked to the $891 million budget figure. Prices had risen so much that this would mean a budget increase of several hundred million. But the economic policy advisers fought back and stuck to their position. The President accepted it.[50] Kissinger's speech, therefore, went only slightly further than Ford's of September, saying that "an expanded flow of food aid" was necessary and that the United States would "increase its food aid contribution."[51]

Advocates of a more specific US commitment continued their campaign at the conference itself, where the presence of a large number of church, international welfare, and "world hunger lobby" representatives acting as observers served to

[50]This account, based on interviews, is essentially consistent with the account in Daniel J. Balz, "Agriculture Report: Politics of Food Aid Presents U.S. With Policy Dilemma," *National Journal*, (November 23, 1974): 1762.

[51]*State Department Bulletin*, December 16, 1974, p. 826.

heighten the pressure. They succeeded in getting the US delegation to cable Ford seeking authority to promise a million ton food aid increase. But Ford resisted, and the World Food Conference closed with no clear decision about how much the US would provide in food aid for a fiscal year already four and one-half months old. State had won a presidential commitment to an increase, and the economic advisers had won the principle of flexibility with respect to the domestic price situation and no immediate public announcement. Finally, USDA had won the assurance it most coveted, that any PL 480 expansion would not come out of the rest of the Agriculture budget.

The issue of volume of aid now became entwined with a struggle over how it should be allocated. Kissinger in 1974 had apparently become more sensitive to food aid's humanitarian uses—and even more sensitive, perhaps, to the value of taking a humane public stance. Hence he titled his World Food Conference address "The Global Community and the Struggle Against Famine," and included in that comprehensive treatment of the world food problem not one solitary mention of the relationship of food to other US foreign policy objectives. But the positions his department took in interdepartmental debates one month later left little doubt that the secretary continued to see PL 480 primarily as a tool for political influence. At a December 5, 1976 meeting, the State Department presented three FY 1975 food aid options for interdepartmental consideration. Each included a total amount and an allocation for that amount, and political-security targets were given overriding priority in each.[52] An NSC staff aide was unwise enough to declare that, "to give food aid to countries just because people are starving is a pretty weak reason." Interestingly, it was the Office of Management and Budget officials who pressed for consideration of an allocation alternative giving greater priority to the neediest countries. They wished to demonstrate that such needs could be met without spending the maximum total amount, which State favored. So the paper prepared for the President several days later included a "low option" of $1 billion and a "high option" of $1.4 billion but also two "middle options" of $1.2 billion, one with State's preferred allocation and one (OMB's) with greater humanitarian emphasis.[53]

Meanwhile, the US Senate was watching, and taking action on its own. On December 3, the FY 1975 foreign assistance authorization bill came to the Senate floor. On December 4, Senator Mark Hatfield denounced a "food aid policy" in which "preserving puppet regimes is more important . . . than preserving the lives of millions of people."[54] Senator Humphrey, the bill's floor manager, won adoption of an amendment which, as later modified in conference, allowed no more than 30

[52]Under the middle option, $612 million in Title I aid was to go to Cambodia, Vietnam, South Korea, Indonesia, Chile, Pakistan, and the Middle East; $194 million for India, Bangladesh, and Sri Lanka.
[53]Dan Morgan in *Washington Post,* December 9, 1974; William Robbins in *New York Times,* December 9, 1974.
[54]*Congressional Record,* December 4, 1974, p. S20602 (unbound).

percent of FY 1975 Title I concessional food aid to go to countries not on the United Nations' list of 32 "most seriously affected" by the world economic crisis. Humphrey was in effect offering the administration a bargain: the larger the total Title I program, the more could be allocated to foreign policy purposes. Though the immediate effect of the Humphrey amendment was to delay the final budget decision still further, as the administration sorted out its meaning and Kissinger bargained with Humphrey on how the amendment would be interpreted, its ultimate impact was both to increase the aid total and to raise the share allocated to humanitarian purposes. For as grain prices declined in December and January, and other foreign demand seemed to wane, the economic policy community's resistance to increased food aid waned also. Finally, on February 4, Butz announced that the Ford administration would increase international food aid to a total of $1.6 billion, including transportation costs.[55]

While the delay in reaching a decision meant that this target would not be achieved, the $1.2 billion in food aid actually shipped in FY 1975 was the largest dollar amount since FY 1968. Moreover, three "MSA" countries, Bangladesh,[56] India, and Pakistan, led the list of recipients.

Like the earlier policy episodes treated here, the food aid issue was exacerbated by the low level of grain reserve stocks. And through most of the 1972–75 period, the United States government and the world community were deliberating actively on a possible system of international grain reserves with agreed-upon rules of access and allocation in time of shortage. Such a system, proponents argued, could dampen grain price fluctuations, help guarantee market access for commercial importers, and be available for famine relief and other needed food aid. But the US government moved very slowly on the reserve issue, and the international system it finally proposed was limited in size, uncertain in efficacy, and not at all tailored to the views of the other national governments whose collaboration would be required to put it into effect.

[55]*New York Times,* January 21, 1975, *New York Times* (Anthony Lewis), January 23, 1975; and *New York Times,* February 4, 1975.

[56]Unfortunately, most PL 480 grain sent to Bangladesh arrived after that country's food crisis peaked in November 1974. Only 68,000 tons of US foodgrain aid reached Bengali ports in August-November, though US shipments of Title I wheat to that country totalled 558,000 tons for FY 1975 as a whole. A major international development organization estimated 20–30,000 deaths by starvation during that period when "arrivals came too late," and a rough extrapolation by Lester R. Brown yielded an estimated increase in deaths of ten times that amount during that fall. (*New York Times,* October 27, 1976.) Of course, internal distribution problems, and the "political" allocation of PL480 grain by the Bangladesh government, also contributed to the disaster.

For statistical information, see "Schedule of Vessels Arrived/Expected at Bangladesh Ports Carrying Foodgrain, Other Foods, and Fertilizers, August 1974-January 1975," Annex G to report of December 13, 1974 (BD-4094) from the US Agricultural Attaché, and USDA/FAS, "Title I, PL 480: Total Amounts Shipped," p. 7. This U.S. policy-making episode is treated more extensively in the broader Brookings study from which this article is drawn.

The food reserves proposal of 1975[57]

Background

From the turnaround in the world food situation of late 1972 until early 1974, the public face of the US government's approach to food reserves was predominantly negative. The thrust of public commentary on stocks was, in effect, that "the US government has gone out of the commodity business.... and we want to stay out of the business of managing stocks of farm products for the nation and the world."[58]

In 1974, however, more positive statements from those in authority began to be heard. In his United Nations Special Session speech of April 1974, Secretary of State Kissinger declared American readiness "to join with other governments in a major worldwide effort to rebuild food reserves." To the General Assembly the following September, President Ford made this a commitment to creating a reserve "system." More detailed information about what such a system would entail was offered by Kissinger in his World Food Conference speech that November. Yet, it took another year for the US government to arrive at agreement on what was, on balance, a very modest specific proposal, which Assistant Secretary of Agriculture Richard Bell presented on September 29, 1975, to the International Wheat Council. The US proposed accumulation of a 30 million ton reserve—25 million tons of wheat and 5 million tons of rice. Reserves would be "nationally held," but used according to "internationally agreed rules or guidelines" regarding when stocks were to be acquired or released. These guidelines would be tied to "a quantitative indicator based upon stock levels and deviations in production from the long-term production trend." Participants in the system would "receive assured access to supply at market prices," as well as preferential consideration in times of very severe shortage; non-participants would not.[59]

The US proposal was coolly received. One reason was that the EEC countries preferred price triggers for acquisition and release of stocks, since their Common Agricultural Policy was based upon price indicators. Moreover, European countries wished to deal with reserves as part of a comprehensive commodity arrangement, which the US resisted. Another reason was that by the time the US got its proposal together, the international food crisis had receded. With grain prices falling and stock replenishment beginning in any case, the issue had lost its urgency. Importing countries could now afford to take their time about negotiating, for they no longer needed to worry about access to grain in the short term. The international "buyers' market" was returning.

[57]This section draws particularly on interviews; Philip H. Trezise, *Rebuilding Grain Reserves: Toward an International System* (Washington, D.C.: Brookings Institution, 1976); and Daniel J. Balz, "State-Agriculture Feud Delays Grain Reserve System," *National Journal* (June 28, 1975): 951–59.

[58]Earl L. Butz, quoted in Daniel J. Balz, "Economic Report: World Food Conference Prompts U.S. Farm Policy Review," *National Journal* (June 1, 1974): 804.

[59]For summaries of the U.S. proposal, see Trezise, *Rebuilding International Grain Reserves,* pp. 52–55; and *National Journal* (November 11, 1975): 1427.

Analysis

Calls for a system of reserves to insure "world food security" had become public fare by mid-1973. Yet, the US government could not come together on a specific proposal until 1975. One of the reasons for this delay was that, to many in the farm policy community, reserve stocks were a curse, "overhanging the market" and depressing prices. In the much happier (for them) economic climate of 1973 and 1974, they associated proposals to establish ongoing reserve stocks with a return to the depressed market conditions of the prior two decades. Secretary Butz encouraged this association since he was reluctant to assure farmers economically-meaningful supports to brake falling prices, and could hardly call upon them to accept the restraints on price rises which an effective reserve system would entail. Butz argued, moreover, that if the US government stayed out of the commodity business, farmers and traders would accumulate greater stocks themselves, as would importing countries.

The foreign and development policy communities, on the other hand, were very interested in food reserves. For foreign policy officials, a system of food reserves might insure against future shocks to bilateral relations like the soybean embargo and provide a vehicle for assuaging world food emergencies. It might also provide a breakthrough for international cooperation in the long-abrasive sphere of agricultural trade, and a constructive response to LDC pressure for a new international economic order. Development advocates supported it for the latter reason, and because it could contribute to more generous food aid policies in time of need. Ultimately, it was foreign policy concerns which prompted US government movement on the issues. In the wake of the soybean embargo, a comprehensive interagency study of international food policy was ordered in the summer of 1973. When this analytic effort proved inconclusive, a followup study focusing specifically on food reserves was ordered. By early 1974, a minimal consensus had emerged within the US government: there *should* be some international stock arrangement, and it should *not* be controlled by an international agency.

But progress toward greater specificity came hard. One reason was the disappearance of presidential leadership as Nixon became enveloped in Watergate.[60] Second, the position of the economic policy community was ambivalent. The Council of Economic Advisers' report of January 1974 generally endorsed stockpiling. But if senior economic policy officials were more positive than Secretary Butz about the price-stabilizing potential of reserves, and less adamant against government stock ownership or control, they shared his general preference for free market approaches over governmental supply management. Hence, if they initially took a tolerant attitude toward food reserve proposals, they did not embrace or press them as a prime cure to existing economic ills. Finally, food reserves policy making

---

[60]Watergate contributed to instability in economic policy coordinating institutions. In May 1974, economic "czar" Shultz departed, replaced by William Simon at Treasury and Kenneth Rush in the White House. Then, when Nixon resigned, Rush departed, and Ford instituted the Economic Policy Board to coordinate all domestic and international economic policy decisions.

moved slowly because there was no way a system could be established in 1974 which would alleviate then current food shortages. Even if international agreement on a system could be quickly reached—and no one argued it could—actual replenishment of reserves was dependent on growth in production or on lower consumption, perhaps as a result of higher prices. Thus reserves were essentially a long-run proposition in a government overloaded with short-run food policy concerns.

The State Department's one important source of leverage, however, was the upcoming World Food Conference. Ambassador Edwin Martin was effective in pushing the reserve issue as US coordinator for the conference, and Kissinger was able to win interagency clearance for a Rome Conference speech which outlined six general "elements" of an international reserve system. After the conference, Kissinger and his Assistant Secretary for Economic Affairs, Thomas Enders, were able on November 12 to win presidential approval for the establishment of yet another interagency food committee, the International Food Review Group (IFRG), to coordinate follow-up for the World Food Conference. Kissinger was to serve as chairman while Enders acted as the head of the interagency working group. For several months thereafter, deliberations of reserves moved to this forum.

The IFRG itself was, like most such Cabinet committees, a formal umbrella rather than an active forum. But Enders employed the working group actively to expedite development of a US proposal. In these meetings, Enders reportedly pushed his ideas regarding the content of the US proposal, particularly on the most important and controversial issue, establishing guidelines for the acquisition and release of reserve commodities. Enders sought as tight a system as possible, with large stocks, and specific and binding guidelines built on agreed price indicators. But Butz and Bell held out for a looser, less binding and less interventionist system. In the end, Agriculture simply outlasted its opposition. One reason why USDA could do so was that State's specific proposal generated strong resistance in the economic policy community. To most economic policy officials, what Enders wanted looked too much like the type of price-regulating international commodity arrangement for which the Third World was pressing generally, and to which these officials were ideologically opposed. Thus CEA, in particular, cooled on the whole notion of an international reserve system.

In the face of this strong opposition, Enders pulled back from his drive for price triggers and accepted quantitative guidelines early in 1975. But the interagency dispute continued, especially over the thorny question of how to deal with countries like the Soviet Union that might not join the system. For State, it was essential for a system to give preference to members in time of shortage. To Agriculture, this meant export controls, which it opposed for reasons of both economic doctrine and self-interest. In particular, it did not want to risk alienating the Russian market. Enders sought to use a Kissinger speech to force a breakthrough, and he won Butz' eleventh-hour clearance to a pledge that the US would "formally propose a comprehensive international system of reserves" in May.[61] But thereafter interagency conflict re-emerged, and the promised proposal did not materialize.

The final compromise was instead engineered by economic policy-makers. By June, Economic Policy Board officials were pressing for a resolution of the interagency dispute. On June 13, Seevers' position on the Council of Economic Advisers was filled by Paul MacAvoy, who thereby became chairman of the Food Deputies Group. MacAvoy was generally skeptical about international commodity management arrangements, but State officials persuaded him that what was now at issue was not a price-fixing but a buffer stock scheme, and MacAvoy concluded that this made sense. So the issue was recast in the form of an economic analysis problem and econometric studies were ordered under MacAvoy's Food Deputies Group. The results, reportedly, were generally favorable on the impact of a system on the overall world food situation, and it was concluded that the system would also have a slight burden-sharing effect in practice. Based on this study, a new consensus was reached in mid-July, and pinned down at a Cabinet session led by Kissinger later that month. The final agreement was surfaced publicly in Kissinger's September 1 speech to the United Nations Seventh Special Session, and in complete form in the proposal submitted to the International Wheat Council on September 29.

The final proposal was stronger than it might have been had not State persisted. This was particularly true on the discrimination issue, where the proposal provided the participants would "receive assured access to supplies" and non-participants "would not be assured of obtaining access."[62] But in pressing for a tight, price-based system of grain stock management, State had proposed arrangements at variance with the values of officials who led USDA, CEA, OMB, and Treasury in 1974 and 1975—and in *their* spheres of primary policy concern. Kissinger had strong leverage with Ford, and Enders was very adept bureaucratically. But since they did not forge strong alliances with key economic or agriculture policy officials, their effectiveness was limited to issues and occasions which they could define as *foreign* policy more than *economic* or *agricultural* policy. Had they not exploited the World Food Conference and Kissinger's role as foreign policy spokesman, there might not have been any US reserves proposal. But the lack of a shared perspective with either the economic or agriculture policy community limited the substance of what they could achieve.

While these food aid and grain reserves debates were being brought to their conclusion, American food policy-makers were also confronting anew the problem of Russian grain purchases and their domestic price impact. This time neither the Russians nor the grain companies went unconstrained, and farm policy values were

---

[61]"Strengthening the World Economic Structure," Address by Secretary of State Henry A. Kissinger before the Kansas City International Relations Council, May 13, 1975, reprinted in *Department of State Bulletin,* June 2, 1975, p. 718.

[62]For the text from which these quotations are taken, see U.S. Information Service, *Wireless Bulletin from Washington,* September 30, 1975.

reined in to accommodate economic and foreign policy goals as well. But the way the US government achieved this restraint outraged the farm policy community, undermining the political basis for balanced policy over the longer term.

Soviet grain sales and domestic inflation: 1974–1975 [63]

Background

After their large purchases in 1972–73, the Russians stayed out of the US grain market in 1973–74. But their crop in 1974 was down, and that fall they re-entered the US market suddenly, for 3.2 million tons of grain, although not without some prior diplomatic consultation. USDA was notified of Soviet grain purchases immediately by the grain companies, under reporting procedures then in operation. As instructed, the department passed on this information directly to the White House.

This was the fall when US grain supplies were tightest. Consumer food prices were again rising rapidly; there was evidence that the Russians were in the market for at least another 2 million tons. And *everyone* remembered 1972! Thus, though the sale was quite small compared to 1972,[64] the Administration responded quickly. One day after receiving notification of the new transactions with the Russians, Secretary of the Treasury William Simon summoned representatives of the grain companies to a White House meeting, where in the presence of Simon, Butz and other officials, President Ford told the company representatives that the sales should not go forward.[65] He cited US political pressure and the danger that Congress might force export controls if the sales were not stopped. Butz then summoned grain company representatives to an overflow meeting at the Department of Agriculture to announce the enforcement of a new, "voluntary" system under which companies would obtain prior approval at USDA for all sales in excess of 50,000 tons to any country. Shortly thereafter, Secretary Simon led a mission to Moscow which re-negotiated the contracts, ending up with the same total amount of grain but reversing the amounts of wheat and corn.

---

[63]This section draws particularly on interviews; Congressional hearings as cited; Daniel J. Balz, "Soviet Grain Purchases Prompt Informal Export Controls," *National Journal* (September 6, 1975): 1259–64; and Raymond F. Hopkins, "Global Food Management: U.S. Policymaking in an Interdependent World," in J. S. Nye, Jr., Robert O. Keohane, et al., "Organizing for Global Environmental and Resource Interdependence," Appendix B to the *Report of the Commission on the Organization of the Government for the Conduct of Foreign Policy* (Washington: GPO, 1976), pp. 141–44.

[64]The 2.3 million tons of corn and 900,000 tons of wheat were less than 2 percent of US production, respectively, for these crops. The 1972 wheat sales were about 25 percent of US production.

[65]Edward W. Cook, Chairman of the Board of Cook Industries, asked that the government put its "request" in writing, and Simon sent him a mailgram stating: "These contracts are *not in the national interest at this time* and Cook Industries should not proceed to implement them." (Emphasis in original.) A similar mailgram was sent to Continental. For the full text, see US Senate Government Operations Committee, "Sales of Grain to the Soviet Union," Hearing, October 8, 1974, pp. 20, 37.

For the next few months, monitoring of exports was interdepartmental. Then, as market conditions eased and prices fell, monitoring was relaxed. On January 29, Secretary Butz announced the lifting of the prior approval system for wheat and soybeans; on March 6, all prior approval requirements were ended, though the reporting requirement for sales contracts was retained. Then, in late spring and early summer 1975, evidence mounted that Russian crop problems would bring estimates of that year's grain harvest well below the 1972 level. On July 16, USDA announced the first 1975 sales of US grain to the Soviet Union. Eight days later, with 10 million tons of grain already contracted, Agriculture asked exporters to give advance notice of any further grain sales to Russia, and indicated that the US expected no more sales would be completed before the August 11 corn crop report. When that report showed some deterioration, Butz announced that the "temporary suspension" of sales to Russia would continue until the September crop report. Everybody remembered 1974 and what happened to US corn that year.

At this point, the US labor movement made a dramatic public entrance into the issue. Maritime unions wanted the Russians to pay higher shipping rates and use US bottoms for a larger proportion of their shipments. Moreover, the US-Soviet Maritime agreement was due to expire at the end of the year. Aligning their interests with those of consumers fearing a repeat of 1972, AFL-CIO President George Meany announced on August 18 that members of the International Longshoremen's Association would refuse to load grain bound for Russia unless the administration promised that the interests of consumers—and the shipping industry—would be protected. Meany was also urging that a "wheat board" outside USDA be established to manage exports. As the unions moved to implement their boycott and court restraining orders temporarily blocked them, Secretary of Labor Dunlop used his strong relations with the labor movement to move forcefully and publicly into the issue. He was determined that the American economy should be protected from food price inflation. Ford and Dunlop met with Meany and five other labor leaders at the White House on August 26, along with OMB Director James Lynn and economic adviser William Seidman. No resolution of the issue was achieved, and the president assigned Dunlop the task of finding a solution. On September 9, they met again (with Kissinger and Butz also present) and an agreement developed by Dunlop *was* reached: the unions would suspend their boycott for a month; the moratorium on new sales to Russia would be extended until mid-October, while the administration sought to negotiate "a longer-term and more certain purchase understanding with the Soviet Union, providing, among other features, for certain minimum purchase" of grain.[66] That same day, yet another food policy-making unit was established to oversee the negotiations. It was designated the "Food Com-

[66]*New York Times,* September 10, 1975. See also a chronology prepared for the Senate Agriculture Committee by the Congressional Research Service, in "Who's Making Foreign Agricultural Policy," *Hearings,* 1976, pp. 126–29, and Robert G. Kaiser, "Old Grain Policy Unworkable, US Officials Found," *Washington Post,* September 11, 1975, reprinted ibid., pp. 111–113.

mittee'' of the Economic Policy Board and the National Security Council, co-chaired by Kissinger and Simon.

On September 10, Under Secretary of State for Economic Affairs Charles W. Robinson left for Moscow to begin negotiations. That same day, the State Department quietly requested, through its Warsaw Embassy, that Poland stop buying grain in US markets, and Poland complied. On September 19, a new US-Soviet agreement on shipping rates was announced. On September 29, Secretary Butz and the Polish Minister of Agriculture reached agreement on regularizing Polish purchases over a five-year period, and a formal exchange of letters confirmed this in November. On October 10, President Ford announced he was lifting the Polish embargo because of record US wheat and corn crops, and on October 20 he announced the signing of a five-year grain trade agreement with the Soviet Union and the lifting of that embargo.

Effective October 1, 1976, the agreement committed the Soviet Union to purchase at least six million tons of wheat and corn each year. It also guaranteed that the US would not impede Soviet purchases of up to eight million tons, unless US supplies were extraordinarily low. If the Russians wished to buy more than eight million tons, intergovernmental consultations were required. For 1975–76, the Russians agreed to consult if they wished to purchase more than 7 million tons beyond the 9.8 for which they had already contracted.

Analysis

The outcome in both 1974 and 1975 was a balancing of food policy goals and interests, a far better balancing than had occurred in 1972 and 1973. The domestic economy was protected from unlimited Soviet grain purchases, but such purchases were continued and, to some degree, regularized. This both advanced and symbolized the foreign policy goal of getting Russia to behave more responsibly in international markets. All of these gains were limited ones, but the trade-offs and political pressures were difficult as well. Perhaps most important, the US government had effectively avoided the sins of 1972 and 1973; i.e., all major policy values were taken into account, and all were to some degree protected.

Restraint was accomplished, essentially, through an alliance between the economic and foreign policy communities. But the farm community was up in arms. In vetoing a bill raising price support levels the previous spring, President Ford had declared (at Agriculture Department initiative): ''We have now eliminated all restrictions on exports and we are determined to do everything possible to avoid imposing them again. Our farm products must have unfettered access to world markets.''[67] Now the administration had closed the door to deny farmers that

---

[67]*Weekly Compilation of Presidential Documents,* May 5, 1975, p. 475.

market reward, the Russians had gone to other markets during the three month "embargo," and the summer rise in farmers' grain prices gave way to a fall decline. A galling symbol of farmers' losses was the evidence that their voice in the federal government, the Department of Agriculture, had been either ignored or overridden in these decisions. There was the new "Food Committee" with two non-USDA chairmen and Butz only one of eight members; the photograph of George Meany and Gerald Ford negotiating grain export policy at the White House, which was reprinted in papers throughout rural America; the suspension of exports to Poland negotiated by State. Asked, "Have you lost the power to make agricultural decisions in the Administration?" Butz replied, "No, sir. I am free to decide what time we set our office hours."[68] Senator Robert Dole said the following January, "I am not certain President Ford will ever recover from that in rural America."[69] "Embargoes" became a vocal and visible issue in the 1976 election campaign.

Thus, the very way that balanced policy-making was achieved served to outrage the farm policy community. And the pattern in 1975 replicated 1974. The earlier episode took place during a serious, coordinated US government effort to hold exports down as the drought in the corn belt cut back supplies. Monitoring the situation and developing the ongoing analysis was the responsibility of Seevers' Food Deputies Group. USDA had the operational lead, including dealings with the Russians: Secretary Butz conferred with Ambassador Dobrynin about the tight situation and sought to ascertain Russian buying intentions; he and his subordinates kept in close touch with the grain companies and gave strong restraining signals to most of them. But the Department apparently wanted only 1 million tons of corn in total sold to Russia, not a million each by Continental and Cook. And its guidance to the latter was considerably less stringent. So more was sold than planned; the press gave prominence to the story; Simon saw a policy crisis which his leadership could help avert; and Ford was moved to intervene.

Most non-USDA actors saw the crisis as a product of Department of Agriculture mismanagement and its lack of ability or willingness to restrain commercial agricultural interests. So USDA was supplanted operationally. Simon led the renegotiating mission to Moscow, and a new operational committee was established under Seevers' chairmanship. Its charge was to oversee the new prior approval system for exports and negotiations with foreign buyers to limit their purchases.

But this informal export control system was not at all popular in the farm community, as Ford discovered when he campaigned in the Midwest before the November mid-term election. USDA, while recognizing the need for (or at least the political inevitability of) some form of export management activity, wanted a system which was both less stringent and more under USDA control. Seevers did not

---

[68] White House press conference of October 20, 1975 on the Soviet grain agreement, reprinted in House Committee on International Relations, "United States Grain and Oil Agreements with the Soviet Union," Hearing, October 28, 1975, p. 61.

[69] Senate Agriculture Committee, "Who's Making Foreign Agricultural Policy," p. 15.

like the chairman role because this committee was too operational, he thought, for the Council of Economic Advisers to lead. So Agriculture proposed that Bell be made chairman. With Bell as chairman the committee continued to function for a while, but less frequently as the supply situation eased (partly because US farmers sharply reduced corn feeding to livestock) and the export target was raised.

So by the time the Russian issue re-emerged in 1975, Agriculture was once again in control of export monitoring. And with farm prices declining steadily through the winter and spring and bumper 1975 grain crops likely, the Department badly needed new Russian sales to bolster the market.[70] In dealing with both the Russians and the grain companies, Butz and Bell were now playing a very active role, one facilitated by the fact that neither the Soviet Union nor the grain companies wanted a replay of 1974. When signs accumulated that the Russians might be re-entering the market, and on the scale of 1972 rather than 1974, Butz and Bell set a quantity—10 million tons—and communicated it to the Russians and the grain companies without getting formal interagency clearance. They surfaced the number publicly as a *prediction* of what Russia might buy, but enforced it as a *limitation*. "It was quite clear," said a grain executive, "Mr. Butz and Mr. Bell said we could spare 10 million tons."[71] By the end of the month, Bell was stating publicly that the Russians had in fact contracted for 9.8 million tons of grain out of the 1975 US crop, and that they did not "expect" any more sales until the August 11 crop report.[72] At the end of August, Bell could say with some justification, "This thing has unfolded just about as we had intended."[73]

Thus, in the summer of 1975 the Agriculture leaders were playing an active, and rather uncharacteristic, export management role. Operating under the threat of having responsibility once again wrested from them, they pursued a rather flexible and sophisticated course and did, in effect, what they had long been criticized for not doing, i.e., restraining commercial agribusiness interests in the name of other policy concerns. But Butz had built his constituency around his unabashed championing of commercial agricultural interests, achieving unusual popularity in the process. This made the restraining role, difficult for any USDA leadership, especially difficult for *this* leadership. When Butz and Bell enforced a lid of 10 million tons on sales to the Russians that July and August, they had to do so semi-covertly, so as to minimize cries of betrayal from grain interests.

But this course had risks of its own. A September 1975 *National Journal* article concluded that in "choosing not to explain in any detail the approach they are taking, Administration officials risk a perpetuation of the uncertainty that exists any

---

[70]USDA would estimate on July 31 that the sales to Russia contracted during that month would increase the average price of wheat in 1975–76 by 75 cents a bushel above what it would be in the absence of such sales. The comparable figure for corn was 30 cents. (US Senate Government Operations Committee, "Grain Sales to the Soviet Union," Hearings, July 31, 1975, p. 31.)

[71]Balz, "Soviet Grain Purchases," p. 1262.

[72]Testimony in "Grain Sales to the Soviet Union," p. 26.

[73]Quoted in Balz, "Soviet Grain Purchases," p. 1264.

time the Russians move into the market."[74] Reuben Johnson of the National Farmers Union expressed similar concern: "I don't trust any behind the scenes hanky-panky between Butz and the grain companies to protect the consumer."[75] Such distrust was magnified because USDA had, as reported in the press, proposed to sell more grain to Russia that summer than other agencies would accept before the 1975 crop information was firmer. Lack of trust of USDA pervaded the executive branch also, as it had in the 1973 soybean embargo.

A brokering role requires trust from the major parties at interest, especially when an issue heats up. USDA was widely distrusted in the economic and foreign policy communities, and by politicians and lobbyists who gave voice to their concerns. Butz had fueled this distrust by catering to a narrow constituency. George Meany now used it to achieve his objectives; Dunlop played on it, and on Meany's intervention, to push through changes in food policy, and the reorganization of food policy-making which he saw as essential to subordinate USDA to a broader public interest. In that political context, President Ford adopted the plan, as almost any president probably would have, and power slipped away from USDA again.

The Butz USDA could not coordinate when crisis came and prices rose or threatened to rise. But others could not coordinate once crisis faded and prices fell.

In both October 1974 and August 1975, the shift of power away from USDA proved temporary, for two related reasons. First was the reaction from the farm policy community, which was split on Earl Butz and his free-market policies but relatively united against these particular interventions in export markets. Second was that the counter-pressure from the economic and foreign policy officials diminished as the crisis receded; their attention turned to other issues, particularly the attention of the senior officials who had forced the shift, while the farm policy community continued to concentrate on food. Thus in early 1975 Bell won the chairmanship of the export management committee, which then met less and less as the issue lost its urgency. In March 1976, with farm prices falling and the autumn election approaching, Butz succeeded in getting President Ford to announce in a speech to the Farm Forum in Springfield, Illinois, the abolition of the EPB/NSC Food Committee and the International Food Review Group, and their replacement with an Agricultural Policy Committee chaired by Secretary Butz.[76]

The way the Ford Administration balanced food policy concerns was through abrupt shifts in the locus of power as circumstances changed and policies changed with them. These shifts had "very disruptive market effects," as Gary Seevers wrote later,[77] and disruptive political effects as well. The Ford Administration coped with food crises better than its Nixon predecessor. But partly because of the approach of its Agriculture Department leadership and the reaction this approach

[74]Ibid.

[75]Quoted ibid.

[76]Remarks on March 5, 1976, in *Weekly Compilation of Presidential Documents,* 1976, pp. 338–45.

[77]Gary L. Seevers, "Food Policy: Implications for the Food Industry," *American Journal of Agricultural Economics* (May 1976): 274.

provoked, it left the problem of building an institutional and political base for longer-term balanced food policy to its successor.

Conclusion

Food policy requires reconciling a range of conflicting but legitimate policy concerns. There is no generally-accepted set of priorities among these concerns, because different policy communities weight them differently. One would therefore expect the food policy process to be somewhat untidy, especially in a period when sharp price rises increased the stakes of governmental policy actors and their outside constituencies.

This expectation is amply confirmed in the episodes examined here. Moreover, they suggest that untidiness may be not only inevitable but sometimes desirable. Newspaper headlines and the clash of competing advocates give visibility to particular issues, reducing the chances that an important policy concern will be excluded from the debate.[78] Perhaps the tidiest of the five cases reviewed here in terms of regularity of procedures and clarity of responsibility is the response to the first Russian grain sales—at least until January 1973. In terms of policy outcome, it ranks with the worst.

Food policy making in 1972–76 was further complicated by the newness of the situation. Officials who addressed it had no experience with a world which might buy more grain than America could afford to sell, or with a market where corn and soybean prices tripled and wheat prices quadrupled in periods of seven months to two years. In such circumstances serious miscalculations are inevitable, and one reassuring conclusion from the experience examined here is that learning did in fact take place. The episodes of 1974 and 1975 were better handled in the limited but important sense that no areas of policy concern were grossly slighted as was domestic economic policy in 1972, farm and foreign policy in 1973, and development policy in both years. The least common denominator compromise on food reserves is a reminder that balanced policy making does not assure creative or effective policy in terms of the problem addressed. But it *was* a gain that the substantively and politically difficult crises of fall 1974 and summer 1975 were handled without either formal export controls or another great grain robbery, and that officials coping with them *knew* more—about what the Russians and the grain companies were doing, and about the informal means available for influencing international grain transactions.

But the learning was limited. In every episode examined except food reserves,

---

[78]For an argument stressing the value of politicization and controversy in drawing attention to neglected concerns, see Robert O. Keohane and J. S. Nye, "Organizing for Global Environmental and Resource Interdependence," Appendix B (Volume 1) to the *Report of the Commission on the Organization of the Government for the Conduct of Foreign Policy,* pp. 52–54.

policy and power shifted both suddenly and too late to salvage important concerns. The return to a more humanitarian food aid policy came too late for Bangladesh. The White House takeover of farm policy in January 1973, and the soybean controls imposed the following June, came after time had sharply narrowed the options that were open. And in these two cases, as in the grain sales 1974 and 1975, the eleventh-hour shifts in power and policy were products of the actual and perceived insensitivity of the primary food policy department to anything but narrowly construed farm policy concerns. For other actors, concern over food policy is intermittent, a function of how it affects their nonfood concerns. But for the Department of Agriculture, food and agriculture are the primary, ongoing business. USDA has the in-depth expertise; it has the day-to-day ties with the community and other interest groups for which agriculture is also the central occupation. In non-crisis periods, USDA is bound to predominate. However, if it does not respond to food policy concerns broader than those of the commercial agricultural establishment, it is bound to lose the action when crisis forces presidential intervention to assuage these other policy concerns.

It is normal, of course, for any department to be parochial because any department has, by definition, less than government-wide responsibilities and hence less than a society-wide constituency. An endemic problem of government organization is to build counterweights to such parochialism. In the US executive branch, such counterweights are generally interagency committees and/or analytic/coordinating staffs with links to the presidency. The entities which entered the cases examined here fall into two categories—those created specifically for food issues, and those with some broader policy mandate.

About the specific food groups, enough has already been said—those around the assistant secretary level were essential for handling the post-1972 issues, and while the experience of each differed, their contributions were substantial. Somewhat uneven was the impact of the more general coordinating units: the National Security Council; the Council on International Economic Policy created by Nixon in 1971; the Council on Economic Policy, which was Shultz' formal leadership vehicle in 1973; and Ford's Economic Policy Board. Usually it was in the direction of broadening the range of policy values given consideration, as when the NSC opened food issues to broad interagency study after the soybean fiasco, or when the EPB insisted that Kissinger's proposed food aid pledge be analyzed for its impact on domestic grain prices. But they sometimes also tended to press their own particular perspectives—the NSC pushing political allocation of food aid; the EPB its overriding concern with the domestic economy. Only toward the end of the period reviewed here had the staff of a coordinating body—the Economic Policy Board—established itself as an ''honest broker'' trusted, in the main, by officials in competing agencies—State and Agriculture. And then, for political reasons, President Ford removed food problems from its formal jurisdiction, though it continued to play a role in monitoring food issues through the non-crisis year of 1976.

But there were limits to the ability of any central staff organization to promote coordinated, balanced food policies without Department of Agriculture leadership which 1) was sensitive to the need for balanced policies, 2) had engaged in building a constituency for such policies, and 3) employed its information and analytic talent and expertise to help develop such policies. The department will continue, again by definition, to be both farmer and agribusiness-centered. But it does not seem beyond the realm of possibility for its leaders to build a constituency which includes consumers, and to engage in international food institution-building as a primary responsibility. It was probably inevitable that, as non-farm policy values became more important in 1972–76, the department would have to share food policy-making to a greater extent, and that power would shift to some degree to economic and foreign policy institutions. The belated and then rather extreme way that it shifted seems largely the product of the particular parochialism of the Butz regime. A Secretary less ideologically determined to minimize government management of commodity markets, and more concerned with the economic, foreign, and development policy effects of food policy actions, could have made the process of adjustment far smoother. Orville Freeman in 1961–68 actively pursued such broader policy values. He even sought, unsuccessfully, to have his bailiwick renamed "Department of Food and Agriculture."[79] With the attrition of agriculture's political base in the Congress and in society and its consequent need to broaden its support, such a change may now be feasible if an administration is determined to pursue it.

What is important, of course, is not the name but the orientation, i.e., the way a Secretary (and his President) conceives of his role and goes about building and maintaining his constituency. Nor would major reorganization be necessary or even desirable. It is preferable that some formal responsibilities for agricultural trade negotiations, food aid, and the impact of food on the broader economy remain outside USDA in order to maintain the institutional links of other concerns to food policy, and to counteract what will inevitably be some USDA bias toward commercial agriculture and its interests. But a reorientation would enable the Secretary and his chief subordinates to take the lead on more issues, both lightening the coordinating burden of the White House and making it easier for the White House and other departments to exercise food policy leadership in cases where it is impossible for Agriculture to do so.[80]

Such a reorientation is not unconnected to the substantive views of the Secretary and his supporting cast. Constructive USDA leadership on food reserves requires that top USDA officials believe in their potential value for farm, economic, and foreign policy purposes. It also requires a commitment to develop an approach

---

[79]Weldon V. Barton, "Food, Agriculture, and Administrative Adaptation to Political Change," *Public Administration Review* (March/April 1976): 150.

[80]Calls from within the Agriculture Department for responsiveness to a wider range of concerns and constituencies include: Don Paarlberg, "The Farm Policy Agenda," Address to the National Public Policy Conference, Clymer, New York, September 1975; "USDA and Food Policy Decisionmaking: A Report of the Agriculture Department's 1976 Young Executives Committee," January 1977; and USDA/ERS, "Agricultural-Food Policy Review," January 1977.

to reserve accumulation and management which protects agricultural interests and can be presented to them as protecting their interests. But because reserves is an international issue so linked to USDA's primary area of domestic concern—commodity markets—it is probably impossible for the US government to develop strong policies on this issue without Agriculture in the lead, or at least in a sympathetic, supporting role. And more consistent government handling of short-supply crises like those of 1972–75 will depend heavily on the substantive responsiveness of the department's leadership to the concerns of the non-farm policy communities. For it is USDA which will be sending out most of the signals to food producers and food traders. If it fails to help set the stage for food policy actions which accommodate non-farm concerns at some cost to producers, then the reaction of the farm community is likely to be a replay of 1975.

Stronger, broader-gauged USDA leadership would not eliminate food policy conflict, nor should it. Food policy affects too many major governmental and societal concerns to be the province of a single department. USDA will inevitably be, to some degree, commercial agriculture's representative in the federal government, and its secretary will need to play—publicly—the role of farmers' advocate. But though pressure and precedent are against it, he must seek to play a broader role as well.

For in the management of food policy the US government faces a dilemma common to other policy areas as well. The department with most of the information and day-to-day action tends to emphasize one set of policy concerns to the neglect of others. Yet to remove effective power from it to White House-based coordinating groups brings problems of its own: a separation of ''policy'' from detailed information and operational responsibility; a complicating of communications with the Congress and the public; a tendency toward closed policy-making which further weakens the Cabinet departments and often the Cabinet members themselves. And once one applies this White House-based ''solution'' to enough policy areas, the biases toward particular policy interests and the boundaries between departments and agencies become replicated in the organizational and jurisdictional divisions within the President's Executive Office. There is no perfect solution for food policy, any more than there is one for the issue of whether foreign policy leadership (short of the President) can come best from the Secretary of State's office or from the National Security Council staff. But the broader the constituency which a Secretary of Agriculture can make his own, the wider the range of policy concerns he and his subordinates show sensitivity to and seek to accomodate, the greater the share of governmental food policy leadership they are likely to be able to assume; and the better the overall food policy process is likely to function. Conflict will remain, but it will be less of a zero-sum game.

3

Shifting and Sharing Adjustment Burdens: The Role of the Industrial Food Importing Nations

Robert L. Paarlberg

Too often world food problems are viewed as North-South problems, as matters to be resolved between rich and poor. In fact, most world food trade takes place entirely among the rich. The industrial nations of the European Community, Japan, and the USSR import more food today than all of the poor countries combined. These industrial food importing nations make a dubious contribution to the stability and security of the world food system. In different measure, they seek to shift adjustment burdens onto others, to enjoy something of a free ride. All have subsidized production for export in times of world surplus, and all have stepped ahead of poor countries to purchase high priced imports in times of scarcity. To these burden-shifting trade policies, the USSR in particular adds its own troublesome non-participation in most multilateral efforts at world food policy management. Prospects for improved burden sharing in the future are dim. Fortunately, the world food system still gains most of its stability and security from separate production decisions within nations, rather than from collective storage, trade, or aid decisions among nations.

Problems in the world food system appear as moving targets. As late as 1972 the major problem was widely judged to be one of chronic oversupply, and depressed prices. Its source appeared to be "absurd production stimulation" in "non-efficient areas" such as Western Europe and Japan, where farmers produced unneeded quantities of expensive food in response to "abnormal price supports."[1] Experts,

Robert L. Paarlberg is an Assistant Professor of Political Science, Wellesley College, and a Research Fellow, Center for International Affairs, Harvard University.
[1]See Harald B. Malmgren, *International Economic Peacekeeping in Phase II* (New York: Quadrangle Books, 1972), p. 145.

such as D. Gale Johnson, predicted that by 1980, if these policies were not corrected, excess production within the wealthy industrial states would provoke a major disruption of world agricultural trade.[2] The solution appeared to be reduced production incentives within Western Europe and Japan, together with reduced food trade barriers, thereby permitting increased world reliance upon the most efficient source of supply, North America.

As predicted, the "disarray" of world agriculture did increase after 1972. But scarcely in the direction of continued surplus accumulation. As Hopkins and Puchala described, world food production declined in 1972, for the first time in two decades, while the Soviet Union reversed its pattern of trade, and imported a record 30 million tons of grain. A succession of poor crops, in Asia, in the US in 1974, and in the Soviet Union in 1975, delayed an immediate rebuilding of reserve stocks, so at the end of the 1975/76 marketing year world stocks of grain stood at nearly a thirty-year low as a percent of the previous year's consumption.[3] This sudden scarcity restructured the world food policy debate of 1973–76. "Food security" replaced "surplus disposal" as a dominant concern, and the poor food importing nations of the Third World became the visible object of concern. Much less attention was paid to "absurd production stimulation" in "non-efficient" areas such as Western Europe and Japan.

Now, following the record harvests of 1976 and 1977, world food policy concerns have come full circle. As short term commercial demand is more than met, surplus stocks accumulate, prices fall, and import restrictions again take hold. Export competition among rich surplus producers replaces import competition among the poor. Earlier predictions of chronic oversupply come back into fashion.

But essential world food problems lie unchanged beneath the surface tides of current fashion. Food security, even when defined narrowly as the commercial availability of food supplies at reasonable and at reasonably stable prices (See Seevers) is not so easily attained. Under present policies, market scarcities can return with the first year or two of poor weather. And in the meantime, whatever the condition of the world food market, most food trade will continue to take place among the rich. In times of both scarcity and abundance, the European Community (of the Nine), Japan, and the Soviet Union together import more food than all of the poor developing nations of South Asia, East Asia, Southeast Asia, Africa, the Middle East, Central America, and South America combined. For this reason, it is essential to clarify the impact which these industrial nations have upon the world food system, whatever the future condition of the world food market.

This essay will review the role which each of these three wealthy industrial food importing regions—Western Europe, Japan, and the USSR—played during the recent food crisis, the role which each has played during periods of supply abundance, and the role which each might play in meeting future dilemmas of global food security, stability, equity, and efficiency. What follows is a comparison of the changing market position of these three regional actors, a review of the domestic farm policies and the international food trade policies of each, and finally a summary of multilateral, bilateral, and unilateral measures which might be taken to ensure their contribution to a secure world food system.

The industrial food importing nations: apparent similarities and critical differences

The European Community, Japan, and the USSR are all wealthy industrial regions which import very large quantities of food. Over the period 1973–75, the net grain imports of each of these three regions averaged between 10–20 million metric tons per year (See Table 1). Together, they import more grain on the average than the entire developing world.

Table 1   **Industrial nation net grain imports 1973/74–1975/76**

(MILLION METRIC TONS)

	1973/74	*1974/75*	*1975/76*	*1973/74–1975/76 average*
European Community Nine	13.3	11.1	13.1	12.5
Japan	19.2	18.5	19.2	19.0
USSR	5.6	.3	26.4	10.8
Total	38.1	29.9	58.7	42.2
Developing World Total	26.6	35.9	30.6	31.0

Source: US Department of Agriculture, ''World Agricultural Situation,'' WAS-10 (July 1976), Table 10, p. 15.

These industrial food customers also import grain for a less urgent purpose than most of the developing world. The vast majority of these rich nation grain imports, close to 85 percent, come in the form of coarse grains such as corn, to supply feed for livestock. By contrast, the developing world imports almost all of its grain to supply human needs directly—an average of 96 percent consists of wheat. Moreover, rich nation imports show continuing potential for growth. While human caloric intake does tend to ''flatten out'' at high income levels, primary cereal consumption in all forms, including animal products, does not. Between 1964 and 1974, *per capita* cereal use in all forms increased 11 percent in the EEC, 17 percent in Japan, and 29 percent in the USSR,[4] compared to a *per capita* increase of less than 5 percent in most poor countries. As these wealthy food customers continue to develop a taste for animal protein, their claim on world supplies will continue to increase.

As all three of these wealthy regions import large quantities of food, largely to support livestock production, they may appear to place parallel demands upon today's world food system. But trends over time show that the import needs of these three regions have been highly dissimilar. Only a dozen years ago the EEC imported *more* food from abroad than today, Japan imported much *less,* and the USSR was consistently a *net exporter* of food. So when the world food system entered its recent period of relative scarcity and insecurity, the import claims of Japan, and particularly the USSR, were rapidly increasing, while those of the EEC were actually in some decline (See Table 2).

Table 2   Industrial nation net grain imports

(MILLION METRIC TONS)

	1960/61–62/63 average	1973/74–74/75 average	Net change
European Community Nine	21.5	12.5	−9.0
Japan	5.3	19.0	+13.7
USSR	−7.3	10.8	+18.1

Source: US Department of Agriculture, "World Agricultural Situation," WAS-10 (July 1976), Table 10, p. 15.

Second, the response of these three wealthy food importing regions to the tightened world supply of recent years also showed considerable variation (See Table 3). The EEC did encourage a very modest reduction in the use of grain to feed livestock soon after the 1972/73 decline in world food production. But in Japan, livestock feeding continued to increase (from its very low level) until 1975/76. And in the USSR livestock feeding also continued to increase until 1975/76, to surpass even the US level in 1974/75, a year of very tight world supplies. Not until its own disastrous harvest of 1975, and only in the face of physical barriers to further feed grain imports, did the USSR finally reduce the feeding of grain to animals.

So the EEC has steadily reduced its claims upon the world food market, by subsidizing its own domestic production and by moderating its livestock feeding in times of short supply. By contrast, Japan and the USSR have rapidly increased their food imports. And the Soviet Union, in particular, was slow to moderate its use of

[4]Egbert de Vries and J. H. Richter-Altschaffer, *World Food Crisis and Agricultural Trade Problems* (Beverly Hills: Sage Publications, 1974), p. 5.

imported grain for animal feed during the world food emergency of 1973–75. These are gross distinctions, however. A closer look at the domestic and foreign agricultural policies of each of these three industrial importing regions is necessary to clarify and to qualify the role of each in the world food system.

Table 3   Industrial nation grain fed to livestock

(MILLION METRIC TONS)

	1969/70–71/72 average	1972/73	1973/74	1974/75	1975/76
European Community Nine	68.8	72.2	72.3	70.9	70.0
Japan	9.3	10.4	12.1	13.1	11.8
USSR	89.0	98.0	105.0	107.0	85.0
US	136.5	148.5	143.2	106.4	120.2

Source: US Department of Agriculture, "World Agricultural Situation," WAS-10 (July 1976), Table 14, p. 21.

The European Community

The enlarged European Community relies upon the world market to provide for roughly 20 percent of its very large coarse grain consumption.[5] In protein-rich animal feed concentrates the EEC is 80 percent dependent upon external supplies. Yet the Community would be far more dependent upon external food supplies today had it not invested so heavily in farm policies which protect and promote its own agricultural production.

Domestic farm policies

European agriculture has long been an industry in relative decline. Over the past two decades the agricultural work force has been decreasing by nearly 5 percent per year. And many of those who remain on farms face difficult commercial circumstances. Two thirds of the farms within the Community are smaller than 25 acres, and half of those individuals running farms are 57 years of age or older, poorly educated, and ill-prepared to adopt mechanized farming techniques.

It is the announced policy of the EEC to protect this endangered farm population from the prospect of an even more rapid and painful economic decline. Indi-

[5]The enlarged Community imports twice as much food as all of the non-member states of the Western European region combined. Western European nations outside of the EEC, such as Spain, Portugal, and Greece, are increasing their food imports more rapidly, but the EEC itself still dominates the import trade of the region.

vidual governments had undertaken programs to support farm prices and to protect domestic producers from external competition for many years before the 1957 Rome Treaty. In some countries, especially France, farmers have long demanded such protection, in their role as a powerful political interest group. Over the period 1962–67, however, these separate national farm policies were strengthened and joined into one. This Common Agricultural Policy (CAP) did not eliminate entirely the separate role of national governments.[6] But under the CAP, a common market organization does now extend to cover more than 91 percent of all EEC farm produce, and common support prices are offered for more than 70 percent of all farm production.[7] Prices of individual agricultural commodities are established annually by the EEC Council of Ministers (in terms of ''units of account'') and are maintained by variable levies on low-priced imports from abroad, and by official purchases of excess supplies at home.

The CAP has neither reversed the decline nor increased the efficiency of European agriculture. Farm incomes have grown, but at a rate sometimes slower than in other sectors of the economy. And the largest benefits of the CAP price support system fall where farm size and production are already large, so income gaps between the rich and poor farming regions of the Community have actually widened. Meanwhile, the structural weakness of European farming remains essentially uncorrected. Average farm size has grown by only 7.4 acres since 1958, and with 10 percent of its population still in agriculture the EEC is still far from approaching former Commission President Sicco L. Mansholt's vision of a 6 percent farm population by 1980.

Meanwhile, the costs of the CAP to consumer and taxpayer have been very high. Separate estimates (in the years 1966/67 and 1967/68) placed annual combined consumer and taxpayer costs of all EEC farm programs at a hefty $12–14 billion.[8] Furthermore, these costs are not equally borne within the Community. Those member states with small farm populations and large food imports, such as Germany, carry the heaviest cost. Germany's burden is magnified by a cumbersome system of fixed ''green exchange rates,'' which were designed to protect CAP prices from the instability of the current ''floating'' exchange rate system. Disparities which have developed between ''market'' and ''green'' exchange rates work to the disadvantage of nations, such as Germany, which have enjoyed appreciating currency values. Even Italy, a relatively poor member state with a depre-

[6]See Denis K. Britton, ''National Policies Within the CAP,'' *Food Policy,* Vol. 1, No. 5 (November 1976): 405–12.

[7]*Bulletin of the European Communities,* Supplement 2/75, ''Stocktaking of the Common Agricultural Policy'' (Communication from the Commission to the Parliament and the Council, transmitted on 27 February 1975), p. 8.

[8]See G. R. Kruer and B. Bernston, ''Cost of the Common Agricultural Policy to the European Economic Community,'' *Foreign Agricultural Trade of the United States* (Washington: Department of Agriculture, 1969), pp. 7 and 12, and Dennis Bergmann et al., *A Future for European Agriculture,* Atlantic Paper 4 (Paris: Atlantic Institute, 1970), pp. 8–9, 62, as presented in Johnson, *World Agriculture in Disarray,* pp. 45–51.

ciating currency, finds itself disadvantaged, by having to pay to support the surplus production of prosperous farmers in France and Holland. France, a food exporting nation with a large farming population, and in recent years a depreciating currency, enjoys the strongest relative advantage under the CAP pricing system. The French have insisted upon this relative advantage in agriculture, since the inception of the Common Market, to compensate for the advantage which they consider West Germany to have received in a wider market for manufactured goods.

The effects of the CAP upon Europe were considerably altered when world food prices increased sharply after 1972. When these prices grew to surpass even the high support prices maintained within the EEC, the protective machinery of the CAP suddenly became an instrument for keeping consumer prices lower and limiting incentives for producers. In the summer of 1973 the EEC levies changed from tariffs on food imports to taxes on exports. This discouraged sales on the world market and moderated domestic food price inflation. In Great Britain this timely reversal helped also to moderate adverse views toward Community membership, which was then under reconsideration. Government ministers explained to Parliament in 1974 that the CAP was actually keeping down the cost of British food, rather than increasing that cost. But by protecting internal price levels in this fashion, the CAP severely distorts the free flow of international agricultural trade.

Food trade policies

Support and stabilization for farm prices within the Community requires protection from more efficient foreign producers and from price fluctuation overseas. Separate European states had long protected themselves from North American competition by placing fixed tariffs against food imports. But today the CAP protects the Community as a whole by means of its variable levy system. During periods of global market surplus, as during the late 1960s and early 1970s, when the total charges of this levy system are converted into *ad valorem* equivalents, it becomes clear that the common policy has in effect increased average protection levels from the pre-CAP period. Comparison between 1959 and 1968 shows a protection level increase from 19 percent to 137 percent in dairy produce, from 14 percent to 52 percent in meat, and from 14 percent to 72 percent in cereals.[9] Not surprisingly, Europe has become a declining market for exporters, as noted earlier.

In addition to restricting imports, the EEC has also subsidized exports during most of its operation. The high domestic target prices of the CAP, when unaccompanied by acreage restrictions, tend to generate surplus production. Disposal of these surpluses has been accomplished, in part, by offering export subsidies which permit the sale of food abroad at or below the world price. These subsidy payments, mostly to promote export of grains, dairy products, and sugar, totaled over $1 billion in 1969. In 1970 the Community subsidy for soft wheat exports was actually

---

[9]Malmgren, *International Economic Peacekeeping in Phase II*, p. 123.

larger than the world price to which it was being added.[10]

Such very large export subsidies have seriously disrupted patterns of international trade and production. They have often forced efficient producers in North America to store grain in large quantities, and even to withdraw land from production to avoid downward pressures on price, while allowing less efficient European producers to continue to export their own grain surplus with little regard to the effect on world prices.

Scarcity does not eliminate the disruptive effect of these EEC food trade policies. When world food supplies tightened, from 1972 to 1976, EEC export subsidies were discontinued and replaced by export taxes. Prices within the EEC were to be held down by reducing exports. Export taxes on wheat eventually grew to equal more than two thirds of the already high domestic price.[11] Having earlier dumped Europe's surplus onto a saturated world market, the CAP was now holding European produce away from a tight world market, in hopes of containing runaway food price inflation at home. All the while, the EEC continued to import substantial quantities of food. These trade practices raise questions about the overall contribution which European food policy makes to the security and stability of the larger world food system.

The contribution of the European Community to world food security and adjustment

In certain respects the EEC takes a "free ride" on the world food system.[12] In times of oversupply, the EEC made things worse by restricting imports and subsidizing exports; in times of shortage, the CAP has reduced EEC exports even while the EEC has continued to bid against less wealthy food deficit nations for a high volume of imports. Such policies show considerable disregard for the goals of stability and security in external food markets (See Seevers).

The contribution of the EEC to global food security, however, has not been entirely negative. First, even while the EEC introduced its 1973 export tax on cereals, it continued to honor its considerable obligations with respect to Third World food aid. EEC financial contributions for food aid increased from less than $7 million in 1965 to nearly $450 million by 1974, or roughly 30 percent of the OECD total.[13] Second, to complement these food aid policies, the EEC has recognized a special obligation to provide access to exchange-earning agricultural exports from the Third World. The Community's Mediterranean Policy, its Generalized

[10]Werner J. Feld, "Trade Between the US and the European Community: Differing Expectations in a Changing Power Relationship," *Journal of International Affairs,* Vol. 28, No. 1 (1974): 11–12.

[11]DeVries and Richter-Altschaffer, *World Food Crisis and Agricultural Trade Problems,* p. 94.

[12]For an elaboration of the notion of a "free rider," see Mancur Olson, Jr., *The Logic of Collective Action* (Cambridge: Harvard University Press, 1965), pp. 22–36.

[13]While the US failed to negotiate a reduction of barriers to agricultural trade in the Kennedy Round of the GATT negotiations, the US at least did persuade the EEC to enter into the 1967 Food Aid Convention, which pledged the EEC to contribute more than 20 percent to a 5 million ton food aid program for developing countries.

Preference Scheme (GSP), and the 1975 Lomé Convention, offer privileged access to the European market for a growing number of poor nation exports. The Lomé Convention dramatically expanded trade concessions earlier offered to 46 underdeveloped African, Caribbean, and Pacific (ACP) states, 18 of which are listed by the UN as among the world's poorest. These countries now enjoy duty free access to the Community for 96 percent of their agricultural production. The Lomé Convention may only bring a limited increase in trade, since most ACP products, apart from sugar, do not compete with major EEC commodities. Further, the EEC has various non-tariff barriers to trade, including quality controls and previous bilateral agreements; these cancel some access provisions of the Convention. But Lomé does provide a new export stabilization agreement (Stabex) to guarantee the monetary value of many Third World exports to the Community.

Yet the EEC makes its most important contribution to world food security simply by maintaining an indigenous capacity to produce a significant proportion of its own food. The EEC is by no means self-sufficient in food, but since full implementation of the CAP, annual grain imports have fallen from above 20 million tons in the early 1960s to an average 12.5 million tons by 1975. By 1973, owing in part to the CAP, the Community was 100 percent self-sufficient in wheat, barley, cheese, poultry, eggs, potatoes, pork, beef, and veal. The Community was more than 90 percent self-sufficient in oats, butter, rye, sugar, and fresh vegetables.[14] When the sudden scarcity crisis burst upon international food markets in 1972, it was fortunate that EEC food import needs were in decline. If the "more efficient" farm regions of North America had been permitted to take over the feeding of Western Europe earlier during the 1960s, then the US grain surplus would have been depleted much sooner. US cropland would have already been in full production in 1972, and so there would have been a smaller excess capacity available after 1972 to meet the unexpected explosion in overseas demand. In short, a measure of European self-sufficiency in food supplies, even with the loss of some production efficiency, can be beneficial to world food security.

European self-sufficiency in agriculture remains a controversial policy, however.[15] The recent FAO Director General, A. H. Boerma, presented a draft strategy for international agricultural adjustment in 1975 which conceded that "a substantial degree of self-sufficiency" was an appropriate goal for those less developed countries with "limited opportunities for earning foreign exchange." But he warned: "Any general tendency for developed importing countries to adopt policies aiming at further increases in their self-sufficiency would represent a less effective use of resources available for agricultural production."[16] Limited self-sufficiency and increasing "interdependence" in the world food trading system is naturally favored

---

[14]Gordon MacKerron and Howard J. Rush, "Agriculture in the EEC: Taking Stock," *Food Policy,* Vol. 1, No. 4 (August 1976): 294.

[15]See, for example, J. P. O'Hagan, "National Self-Sufficiency in Food," *Food Policy,* Vol. 1, No. 5 (November 1976): 355–66.

[16]*Director-General's proposed strategy for International Agricultural Adjustment,* FAO Conference 18th Session. C75/18, August 1975, p. 15.

by net exporting regions, such as North America, but it is understandably trouble-some to some net importers. In the absence of a global food regime which guaran-tees market access, and in the absence of predictable weather to guarantee high levels of production, interdependence will at times endanger the security of food importing states. As long as North American production remains vulnerable to unpredictable weather, as long as the global food distribution system remains vul-nerable to technical limitations or to political uncertainties, and as long as food itself remains scarce in relation to nutritional needs, some of the less efficient producing regions, including Western Europe, may do well to maintain a "redundant" produc-tion capability.

Of course, the CAP has not been the most efficient means to promote European production capabilities. Its original motive was not to increase world food security, but rather to support very narrow domestic political constituencies. In its support for these powerful domestic farming interests, the CAP has placed heavy reliance upon price policy instruments alone; these do little to improve income distribution or to promote structural reform. If more CAP funds had been directed originally toward farm modernization, high European production could have been attained at higher political cost but at lower economic cost and with less external disruption.

Still, if we must face recurring food scarcities, any policy which promotes the production of more food deserves to be measured by a less rigid standard. The CAP may perpetuate an inefficient division of international agricultural labor, but its direct costs are largely borne by Europeans, and over time it has worked to reduce the total quantity of EEC food imports. By comparison, the agricultural policies of some other wealthy food importing nations have had less favorable effects.

Japan

Japan's 110 million people (slightly over half the US population) live in a land area smaller than the size of the State of Montana. Only 15 percent of this land can be brought under cultivation. Yet Japan still provides for nearly 73 percent (by value) of its own food needs. By any standard this is a remarkable performance, particularly since per capita intake of meat in Japan has tripled since 1960.[17]

Japan's agricultural position, however, unlike that of the EEC, is one of increasing import dependence. Precisely at a time of uncertain international supply, Japan has emerged as the world's largest consistent importer of food. Japan's net grain imports increased from an average 5.3 million tons in the early 1960s to 14.4 million tons in 1969–72, and to the present level of nearly 20 million tons by 1973/74. In times of scarcity, this rapidly growing Japanese claim on the world food market can constitute a danger to less wealthy food deficit nations. It is also cause for some apprehension within Japan, where farm policies that once encouraged a high degree of food trade interdependence have now come under critical review.

[17]Larry F. Thomasson, "Self-Sufficiency Goal Raises Many Questions," in US Department of Agricul-ture, Foreign Agricultural Service, *Foreign Agriculture*, Vol. XIII, No. 40 (October 6, 1975): 28.

Japanese farm policies

Modernization of Japanese agriculture dates from the Meiji Restoration, which abolished feudal land tenure in 1868. A further reform enacted under US military occupation after World War II released nearly 30 percent of Japan's cultivated area from landlord ownership. But small average farm size and incomplete mechanization left Japan's agriculture ill-prepared for the high rate of economic growth which was to follow. In 1961 new farm legislation was enacted to support declining farm incomes during the transition to full industrial development. These Japanese support programs bear some resemblance to those enacted at roughly the same time by the EEC, and like the farm policies of the EEC, they have produced mixed results.

First, Japan's support policies have encouraged vast quantities of surplus rice production. Roughly 40 percent of the annual budget of the Ministry of Agriculture and Forestry has been devoted to supporting domestic rice prices, often at levels two or three times above the world price. Even in 1973, when the world price of rice had increased by 300 percent to an astonishing $636 per ton, Japan's domestic producers were being offered more, out of public funds.[18] The generosity of these farm support policies reflects the political leverage which rural constituencies enjoy within the ruling Liberal Democratic Party. The rice program produces an unmanageable surplus, some of which can be sold abroad under export subsidy. Yet to control surplus rice accumulation, farmers must also be paid not to produce. In 1970 almost 10 percent of the country's precious fields were actually left uncultivated. Despite the enormous public expense of these farm support policies ($3.1 billion for farm subsidies in 1975), agricultural incomes in Japan have continued to lag behind industry.[19]

Most important for the global food system, Japan's farm policies do not provide needed supplies of feed grain for livestock, to satisfy growing consumer tastes for animal protein. Between 1961 and 1971, while Japan produced an enormous rice surplus, its grain production actually *decreased* by 2.2 percent annually. Over the same period, grain consumption was increasing every year by 3.3 percent, spurred on by the growing dietary expectations which seem to accompany affluence throughout the world. Rice still provides for about one third of Japan's caloric intake, but since 1960 per capita consumption of animal products has nearly tripled. This dietary revolution has brought with it an increased requirement for feedgrain imports, which have grown since 1960 by a factor of five. Japanese wheat imports simultaneously doubled in volume, while soybean imports increased by a factor of

[18]US Department of Agriculture, Economic Research Service, ''World Food Situation and Prospects to 1985,'' Foreign Agricultural Economic Report No. 98 (December 1975), p. 24.

[19]Average farm size has increased since World War II by only .2 acres, and 74 percent of the Japanese agricultural labor force now consists of women or of males over 60 years of age. Farm households survive, typically, by seeking more than half of their income from employment beyond agriculture. The Japanese government has recently emphasized the need to contain this situation by developing more farming operations by ''full time male farmers.'' See Japanese Ministry of Agriculture and Forestry, ''The State of Japan's Agriculture: A Summary Report,'' Tokyo, Japan, 1975, p. 19.

three. Because of these rapidly increasing imports, Japan's "self-sufficiency" in wheat declined from 39 percent in 1960 to a mere 4 percent today, while self-sufficiency in coarse grain declined from 49 percent to 2 percent. When the world food market suddenly tightened in 1972, Japan had to reassess this drift toward a growing reliance on food imports.

Japan's food trade policy

Before 1972, Japan's heavy dependence on overseas grain supplies had not been cause for anxiety. Japan recognized its own comparative disadvantage in wheat and soybean production, and made a conscious decision to buy from abroad. The world market was in a condition of oversupply, prices were low, and Japan's own trade balance was particularly strong with the US, its primary source of food imports.

But following the market reversals of 1972, and then the oil shock and the brief US imposition of export controls on soybeans in 1973 (see Destler) Japan began to reassess its growing food trade dependence. Public concern was aroused by a government study which indicated that if Japan's food and animal feed imports were halted, and if every available acre of land were farmed (for example, if the nation's golf courses were given over to sweet potato cultivation), levels of nutrition would still fall back to the very low standard of the immediate postwar period.[20]

In response to such apparent dangers, the Ministry of Agriculture and Forestry adjusted its budget after 1973 to cut expenditures for rice and to provide increased support for wheat, barley, and soybeans. And in 1975, in a watershed report to the Cabinet, Japan's Advisory Council on Agricultural Policy set a 10-year target of 75 percent (by value) self-sufficiency in aggregate food supplies. This meant reversing the decline in self-sufficiency (from 90 to 73 percent) that had been recorded since 1960.[21] The report first called for expanding domestic production of all crops and livestock. "Whatever we can produce in Japan we should," Ministry officials proclaimed. Secondarily, the plan projected reduced growth in per capita animal protein consumption. In combination, these measures were designed to hold the annual increase in import demand for feedstuffs to about .4 million tons per year, versus the .65 million tons per year noted over the past decade. In April 1976, as a further means to reduce food import dependence, a movement began to re-substitute rice for bread in school lunch diets.

In addition to increasing its agricultural self-sufficiency, Japan has also been seeking to diversify its overseas sources of food supply. Following the 1973 em-

[20]See "Farming," *Business Japan* (October 1975): 17.
[21]See Japanese Ministry of Agriculture and Forestry, "Long Term Prospects of Production and Demand of Agricultural Products in Japan," Tokyo, Japan, August 1975. For an extended analysis of this important document see US Department of Agriculture, Foreign Agricultural Service, *Foreign Agriculture*, Vol. XIII, No. 40 (October 6, 1975).

bargo, soybean imports were increased from Brazil and from the PRC, and the US market share of Japan's feed grain imports fell from 71 percent to 59 percent. To secure this remaining share, Japan reached an informal agreement with the US, in August 1975, recognizing Japan's intention to buy 3 million tons of wheat, 3 million tons of soybeans, and 8 million tons of feed grains in each of the coming three years, and also recognizing the intention of the US to make these amounts available.[22] Japan continues to seek such long-term import agreements, and has now initiated a modest food stockpiling program, to ease its near total dependence upon "pipeline" supplies.[23]

It is too early to judge the absolute impact of these recent shifts in Japan's food trade policy, away from unguarded dependence upon overseas supplies. Despite high support prices and incentive payments to soybean producers, total Japanese oilseed production decreased in 1976, while the dollar value of agricultural imports from the US increased by 16 percent. It will certainly not be easy, moreover, for Japan to curb the dietary expectations of its large and affluent population. Even while wheat output declines, bread consumption continues to rise at the expense of noodles and rice. Nor will Japan's economy find it easy to absorb the budgetary and inflationary costs of increasing agricultural self-sufficiency. Official estimates put the cost of reaching optimal 1985 self-sufficiency goals at $86 billion, which is roughly twice the total cost of all of Japan's food imports over the entire period 1960–72.[24] As a world food surplus returns, as food prices come down, and as the memory of the 1973 soybean embargo continues to fade, it seems likely that Japan will lose interest in agricultural independence.

Japan's contribution to world food security and adjustment

Japan's position in the world food system is not so burdensome as its increasing dependence on food imports alone would imply. Against great odds, Japan has remained self-sufficient in many foods, particularly rice, and it now hopes to slow the increase in its purchase of grain from abroad. Further, it has made efforts to adjust its imports, when necessary, to reduce pressure on supply. Together with the EEC, Japan honored a US request in 1974 to cut its purchase of corn by 10 percent in that very tight crop year.[25]

Also, despite its difficulties at home, Japan has shown some increased interest in providing food aid and in promoting international agricultural development. In 1965 Japan's food aid contributions made up less than 1 percent of the OECD total, but by 1974 this figure had increased to 5 percent, and Japan had funded more than

[22]Philip H. Trezise, *Rebuilding Grain Reserves* (Washington: Brookings, 1976), p. 31.

[23]Ichiro Suzuki, "Need for Imports of Feed Cereals to Continue," *Business Japan* (January 1977): 105.

[24]Thomasson, "Self-Sufficiency Goal Raises Many Questions," p. 28.

[25]United States Senate, Hearings before the Permanent Subcommittee on Investigations, "Sales of Grain to the Soviet Union," October 8, 1974 (GPO: Washington, D.C.), p. 51.

one hundred aid projects for Third World agricultural development.[26] In 1975 Japan established a new International Cooperation Corporation to further encourage food production in poor Asian countries. A dominant purpose behind these projects is clearly to develop new sources of overseas supply. But such new sources nonetheless add to worldwide food security.

All things considered, however, Japan remains something of a burden on the world food system. Its dubious contribution to food security actually extends beyond its growing reliance on feedgrain imports. Notably, Japan is the nation with the world's largest fish catch. For the past 50 years Japan has consistently taken more fish from the ocean than any other nation in the world. In the years after 1964, Japan's annual fish catch grew at an annual rate of more than 5 percent, nearly doubling by 1972 to reach 10 million tons, or roughly 15 percent of the world total.[27] Japan has continued to supply nearly half of its domestic animal protein consumption with fish products. By doing so it tries to moderate its dependence on feedgrain imports. Until recently this seemed a responsible food supply strategy.

But after 1970 the world fish catch for all nations reversed its historical trend of steady growth and went into decline, prompting speculation that the global catch of table grade fish had finally approached a maximum sustainable yield.[28] Japan's own distant water fish catch subsequently declined as well, by 7 percent in 1974, reflecting not only Japan's economic recession and increased marine fuel costs, but a genuine strain on world supplies. Specifically, Japan's take of endangered Alaskan pollock in 1974 dropped to one third of the amount taken during the previous year. This declining distant water fish catch posed a clear threat to Japan's own food security. But it also posed a threat to the future food supply of other nations, including those developing nations which have yet to enter the competitive marine fishing industry.[29]

Finally, it must be observed that Japan's own continued rate of growth of population also places considerable pressure on global food supplies. Japan was generally credited with having done well to reduce its rate of growth of population to just above 1 percent soon after World War II. But this progress in reducing population growth has not continued. Japan's population continues to grow at 1.2 percent every year, roughly double the annual rate in Europe and North America.[30] For a nation of 110 million, poorly endowed with resources to produce food for such

[26]Harlan J. Dirks, "Japan's Strategy to Stabilize Food Supplies," US Department of State (Sixteenth Session Senior Seminar in Foreign Policy, 1973–74), p. 13, and Anne de Lattre, "Food Aid," *OECD Observer*, No. 81 (May-June 1976): 14–16.

[27]Takashi Nakamura, "Fishing Continues Good Despite Restrictions," *Business Japan* (March 1976: 63–64.

[28]Lester R. Brown, *By Bread Alone* (New York: Praeger Publishers, 1974), p. 149.

[29]Japan's distant water fishing activities are now coming under the restriction of national coastal fishing waters which extend out to 200 miles. Nearly half of Japan's distant water catch has been taken within 200 miles of other nation's shores, most conspicuously the US and the USSR.

[30]Lester R. Brown, "The Politics and Responsibility of the North American Breadbasket," Washington, D.C., Worldwatch Institute, Worldwatch Paper 2, October 1975, p. 14.

numbers, and already the largest customer on the world food market, continued population growth can only promise a growing reliance upon overseas and ocean food supplies.

So Japan, for all that it has done, is likely to turn to the world market for ever larger quantities of food. In the event of renewed market scarcities, Japan's very large imports will place something of a burden on the world food system. Among the wealthy food importing nations, however, its contribution to food security is not so burdensome as that of the Soviet Union.

The Soviet Union

The Soviet Union imports, on average, less food than either the EEC or Japan. Yet its domestic and foreign agricultural policies made a much greater contribution to the recent destabilization of the world food system. During most of the postwar period, the Soviets were only marginal participants in the world food system. Their dramatic entry into the world market in 1972 was the direct result of changes in food trading policy. But beneath this event lies the enduring constraint of Soviet farm policy, the under-performance of Soviet agriculture itself.

Soviet farm policy

Much of the Soviet Union is either too cold or too dry to support agriculture. The USSR has rich soil and a land area nearly three times the size of the US. But more than half of this area lacks adequate and reliable moisture, and much of the remaining half, the well-watered half, is unsuitable to farming because the growing season is too short and too cold. Odessa, in the Southern Ukraine, falls on the same northern latitude as Duluth, in the State of Minnesota.

Together with a harsh climate, serfdom and Tsarist oppression had constrained Russia's agricultural development long before the October 1917 revolution. But following that revolution, the Soviet leadership managed to perpetuate Russian agricultural underdevelopment by draining resources from the rural sector to speed industrial growth. The small land-owning peasantry in Russia was viewed as a potential breeding ground for capitalist counterrevolution, so its sacrifice was scarcely mourned by the early Bolsheviks.[31] The sacrifice of the rural sector was most visible during the early Stalinist period, when a campaign to "eliminate" the kulaks (prosperous farmers), forced collectivization, and state confiscation of farm produce actually reduced food production. A rural famine in 1932–33 cost an

---

[31] As early as 1901, Lenin set forth the orthodox view of agrarian questions: "To attempt to save the peasantry would mean a useless hindrance to social development." Cited in Lazar Volin, *A Century of Russian Agriculture* (Cambridge: Harvard University Press, 1970), p. 98.

estimated 5 million lives. And even 20 years later, in 1953, at the time of Stalin's death, the Soviet Union had yet to produce as much food annually as it had produced before the Revolution, in 1913.[32]

Under the more concerned leadership of the Khrushchev-Brezhney era, Soviet farming has vastly improved. The proportion of state investment devoted to agriculture has increased in every one of the post-Stalin Five Year Plans. In the two plans covering the period 1966–75, the state invested twice as much in agriculture as in the preceding 50 years combined. And in the upcoming plan period (1976–80), proposed investments in agriculture will increase an additional 31 percent, while the rest of the economy will get an increase of only 24 percent.[33] These massive investments have had a strong impact. Over the decade prior to the 1975 harvest setback (when crops fell 75 million tons or 33 percent below the production target), Soviet cereal production had increased at a respectable average annual rate of 3 percent.

Increases occurred despite the state and collective farming system of the Soviet Union which remains a barrier to flexible and efficient food production. Because the Soviet Union is so large, because its agricultural conditions are so various, and because its weather is so unsteady, it suffers more than otherwise from a farming system founded upon inflexible central direction. Central direction stifles farm level management, while collateral requirements for "uninterrupted" plan fulfillment discourage innovation and transition to new farming techniques.

These problems of Soviet agriculture have not gone unnoticed, and the current Soviet leadership does take a considerable interest in the availability of domestic food supplies. Following the 1970 Christmas food riots in Poland, which brought down the Gomulka regime, the Soviet party leadership determined that it must maintain a selection of cheap food products, including an increased variety of meat products, on its own retail shelves at home. Unfortunately, this intense political interest in cheap food only compounds the plight of Soviet agriculture. The requirement to hold down retail prices makes more difficult the task of expanding production. State retail store prices for both bread and beef in the USSR have not been increased since 1962. In 1974 they were actually lower than prices in Europe and in North American. Despite the growth of costly government subsidies which help to compensate for these low retail prices, the rural sector has received little added incentive to increase its production. Prices actually received by state and collective farm producers in the USSR have not increased since 1970.[34]

Effective reform of Soviet agriculture is blocked by a widespread leadership preference for very large operations run by central production command.[35] Those

[32]US Department of Agriculture, "The World Food Situation and Prospects to 1985," p. 14.

[33]For a detailed review of the 1976–80 plan, see David M. Schoonover, "Soviet Agriculture in the 1976–80 Plan," presented at the annual meeting of the American Association for Advancement of Slavic Studies, St. Louis, Missouri, October 7, 1976.

[34]US Department of Agriculture, "The World Food Situation and Prospects to 1985," p. 30.

[35]Politburo member Gennadi Voronov saw his career come to a premature close in 1973, for having championed the agricultural reform policies of Ivan Khudenko, who had actually demonstrated that

who advocate the alternative of decentralized management techniques may endanger their political future. In the months following the 1975 harvest failure, the Soviet Minister of Agriculture, Dmitri Polyansky, who opposed excessive centralization, was disgraced and removed from his post and from the politburo, while those responsible for farm policy within the party secretariat were untouched.[36] In June 1976, the Central Committee then endorsed a policy of "agro-industrial integration," yet another step away from the alternative of decentralization.

It is unlikely that this vicious circle can soon be broken. Consumer demands in the USSR are expected to continue to grow faster than plans or incentives for domestic production. "Consumption norms" have been established by the Institute of Nutrition at the Soviet Academy of Sciences which indicate continued hopes for dietary improvement. Per capita meat consumption will have to increase by more than 40 percent from its 1975 level to reach the Academy's "norm."[37] But plan guidelines for the 1976–80 period allow for only a 3 percent growth in per capita meat consumption during a protracted recovery from the distress slaughter of 1975–76. This is a dramatic retreat from the 21 percent growth rate of the previous plan period.[38]

In the meantime, the Soviet Union is left with only one politically acceptable response to a production shortfall: it must import food. Even the scaled down goals of the 1976–80 plan will require the availability of an average 215–220 million tons of grain every year. Until 1976 the USSR had managed only one crop in excess of 200 million tons. If the Soviet Union continues to enjoy good weather and manages an average annual production of 200–210 million tons, it will still have to import an average 10–15 million tons of grain every year if it hopes to reach planned consumption goals.

Soviet food trade policy

It was once the policy of the USSR to hide its agricultural setbacks from the outside world by refusing to import food during times of domestic shortage. Indeed, the Soviet Union often continued to *export* food during times of short supply. Food exports were continued during the famine of 1932–33, and Khrushchev himself described widespread starvation, accompanied by instances of cannibalism, which occured in the Ukraine during the poor harvest year of 1946, while Stalin insisted upon continuing food exports to Poland and East Germany.

Today it is Soviet policy to import food in times of production shortfall and to

---

decentralization could increase productivity. Khudenko himself was accused of embezzlement in a rigged trial and died in a prison hospital in 1974. See *The Economist,* January 15, 1977: 69.

[36]Following the demise of Polyansky, the Peoples Republic of China taunted the Soviets with the observation that "During the 23 year period administered by Khrushchev and Brezhnev, a total of 8 ministers of agriculture have been dismissed from office—one scapegoat in less than every three years." See *Soviet World Outlook,* Vol. 1, No. 4 (April 15, 1976): 7.

[37]Richard E. Bell, "The New Soviet Five-Year Plan: Its Meaning and Implication for American Agriculture," US Department of Agriculture, USDA 1372–76, May 12, 1976.

[38]See Schoonover, "Soviet Agriculture in the 1976–80 Plan," p. 11.

hide agricultural failure from its own population. In the four years following the bad harvest of 1972, the USSR imported more than 53 million tons of grain from abroad. It has yet to disclose the magnitude of this new import dependence to its own citizens.

But the Soviet Union has also hidden its import needs, before the fact, from the world market, and in so doing it becomes more than just another wealthy customer in that market. By concealing its total needs and by dealing simultaneously and in great secrecy with a half dozen private exporting firms, the Soviet Union was able to complete its 1972 grain purchase from the US within a few weeks time, at very low prices (See Destler). This purchase, a record 19 million tons, contributed to a dramatic market price increase, up from $1.65 to more than $5 per bushel.[39] By then the Soviets were safely out of the market, and other nations were left to meet their customary import needs at a prohibitive price. India, for example, purchased 1.5 million tons of wheat in January 1973, at nearly twice the price paid by Russia during the previous summer. This single purchase cost India, an "ally" of the USSR, nearly one-fifth of its depleted hard currency reserves.[40]

Significantly, not even the private US grain export companies were able to escape the bite of these Soviet purchasing tactics. None had fully anticipated the timing or the size of the 1972 purchase, and by GAO estimates three of the five companies dealing with the Soviets actually sustained losses on the sale of .9 to 1.9 cents per bushel. Cargill claims to have lost more than $600,000 in the Soviet deal, by selling too soon and buying too late.[41]

Over the entire period 1960–73, the USSR alone was responsible for 80 percent of all deviation from trend in world wheat imports.[42] This uneven and unpredictable food trading style reflects more than the considerable variability of Soviet harvest conditions. Buying when the price is low, the Soviets speculate against future world needs. The large 21 million ton net increase in Soviet grain imports noted in 1972/73 followed only a 13 million ton production shortfall. And while this purchase was still in the process of being delivered, the Soviet Union offered a 2 million ton "loan" of wheat to India, and even suggested a "resale" to the US, at the much higher market price. Little wonder that after 1972 the US eventually acted to contain the disruptive effect of these Soviet food trade policies (See Destler). The five year grain agreement of October 1975 stabilizes sales by setting a 6–8 million ton lower and upper limit on annual Soviet purchase of wheat and corn from the US.[43] The possibility of another Soviet "grain robbery," of the kind which upset

[39]US Senate, Committee on Government Operations, Report of the Permanent Subcommittee on Investigations, "Russian Grain Transactions" (GPO, Washington, D.C.), July 29, 1974.

[40]James Trager, *The Great Grain Robbery* (New York: Ballantine Books, 1975), p. 130.

[41]Comptroller General of the US, "Exporter's Profits on Sales of US Wheat to Russia" (GPO, Washington, D.C.), February 12, 1974, p. 25.

[42]US Department of Agriculture, "The World Food Situation and Prospects to 1985," p. 42.

[43]See Robert L. Paarlberg, "The Soviet Burden on the World Food System," *Food Policy*, Vol. 1, No. 5 (November 1976): 392–404.

the world food market in 1972, is now greatly reduced. But, unfortunately, the burden which the USSR places on world food security has not been entirely eliminated.

The Soviet contribution to world food security and adjustment

While facing new constraints on entry into the world food market, the USSR continues to take something of a ''free ride'' on the world food system. While others, including the EEC and Japan, discuss new means to exchange information, to promote Third World agricultural development, to increase food aid to hungry poor countries, and to rebuild world food stocks, the USSR prefers to stand aside.

The Soviet Union did send representatives to the 1974 Rome World Food Conference. But it still refuses to join the international agency most directly concerned with ongoing food issues, the Food and Agriculture Organization (FAO). The Soviets remain outside the FAO at least partly to escape the information sharing obligations of that organization. For example, they have refused to participate in the new Global Information and Early Warning System established in November 1974 under the aegis of the FAO. The Soviet Union sends observers to FAO conferences to learn what they can about the agricultural policies and prospects of others, but they decline to participate themselves.

The Soviet Union has also refused to join other common food management efforts which grew out of the Rome Conference. The most important of these, and so far the most tangible result of that conference, is the $1 billion International Fund for Agricultural Development (IFAD). The Fund has so far received a pledge of financial support from both the OECD and from the OPEC nations, but it receives no support at all from the USSR which has acceded only to those World Food Council proposals which have no budgetary implications.

The Soviet Union is a member of the London International Wheat Council. But Soviet participation in the Council, especially in its discussion of a proposed international grain reserve system, begun in 1975, is quite limited. It has enjoyed opportunities, however, to exacerbate US-European Community differences over the uncertain jurisdiction of the Council, as opposed to the GATT, over grain reserve schemes (See the article by Nau in this volume). All the while, the Soviets refuse to discuss their own grain reserve policy. They consider that policy to be an element of their strategic posture, and not a matter subject to international discussion or inspection, let alone control.[44]

Unfortunately, efforts to create world food reserves without Soviet participation are less likely to provide adequate security. As the world's largest and most irregular producer of wheat, and as the world's most disruptive grain trading nation, the Soviet Union has a special obligation to share in the financial burden of carrying an

---

[44]It is widely assumed that the USSR holds large underground ''war reserves'' of grain which may not be drawn down in peacetime.

international grain reserve. Further, as a developed nation second in wealth and industrial capacity only to the US, the Soviet Union surely has some obligation to contribute to Third World agricultural development. At the very least, the Soviet Union should be expected to share adequate "early warning" information on its own agricultural performance and import needs. But the Soviet Union has denied having such obligations. By refusing to participate in common global efforts at food policy management, the Soviet Union narrows the range for cooperation among those who do participate.

The USSR, among the wealthy food importing nations, has introduced the greatest disruption into the international grain market, and has also made the smallest contribution to collective efforts to recover food security and to restore price stability. The Soviet Union, as a very large industrial nation unblessed with adequate natural agricultural resources, is reluctant to modify its own farm policies, and is ill-disposed to join international efforts at food policy cooperation. Yet it is equally impatient to achieve dietary affluence, and just wealthy enough to do so by disruptive entry into the world food market, frequently at the expense of more needy and more reliable customers. In different measure, the EEC and Japan have also added to world food problems by taking something of a free ride on the world's food system, through protective policies which force trade and production adjustments onto others. But during the recent period of food scarcity, these nations did seek to moderate import needs, they did extend assistance to poor food deficit nations, they did share information on their own agricultural performance, and they have joined in efforts at multilateral food policy management. By contrast, the USSR sought to increase its commercial access to the food supplies of others while contributing little to the maintenance of those supplies.

Conclusion and recommendations

Any conclusion which looks to the immediate future must be hedged against the enormous changeability of the world food market. Several years of good weather have restored that market to its traditional state of oversupply. Still, the more critical danger of scarcity can reemerge with only one or two years of bad weather. Under such changeable conditions, the policies of the wealthy food importing nations must be judged along several dimensions at once. Policies which contribute the most to world food "security" in times of scarcity may be incompatible with those which guarantee efficient production and harmonious trade in times of abundance. Alternatively, the politically motivated policies of some wealthy food importing nations may contribute neither to food security, nor to efficiency, nor to harmonious trade. Under such various circumstances, three different kinds of remedial action can be imagined: multilateral, bilateral, and unilateral action.

Multilateral measures: a global grain reserve

A majority of the 134 nations at the 1974 World Food Conference accepted a resolution which called for creation of nationally held world grain reserves, to restore security and stability to the world food market. The creation of such reserves was to require participation from all of those wealthy food importing nations who held a strong interest in market stability and security. The US underlined this requirement in September 1975 by proposing to the International Wheat Council in London a reserve plan with shares calculated from trade volume, GNP, and production variability. This was a formula clearly designed to require heavy participation from the EEC, Japan, and the USSR.[45] This US plan did not meet with wide or immediate approval. World carryover stocks were increased in 1976 and 1977 in the absence of any specific multilateral commitments.

Of course, a multilateral commitment to share the burden of reserve accumulation does not have to await the unlikely approval of all wealthy food importing nations. An agreement could be reached with limited participation, prohibiting release of stocks to "non-members" in times of shortage. But such a restriction would immediately require multiple pricing systems, complicated control over end-use of grain shipments, and extraordinary membership discipline. In times of tight supply, participating nations would be heavily pressured by domestic farm interests to release some of their stocks for lucrative commercial sale to a wealthy paying customer such as the USSR. In practice, a restrictive system might discriminate against the USSR just enough to create diplomatic problems for the US, which would be the principal "enforcing" state, but not enough to protect reserve stocks from Soviet purchasing power—the worst of both worlds.

In the face of such difficulties, major participants in the world food system have not yet placed full reliance upon any system of multilateral grain reserve management. For that matter, they have made little or no progress toward the multilateral reduction of barriers to harmonious food trade. Seeking a second best solution, greater reliance has been placed upon "bilateral" food security, food trade, and even food aid agreements. (See Hopkins and Puchala, which describes those systems in which "bilaterals" are dominant.) The most dramatic example is the previously mentioned 1975 Moscow agreement.

Bilateral measures: a second look at the Moscow Agreement

The October 1975 US-Soviet agreement, and also the August 1975 food trade understanding reached between the US and Japan, seem to provide an alternative model for dealing with wealthy food importing nations. The understanding with Japan was intended to reassure that nation of its access to the US market, and to underscore what has long been Japan's policy, as well as the policy of the EEC, to

---

[45]Trezise, *Rebuilding Grain Reserves,* pp. 52–54.

signal food import needs well in advance. Since 1975 the US has extended similar bilateral assurances to Romania, Poland, and Israel. The US-Soviet agreement is a more ambitious measure. Its purpose is not merely to stabilize trade, or to restrict Soviet access to US supplies in times of scarcity. By placing a 6 million ton *lower limit* on annual Soviet purchases, it also seeks to pressure the Soviet Union into carrying a larger share of the world's food reserves in times of abundance. That is, it seeks to accomplish through bilateral restriction precisely what has so far defied multilateral management.

In this respect, the success of the 1975 Moscow agreement is by no means assured. In their 1976–80 five year plan, the Soviets have budgeted 3.5 billion rubles to construct 34 million tons of new off-farm grain elevator storage capacity. This is a promising sign. Yet the bilateral agreement does not control Soviet grain exports, which could be increased in times of abundance in lieu of still greater grain storage efforts at home. Subsidized exports to Eastern Europe or to other overseas customers could throw the stockpiling burden back upon the US.

Moreover, it is not clear that the hasty negotiation of the Moscow agreement (partially undertaken in vain hope that Russia might offer low priced petroleum in return for a lifting of the temporary US grain embargo) fits neatly into any larger vision of a viable international food trading regime. With the further proliferation of bilateral trade agreements, the world food system might lose a valuable degree of its own internal freedom. Larger price and supply fluctuations would be forced onto those states not protected by agreements of their own. It is not for nothing that the US, for example, sought to avoid such agreements over most of the past 30 years.

In truth, it is hard to imagine any low cost means, bilateral or otherwise, to pressure the USSR into a stronger contribution to global food security. Despite its recent high volume of imports, the USSR remains largely self-sufficient in food supplies. Even before the record harvest of 1976, over the four-year period of scarcity which included the massive import years of 1972 and 1975, Soviet *domestic* grain production was sufficient to satisfy 92 percent of all national requirements. External food supplies are convenient to Soviet planners, particularly when they can be purchased on US credit at prices held low by export subsidies, as in 1972. But the USSR, the world's largest producer of wheat, is scarcely vulnerable to a bilateral or multilateral ''food weapon.''

Unilateral measures: burdens and blessings of self-reliance

Multilateral and bilateral policy measures are those which enjoy greatest favor among today's outward looking architects of a new global food regime. Yet outward looking policies are not generally favored by the wealthy food importing members of such a regime. The EEC, for example, considers its own inward looking agricultural policies to be non-negotiable. The Japanese also pay close attention to the domestic political aspects of farm policy, and have acquired certain suspicions concerning food trade interdependence. The Soviet Union remains aloof from all multilateral food management schemes. In different measure, each of these wealthy food customers prefers to tend to its own internal needs, and to force most adjustment burdens onto others.

These introverted and "unilateral" industrial nation food policies may distress those with global perspectives. But they are at the same time a predictable feature of today's world food regime. The world food system, after all, is not yet characterized by the same advanced degree of interdependence that exists, for example, in the world energy system. Over the period 1970–75, despite high absolute volumes of international food trade, only about one-eighth of the world's grain production entered the world food market. The rest was grown, harvested, stored, marketed, and consumed, entirely within national or community borders, not across borders. Since most states, including wealthy importing states, are largely self-reliant in basic food supplies, it is easier for them to give priority to unilateral, self-directed food policies.

Fortunately, unilateral and self-directed food policies are not always destructive of world food security. In the case of the EEC, concern for the political and economic interests of farming populations at home did contribute to increased production, and in times of scarcity, to food security abroad. The protective policies of the EEC have built a sometimes useful redundancy into the world's food production system. In similar fashion, Japan's rice support program has prevented that nation from becoming excessively dependent upon overseas supply in times of scarcity. Of course, the USSR has not demonstrated a similar concern for the security of its own farming population. The Soviet political system is much less responsive to the needs of its own rural sector. In part for this reason, its unilateral policies are much less compatible with a secure international food regime.

Looking to the future, it is likely that progress toward global food security will continue to be made largely through unilateral (national or regional) food policy initiatives. These must include stockpiling initiatives in North America, and production initiatives in the Third World. The EEC, Japan, and the USSR may neither join nor challenge these initiatives; they have emerged from the recent experience of food shortages convinced, as always, in the logic of self-protection and self-help. This introverted policy perspective undoubtedly continues to diminish prospects for free and perfectly harmonious world food trade. But it can scarcely be otherwise. Global food policy adjustment will not soon replace domestic political adjustment as the most cherished policy objective of most national policy leaders. Thankfully, these domestic policy objectives remain tolerably compatible, in most instances, with the security and stability of a somewhat compartmentalized world food system.

4

The Politics of Food Scarcities
in Developing Countries

Norman K. Nicholson and John D. Esseks

Barring the global catastrophe envisioned by the Club of Rome, poverty will prove a more intractable problem than low productivity in the Third World. Much greater attention will have to be paid to the distribution of income, jobs, and foodgrains in the future if increases in production are to actually reduce hunger. The failure of many countries to manage their food supplies adequately and to provide basic food security to their populations is explained both by an urban bias in planning and by the sheer administrative complications and costs of stabilizing the foodgrains markets. For many countries dependency was politically easier. Major efforts to increase basic food production are essential in most developing countries, but the political adjustments associated with that decision may be difficult. The institutional patterns required to induce an agricultural revolution will challenge existing patterns of power and social stratification.

The food problem in many Third World states is basically that they have become or will shortly become incapable of meeting rising domestic demand from population growth and higher personal incomes through increased production or commercial imports. As Hopkins and Puchala discuss, by the mid-1980s the aggregate food-grain import needs of LDCs and other deficit countries (e.g., Western and Eastern Europe) are expected to exceed the production capacities of exporting states. In the

Norman K. Nicholson and John D. Esseks are associate professors of political science at Northern Illinois University, where they specialize in political economy. During 1977 and 1978, Norman Nicholson has been on leave, serving as a Senior Social Science Adviser for the United States Agency for International Development.
The authors are very grateful to the following for their helpful comments on an earlier draft of this paper: Edgar Owens, Rollo Erick, Tom Dobbs, Donald Puchala, and Raymond Hopkins.

resulting high-priced commercial markets, the poor in many LDCs will be outbid by rich importing countries. Moreover, food aid from developed OECD countries, especially the major grain exporters, is both limited and undependable. In the tight supply year 1973, US aid, which makes up well over half of all food aid, dropped in volume by about 40 percent from the 1972 level; and in 1974 shipments declined by a further 50 percent.[1]

With domestic production decreasing or stagnant relative to population, commercial imports too expensive, and food aid scarce, many LDCs are likely to see nutritional levels deteriorate, perhaps to the point of widespread starvation if the world scarcities of 1973–1975 recur. In the process, there are likely to be attendant political ills: mass-scale unrest from soaring domestic food prices, insatiable demands from public-sector employees for compensating wage hikes, and increased corruption as governments distribute relief and ration food.

The developing countries as a whole have come to hold an increasingly dependent position in the world food system. Exporters have become importers, reliance on food aid or assistance to meet balance of payments deficits has grown for non-OPEC countries,[2] and efforts to expand production in promising areas, such as the Sudan and Brazil, have yet to be realized. This food dependency and vulnerability to scarcity spills over into balance of payment, developmental and political stability concerns. The riots which occurred because of a rise in food prices in Cairo in spring 1977 illustrate this point well; the rise (later rescinded) was brought on by pressure from foreign lending agencies, and by planners trying to improve production incentives for Egypt's farmers.

The LDCs do not play a role in creating regime norms, except through their dependency. Rather they are the target of the concessional trading system, of funds to foster development, and requests to undertake "reforms"—regime practices often inconsistent with each other and with the domestic policy preferences of less developed states, as we shall see in detail later.

The problem cases

Not all LDCs face this destiny; only the most vulnerable. Developing countries can be classified into four groups.[3] The first group comprises traditional food

[1]These rough percentages are derived from data on food aid shipments of two major kinds: those under Title I of Public Law 480, which provides for sales on concessional terms (20 to 40 years for repayment, low interest rates) and those under Title II of the act, which provides for grants. The data for Title I shipments were given for calendar years as follows: 1972, about 6 million metric tons; 1973, 3 million; and 1974, 1.2 million. Title II figures were given for fiscal years as follows: 1972, 2.5 million metric tons; 1973, 2.1 million; and 1974, 1.4 million. Sources: United States Congress, *1973 Annual Report on Public Law 480* (House Document No. 83–362, Washington, D.C., 1973), pp. 8, 50; and "The Annual Report on Activities Carried Out Under Public Law 480, 83rd Congress, as Amended, During the Period January 1 through December 31, 1974" (preliminary draft, Agency for International Development, 1975), pp. 1, 95.

[2]See USDA Economic Research Service, "World Economic Conditions in Relation to Agricultural Trade," WEC 12 (Washington, D.C., August 1977), p. 7.

[3]US Department of Agriculture, Economic Research Service, *The World Food Situation and Prospects to 1985* (Washington, D.C., 1974), pp. 81–83.

surplus states, e.g., Thailand, Burma, Nepal, Kenya. With reasonably high further investments and good management in the food-farming sector, these nations should be able to continue to feed themselves, at least in basic foodstuffs. The second group consists of financially self-sufficient states, e.g., Algeria, Indonesia, Iran, Morocco, Nigeria. Though not self-reliant in food, they have high foreign exchange earning ability from oil, phosphates, or other raw materials. A third group of states is more vulnerable. They cannot afford the import consequences of stagnant food production, but either have already "made definite progress with the Green Revolution," e.g., Pakistan, the Philippines, Turkey, or, as in parts of Latin America, they have unexploited potential in good climates and underutilized land. The fourth group consists of severely disadvantaged countries. They face limited foreign-exchange earning capacities, population pressures (India, Bangladesh, Sri Lanka), and/or unfavorable climates (the drought-prone African states neighboring the Sahara) which threaten periodic or near-chronic food scarcities. In these states (basically in South Asia and sub-Saharan Africa), high population density relative to food-producing resources keeps them close to or below the margin of minimum nutrition (see Austin). They find it difficult to arrange for foreign exchange to cover both currently needed food imports and Green Revolution inputs (fertilizers, irrigation equipment) which might eventually reduce import dependence. Our paper concentrates on these two problem areas.

The shape of the problem

The best assessments of the progress in reducing food insecurity, or lack of it, is the trend in countries' ability to increase per capita food production and to reduce dependence on food imports. Unfortunately, both food output and population estimates for LDCs are often of questionable reliability. We try to illustrate this by producing, in Table 1, two separate time series of per capita food production for each of the 28 countries surveyed—estimates offered by the Food and Agricultural Organization (FAO) and the US Department of Agriculture (USDA).[4] For 15 of the 23 African states surveyed, the two series agree that food production either failed to keep pace with population (e.g., Ethiopia, Liberia, Nigeria) or improved only a few percentage points from the 1961–65 base (Benin, Guinea, and Madagascar), as the 1971–74 averages in group A of Table 1 show. Staying close to the base index tended not to be much of an achievement, since African states were then and are now among the world's most nutritionally poor countries. According to FAO estimates for the early 1960s, the average daily supply of calories per person in Africa was below the level required for good health and about two-thirds the level prevailing in the developed world.[5] In nine of the above 15 problem countries, the loss of stagnation in food outputs per capita can be attributed in varying degrees to short-

---

[4]The 28 countries in question were ones for which both FAO and USDA per capita food production estimates were available. See Table 1 for specific bibliographic references.

[5]Cited by Donald Heisel, "Food and Population in Africa," *Current History,* June, 1975): 261.

Table 1 Indices of per capita food production: 1961–74 USDA and FAO estimates

1961–65 AVERAGE = 100

		1961–65 Average	1966	1968	1970	1972	1974	1971–74 Average
A. Stagnant or Declining Output (Africa)								
Benin	*USDA*	100	92	94	93	91	99	94
	FAO	100	102	104	108	96	106	102
Ethiopia	*USDA*	100	100	103	100	91	87	91
	FAO	100	101	101	103	99	90	96
Ghana	*USDA*	100	99	91	88	83	87	87
	FAO	100	93	91	101	104	101	104
Guinea	*USDA*	100	93	108	106	107	104	107
	FAO	100	97	105	102	94	92	94
Kenya	*USDA*	100	99	100	95	97	95	94
	FAO	100	109	107	107	102	96	99
Liberia	*USDA*	100	97	83	83	85	94	89
	FAO	100	98	92	93	95	102	96
Madagascar	*USDA*	100	105	108	107	107	103	104
	FAO	100	102	102	98	90	93	92
Mali	*USDA*	100	92	82	87	66	67	68
	FAO	100	98	91	90	74	72	75
Niger	*USDA*	100	100	98	96	73	71	71
	FAO	100	110	103	96	81	70	73
Nigeria	*USDA*	100	94	83	96	96	92	93
	FAO	100	88	88	91	85	79	82
Senegal	*USDA*	100	89	82	66	63	91	82
	FAO	100	91	87	69	59	75	75
Sierra Leone	*USDA*	100	95	97	94	97	95	97
	FAO	100	111	107	107	109	107	107
Togo	*USDA*	100	112	115	105	98	93	96
	FAO	100	115	119	114	84	87	89
Uganda	*USDA*	100	107	109	105	97	85	93
	FAO	100	99	101	108	101	94	98
Upper Volta	*USDA*	100	91	86	79	68	78	70
	FAO	100	106	106	102	86	60	78
B. Increased Outputs (Africa)								
Ivory Coast	*USDA*	100	107	107	112	115	128	120
	FAO	100	93	105	111	116	121	119
Malawi	*USDA*	100	127	106	109	129	123	123
	FAO	100	121	112	109	126	122	122
Rwanda	*USDA*	100	101	116	121	112	99	111
	FAO	100	106	107,	119	112	96	110
Zaire	*USDA*	100	109	114	122	108	115	111
	FAO	100	107	121	118	115	127	118

C. Widely Divergent Indices

Burundi	*USDA*	100	107	105	110	107	82	101
	FAO	100	105	105	129	171	181	165
Cameroon	*USDA*	100	102	105	95	94	95	95
	FAO	100	105	121	122	124	121	122
Tanzania	*USDA*	100	111	100	102	103	86	97
	FAO	100	110	107	124	114	109	113
Zambia	*USDA*	100	122	81	92	157	135	129
	FAO	100	113	102	99	99	103	100

D. South Asian Countries

Bangladesh	*USDA*	100	91	101	95	80	85	85
	FAO	100	91	100	92	78	80	82
Burma	*USDA*	100	85	92	92	83	88	88
	FAO	100	86	94	94	84	90	90
India	*USDA*	100	89	100	109	98	95	101
	FAO	100	91	99	105	97	96	100
Pakistan	*USDA*	100	101	119	132	118	121	120
	FAO	100	99	116	120	114	113	114
Sri Lanka	*USDA*	100	89	110	120	100	108	102
	FAO	100	96	101	98	93	97	94

Sources: U.S. Department of Agriculture, *Indices of Agricultural Production in Africa and the Near East, 1956–75* (Washington, D.C., 1976, Statistical Bulletin No. 556); USDA, *Indices of Agricultural Production for the Far East and Oceania, Average 1961–65 and Annual 1966–75* (Washington D.C., 1976, Statistical Bulletin No. 555); and Food and Agriculture Organization, *Production Yearbook, 1974* (Rome, 1975), Vol. 1, pp. 29–30.

term climatic factors, namely the multi-year Sahelian drought of the early 1970s.[6] However, in five of those nine cases, downward or stagnating trends began before the drought.[7] Significantly upward trends—with per capita food outputs increasing by more than 10 percent—are displayed by only four of the sub-Saharan African countries surveyed: the Ivory Coast, Malawi, Rwanda, and Zaire (group B in Table 1). For another four states (group C), the FAO and USDA estimates diverge too greatly, underlining the problem of reliable data, and prohibiting sensible conclusions. The FAO, for instance, estimates that in 1974 Burundi had increased its per capita production 81 percent over the 1961–65 base, while the USDA thought it had fallen 18 percent.

Among South Asian states (group D) FAO and USDA estimates indicate that Bangladesh and Burma failed to expand food production as rapidly as population growth and India was stagnant: its 1971–74 average was virtually unchanged from that of 1961–65. The indices for Sri Lanka are too divergent for conclusions. Only Pakistan appears to have achieved significant progress, with the FAO and USDA estimates showing 14 to 20 percent increases in food outputs per person.

[6]Ethiopia, Ghana, Guinea, Kenya, Mali, Niger, Nigeria, Senegal, and Upper Volta. Agency for International Development, *Special Report to the Congress on the Drought Situation in Sub-Saharan Africa* (Washington, D.C., 1975), pp. 17–44.

[7]Ethiopia, Ghana, Mali, Nigeria, and Senegal. See the sources listed in Table 1.

Table 2   Indices of food imports, 1962–73, based on current market values

1962–65 AVERAGE = 100

	1962–65 Average	1967	1969	1971	1973	1971–73 Average
African Countries:						
Cameroon	100	123	134	190	247	210
Ethiopia	100	159	110	174	152	144
Ghana	100	90	85	87	126	93
Ivory Coast	100	n/a	260	308	412	367
Kenya	100	67	165	224	247	235
Liberia	100	119	95	146	206	168
Madagascar	100	82	120	157	205	168
Malawi[a]	100	84	92	149	205	179
Mali	100	108	184	247	563	364
Nigeria	100	93	147	245	359	292
Senegal	100	106	136	131	237	170
Sierra Leone	100	130	118	151	246	181
Tanzania	100	135	222	268	411	383
Togo	100	138	114	129	255	190
Uganda	100	170	517	561	551	543
Zaire	100	107	97	96	173	131
Zambia[a]	100	n/a	172	297	153	222
South Asian Countries:						
Burma	100	n/a	29	43	23	29
India	100	158	103	67	118	76
Pakistan	100	131	60	67	136	90
Sri Lanka	100	103	90	93	125	102

1971–73 AVERAGE, ALL COUNTRIES = 219

Note: [a] 1964–65 average.
Source: Food and Agriculture Organization, *Trade Yearbook,* 1968 and 1974 (Rome, 1969 and 1975).

A survey of food imports from 1962 to 1973 is presented in Table 2.[8] In 21 sub-Saharan and South Asian countries (i.e., those for which data were available) there was a general, substantial rise in the money value of food imports. If we compare averages for 1971–73 with the 1962–65 bases, we find a mean increase of 119 percent. Some twelve of the twenty countries (see group B, Table 3) could "afford" their increased food bills. The ratios of their food imports to export revenues were no higher in 1971–73 than in 1961–65; export earnings rose enough to offset the higher food bill. However, for the other countries (see group A), the reverse was true; food imports became more expensive, relatively as well as absolutely. Relative increase or not, many countries in both groups continued to have

[8]Data on the money value of food imports were available also for 1974. However, world market prices for grain were unusually high that year, as well as in 1973. Including both 1973 and 1974 figures would tend to distort excessively the comparisons in Tables 2 and 3 (that is, the averages for the early 1970s versus the 1962–65 bases). Therefore, we chose to omit the 1974 data.

high foreign food bills. India's food imports in 1971–73 averaged 16 percent of its total export earnings; Pakistan, 18 percent; Zaire, 20 percent; Sierra Leone, 21 percent; Sri Lanka, 48 percent; and Senegal, 51 percent.

Table 3   Food imports as percentage of total export earnings 1962–73

	1962–65 Average	1967	1969	1971	1973	1971–73 Average
A. *More Costly Dependence*						
Senegal	43.6	41.0	58.5	55.0	64.5	51.3
Sri Lanka	40.5	46.5	44.0	45.0	54.0	48.0
Sierra Leone	18.0	30.1	16.5	22.1	23.5	21.3
Zaire	18.2	17.3	17.0	18.5	21.6	20.3
Ivory Coast	11.0	n/a	15.4	18.2	13.0	16.6
Tanzania	5.2	5.5	8.0	9.0	10.1	11.0
Uganda	2.3	3.4	8.5	8.0	6.5	7.3
Zambia	4.2	n/a	4.0	9.1	2.8	6.0
B. *Less Costly Dependence*						
Pakistan	31.3	31.0	13.2	13.5	24.0	18.0
India	32.0	51.0	29.0	16.0	21.0	16.0
Togo	19.0	19.1	11.5	11.4	18.2	15.3
Madagascar	14.3	10.2	14.0	14.0	13.1	13.0
Ghana	19.3	19.3	16.0	15.5	12.4	12.5
Kenya	14.0	8.0	11.6	14.0	10.0	12.1
Malawi[a]	14.0	8.0	9.1	11.0	11.0	11.1
Cameroon	9.4	11.0	7.0	10.4	8.0	9.4
Liberia	14.0	11.0	6.0	8.4	9.1	8.5
Nigeria	11.1	9.0	10.5	9.0	7.0	8.0
Burma	10.0	n/a	5.6	8.6	5.5	6.2
Ethiopia	6.0	9.1	5.3	8.0	3.6	5.2

Note: [a] 1964–65 average.
Source: Same as for Table 2.

An alternative to focusing on monetary indicators of food import dependence is to look at physical or volume dependence. The "problem" countries identified in Table 3, i.e., those which had relatively higher food import bills (group A), tend also to be those which in 1971–73 were more dependent than in 1961–65 on imported grain relative to total domestic consumption. Such concurrence increases the threat to consumption levels. The increased cost of food imports makes them a conspicuous target for cutbacks by government action. But any cutback will obviously affect consumption most where it depends upon imports (see Table 4).

This likelihood was realized for at least seven African countries where production lagged behind population growth and imports failed to fill the gap. In these states, averages for per capita consumption of cereals, 1973–75, were below

Table 4   Cereals imports[a] as percentage of total cereals consumption (by volume) 1961–73

IN PERCENTAGES

	1961–65 Average	1967	1969	1971	1973	1971–73 Average
A. Increased Import Dependence						
Ethiopia	.3	.7	.9	1.3	2.7	1.5
Ivory Coast	24.0	20.2	31.5	28.2	29.5	31.3
Liberia[b]	26.2	36.2	36.3	30.0	17.7	26.5
Madagascar	3.8	2.0	3.8	6.0	17.7	13.3
Nigeria	2.4	3.6	4.8	8.3	8.7	7.7
Senegal	76.7	68.3	67.8	79.1	90.0	86.1
Sierra Leone[c]	11.1	15.8	13.0	21.0	18.6	18.7
Tanzania	6.3	4.3	7.6	8.3	16.5	11.6
Upper Volta	1.8	4.4	4.0	7.0	10.5	8.4
Zaire	36.2	31.2	24.9	32.9	38.4	36.4
Zambia[d]	4.7	4.6	11.6	7.7	10.1	9.3
B. Decreased Dependence						
Ghana	25.3	19.0	23.9	21.6	25.7	22.3
Guinea	18.1	18.7	16.4	17.8	13.2	15.7
India	8.3	11.0	4.5	2.3	4.5	2.8
Kenya	5.8	.2	1.1	7.2	3.4	4.2
Pakistan	19.3	26.4	9.9	10.8	9.7	11.3
Sri Lanka	54.6	52.7	48.3	48.2	52.1	49.7

Notes: [a]Wheat, coarse grains, and rice unless otherwise indicated. [b]Rice only. [c]Wheat and rice. [d]Wheat and coarse grains.
Sources: U.S. Department of Agriculture, *Foreign Agriculture Circular: Reference Tables on Wheat, Corn, and Total Coarse Grains Supply-Distribution for Individual Countries* (Washington, D.C. 1976); and ibid., *Reference Tables on Rice Supply-Distribution for Individual Countries* (Washington, D.C., 1976).

1961–65 baselines (see Table 5). Available data on the seven indicate both lower or stagnant output relative to population and import volumes which did not compensate for this.[9] Consumption by the poorest in these countries, of course, dropped.

In addition to an imbalance between supply and need for food, inequitable distribution of income is also a problem. Malenbaum proposes that in many Third World countries one-third or less of the population consumes more than half of the available food.[10] Even in a country such as India, which has barely managed to match food production to growing population, there are large regional variations in consumption. Differences among classes are even more striking. With continuing population growth projected for the long term, the magnitude of the world population threatens to exceed its capacity to produce food. In the short term, that is in the next decade or two, the inability to provide jobs and income to increasing numbers

[9]See the entries for those seven countries in the following sources: US Department of Agricultural Service, *Foreign Agriculture Circular: Reference Tables on Wheat, Corn, and Total Coarse Grains Supply-Distribution for Individual Countries* (Washington, D.C., 1976) and *Foreign Agriculture Circular: Reference Tables on Rice Supply-Distribution for Individual Countries* (Washington, D.C., 1976).

[10]Wilfred Malenbaum, "Scarcity: Prerequisite to Abundance," *Annals of the American Academy of Political Science*, no. 420 (July 1975): 76.

of the poor, rather than the physical lack of food, is the problem. There are economic and social barriers to meeting the needs of all humans for food. It is a crisis of planning and implementation when production grows but not consumption. Poverty is as much a part of the world food crisis as food shortages.

Table 5 Indices of per capita consumption of cereals[a] 1961–75

1961–65 = 100

	1961–65 Average	1967	1969	1971	1973	1975	1973–75 Average
A. Lower Consumption							
Ethiopia	100	105	112	107	78	95	85
Kenya	100	91	86	69	88	82	83
Liberia[b]	100	81	80	79	77	76	76
Nigeria	100	78	93	71	69	79	75
Senegal	100	113	105	124	107	86	95
Sierra Leone[c]	100	95	90	117	94	98	99
Upper Volta	100	88	75	79	67	69	68
B. Higher Consumption							
Ghana	100	118	110	121	150	127	137
Guinea	100	128	115	114	106	101	104
India	100	100	105	103	107	105	104
Ivory Coast	100	121	139	141	121	122	119
Madagascar	100	112	103	106	108	118	115
Pakistan	100	107	123	111	117	114	115
Sri Lanka	100	104	110	115	108	102	108
Tanzania	100	87	86	105	126	131	122
Zambia[d]	100	146	154	135	116	123	121
Zaire	100	95	120	133	150	163	157

Notes: [a] Wheat, coarse grains, and rice, unless otherwise indicated. [b] Rice only. [c] Wheat and rice. [d] Wheat and coarse grains.
Sources: Same as for Table 4.

The problem of income distribution is one which cannot easily be handled within the context of food policy in isolation from other aspects of national development strategies and international patterns of resource flows. It may be possible, as in the case of Sri Lanka, to heavily subsidize food distribution, to use "food for work" projects to provide subsistence to unemployed workers, or to target relief supplies directly to the destitute where they are geographically concentrated (e.g., the Bengali refugees in Indian camps in 1971), but these distributional solutions are inherently limited in their impact and are difficult to sustain. Thus, although we shall concentrate on the distributional politics and problems of food policy in this paper, we must indicate at the outset that neither concessional supplies of food from the United States nor higher agricultural productivity in the agricultural sector in the Third World will in and of themselves eliminate the hunger problem. Only where these food policies are integrated with programs to redistribute productive assets more equitably and with investment patterns which emphasize maximum employment generation can we expect a substantial reduction in real, as opposed to statistical, world hunger.

In summary, we see in the two regions of South Asia and sub-Saharan Africa many countries whose production, import, and/or consumption records are not encouraging. From the early 1960s to the mid-1970s, their per capita food outputs declined or were stagnant; they remained significantly dependent on costly food imports or food aid; and/or their actual consumption levels (at least for cereals) declined. Some countries were "problems" in all three respects, e.g., Ethiopia, Senegal, and Sierra Leone.

By drawing on experiences of these areas, we can anticipate the kinds of policy adjustments and related policy outcomes in LDCs generally as they cope with high production targets, chronic, widespread malnutrition, and threat of mass famine. The discussion that follows is based largely on the experiences of India and selected African countries and is divided into two sections: problems and related policies concerned with distribution and policy problems for food production.

The politics of distribution

The international movement of concessional grain supplies into Third World countries may have one of three possible distributional goals. First, the aid may be intended merely to relieve the intense shortfalls of supplies associated with natural disaster and crop failure—as famine relief. These programs typically do not make class distinctions among recipients and generally make very limited contributions to the economic rehabilitation of the poor. Second, the food aid may be designed to provide long-term supplements to the income of specific target groups in the form of subsidized food supplies, "food for work" programs, or highly specialized nutritional programs. These programs often have a very limited clientele and seldom have any immediate impact on the structure of poverty in Third World countries. They are essentially remedial in character rather than developmental. Third, food-grains programs are designed to stabilize prices and counter inflationary trends associated with the development process in many countries. In the long term, this use of foodgrains probably has the greatest impact on the structure of poverty through the contribution it makes to speeding investment. On the other hand, such a food program has little direct effect immediately on the poor and may well serve to depress agricultural prices and reduce production incentives in agriculture in the recipient country. The two effects are, of course, related. It is difficult to improve the lot of the poor if agriculture is depressed and most of the poor are found in the rural areas. The politics of food distribution will differ greatly depending on the type of distributional strategy intended by the international donor and the recipient government. (It should not be assumed that these two are necessarily congruent.)

For twenty years (1954–75) surplus grain stocks moving through the concessional system of the global regime provided (friendly) developing nations with an inexpensive and politically attractive solution to their food problems.[11] In terms of

[11] During the decade of the sixties imports of grain averaged 7.7 percent of India's domestic production,

famine policy these stocks supplied the essential "insurance" against erratic weather. But that is not the only function concessional sales and gifts performed. In India, for instance, they were used, somewhat ineffectively, as an anti-inflation device to compensate for extensive deficit financing. It is also clear that, given the apparent stagnation in Indian agriculture and the difficulty of persuading subsistence farmers to part with their produce on the market, American grain was used by Indian planners to avoid the necessity of what they perceived to be fruitless investment in the agricultural sector.

As the amount of food moving in concessional systems decreased relatively and absolutely after 1972, countercyclical policies, once accomplished solely through import policy, must now be controlled by regulation of national foodgrains supplies and markets. This involves the control of price levels, whether for famine, welfare, or anti-inflation reasons. Restrictions on the physical movement of grains are likely to be necessary, at least where areas of high demand and high income compete for stocks with areas of high need and low income. Stocks will also have to be maintained as reserve for famine and, once established, the system may prove useful for "buffer stock operations" to even out price fluctuations. Finally, given the collapse of income earning capacity in certain regions due to weather or within certain classes due to the structure of the economy, it may be advisable to target supplies specifically to the "vulnerable population." Each of these functions will require the development of new institutional capacity by the government. The total cost of this operation is likely to be high, and a number of difficult decisions must be made regarding the allocation of costs and benefits of the system.

The Indian case

In India the distinction between short, intense periods of deprivation (famine) and the growing incidence of continuing destitution is fairly clear. While famines have been largely alleviated, chronic hunger remains a difficult problem. India's institutional development for dealing with the facts of hunger goes back more than two decades and provides many lessons. Moreover, the Indian case is particularly important as it illustrates how even minor shortfalls in production can escalate to major political consequences in the absence of effective management.

As a first step it is important to recognize the magnitude of the task at hand. In 1973, Ali Khusro estimated that India required, at minimum, a buffer stock of about five million tons a year to provide adequate security.[12] Taking into account procurement costs, handling, storage costs, and storage construction, the total cost for each million tons was calculated to be about $119.6 million in non-recurring

---

for example. More to the point these imports represented 20.4 percent of the *marketed* supply of grain. See V. S. Vyas and S. C. Bandyopadhyay, "National Food Policy in the Framework of a National Food Budget," *Economic and Political Weekly,* "Review of Agriculture" (March 1975): A2–A13.

[12]*Indian Foodgrain Marketing* (New Delhi: Institute of Economic Growth, 1973) pp. 18–26. Refer also to John Moore et. al. *Indian Foodgrain Marketing* (New Delhi: Institute of Economic Growth, 1973).

costs.[13] In fact, a stock of eight or nine million tons has proven barely adequate to cover the deficits of the seventies. The operative costs of the public-sector Food Corporation of India, which handles these stocks, has proven higher than expected.[14] A careful analysis of the costs of the Corporation indicated that for each quintal of grain, purchased at Rs. 80, the necessary mark-up for the Corporation was Rs. 25, or 31 percent (one rupee = $0.13). Furthermore, the longer a stock was held in reserve the larger that figure would be. On a stock of 8.9 million tons handled in 1972–73, losses in storage and handling alone were estimated at a value of $28.0 million. In addition, rising foreign and domestic prices have forced the government of India to subsidize the operation in the amount of $196.3 million in the same year. In comparison, the entire proposed central government expenditure on agriculture for 1971–73 was $584.2 million. This enormous expenditure and a staff of 38,000 at the central level alone (in many cases actual procurement and distribution of grain is handled by state level officials) is the price of a national system of food crisis management.

India's present massive system of foodgrains management evolved slowly after the inflationary effects of the second five-year plan (1956–57 to 1961–62) led to a public outcry against rising prices. At that time, the state's role consisted of little more than allocating imported stocks and making the arrangements for their dispatch to the larger cities. Stocks were not maintained against emergencies, no buffer stock operations were attempted to stabilize prices, and there was no serious attempt to use food stocks as a device for economic planning.[15] There were certain left-wing politicians and Planning Commission economists who called for greater control over both imported and domestic stocks, but the flood of American grain during the late 1950s relieved the pressure and delayed full institutional development for nearly ten years. It was only in 1964 that the government of India accepted a proposal for the establishment of a central foodgrains trading organization (Food Corporation of India), and not until 1968 that the organization became fully operative with complete control over interstate movement of foodgrains and sole responsibility for management of imported stocks.

The Food Corporation was but one part of a package of institutional innovations and policy departures undertaken in the period 1960–65. The poor accomplishments of "community" oriented development programs in the fifties and the growing fear of the economic and political consequences of rising prices persuaded the government to adopt a new strategy aimed mostly at the individual commercial farmer. In this context the Corporation was expected to accomplish its ends through market operations and, if need be, to support farm prices in order to provide incentives.

[13]The data following on operating costs come from *Report of the Committee on Cost of Handling of Foodgrains by Food Corporation of India* (New Delhi: Government of India, 1974), pp. 23; 40–41.

[14]These dollar figures were converted from rupees at the official exchange rate then prevailing, one rupee = $0.13

[15]N. K. Nicholson, "The Politics of Food Policy in India," *Pacific Affairs*, Vol. 41, no. 1 (Spring 1968): 34–9.

From a long-term perspective it was the surpluses of the good years and not the shortfalls of the bad years that were the problem—for the commercial farmer.[16] The latter problem could continue to be managed through imports.

In 1965, there was already a huge, but chaotic, public operation on foodgrains, characterized by a complex set of arrangements between New Delhi and the respective state governments. Most deficit states were badly in debt in their foodgrains operations, it was impossible to keep track of stocks, and such internal procurement of grain as did take place was entirely at the whim of respective state governments. Many in Delhi, therefore, perceived that the establishment of an autonomous, compact, and professional state trading organization would improve the situation. With its own capital, its own procurement organization, and its own interstate distribution system, the Corporation could reduce costs and confusion. So long as most stocks were in fact imported, this was not a difficult decision to implement.[17]

However, the food crisis of 1967 eliminated any semblance of autonomy for the Corporation. Prices, distribution arrangements, and interstate allocations became matters of intense political concern subject to day-to-day control by the Ministry of Food. Finally, the crisis ended any hope that the Corporation might actually establish itself as an independent force in the markets of the surplus states. As in the past, state governments became reluctant to permit external control of their food stocks and preferred to operate as the "agents" of the Corporation, maintaining their physical control over procurement.

Moreover, many national-level politicians and administrators were not eager to bear the responsibility of controls. As market prices are disrupted, the functions they perform must be absorbed by administrative agencies. These price functions include: adjustment of supply and demand, income distribution, resource allocation, and capital formation.[18] The regulation of the supply of food to one region or section of the population will affect supplies available to other regions and sections. This almost inevitably leads to demand for the extension of government protection to a larger and larger portion of the population. Most importantly, as Myron Weiner

[16]The basic document in this change was the Ford Foundation report, *India's Food Crisis & Steps to Meet It* (New Delhi, Ministry of Food and Agriculture and Ministry of Community Development and Cooperation, 1959). Regarding price policy two subsequent reports indicate clearly the direction of thinking, in the Government of India: *Agricultural Price Policy in India* (New Delhi: Directorate of Economics and Statistics, Ministry of Food and Agriculture, 1966), and *Report of the Foodgrains Policy Committee* (New Delhi: Department of Food, 1966). In agricultural policy the innovations are presented in *Modernizing Indian Agriculture* (New Delhi: Ministry of Food, Agriculture, Community Development, and Cooperation, 1969). Also see N. K. Nicholson, "Rural Development Policy in India: Elite Differentiation and the Decision Making Process" (DeKalb: Center for Governmental Studies, Northern Illinois University, 1974); D. Brown, *Agricultural Development in India's Districts* (Cambridge: Harvard University Press, 1971).

[17]This interpretation was derived from extensive interviews by Nicholson in India in 1974 with officers and politicians involved in making the decision or in the early implementation of the decision.

[18]John Mellor, "The Functions of Agricultural Prices in Economic Development," in *Comparative Experience of Agricultural Development in Developing Countries of Asia and the South-East since World War II* (Bombay: Indian Society of Agricultural Economics, 1971), pp. 122–40.

argues in *Politics of Scarcity*, once a government enters into controls, like it or not, it does become *responsible* for vagaries of weather and market.[19] The administrative and financial cost of the operation aside, the political cost of failure to meet these responsibilities, once accepted, are enormous. Driven to avoid such failure, governments will be tempted to expand their control over the nation's food supplies, both at the production and distribution end of the chain. This, in turn, disrupts existing distribution of functions between public and private sectors, threatens existing distributions of political and administrative authority, and adds massively to the bureaucratic weight of government on the citizenry. The sources of political crisis are far broader than the cries of the hungry.

The moment one accepts the inevitability of securing a substantial portion of its emergency reserves domestically, the problem of price levels presents itself. Those affected by hunger have little income earning capacity and cannot pay market prices for food. A subsidy is the obvious answer. But the cost of a subsidy is not to be measured only in budget terms. On the contrary, Morris Morris argues, the real cost is the missed opportunity for alternative investment.[20] Given the difficulty of raising taxes in Third World countries, the transfer payments which relief expenditure represents are not usually transfers from the rich to the poor but from the poor to the poor. Every rupee of relief could have been used toward productive investment elsewhere.

The alternative strategy is to restrict the price the government must pay for the grain in the first place. One method is a statutory levy on all farmers. This has the advantage of increasing the "market surplus" because it operates even on subsistence farmers. Few state governments were willing to accept the administrative cost of such a measure, however, and no one has forgotten the Congress Party defeats in the 1952 elections in areas where this method was employed.[21] If the government decides to buy in the market, however, the presence of such large "commercial" purchases will tend to force prices up, to the advantage of the better capitalized farmer who can wait to take advantage of the unusually high prices which prevail after the government has drained the market.[22]

---

[19]M. Weiner, *The Politics of Scarcity* (Chicago: University of Chicago Press, 1962), Chapter 9.

[20]Morris D. Morris, "What is a Famine," *Economic and Political Weekly* (November 2, 1974), 885; "Needed: A New Famine Policy," ibid., (February 1975): 283. See also N. S. Jodha, "Famine and Famine Policies: Some Empirical Evidence," ibid., (October 11, 1975): 1609.

[21]For a discussion of the politics of decontrol, see Norman K. Nicholson, "Politics and Food Policy in India," thesis presented to the Graduate School, Cornell University, for the Degree of Doctor of Philosophy, June 1966, Chapter 2.

[22]This possibility was demonstrated in the report by the Directorate of Economics and Statistics, Ministry of Food and Agriculture, *Report on Market Arrivals of Foodgrains—1958859 Season* (New Delhi: 1959).

The question of the effect of this control system on incentives has frequently been raised in public debate and in academic circles. Several answers are possible. First, the disincentive effect will depend on the extent to which higher prices would, in fact, be reflected in higher investments by the farmer. It could reasonably be argued that, in the absence of new technology, extensive farm investment was not to be expected. Second, controlled prices may be offset, from the perspective of the farmer, by higher average prices if the government does actually support the price at harvest and in bumper years. Third, some disincentive may be justified by the responsibility of the government to prevent starvation if this is what the grain is actually used for and there appears no other way to do the job.

For the government of India the Green Revolution has largely resolved this problem. The new hybrid wheats have had a dramatic impact on the northern wheat regions of India, especially in Punjab and Haryana. In an area of high productivity and commercial farming, the procurement task is greatly reduced. The government of India prohibits export of grain from the region, thus limiting demand; the state marketing federations then enter the markets as the monopoly wholesale agents of the government. In 1972, India procured 7.7 million tons of foodgrains internally. Of that total roughly 5 million tons were procured in Punjab and Haryana.[23]

This arrangement is not simply fortuitous, however. The surplus exists because of previous investment in the region which has encouraged commercial agriculture and because of research investments that produced the new technology.[24] Furthermore, it is sustained politically because the state government, in effect, supports harvest prices with its procurement operations and prevents the normal seasonal decline.[25] The stocks thus procured by the state government then become resources in political bargaining with the national leadership. In short, India's food system reflects a continual balance of political administrative, and economic costs in selecting a strategy for securing adequate stocks.

In summary, India now has the capacity to secure and store large reserve stocks, it has the capacity to manage a national foodgrains budget and interstate allocation system (averaging 7.4 million tons between 1969–72), and above all is committed to this as a continuing public function. The cost is high and the system is not free from many difficult problems, but it represents a substantial increase in the institutional capacity of the government. The test of the system in the Bangladesh war proved its utility. Ten million refugees were fed with grain stocks approaching nine million tons with an efficiency that probably few developed nations could guarantee.[26]

The African case

No tropical African government has a capability comparable to India. Where they exist, state food marketing agencies appear to lack the purchasing networks, pricing policies, and other means with which to secure large quantities of foodstuffs

[23]Statistics on foodgrains production, procurement, pricing, and distribution can be found in *Food Statistics,* published annually by the Directorate of Economics and Statistics, Ministry of Agriculture, New Delhi.

[24]See N. Krishnaji, "Inter-regional Disparaties in Per Capita Production and Productivity of Food-grains," *Economic and Political Weekly* (Special Number, August 1975): 1377. See also John Mellor, *The New Economics of Growth* (Ithaca: Cornell University Press, 1976), Chapter 3; S. S. John & M. S. Mudahar, "The Dynamics of Institutional Change and Rural Development in Punjab, India" (Ithaca: Rural Development Committee, Center for International Studies, 1974).

[25]N. Krishnaji, "Wheat Price Movement," *Economic and Political Weekly* (June 1973): A–42.

[26]A review of the relief problems can be found in the following documents: *Relief Problems in East Pakistan and India* (in two parts), United States Senate, Committee on the Judiciary, Subcommittee to investigate problems connected with refugees and escapees (Washington: June 28, 1971, and October 4, 1971); Senator Edward Kennedy, *Crisis in South Asia,* United States Senate, Committee on the Judiciary, Subcommittee to investigate problems connected with refugees and escapees (Washington: November 1, 1971).

relative to consumption needs.[27] For example, Kenya's Maize and Produce Marketing Board was charged by statute to ensure adequate supplies of maize through stocking in good years, selling from reserves in lean years, and arranging for imports to cover domestic deficits. However, according to Leys, in both the 1965 and 1970–71 droughts the Board proved unequal to these responsibilities, being unable either to stock sufficiently before the droughts or to prevent illegal exports and a flourishing internal black market during the scarcities.[28]

Kenya has been unusual in tropical Africa for its large grain storage capacity—with its maize-stocking facilities equal to about a half year's demand.[29] In the other drought-prone states of the region, storage capacity has been very low relative to total consumption needs. Mali as of 1974 could store about 34,500 metric tons or roughly 4 percent of the expected consumption of the staples sorghum and millet for the 1974–75 crop year.[30] Chad's storage capacity in the same year was estimated at only 11,000 metric tons.[31]

The first and last steps in a food distribution system are the same—identifying the needy. The first step is to identify correctly the start of a crisis and to set in motion the public response mechanisms. The last step in the chain of events is to assure that the food reaches the needy and that the crisis does not destroy their earning capacity. This last point is often omitted in discussions of famine. If the diversion of funds is not to continue ad infinitum, it is essential that those affected by crop failure not be forced to sell their land, tools, or animals. Once this happens the region may take years to recover. The argument is essentially the same if the target group is not one hit by famine but one which has been historically destitute. The only way out of continued dependence on government is to increase their earning capacity.

Both the identification and management of crises depend to a large extent on the degree to which governments have *already* invested in development in the affected regions. Without communication facilities and officials penetrating into every village, hunger may well become widespread before anyone knows about it. This was the case in Bengal in 1943, where over a million starved, and in the Sahel and Ethiopia in 1973, where deaths in both areas may have numbered in the tens of thousands before their governments became aware of the mass scale of suffering.

One of the first clear indications of a drought crisis received by Ethiopia's central government was the appearance on the outskirts of the capital city itself of

---

[27]See the discussions of state agencies in Kenya and Sierra Leone in William O. Jones, *Marketing Staple Food Crops in Tropical Africa* (Ithaca, New York: Cornell University Press, 1972), Chapters 7, 8.
[28]Colin Leys, *Underdevelopment in Kenya* (London: Heinemann, 1975), pp. 106–7.
[29]Ibid., p. 108.
[30]See *War on Hunger* (A Report from the Agency for International Development), vol. 8 (August 1974): 27; and Food and Agriculture Organization, "Mission Multi-Donateurs Dans la Zone Zahelienne: Republique du Niger" (Rome: 1974): 2.
[31]Agency for International Development (US), "Development Assistance Program: FY 1975, Section Three: Chad, Cameroon, Central African Republic, and Gabon" (Washington: 1975), pp. 1–19.

about 1,500 destitute peasants.[32] They had left their farms about 200 miles to the north in quest of food. Similarly, Sahelian governments began to suspect a crisis when nomads, with their livestock lost, were reported flocking to administrative centers to obtain food and water.[33] In other words, the central governments began to appreciate the situation only *after* crops and animals had been destroyed and food reserved from previous years had been totally consumed. There was apparently little effective anticipation of the crisis, such as readying relief stocks so that livestock could have been saved and farmers permitted to remain in their villages. This lack of official anticipation seems condemnable since rains had been poor in the immediately preceding two or more years. The 1972 rainy season should have been watched with care.

The capacity to monitor, however, was limited by physical and political obstacles to communication between countryside and capital. Shepherd reports that in 1973 eight out of ten Ethiopians "lived a full's day walk from any road."[34] Their needs were represented to the center, if at all, through a feudal-type system of governance. In the Sahel the 1970–73 drought tended to be most severe in northern areas, closer to the desert, where communications were poor, but also where the inhabitants were mostly nomads who by tradition avoided contact with government. In addition, the Sahel's governments, like most of Africa, accorded a low priority to agriculture in their spending programs (see Table 6) and, hence, had few cadres in food-producing areas who could develop informed reports on the drought's impact on production.

Yet another factor in the Sahel was the absence of a recent-memory precedent of drought with sufficiently high political costs to make governments wary. Among such costs (which developed during 1973) were thousands of refugees crowding in and around cities and towns, severe losses of export revenues (because of reduced harvests of cash crops and livestock), and numerous starvation deaths blamed on the incumbent elites by their political rivals. The last major drought in the Sahel occurred in 1912–14.[35] In effect there was no "Bengal famine" (India, 1943) to sensitize central governments to the imperative of preparing for another mass-impact drought. Adequate preparations would have been costly. These costs include the development of data-gathering capacities sufficient to assess the food crop and livestock losses, the amounts of food reserves not yet consumed, and the deficits needed to be covered by imports. In the absence of these and other assessments, external relief sources could not determine how much help was needed. For exam-

---

[32]Jack Shepherd, *The Politics of Starvation* (New York: Carnegie Endowment for International Peace, 1975), p. 1.

[33]Victor D. DuBois, "The Drought in West Africa: Part I," *American University Field Staff Reports: West African Series,* vol. 15 (no. 1, 1974): 3.

[34]*The Politics of Starvation,* p. 4.

[35]Derek Winstanley, "Climatic Changes and the Future of the Sahel," in *The Politics of Natural Disaster: The Case of the Sahel Drought,* edited by Michael H. Glantz (New York: Praeger Publishers, 1976), p. 198. See also p. 164 of the same volume.

ple, on April 18, 1973, the French Foreign Ministry estimated that the drought-afflicted Sahelian states would require 530,000 tons of emergency food before the end of the crop year. The FAO thought otherwise, announcing on April 20th that the need would be 713,000 tons.[36]

Whatever the correct level, relief arrived too late in 1973 to prevent tens of thousands from dying.[37] It arrived late largely because the process of persuading donors to make commitments and to start shipping began too late. And the tragic delay in this process was due mostly to the Sahelian government's own failure to appreciate the seriousness of the drought. It did not declare a "state of emergency" and make urgent appeals for external aid until March 1973, about four to five months after it should have been clear that the 1972 harvests were extraordinarily poor and the pasture cover woefully inadequate.[38] A similarly tragic time gap occurred in Ethiopia: severe crop failures occurred in the fall of 1972 but no request by the Haile Selassie government for foreign relief assistance was made until April 1973.[39]

India's government, having experienced recurring crop failures and knowing their potentially high human and political costs, has invested in elaborate administrative mechanisms to alert it to famine threats and then to implement distributive programs. However, even when adequate staff is in place, the task of spotting the crisis is far from easy. As Morris indicates, distress signals are often difficult to read.[40] High prices may signal growing demand as much as food shortfalls. Migration may be merely the movement of surplus labor to jobs in other areas. Liquidation of assets (cattle, gold, stocks of produce) may be, in effect, a private insurance system at work. If officials are too callous, they flirt with death. If they are too generous, scarce resources and food stocks are depleted unnecessarily or prematurely, development plans are disrupted, and peasants may even be encouraged to take unnecessary risks at public expense, e.g., planting highly valuable but vulnerable crops.

Food administrators in India have concluded over the years that the task of identifying the needy in individual terms is almost impossible. And given the fact that it is also impossible to control the general price level, they seek an intermediate solution—fair price shops in selected areas. The fair price shop is an outlet for government food stocks at controlled prices (stocks being either imported or domestically procured). This technique targets specific regions of high demand and attempts to supply those regions with a basic minimum ration at controlled prices.

[36]"The Drought in West Africa: Part II" (no. 2, 1974): 6.

[37]A field survey by the US Public Health Service estimated for Mauritania, Mali, Niger and Senegal that "the maximum number of deaths due to famine this year (1973) is calculated at 101,000." Public Health Service, "Nutritional Surveillance in West Africa" (July–August 1973), reprinted in *Disaster in the Desert*, by Hal Sheets and Roger Morris (New York: The Carnegie Endowment for International Peace, 1974), pp. 131–36. Shepherd reports, "In Ethiopia alone, at least 100,000 people starved to death in 1973 alone...." *The Politics of Starvation*, p. xiii.

[38]"The Drought in Africa: Part II," pp. 2–4.

[39]*The Politics of Starvation*, p. 17.

[40]"Needed: A New Famine Policy," p. 283.

This does not, of course, provide jobs for the jobless or prevent the rich from bidding up the prices on the "free" market. Organized workers are easy to target with such a system because they can be identified at their work place. But the bulk of the population must be supplied in its neighborhood, irrespective of income. The number of fair price shops in India at the end of 1972 was 165,000. Although government officials admit they have no clear information on urban-rural distribution patterns or allocation of stocks among cities of different size,[41] they assume that the rural areas can feed themselves and, leaving aside periods of intense famine, have centered public distribution in the cities. It would also appear that the small and medium sized towns tend to be neglected. It is a widespread, though unproven, assumption that the effect of the system is to offset the effect of inflation on the big city work force and not to provide protection for the poor. We shall return to this point, but the system would appear to trade the Punjab farmer a stable price in return for a stable price to the urban worker, neglecting the rural poor and small towns. Overall, the system has little effect on the effective price structure (the one facing most people) and does little to help the destitute.[42] Thus, its determinants must be viewed as almost entirely political. This compromise between the larger wheat farmers, who market most of the grain, and the urban workers/middle class has one efficacious result—it provides stocks which can be distributed in case of famine. The system has offered no real solution, however, to the problems of the chronically poor.

In the Sahel and Ethiopia during 1972–74, governments were both late in identifying the crisis and in distributing relief supplies. They had no "system"— even one favoring the better off workers and farmers—which could be activated once the famine threat was identified. With very few "up-country" food reserves, they had to rely mostly on supplies shipped from abroad and on transportation means which were unsuitable for carrying large quantities of basic foodstuffs inland from ports. Severe bottlenecks developed at ports, along typically single-track railroads leading from ports, and at bridgeless rivers and other natural obstacles.

---

[41]*Report of the Study Team on Fair Price Shops* (New Delhi: Ministry of Food and Agriculture, Community Development, and Cooperation, 1966), especially p. 57.

[42]The effect of the distribution on prices in Punjab appears to be one of stimulating prices. See N. Krishnaji, "Wheat Price Movements," *Economic and Political Weekly,* Review of Agriculture, (June 1973): A–42.

On the whole, over the past two decades the index of food prices has risen faster than the wholesale price index and terms of trade have favored the farmer. See, V. S. Vyas & S. C. Bandyopadhyay, "National Food Policy in the Framework of a National Food Budget," *Economic and Political Weekly,* Review of Agriculture (March 1975): A–2. In fact, the distribution system appears to stimulate demand and as price is determined by demand more than supply—due to the fact that aggregate production is unresponsive to prices—the system may actually encourage price increases. See S. K. Chakrabarti, "Relative Prices of Cereals: 1952–70," *Economic and Political Weekly,* Review of Agriculture (June 1975): A–43; National Council of Applied Economic Research, *Structure and Behavior of Prices of Foodgrains* (New Delhi: NCAER, 1969), Chapter 7; R. Tamarajakshi, "Inter-Sectoral Terms of Trade and Marketed Surplus of Agricultural Produce 1951–2 to 1965–6," in *Comparative Experience of Agricultural Development in Developing Countries* (Bombay: Indian Society of Agricultural Economics, 1972): 141. On the issue of the destitute, see V. M. Dandekar & N. Rath, "Poverty in India," *Economic and Political Weekly* (January 2, 1971): 25, (January 9, 1971): 106.

Table 6 Percentage of government expenditures allocated to agriculture[a]

	1963	1964	1965	1966	1967	1968	1969	1970	1971	1972	1973	Average for all years
Kenya	n.a.	17.9[b]	18.1[b]	14.3[b]	12.4[b]	12.5[b]	12.8[b]	11.0	9.0	10.0	12.1	13.0
Malawi	n.a.	8.8	n.a.	10.4	n.a.	12.5	n.a.	n.a.	11.9	15.4	15.4	12.4
Tanzania	13.6[b]	11.8[b]	8.6[b]	8.3	n.a.	n.a.	n.a.	10.2	11.3	9.5	9.9[c]	10.4
Uganda	n.a.	8.1[b]	6.7[b]	8.5[b]	8.0[b]	8.2	6.6	9.5	8.7	n.a.	n.a.	9.1
Ivory Coast	n.a.	n.a.	n.a.	n.a.	n.a.	n.a.	n.a.	8.8[c]	6.3[c]	6.8	8.4[c]	7.6
Ghana	6.4	5.4	8.8	7.5	7.4	6.5	5.3	5.1	4.9	5.6	6.5	6.3
Rwanda	n.a.	n.a.	n.a.	4.6	5.9	5.1	4.9	5.1	4.6	n.a.	n.a.	5.0
Ethiopia	n.a.	n.a.	3.0	2.7	2.8	4.2	n.a.	3.6	5.0	8.7[c]	8.4[c]	4.8
Sierra Leone	n.a.	n.a.	n.a.	n.a.	n.a.	3.6[b]	3.1[b]	4.8[b]	4.9[b]	3.5[b]	7.8[b]	4.6
Liberia	n.a.	n.a.	n.a.	n.a.	n.a.	1.8	1.8	1.5	2.7	3.8	3.8	2.6

Note: [a] Actual recurrent and capital expenditures, unless otherwise indicated. [b] Fiscal year. [c] Estimated.

Sources: Kenya: Irving Kaplan, et al., *Area Handbook for Kenya* (Washington, D.C., 1967); Kenya, *Economic Survey, 1970* (Nairobi, 1970); United Nations. *Survey of Economic Conditions in Africa, 1973* (New York, 1974). Malawi: Harold D. Nelson, et al., *Area Handbook for Malawi* (Washington, D.C., 1975); *Survey of Economic Conditions in Africa, 1973*. Tanzania: Allison B. Herrick et al., *Area Handbook for Tanzania* (Washington, D.C., 1968); *Survey of Economic Conditions in Africa, 1973*. Uganda: Uganda, *Statistical Abstract* [5], 1967 (Entebbe, 1967); 1970 (Entebbe, 1970); and 1971 (Entebbe, 1971); Allison B. Herrick, et al., *Area Handbook of Uganda* (Washington, D.C., 1969).

Food spoiled. Other relief supplies were diverted to commercial markets for the profit of local officials.[43]

By late 1974, the high political stakes of mismanaging famine relief became clear. Three civilian governments of drought-stricken countries fell to military coups: those of Upper Volta (in February 1974), Niger (April), and Ethiopia (September). Urban workers protested soaring food prices, student groups blamed government for the suffering of drought victims, and rumours circulated that officials were profiting from sale of relief supplies.[44] Such signs of popular disaffection encouraged the military in their ambitions and gave them grievances with which to justify their takeovers before national and foreign audiences.

The politics of production

Besides developing the institutional capability to distribute large quantities of relief supplies with reasonable efficiency and equity, vulnerable LDCs should also follow India's example in trying to increase domestic food production.

In sub-Saharan Africa food farming has tended to be a seriously neglected sector. The region's governments have spent relatively little on agriculture (even though from 60 to over 90 percent of their people obtain their livelihoods from that sector). Among the 10 African countries surveyed, the highest average allocation was only 13 percent, found in Kenya, the most industrialized of the states. The lowest was 2.6 percent in Liberia, and the median 7.6 percent. (See Table 6.) In comparison, the state government of Punjab (India) devoted 11 percent to agriculture in 1974–75, without taking into account federal government expenditure in the state.[45] African governments' relative neglect of agriculture has meant little research on food crops, weakly staffed extension services for food farming, and inadequate investments in farm-to-market transportation so that many areas of potentially significant surpluses are cut off from town consumers and, hence, have no incentive to produce in surplus of family and local needs.[46]

What will induce less developed states to invest more heavily in food farming, as the Indian governments have begun to do? Among the persuasive local factors may be the 1973–75 famine experiences, the increasing foreign exchange drain from food imports, and soaring domestic food prices. Between 1970 and 1974, food prices rose by a reported total of 74 percent in Tanzania, 85 percent in Ghana, 102

[43]John D. Esseks, ''The Food Outlook for the Sahel: Regaining Self-Sufficiency or Continuing Dependence on International Aid?'' *Africa Today,* vol. 22 (April-June 1975): 46–7; and *The Politics of Starvation,* pp. 60–64.

[44]Jean Copans, ed., *Secheresses et Famines du Sahel* (Paris: Francois Maspero, 1975), pp. 133, 137–38, 140–42; Victor DuBois, ''The Drought in Niger, Part II: The Overthrow of President Hamani Diori,'' *American Universities Field Staff Reports: West African Series,* vol. 15 (no. 5, 1974): 6–7; and *The Politics of Starvation,* pp. 49–50.

[45]*Punjab Budget at a Glance: 1974–75* (Chandigarsh: Government of Punjab, 1974).

[46]See Uma Lele, *The Design of Rural Development* (Baltimore: The Johns Hopkins University Press, 1975), Chapters 3, 4, 6.

percent in Zaire, and 145 percent in Uganada.[47] To these factors might be added external forces in the international food system, including global regime norms. (See the essays by Seevers and Christensen.)

The Indian case

In the early sixties India embarked on what was a remarkable rural development strategy for an underdeveloped nation. Faced with rampant inflation and rapidly increasing demand for food, which threatened to disrupt the entire planning exercise, India opted for a "quick fix." On the advice of the Ford Foundation, the government of India decided to concentrate its investment in the most favored rural areas in order to maximize the marketed surplus.[48] Technical assistance, credit, roads, electricity, and irrigation development were poured into districts (particularly in Punjab and Haryana) with good water supplies and soil fertility, among other advantages. When the new plant varieties appeared, this same investment, particularly credit and irrigation, proved crucial to its adoption by farmers.

In the mid-sixties important new varieties of hybrid wheat and rice were developed. The attraction of these new hybrid seeds was the ability to produce a dwarf plant which was very responsive to high applications of fertilizer. Traditional varieties of grains typically converted the nutrients provided by heavy fertilizer applications into the overall growth of the plant rather than into the growth of the grain. Not uncommonly, the resulting increased growth of the traditional varieties caused the stalks to break, lodging the grain on the ground and resulting in heavy crop losses. In these circumstances, the biological capacity for intensifying grain production simply did not exist; and a technological barrier existed to increased food production. The new hybrids, being genetically dwarf, absorbed increased nutrients in the grain, thus removing the constraint and permitting efficacious use of heavy dosages of fertilizer.

The new varieties were "revolutionary" in two senses. Of course, the genetic breakthrough was a discovery of major importance. In terms of most farming techniques, however, the new varieties' requirements were not dramatically different from traditional varieties; only the results were. It was certainly not uncommon to double or treble yields by shifting from the old to the new varieties. This dramatic increase in farm yields and, therefore, in farm income was what made the new varieties truly "revolutionary." Several consequences followed from this production breakthrough. First, a "revolution" occurred in thinking about the problem of agriculture. Farmers who were presumed to be hopelessly backward and conservative by urban-dwelling government planners suddenly switched to these highly profitable seeds, which demonstrated the potential dynamism of peasants when offered a workable technology. This in turn provided an opportunity for new investment in the rural sector to provide public support for the "revolution."

[47]International Labour Organization, *Bulletin of Labour Statistics,* 2nd Quarter, 1976, Table 9.

[48]See N. K. Nicholson, *Rural Development Policy in India* (Dekalb: Center for Governmental Studies, Northern Illinois University, 1974).

Second, the new seeds worked effectively only when combined with plenty of fertilizer and plenty of water. In consequence, the capital outlay of farmers (for wells) and the production expenditures (for seed and fertilizer) increased rapidly and with them risk. This in turn put pressure on governments to assist the revolution through the provision of credit, stabilization of market prices, and investment in rural infrastructure. Third, the new varieties proved very prone to disease, compared with traditional varieties, and the rice, in particular, was very sensitive to variations in climate and growing conditions. This, in turn, necessitated a heavy public investment in agricultural research (and extension) to protect the "revolution" from genetic failures. Even at the time, some were cautious about the potential of this revolution. The success of the technology depended on large fertilizer imports. Many developing nations lacked governmental systems capable of maintaining the administrative and research support to sustain the highly vulnerable technology. Nevertheless, most observers assumed that the world's food problems had been solved. Today we are less optimistic.

In India, the application of Green Revolutionary technology to favored rural areas proved to be an unqualified success. However, it has meant that eight districts with 0.31 percent of India's cultivated area used 11.4 percent of the nation's fertilizer.[49] Extensive and effective use of fertilizer is the key to increasing rural incomes in the Third World.

It was generally recognized that this strategy was one beset with enormous risk because prospects for the future lay in a restricted geographical region and two crops.[50] Many argued that smaller investment spread over wider areas would produce greater aggregate yield responses. These arguments did not prevail, largely because of the uncertainty of farmers' responses in the more backward areas. In many ways the gamble paid off; Punjab and Haryana can now provide 65 percent of India's buffer stock. Although this has eased some of the government's problems, it has increased others. Nothing was done to reduce inter-regional income disparity; in fact the disparity grew. Nor was anything done to reduce the probability of crop disasters in less favored regions. Indian politics has been strongly affected by these choices.

Such a strategy, in retrospect, made sense only if the United States would insure the gamble with its own stocks. No society on the edge of subsistence would ever have taken such a gamble. In the past, farmers and governments alike have preferred to reduce the risks of famine rather than increase the returns of good years.

[49]See Gunvant Desai, *Growth of Fertilizer Use in Districts of India* (Ahmedabad: Indian Institute of Management, Center for Management in Agriculture, 1973) Chapter 2. See also Gunvant Desai et. al., *Dynamics of Growth in Fertilizer Use at Micro Level* (Ahmedabad: Center for Management in Agriculture, Indian Institute of Management, 1973); Brian Lockwood et. al., *The High Yielding Varieties Program in India,* Part I (New Delhi: Programme Evaluation Organization, Planning Commission, 1971); National Council of Applied Economic Research, *Fertilizer Use on Selected Crops in India* (New Delhi: 1974).

[50]Even at the time, according to the recollections of those involved in the decision, this was widely viewed as a considerable risk. In fact, most of the field trials of the new seeds were not encouraging and the best economic opinion was against building up a dependence on imported fertilizers.

Farmers plan their crop strategies for the worst years. Such a strategy is not applicable today because it is no longer accepted that the agricultural sector is stagnant, and there is an inclination to seek solutions in growth rather than in distributional arrangements. Nevertheless, a policy in which one section of the population secures all the gains of the Green Revolution and another section absorbs all the risks of the global food crises will not prove viable. Nor do enormous transfers of food from the rich to the vulnerable make sense. Rather, a strategy which attempts to increase and protect the productive capacity of each region and population group would appear to be the only viable one for a nation at the margin. It is not enough that governments give more attention to agriculture; they must be concerned with the pattern of that investment.

Greater investment in agriculture is hardly a difficult principle to sell if a nation is close enough to the margin of survival. Unfortunately, the distribution of the costs of such investment still remains to be decided. In most countries of the Third World, and especially in India, agricultural taxes are very low and very regressive. Yet rural incomes have been rising and at least some have derived enormous benefits from public investment. Faced with rising prices and high income taxes, urban interests are likely to take a critical view of rural public investment, focusing on the need first to correct these inequities.[51]

In India the emergence of the commercial farmer, encouraged by the policies of the sixties, has coincided with precipitous increase in government demands in the form of taxes, fees, price controls, etc.[52] This has led to the development, in the early seventies, of the embryos of farm lobbies in several states.[53] Such farm interests were strikingly absent in the decision-making processes of the sixties. It is not that caste and language have disappeared as rural issues. Rather, these appeals are no longer sufficient to win support without sensitivity to the interests and demands of the commercial farming population. In various areas, these farm interests receive further strength from local government systems, cooperatives, and even the new agricultural universities.

Large landed interests had always been a political force in the sub-continent,

[51] See *Report of the Committee on Taxation of Agricultural Wealth and Income* (New Delhi: Ministry of Finance 1972); E. T. Mathew, *Agricultural Taxation and Economic Development in India* (New Delhi: Asia, 1968); A. C. Angrish, *Direct Taxation of Agriculture in India* (Bombay: Somarija, 1972); V. P. Gandhi, *Tax Burden on Indian Agriculture* (Cambridge: Harvard Law School, 1966); S. L. Shetty, "An Inter-Sectoral Analysis of Taxable Capacity and Tax Burden," *Indian Journal of Agricultural Economics,* vol. 26 (July-September 1971).

[52] In 1974, for example, attempts were made by the Finance Ministry to pressure the state governments into adopting agricultural income taxes. In addition, although the central government may not constitutionally tax rural income, the income tax laws were amended to take rural income into account in calculating the *rate* of income tax. Electricity rates were revised upwards by many states during the year and the price of fertilizer was doubled.

[53] The two most obvious were the Kheti Bari Union in Punjab and the Kehdut Samaj in Gujerat. But interviews with Congress party MPs in New Delhi indicated that by 1974 rural MPs from the Northwest were becoming increasingly aware of their common economic interests and some identified the "farm lobby" in the Congress as one of the major components of the attempt to oust Indira Ghandi in 1975 (June).

but post-independence land reforms virtually eliminated this landlord class as a political force in many areas of India. Democratic elections then brought the middle farmers into increasing political prominence: first in the state legislatures, then in the state executives, and finally, by the late sixties, in New Delhi. While never very effective at the national level, the "farm bloc" formed one of the components of resistance to the "leftist" policies of Indira Gandhi in the early seventies. Farm power in the states proved a far more effective buffer to those policies, as programs of further land reform, rural tax reform, and small farmer development were ground to a halt. It was evident that the progressive farm community felt that these new impositions were threats to their newly acquired prosperity and opportunities for social mobility. In Punjab, farm organizations attempted, unsuccessfully, to disrupt government procurement operations. In Gujerat, farm disaffection contributed to the embarrassing defeat of the Congress Party in the 1975 elections—just before the declaration of emergency. In most states the major institutions serving the rural sector—land development banks, marketing federations, primary credit coopera- tives—have all come to be controlled by the farming castes and represent an im- portant base for rural political organization. The *organized* farmer is now a force to be reckoned with in India. This "organization" is not as yet as formalized and national in scope as, let us say, the American Farm Bureau Federation. Neverthe- less, a revolution has occurred in that at least some sections of India's farm commu- nity can and do now demand changes in policy and improvements in public services to serve their interests.

The case for agricultural development in LDCs

It might be expected that the food crisis of 1973–74 would encourage rural investment and perhaps in turn shatter the old alliance of urban and rural elites in many LDCs. The latter would be expected because a heavily regulated urban sector would not accept a virtually unregulated rural sector once economic growth spreads to the farms. In the rhetoric leading up to the Indian political crisis of 1975, for instance, it was evident that the "capitalist" farmer had replaced the "feudal" landlord as the target of the urban left.

Similar shifts in political symbols denote realignments following a change in the rural sector. In Kenya, when African "big farmers" replaced Europeans after the country's independence in 1963, criticism by urban socialists arose. As Table 6 indicated, Kenya's government has ranked among the highest in Africa in terms of the spending priority accorded to agriculture. However, the flow of services (exten- sion, production, and land-purchase credit) tended to favor large-scale farmers.[54] As of 1966 there were reportedly about 750 farms, averaging 800 acres, owned by African civil servants, politicians, and others.[55] While much of the favored position

[54]*The Design of Rural Development,* pp. 75, 81; and *Underdevelopment in Kenya,* p. 101.
[55]Henry Bienen, *Kenya: The Politics of Participation and Control* (Princeton, New Jersey: Princeton University Press, 1974), pp. 169–70.

of larger farms relative to government services may have been due to political connections, another factor was those farms' superior capacity to utilize credit and other inputs. A study in Kenya's Nyeri District found a correlation between farmers' progressiveness on this dimension and their receipt of government services.[56] Moreover, whatever greater rural inequality and critical rhetoric government policies did promote seem to have had only minor political impact thus far. Bienen notes that Kenya's foi..ier opposition party made little headway with this issue.[57] One reason appears to be that many large holdings are in fact owned jointly by groups of persons. Another is that owners tended to settle numerous relatives on their land.[58] Finally, pressure from landless peasants could be met through opening new opportunities (at least for the first decade of independence) by settling them on formerly foreign-owned farms.

No response by the Third World nations which ignores questions of equity will be meaningful, however, for it is the destitute who represent the reality of the world food crisis. Dandekar and Rath presented the dilemma clearly.[59] In 1960–61, they report, 40 percent of India's rural population and 50 percent of its urban population lived *below* a consumption level of one half a rupee a day. In the eight-year period (1960–61 to 1967–68) they examined, the net national product more than doubled. Yet consumer expenditure increased by only 4.8 percent. Were this to continue, they argue, "The gulf between the rich and the poor will widen intolerably and inevitably undermine the democratic foundations of the economy." This aspect of the global food crisis will test the will and ingenuity of planners, administrators and above all, of politicians. They must be able to design a development plan that will direct a greater proportion of the growth in national income to the poor and a choice of technology that will provide them with productive employment. John Lewis has called for a "relevant radicalism," radical in its departure from existing trickle-down growth strategies.[60] Too few planners have taken the advice.[61]

However, a development model is emerging among economists of how to handle the inequality concerns. It takes the form of increasing agricultural productivity sparked by public investment in technology and overhead. The consequent increase in farm income stimulates demand which is then met by expanding small-scale consumer goods industries in smaller towns, close to their market. This in turn, it is hoped, will absorb the excess labor supply—productively. Rising income will

[56]Cited by Charles Elliott, *Patterns of Poverty in the Third World* (New York: Praeger Publishers, 1975), p. 27.

[57]*Kenya: Politics of Participation*, pp. 181–82.

[58]*Underdevelopment in Kenya*, pp. 90–91.

[59]V. M. Dandekar & N. Rath, "Poverty in India," *Economic and Political Weekly* (January 2, 1971): 25; (January 9, 1971): 106. See also P. K. Bardhank, "On the Incidence of Poverty in Rural India of the Sixties."

[60]John Lewis, "Wanted in India: A Relevant Radicalism," *Economic and Political Weekly* (Special Number, July 1970): 1211.

[61]In 1974, these issues led to the resignation of B. S. Minhas, at that time the leading economist on the Indian Planning Commission. This signaled the impending economic collapse which led to the declaration of emergency in June 1975. His book, *Planning and the Poor* (New Delhi: S. Chand, 1974) takes on particular significance in the light of subsequent events.

hopefully slow population growth and also increase effective (market) demand for foodgrains. These, in turn must be supplied by an increasingly productive *domestic* agriculture. There are variations on this theme but the basic outline is recognizable.[62] The recent history of Punjab fits the new development model. Double cropping has increased demand for labor, thus expanding employment opportunities in the small towns.

In many areas, however, the model faces serious institutional obstacles. Where "feudal" landlords are still the rule, land reform and other redistributive measures may be needed. Most of the existing rural institutions may have to be reformed or bypassed because they have been largely captured by local elites who are not inclined to use them to foster greater production.

The widespread weakness of local participatory institutions requires some explanation. The situation is by no means a total disaster. In the Indian state of Gujerat, for example, cotton marketing cooperatives have proved highly effective and progressive. The credit cooperatives in Punjab appear to have been viable and also to have made credit available even to small farmers if they were able to grow the new high-yielding dwarf varieties. Nevertheless, it is true that rural institutions, even in the Indian sub-continent, have been a disappointment.

There are essentially three explanations for the political weakness of the countryside. First, in areas where the new technology is unsuited, agriculture is still stagnant. There has not been enough economic pressure to divert local institutions away from their traditional preoccupation with distributing patronage to undertaking effective developmental roles. Second, in areas with highly unequal land holding sizes, politics is dominated by patron-client relations. The small farmer is dependent on the larger farmer and cannot bring effective pressure to bear for more widespread dispersion of needed inputs such as credit and water and fertilizer. The benefits, if any, tend to be highly concentrated among the few politically powerful "bosses." Third, even in technically dynamic areas with fairly equitable land holding patterns, the local institutions can be rendered ineffective if poorly designed. This was certainly the case with local governments in both India and Pakistan, where indirect elections favored elite control in local bodies and confusion and overloading of functions inhibited accountability. The combined effect of these technological, social, and institutional problems has tended to hamstring even progressive national government efforts in the past.

Finally, state administrators are often as reluctant to accept innovations as rural elites. This need not be because they are somehow part of the "establishment" but because new departures threaten established bureaucratic power structures. Certainly, the Ford Foundation encountered this kind of resistance in trying to imple-

[62]The clearest recent presentation of this model can be found in, John Mellor, *The New Economics of Growth* (Ithaca: Cornell University Press, 1976). A two volume work by Sudhir Sen, *Reaping the Green Revolution* (New Delhi: Tata-McGraw Hill, 1975), *A Richer Harvest* (New Delhi: Tata-McGraw Hill, 1974), is a comprehensive statement of the problems and solutions. An excellent statistical statement on the Indian case can be found in, "A Report to the Nation on the Downtrodden," *Monthly Commentary on Indian Economic Conditions,* Indian Institute of Public Opinion, Annual Number, vol. 5, no. 5, (1973).

ment a program that would have directly benefited rural elites.[63] This suggests that national governments may have to risk classic "redistributive" radicalism in certain regions if the way is to be opened for new investment and new technology. This being the case, class issues are likely to dominate the politics at the margin. A way out of this conflict and the worst effect of food crises can be found with a combination of political skill and an adequate development model, but success is far from guaranteed. Let us look at three sets of basic decisions which must be made and the factors which inhibit adequate responses.

(1) The greatest problem of a food crisis is that it tends to encourage a concentration on the short-term responses to the detriment of *long-term structural changes*. This is especially true where the crisis is viewed as a temporary aberration. A recognition of the permanence of the food crisis and the corollary need for major structural changes is a first requisite of adjustment to the crisis. It is probably true that nothing short of pressure from urban consumers will produce the incentives for policy changes. On the other hand, extractive politics to benefit the urban populace may well substitute for investment and rural structural change if the urban elites are too powerful.[64] Conversely, if rural elites prevail, solutions will be sought in higher agricultural prices, mechanization, and expanding farm size. These changes will increase the marketed surplus, increase farm incomes, but cause hardship for a growing portion of the rural community. Neither of these solutions resembles the labor-intensive consumer goods strategy outlined in the new model. The problem is that in most developing countries it is difficult to imagine the appearance of a coalition of political forces that might produce such a policy.

A labor-intensive strategy of development encouragement requires several policy innovations. First, it requires the existence of the small farm, which tends to be more productive per acre than the large farm and also uses labor more intensively. Mere food shortage is not likely to persuade a government to risk a radical land reform by direct redistribution, however, in light of the present economic and political power of landed interests in most LDCs. This means that the single structural change which could absorb the most rural labor is usually precluded. There are undoubtedly alternative ways of influencing farm size, for example, tax and inheritance policy. However, lack of administrative capacity to administer them and lack of any clear theory on how to go about reform tend to eliminate this option even if the political will exists. The other major source of employment opportunities appears to be small consumer goods industries. This solution is inhibited by a lack of

[63]See N. K. Nicholson, "Rural Development Policy in India: Elite Differentiation and the Decision-Making Process," (Dekalb: Center for Governmental Studies, Northern Illinois University, 1974) pp. 39–43.

[64]A good discussion of the "urban" focus of early agricultural planning in India can be found in C. H. Hanumantha Rao, "Agricultural Policy Under Three Plans," in N. Srinirasan, ed., *Agricultural Administration in India* (New Delhi: Indian Institute of Public Administration, 1969), pp. 116–19. See also M. Lipton, "India's Agricultural Performance: Achievements, Distortions, and Ideologies," in *Agricultural Development in Developing Countries—Comparative Experience* (Bombay: Indian Society of Agricultural Economics, 1972), Chapter 4.

appropriate technology, ideological mistrust of "capitalist solutions" in some countries, urban elites' preoccupation with imported luxury goods, and the lack of a dynamic rural sector to provide a market for these goods. In addition to these problems, the small manufacturers' sector faces strong if not overwhelming competition when seeking government assistance—from heavy industry (supported by international investment), primary commodities development (sustaining food and luxury goods investment), and the growing vested interests of a farmer-dominated cooperative sector. Clearly, there are many more effective claims on public resources than the needs of small industry and market towns. Only public works, supported by landed interests and contractors, is available as a politically popular labor-absorbing program.

The entire farm community will be able to resist urban exploitation on the one hand and increasing concentrations of rural economic power on the other (both inimical to long-term solutions), only if reasonably broad-based rural political participation is encouraged. This may be accomplished by substantial decentralization to local governments, a mass-based party structure, or through lobby activities by broad-based farm organizations.[65] One way or another, however, it must be done. Unfortunately, such structures are often a threat to national or regional leaders, local elites, and to bureaucratic power—a formidable list of adversaries. In India, the power of the local government (panchayats) and the autonomy of the cooperatives which peaked in the mid-1960s has been steadily eroded in most states. In 1974, for example, in Gujerat state in India, no elected governments at any level continued to function. All governmental functions were being performed by administrators. In the same year in Punjab state, both the Apex Cooperative Bank and the Apex Cooperative Marketing Society had delayed over two years in electing their governing boards due to a combination of fiscal and political difficulties. Pakistan is still without functioning rural local governments although the Bhutto regime had been considering the matter for four years. Yet broad-based rural political participation appears to be essential to a proper balance of rural development policies and socially optimal results.

However necessary for effective development over the long run, such participation may appear in the short term to be politically too risky. Tanzania, with its program for socialist rural development, *ujamaa,* is a good example of this paradox. Tanzanian rhetoric calls for broad popular involvement in government.[66] A 1972 reform significantly increased the powers of local government at the expense of central ministries. However, one field study suggests that the farmers themselves

---

[65]See N. Luyks, "Rural Governing Institutions," in M. Blase, ed., *Institutions in Agricultural Development* (Ames: Iowa State University, 1971), Chapter 10; N. T. Uphoff & M. J. Esman, *Local Organization for Rural Development: Analysis of Asian Experience* (Ithaca: Rural Development Committee, Center for International Studies, 1974); D. E. Ashford, *National Development and Local Reform* (Princeton: Princeton University Press, 1967).

[66]See, for example, statements by Julius Nyerere, President of Tanzania, reprinted in *Freedom and Socialism: A Selection from Writings and Speeches 1965-67* (London: Oxford University Press, 1968), pp. 324-25, 353-55.

have had very little influence on policy choices.[67] Another source concurs: "(T)he practical effect of the decentralization policies pursued since 1967 has been to concentrate decision-making power in the hands of administrators, technicians, and political commissioners at Regional and District levels."[68] The problem may derive from the radical nature of the ruling party's rural development strategy, the opposition it has encountered, and the government's unwillingness to give its many farmer opponents formal means to influence policy. The strategy has been to communalize agriculture, and it has been strongly opposed by commercial farmers who feel threatened with loss of income and by poorer peasants who object to being resettled into new communal villages.[69] As long as much of the clientele is hostile to its policy purposes, Tanzania's government, and others like it, pursuing transformationist strategies, may repress grassroots participation. The hostility need not be long-lasting, however, particularly if after trial and error the strategy proves economically successful.[70]

The other factor which appears to be essential to restructuring the rural sector is public investment in agricultural research. It is widely recognized now that a steady program of agricultural technology is essential to rural modernization and to reducing production costs while increasing yields.[71] For many small nations the cost of building educational institutions and research centers will be high, and there may be advantages to internationalization. But one way or another relevant research must be encouraged. Politically, this is probably easier than institutional reform as much of this effort is within the control of the national elites. One can be reasonably optimistic about the future in this area, provided research priorities relate to small rather than large capital intensive farming.

(2) The second set of strategic decisions for developing nations as they consider restructuring the rural sector to handle the emerging food crisis is in defining the *proper relationship between the public and private sector*. This involves decisions about the control of land, the manufacture and distribution of inputs, and the

---

[67]"As the review of *ujamaa* carried out under ARDS [African Rural Development Study] noted, "there are only limited formal procedures for local people to influence TANU [Tanganyikan African National Union, the ruling party] officials, leaving little more than good will to assure these officials will, in fact, protect peasant interests." *Design of Rural Development,* p. 153.

[68]Paul Collins, "Decentralization & Local Administration for Development in Tanzania," *Africa Today,* vol. 21 (Summer 1974): 25. In the same article Collins suggests that an exception to the concentration trend may be the interaction between local farmers and regional officials by means of *Ujamaa* Planning Teams which take officials to villages to assist in drawing up feasible and realistic development plans for the villages. Ibid., pp. 23, 25.

[69]See the discussion of farmer opposition to Tanzania's communalization of farming in *Design of Rural Development,* pp. 155–57.

[70]Chinese experience in this regard is instructive. See B. Stavis, "People's Communes and Rural Development in China" (Ithaca: Rural Development Committee, Center for International Studies, Cornell University, 1974); J. D. Pelzel, "The Economic Management of a Production Brigade in Post-Leap China," in W. E. Willmott, ed., *Economic Organization in Chinese Society* (Stanford: Stanford University Press, 1972), pp. 387–416.

[71]See R. E. Evanson & Y. Kislev, *Agricultural Research and Productivity* (New Haven: Yale University Press, 1975); Y. Hayami & V. W. Ruttan, *Agricultural Development: An International Perspective* (Baltimore: Johns Hopkins, 1971).

control of the grain trade. A related set of decisions concern the development of regulatory policies—crops, prices, input packaging, and marketing. The former set of decisions, regarding nationalization, are typically made on ideological grounds and not on the basis of any particular theory of rural development. The latter decisions, regarding regulatory activity, are usually dictated by the extent to which policy is dominated by governmental purposes. In neither case does the preference, convenience, or efficiency of the farm community appear to be the primary consideration in the decision.

In Indian Punjab, for example, a "crop loan system" specifies the "package" of inputs to be used on a particular crop. Both the loan and the inputs are supplied through the state cooperative system.[72] Yet analysis of the production functions of farmers can find no appreciable difference in the efficiency with which fertilizer is used among farmers relying on the co-ops and those relying on the private sector. Some studies, in fact, suggest that those following the official advice operate less efficiently.[73] In Pakistan Punjab, farmers preferred the larger and more expensive diesel pumps for their tubewells in the mid-sixties, because government regulation of electricity made the more efficient electric pumps too difficult to install.[74] For years in India, until 1965, in fact, foodgrains procurement prices were set without the slightest attempt to calculate the actual cost of production.[75] Extension services more often act as the conduits of official policy than as service agents for the farmer; this has been true in India, Pakistan, Tanzania, and many other LDCs. In spite of these examples, decisions to increase public input or control have not been either entirely pointless or detrimental to farm interests. It simply should be noted that farm preferences typically took a back seat to government needs in these programs.

The basic problem here is twofold. First, policy makers have often failed to treat the farmer seriously as a rational, profit-oriented producer for whom considera-

[72]*Report of the Fertilizer Credit Committee of the Fertilizer Association of India* (New Delhi: Fertilizer Association of India, 1968) pp. 92–96.

[73]P. L. Sankhayan, D. S. Sidhu, and P. S. Rangi, "Efficiency and Impact of Various Fertilizer Supply Systems on Production in Punjab," *Indian Journal of Agricultural Economics* 28 (October/December 1972): 77–84; R. I. Singh, Ram Kumar, & Sri Ram, "Impact of Input Supply Systems on Crop Production in District Moradabad," ibid., pp. 130–36; J. G. Ryan & K. B. Subramanyam, "Package of Practices Approach in Adaptation of HYV," *Economic and Political Weekly*, Review of Agriculture, (December 1975): pp. A 101–10.

[74]L. Nulty, *The Green Revolution in West Pakistan* (New York: Praeger, 1972).

[75]This neglect was corrected in the mid-sixties with the establishment of the Agricultural Prices Commission in the Ministry of Agriculture, which prepares cost of production and price recommendations seasonally for the Ministry. The Commission's cost of production calculations are generally disputed by farm organizations which feel they are too low. The Commission also appears to be of the opinion that within broad ranges, prices do not influence the allocation of acreage, input use, etc. For discussions of various aspects of this problem, see Raj Krishna, "Agricultural Price Policy and Economic Development," in H. M. Southworth & B. J. Johnston, *Agricultural Development and Economic Growth* (Ithaca: Cornell University Press, 1970), Chapter 13. Uma Lele is highly critical of government pricing policies in *Foodgrain Marketing in India* (Ithaca: Cornell University Press, 1971), pp. 220–23. That this is a widespread problem is argued by T. W. Schultz in "US Malinvestments in Food for the World," reprinted in *Agricultural Development in Developing Countries* (Bombay: Indian Society of Agricultural Economics, 1972), Chapter 21.

tions of efficiency are of some significance. This is reflected in the lack of concern for adequate profit incentives. When a government must control and regulate, it usually has been bureaucratic convenience and efficiency which dictated the choice of institutional arrangements and the form of the regulations, not the farmer's. Finally, when restrictions are imposed, too little attention has been paid to finding a mode of enforcement which might contribute mutually to the interests of both government and farmer. There are examples of useful arrangements, but they are all too rare. Punjab's MARKFED (state cooperative marketing federation) exchanges support for harvest season prices for an effective governmental monopoly of wholesale marketing. The Gujerat government trades strict crop and movement controls over the cotton crop for equally strict publicly regulated quality control which improves farm prices.[76]

Far more common are the institutional failures. To assure maximum production rather than maximum profits, extension services have frequently been used to encourage farmers to employ more chemical fertilizer than the farmers found profitable. There are even reports of extension officers being ordered to require farmers to take complex fertilizers they neither wanted nor needed in order to remove stocks that had been over-produced by the factories. This type of unprofessional advice to the farmer clearly weakens the effectiveness of the extension service. Cooperative societies have often been treated as administrative agencies of the government. They are asked to procure foodgrains for government stocks at very low profit margins. They are employed to enforce the use of certain technology packages favored by the government. In fact, governments often have preferred heavily bureaucratized systems of market management rather than reliance on simple market regulating mechanisms because direct physical control over the crop was more amenable to traditional bureaucratic procedures than free market manipulations. The inability of developing nations to implement policies in the rural areas and the high administrative costs which are frequently incurred are all too often due to a failure to reconcile the valid interests of the farmer with the public interests of the government in new and more efficient and reciprocal institutional arrangements.

Finally, politicians desiring control and administrators desiring effective "integration" of policy are far too likely to encourage the concentration of governmental power in the rural areas. It is only slowly that India has learned the cost of this policy.[77] Slowly, however, it has become evident that services must be institu-

---

[76]See N. K. Nicholson, "Local Institutions and Fertilizer Policy: The Lessons from India's Punjab and Gujerat States" (Paper presented to East-West Center Food Institute Conference, INPUTS June 7–17, 1976, Honolulu, Hawaii). Also, "Differential Responses to Technical Change in Gujerat and Punjab: An Analysis of Economic Political Differentiation in India" (Paper presented to American Political Science Association, Annual Convention, San Francisco, September 16, 1975).

[77]A good example is the Small Farmer Program, evolved in the late sixties. It was designed to direct federal resources into programs to help the smaller farmer. Discussions of the problems and programs can be found in V. R. Gaikwad, *Small Farmers: State Policy and Program Implementation* (Hyderabad: National Institute of Community Development, 1971); *Rural Development for Weaker Sections*, Report of a Seminar Sponsored by the Indian Society of Agricultural Economics and the Indian Institute of Management (Bombay: I.S.A.E., 1974).

tionally differentiated if specific rural groups are to be targeted. In addition, it has become evident that differentiation of functions and multiple channels of access to key inputs and services may reduce access costs to the farmer and provide greater flexibility to him in adjusting his combination of inputs.[78] For example, given the additional administrative and political complications of using cooperative credit, it may not be attractive to all farmers. On the other hand, the existence of extensive cooperative credit undoubtedly has its impact on the private moneylenders' rates of interest, level of services, etc. Farmers can be expected to take advantage of the indirect effect of programs in decisions about borrowing as well.

As poor countries have been and are compelled by food shortages to take agriculture more seriously, they are forced (many for the first time) to think much more seriously about the impact of their administrative procedures, institutional patterns, and regulatory policies on the rural sector. Most lack information, experience, and training in evaluating these impacts and taking the appropriate adjustment effects. Hence, program ''errors,'' even if high, should not be an excuse for no effort at all.

(3) *International relations* constitute the third set of decisions. External relations will continue to play a vital role in the strategies employed by Third World nations in their attempts to handle the food crisis. Small nations and those vulnerable to recurrent drought will remain dependent on international reserve stocks. The major grain exporting nations can help to provide the security which will enable these states to risk the radical departures in policy and the high investment rates that will be needed to transform their agricultural sectors. Imported chemical fertilizer will also continue to be a vital component of any development strategies. Fortunately, it now appears that the fertilizer shortages of the 1973–75 period have been rectified and new production capacity will ensure ample supplies at least for the next decade.[79] Nevertheless, fertilizer imports will continue to absorb vital foreign exchange, even if new production reduces the need for costly food imports.

The continuation of a food import strategy in the face of rising international grain prices is, of course, a very restricted solution, generally available only to countries with a strong and reliable export capacity. Furthermore, whether the grain is supplied on commercial terms or as relief supplies under bilateral or international agreements, grave political risks are involved in such dependence. Pakistan and India both felt the pressure from the United States when aid was manipulated to bring a stop to the 1965 war. With the United States supplying most of its fertilizer, Pakistan must be well aware of the intimate connection between the success of its agricultural programs and American views on its nuclear program. The use of food as a diplomatic bargaining tool by the US or other major suppliers may seem

[78]N. T. Uphoff & M. J. Esman, *Local Organization for Rural Development: Analysis of Asian Experience* (Ithaca: Rural Development Committee, Center for International Studies, Cornell University, 1974), pp. 63–75.

[79]P. J. Stangel & J. H. Allgood, ''World Fertilizer Situation 1976-80'' (Paper presented to Food Institute Conference, East-West Center, Honolulu, Hawaii, June 7–17, 1976).

ineffective when applied to the Soviet Union; but in the Third World, food dependence can make countries very vulnerable. This last statement should be treated
with caution, however. We have stressed throughout that food strategies are the
result of a complex set of demands and that there are alternatives available to
developing nations. The costs of dependence are not necessarily determining—they
must be weighed against alternatives. Similarly, in encouraging or discouraging
import dependence, donors such as the United States should keep in mind their
complex goals as well. When used carefully and targeted accurately, food imports
can still be used to encourage job creation and to control inflation in the Third
World.[80]

Developed states can do much to encourage greater production in the Third
World; a most important contribution would be the use of the vast technical capacity
of the US to help solve the complex remaining technological problems of tropical
agriculture.[81] We should recognize, however, that successful agricultural development will alter diets in the direction of more nourishing but less efficient uses of
grain, such as meat, processed foods and milk.[82] The effect of this on poor people
who cannot afford these foods may be deleterious, as Christensen argues in this
volume. This suggests that poverty and inequality will continue to be at the forefront
of international politics in the Third World for some time, regardless of any likely
level of "success" in rural development.

Domestic political constraints and international dependency

We can now summarize briefly some of the domestic political factors which
inhibit or influence solutions to the food crises in various Third World countries and
the potential or real role of international forces upon them. Like any other set of
policies, those aimed at coping with food problems involve gains for some and
losses for others. In consequence, existing political cleavages will often be increased and new ones may appear. Characteristically, seven forms of political
problems appear to surround food issues as increasing population puts pressure on
existing supplies and poverty exacerbates hunger in LDCs.

First, and perhaps most severe in the initial stages, are interregional conflicts
within LDCs. Except in small countries food crises are seldom uniformly distributed
geographically. Typically, rural growth increases intra-country differences.[83]
Planned investment tends to take place in those areas which promise the most
return. Typically the problems of the better endowed regions present problems that

---

[80]See U. K. Srivastava et al., *Food Aid and International Economic Growth* (Ames: Iowa State
University, 1975).

[81]See, for example, W. D. Hopper, "The Development of Agriculture in Developing Countries,"
Scientific American, no. 235 (September 1976): 196–205.

[82]See J. Janick, C. H. Noller, & C. L. Rhykerd, "The Cycles of Plant and Animal Nutrition,"
Scientific American, no. 235 (September 1976): 74–87; Roger Revelle, "Food and Population," *Scientific American*, no. 231 (September 1974): 160–70.

[83]See N. Krishnaji, "Inter-Regional Disparities in Per Capita Production and Productivity of Food-
grains," *Economic and Political Weekly* (Special Number, August 1975): 1377; P. K. Bardhan, "On the
Incidence of Poverty in Rural India of the Sixties," *Economic and Political Weekly* (Annual Number,
February 1973): 245–68.

are both technically and administratively easier to resolve by hard-pressed governments. In consequence, both efficiency and the national interest seem to conspire to increase inequality. There is certainly some evidence of this in India where the Ford Foundation encouraged intensive investment in the best areas for a "quick fix" for the food shortage.

Where geographical cleavages also correspond with ethnic and cultural differences, the redistribution of the gains of growth is even more difficult. The Sahel offers a good example where governmental neglect was largely responsible for the severity of the food crisis there. The ethnic divisions between pastoralists and the farming-town populations on which the region's governments were based contributed to the inadequacy of governmental responses. Even otherwise effective development programs, as in India, have shut ethnic minorities out of the benefits. In India, as elsewhere, minority tribal groups have not fared well at the hands of the dominant group(s).

Nor are different regions likely to have equal access to decision makers. India provides a good example. In Punjab, which is the heartland of the Green Revolution, the success of a farmer depends on his tubewell, a necessity that can easily be secured locally through influence with the local credit cooperative. Electricity, to run the pump, can be assured politically by Punjab's contribution to the central foodgrains pool. In Gujerat state, in contrast, there is little ground water; and it would require a Planning Commission level decision to construct a new dam to provide the needed water. With cotton as the major crop in the region and cotton exports failing, Gujerat has far less influence in New Delhi. Not surprisingly a dam has not been built.

Investments based on the comparative advantage or superior resource base of a given region, therefore, are reasonable policy decisions where ethnic homogeneity or a responsive political structure can provide alternatives or transfer payments to the marginal areas. Where such political mechanisms fail, however, growing tension, conflict, and even separatism may result. In this situation, the current attention of the international aid agencies to the poor developing world may be more important in the political economy of the world than realized. By providing additional resources, new technologies, and foreign pressure, foreign aid can assist the needed transfer payments within LDCs.

The second issue involves the character of rural politics. In most Third World countries rural politics has become the politics of faction and patronage since independence. Rural politics depends, then, on the distribution of favors to clients. Political struggles are for a piece of a very small pie and short of the negative power of rural elites to prevent reform, rural influence is frequently dissipated in factional struggles.[84] This may provide the explanation of why nations with such a large rural population can spend so little on the development of that sector. Coalitions of rural

[84]There have been only a few attempts to relate the character of local politics to policy, and they are as yet somewhat primitive. See S. Hadden, *Decentralization and Rural Electrification in Rajasthan, India* (Ithaca: Rural Development Committee, Center for International Studies, Cornell University, 1974); R. N. Blue & Y. Junghare, "Political and Social Factors Associated with the Public Allocation of Agricultural Inputs in a Green Revolution Area" (Minneapolis: University of Minnesota, Department of Political Science, 1973, mimeo); B. W. Coyer, "The Distribution of Rural Public Policy Goods in Rajasthan"

factions may break down as poverty increases and we may well see the emergence
of class politics in the villages. For the present, however, the inability of the
farmers, save in the most progressive areas, to articulate their economic interest
against rural elites and the urban sector is a fact of life in most Third World nations.

The prevalence of factionalism combined with patronage politics is an under-
standable solution to the political problems of a rapidly changing rural environment.
Within the village traditional loyalties are typically shattered by externally induced
stresses and strains. As the scale of political organization and the degree of political
participation both increase, some basis must be found for alliances among disparate
groups with little experience of working in common. The result is loose alliances
among diverse segments which trade their support for direct and immediate favors.
We have, in effect, a barter political economy. This system is highly efficient in its
use of scarce political resources. Divided as it is into factional segments, there is
often no majority coalition or stable opposition, merely a dominant faction facing a
fragmented opposition. Only those in the dominant faction need to be "paid off"
and there is little need to provide "class benefits" or public goods to a farm
constituency—only favors to supporters. Such a system works quite well, even with
a bare minimum of divisible patronage, as exemplified by Kenyan politics. It is
difficult for such a system to have any progressive impact on public policy. It
develops no real pressure for structural change, no real support for the concentration
of resources and large-scale, long-term investment. Local elites, well off and benefiting from control of the patronage, have little incentive to challenge the system.
They leave policy to the urban elites. Both increasing poverty and rural progress,
however, threaten this political order. No matter in which direction many developing nations move, major adjustments in rural politics are in the offing.

The emergence of class conflict is a third component of the emerging poverty
of the Third World. In the past, rural social units—villages, tribes, and estates—
stood against the hostile outside world. Throughout the Third World a growing
market orientation combined with increasing population pressure have destroyed
that solidarity. One need not assume that that traditional solidarity was necessarily
benign, but it was real. In areas experiencing growth, however, customary ties
collapse; and rural tension is common. For the first time in many countries, therefore, opportunities have appeared for political leaders to win support from the rural
poor who can no longer be controlled by their patrons.[85]

A growing class consciousness among the farm population will, of course,
have a mixed effect. On the one hand, it may encourage governments to pay

---

(Paper presented to Fourth Annual University of Wisconsin Conference on South Asia, November 7–8,
1975); N. K. Nicholson, "Factionalism and Public Policy in India," forthcoming in F. Belloni, ed.,
Party and Faction (CLIO Press).

[85]Francine Frankel, "The Politics of the Green Revolution: Shifting Patterns of Peasant Participation in
India and Pakistan," in T. J. Poleman & D. K. Freebain, eds., *Food, Population and Employment*
(Ithaca: Cornell University Program on Science, Technology, and Society, Praeger Publishers, 1973),
pp. 120–51; Jan Breman, *Patronage and Exploitation* (Berkeley: University of California Press, 1974).

increasing attention to the agricultural sector, which in the long run is probably beneficial. On the other hand, the growing threat of a restive rural poor does not generally incline landowners toward "socially progressive" policies. Curiously enough, redistributive solutions to rising rural poverty make the most sense in those countries which face the least serious resource constraints. In areas such as India and Bangladesh there are undoubtedly areas which might benefit from land redistribution, for example, but in areas like Punjab one could not redistribute further without endangering production. In the final analysis there is simply not enough land to go around. In this context, to paraphrase John Lewis, a good deal of Indian radicalism is irrelevant. In many areas of Latin America and Africa with a dual economy of distinct peasant and modern sectors, however, major redistributive solutions are plausible. In such areas a strong leftist party with a base in the rural poor might be efficacious in forcing incremental reforms. Thus, the growing class conflict in rural areas will undoubtedly mean increased political participation but its significance will depend on the overall resource situation and how that participation is structured. Thus, strong local governments will encourage agriculture but strengthen land-owners against the agricultural laborers. Migration will relieve pressure for land reform but the associated urbanization will increase pressure for lower food prices and greater government control over markets. Unduly rapid commercialization of agriculture without a strong demand for labor and without the political capacity for transfer payments probably encourages extremist movements. Thus, the "new development model" can trigger instability if rural job creation is not achieved.

The fourth element of the emerging political crisis is the role of technology. In the early part of this century in India, manufactured consumer goods destroyed a whole class of village artisans.[86] Today in some areas resumption of cultivation and mechanization may be destroying a class of tenant farmers. Pakistan is a good example,[87] as is Ethiopia. Cohen observed in Ethiopia that a rural development program targeted at small farmers had the unintended consequence of *dispossessing* many of them. Through a demonstration effect, large landowners outside the project area adopted the improved seeds and use of fertilizers which proved successful in the project. And finding that those inputs made mechanization financially feasible and that with machinery they could dispense with tenant farmers, owners drove "thousands of tenants" off the land.[88] The tenants who remained found their rent

[86]M. L. Dantwala, *Poverty in India Then and Now 1870–1970* (Delhi: MacMillan, 1973).

[87]For India, see W. Ladejinsky, *A Study on Tenurial Conditions in Package Districts* (New Delhi: Planning Commission, 1965); Francine Frankel, "The Politics of the Green Revolution . . ."; Edgar Owens and Shaw, *Development Reconsidered,* pp. 86–91; W. Ladejinsky, "Agrarian Reform in Asia: The Green Revolution and its Reform Effects," in R. T. Shand, ed., *Technical Change in Asian Agriculture* (Canberra: Australian National University, 1973) Chapter 12; John Mellor, *The New Economics of Growth,* Chapter 4; L. Nulty, *The Green Revolution In Pakistan,* pp. 25–40; Hiromitsu Kanepa, "Mechanization, Industrialization and Technological Change in Rural Pakistan," in R. T. Shand, *Technical Change in Asian Agriculture,* Chapter 9.

[88]John M. Cohen, "Effects of Green Revolution Strategies on Tenants and Small-Scale Landowners in the Chilalo Region of Ethiopia," *Journal of Developing Areas,* vol. 9 (April 1975): 340–41, 350–51.

rising and sale prices of land climbing out of reach, despite their own higher incomes from Green Revolution inputs. Another unfortunate side effect may be dramatically increasing numbers of very small farms, as an expanding population, a land constraint, and a more productive technology combine to constrict the assets available to the poorest.[89] No one would argue that technology "caused" these problems. Rather, there is now good evidence that technological innovation tends to economize on scarce factors in the production process. Sometimes this is labor, as in the United States, or land, as in Japan. Further, these are not simply economic changes, but, as Polanyi argues, these technical changes almost always help to speed up changes in social relationships with associated changes in power relationships.[90]

The Green Revolution technology has been accused of producing potentially dangerous social side effects in the most affected areas. This argument contends that, due to the intensification of production, landlords have been encouraged to resume cultivation of their own land and eject their previous tenants. Furthermore, it is argued, this terminates any social obligations the rural rich may have had to care for the rural poor by turning "tenants" into "wage laborers." The result, it was predicted in the late sixties, would be rapidly growing immiserization and rural insecurity. Events have raised some question about this prediction and necessitated some reservations. First, there appear to be no particular economies of scale in the new technology. Whether, in fact, operational holdings expand in size, increasing the number and vulnerability of those without land or even tenant's rights depends on a number of factors. Among them are the initial degree of inequality of holding sizes, extent of supporting services to small operators available from the government, the availability of a stable water supply, and the flexibility of existing tenancy arrangements. Second, in most areas the new technology has been labor-deepening and has forced up agricultural wages. Whether this is an advantage to the poor or not depends on other factors. A tradition of payment of wages in kind rather than cash will permit workers to share in the increased productivity and rising prices. If off-farm employment is available, workers may in fact combine the high peak season's wages which the new prosperity premits farmers to pay with additional earnings in the slack season. Rising prosperity in the farm sector may in fact encourage the development of localized business investment that will provide those jobs. Ultimately, the logic of the argument was based on the increasing gap between the landowners and the rest of the rural population, a gap widened by the increased productivity of land. One's reaction to this argument depends on how one evaluates the political impact of the increasing gap compared with the significance of a rapidly

[89]In Punjab, for example, farms of under two hectares constituted 17 percent of all holdings. In 1971, they increased in number until they constituted 57 percent of all holdings. N. K. Nicholson, "Local Institution and Fertilizer Policy . . .," p. 23.

[90]Hayami and Ruttan, Chapter 3. See also K. Polanyi, *The Great Transformation* (Boston: Beacon Press, 1960).

growing real income. The Green Revolution has undoubtedly raised tension and conflict. But the experience of ten years suggests that, within these specific regions, progress has been sufficient to contain them.

Intra-governmental and inter-governmental problems constitute the fifth aspect of political change. The growing economic integration of the agricultural sector into the national economy has a profound influence on government administration. Technical bureaucracies expand and create tension with old guard law-and-order ministries and traditional generalist civil servants.[91] The scale of social organization adjusts to broadened interdependence of rural communities. Local leaders often become irrelevant to the needs of villagers unless they respond by evolving a new brokerage role that dramatically alters authority relationships in rural areas.[92] New levels of government and administration emerge to correspond to the changing scale and functions of government. This tends, in turn, to exacerbate problems of center-periphery conflict. These questions may be so serious as to virtually stalemate rural institutional development, as they have done in Pakistan recently.[93]

It could be argued, in fact, that the success of the rural transformation, and hence the response to the crisis of food scarcity, depends on the transformation of rural governance structures. Efficient allocation of public goods such as roads, irrigation and educational facilities, etc., can in most cases only be made by effective localized authorities. Certainly their effective maintenance depends upon such decentralization. Of course centralized control is necessary for sector-wide policies such as pricing, import-export decisions and credit. Effective mobilization of the collective self-help capacities of the rural population, however, demands considerable initiative in devising and encouraging new economic structures such as water users' associations and cooperative societies. In short, collective decision-making capacities need to be expanded at the local level. For administrators and nationalist leaders who may view power as a zero-sum game, these are particularly difficult decisions. Furthermore, the discretionary power invested in these institutions at the local level is not provided without some risk of wastage, corruption, and misallocation. A local base for opposition activity may also be created inadvertently. Drawing the lines of authority is not easy and new institutions have frequently failed

[91] A severe criticsm of the recent role of government adminstration can be found in M. L. Dantwala, "From Stagnation to Growth: Relative Roles of Technology, Economic Policy and Agrarian Institutions," in R. T. Shand, ed., Chapter 13. See also N. K. Nicholson and Silawar Ali Shan, *Basic Democracies and Rural Development in Pakistan* (Ithaca: Rural Development Committee, Center for International Studies, Cornell University, 1974).

[92] Good discussions of the emergence of brokerage politics can be found in Richard Sisson, *The Congress Party in Rajasthan* (Berkeley: University of California Press, 1972); and S. Javed Burki, *Agricultural Growth and Local Government in Punjab, Pakistan* (Ithaca: Rural Development Committee, Center for International Studies, Cornell University, 1974).

[93] See *Integrated Rural Development Programme* (Islamabad: Ministry of Food, Agriculture and Rural Development, Government of Pakistan, 1973).

because it was inadequately done, but the organization of public authority at the local level is a major variable in the development process.

The sixth political dimension of the food crisis involves international dependency. Few Third World nations have the political capacity or resources to transform the rural sector without assistance. Yet as the Russian-American conflict spreads now to Africa and Latin America, as well as Asia, the costs of dependency become clearer. We have seen the frustration of the Third World leaders in the Cocayoc Declaration and in other international gatherings.[94] In the past, aid bought time and provided external resources for elites. But as the crisis deepens, time runs out and poverty grows faster than external assistance in all but a few politically favored states. It seems unlikely that dependence will be an alternative to domestic reform for many nations much longer. More important, however, is the fact that unless the nation in question has the technical, administrative, and political strength and skill to manage the relationship, dependence may well distort policy and institutional development as severely as colonialism did.

Seventh, and finally, "ideological" questions must play an important role in the emerging solution to each nation's part of the global food crisis. Insofar as "ideology" implies a model of the future (in this sense we could use Mannheim's "utopia")[95] and a broad strategy for the role of government in bringing that future into existence, one should perhaps encourage it. Many nations, including those of the West, have been content to minimize the government's responsibility, dealing with problems in ad hoc fashion and letting solutions emerge from "market" adjustments. This would seem unwise if the future global food system will face shortages anything near as serious as the "doom-sayers" suggest.

The key development problem identified by the Club of Rome, in political terms, is the inability of the future to place demands on the present.[96] All decision makers discount heavily distant events in time. The result is that we are often caught by surprise. Another key problem is that identified by Garnett Hardin as the "commons" problem.[97] Expendable resources, or those which may be overtaxed, are poorly managed if responsibility and benefits are separated. From overfishing of the sea to grain shortages flowing from unregulated markets, this classic problem of political economy is becoming more frequent at the international level. An ideology which supports practical management and philosophical wisdom has never been more needed in directing the power of government, certainly those in developing states.

[94]"Cocayoc Declaration," *Ceres* (November–December 1974).

[95]K. Mannheim, *Ideology and Utopia* (New York: Harcourt, Brace & Co., 1936, Harvest Books ed.), p. 55; Clifford Geertz, "Ideology as a Cultural System," in David Apter, ed., *Ideology and Discontent* (Glencoe: Free Press, 1964), Chapter 1.

[96]See D. H. Meadows and D. L. Meadows, *The Limits to Growth* (New York: New American Library, 1972); H. S. D. Cole et al., *Models of Doom* (New York: Universe Books, 1973); M. Mesarovic and E. Peskel, *Mankind at the Turning Point* (New York: E. P. Dutton, 1974); E. F. Schumacher, *Small is Beautiful* (New York: Harper & Row, 1973).

[97]Garnett Hardin, "Living on a Lifeboat," *Bioscience* (October 1974): 561–68; "Tragedy of the Commons," *Science* (December 13, 1968): 1243–48; W. M. Murdoch and A. Oaten, "Population and Food: Metaphors and the Reality," *Bioscience* (September 1975): 561–67.

All these political problems are not the direct result of low productivity among the rural populace, or of food shortages, such as occurred in 1973–74. However, increasingly the determinant of economic growth and eventual political order in many developing states appears to rest on how agricultural development is managed. Given the significant vulnerability and hence dependency of many LDCs within the current world food system (especially those in South Asia and Africa), the norms of the global food regime regarding the terms on which concessional food aid and agricultural assistance will be provided become important in determining which pattern emerges in individual countries. In short the countries with the least control over the regime are also the ones most affected—politically and economically—by how the system works.

III. Economics, Politics, and the World Food System

5
Food Markets
and Their Regulation

Gary L. Seevers

A food regime not dominated by one or a few entities, without governmental policies separating national markets, and with free access to information would result in a single, integrated *global food market*. Such a hypothetical market would contribute more than the current system to efficiency and stability, although it would not necessarily be superior from an equity standpoint. Such a global food market does not exist. This is primarily because government regulation separates individual national markets. Residual *international* markets, shaped by the domestic and trade policies of major buyers and sellers, exist for major commodities. In the international grain market the United States is preponderant, but American policies in recent years have prevented the US from playing a dominating role. Furthermore, futures trading provides an open reference price. Consequently, the international grain market more nearly approximates "ideal" market features than many other international markets. An expansion of public markets and futures trading, by the United States and other countries, could enhance the effectiveness of international food markets in serving goals of efficiency, stability and security of access.

A discussion of markets is the appropriate starting point for any analysis of world food institutions. With regard to the distributional aspects of the global food system, markets, domestic and international, are the most important distributors of food. Technically, markets are organized practices for buying and selling goods and services among individuals or collective entities. In a broad sense they exist for all human exchanges, though conventionally we think of them principally in their commercial and monetarized forms. With regard to food, the practices and rules that guide exchanges (or marketing) across national frontiers are important elements of the global food regime. Similarly, the resultant transactions, which affect who gets

Gary L. Seevers is a Commissioner on the Commodity Futures Trading Commission. I appreciate the special assistance provided by Joseph W. Willett and his staff in the US Department of Agriculture.

how much food, when and why, are basic determinants of global food system functions.

This essay will evaluate how international food markets function in general, and then with regard to grains, in particular. There are as many criteria to evaluate a food market as there are possible values that such a market could satisfy or frustrate. Analysis here focuses upon three important performance criteria or objectives of the world food system—efficiency, stability, and equity. The achievement of these objectives is influenced by food markets along with other features of the world food regime.

Efficiency. The production of food and its distribution to consumers should be accomplished with the least possible use of resources. If allocated otherwise, resources will be wasted because some could have been devoted to additional food production or more of something else of value. This "efficiency" objective should be considered not only at the moment, but also over time. For instance, a crop-growing practice which would improve production this year but at the cost of reducing production possibilities in future years probably would be undesirable, and contrary to the efficiency criterion. Conversely, a new practice that initially had negative production effects could be justified if it increased production in subsequent years.

Stability. Food should be produced, distributed, and consumed without undue and extreme fluctuations of a transitory nature. Since shifts in food demand tend to be slow and predictable, fluctuations on the supply side pose the principal problem. The occurrence of significant production shortfalls during the 1970s has elevated food security concerns to a higher status, especially in importing countries. Security requires stability, since those who can afford food can maintain access to it even if prices fluctuate upward, while those commanding fewer resources can be severely penalized by even moderate price increases. Food stability and security is achieved when price gyrations are not excessive and when no significant group of people is threatened with reduced food supplies.

Equity. Food should be distributed so that a measure of fairness is attained, not solely in shortfall years, but on a continuing basis. An absolute achievement of this objective would require everyone to receive equal amounts of nutrients (or emotional satisfaction) from their food intake. In practice, the emphasis given equity depends upon affluence. Until recently, a worldwide standard for equity would have been "no starvation" whereas today it more often is considered "minimum nutrition." Economically affluent countries have adopted much higher standards. In the United States, for example, the food stamp program has had a standard that no American family should have to spend more than a certain fraction of its income on the purchase of a nutritionally adequate diet. By contrast, in the Sahel region and in parts of Southeast Asia, the elimination of near-starvation is still the major goal.

Additional objectives could be cited, but these are the primary ones. In the 1972–73 period, the abrupt shift from relative abundance to scarcity substantially altered the priority given to these various food objectives, in the United States and worldwide. I will use these as guides for my overview of how food markets operate, how they are regulated, and how they might be improved.[1]

The operation of food markets

The global distribution of food among nations continues to be carried out primarily through commercial channels in which the participants are both private firms and governmental entities. In this sense, markets are the instruments for determining the price[2] and physical distribution of food, as contrasted with governmental regulation of flows and prices. But while few markets in the real world meet Adam Smith's concept of a purely competitive market,[3] some come closer than others. For instance, the international market for vegetable oils, with its numerous sources of substitution, such as soybean, palm, and peanut oils, is much more competitive on the selling side than the coffee market which is heavily influenced by Brazilian regulation of exports.

Markets may deviate from the competitive model for two reasons: (1) because structural characteristics of the market itself enable private firms to inject monopoly elements; or, (2) more commonly, because governments intervene to regulate and control markets. Governments—both in developed and less developed countries—have a long history of controlling food distribution due to the political sensitivity of food.[4]

A global market: some analytic requirements

Primarily because of governmental regulation, the global food system in existence today cannot be characterized as being subsumed within or interlinked by a

[1]Bergsten et al. discuss "seven criteria against which to judge the effectiveness of any international economic system: efficiency, growth, full employment, income distribution, price stability, quality of life, and economic security." C. Fred Bergsten, Robert O. Keohane, and Joseph S. Nye, Jr., "International Economics and International Politics: A Framework for Analysis," *International Organization,* (Winter 1975): 26–36.

[2]The word "price" will be used as a shorthand for the overall terms of exchange. The specifics in an actual transaction might also include financing, shipping arrangements, contingency clauses, and other terms which together with price determine how attractive the transaction is to buyer or seller.

[3]The observation that few markets are perfectly competitive—or that some are becoming less competitive, or that others are cartelized—is sometimes used in support of government accepting more responsibility for market performance. A more useful concept may be "workable competition" which is a judgmental concept about the degree of competition. Indicators of competition include: the degree of concentration among buyers and sellers, the ability for new competitors to challenge existing firms, the openness of the price-making process, and the receptivity to technological (cost-reducing) advance. A promising line of research would be to apply this concept to international food markets where little careful analysis has been done of market performance. An index might be developed which would rank international food markets according to the degree of competition. Under the workable-competition concept, the relevant policy question becomes: would the benefits of more government regulation designed to improve market performance more than outweigh the various costs associated with additional regulation?

[4]Several major historic experiences with controls are summarized by Mary G. Lacy, "Food Control During Forty-Six Centuries," *Scientific Monthly* (June 1923).

global market. National food systems and markets exist, and they are linked together by economic forces. But, as will be shown, they do not form one integrated market, and this has implications for efficiency, stability, and equity at the global level. The actual structure and functioning of the international food market is most readily observed and easily understood by comparing it to a model "global market." It will therefore be useful for subsequent discussion to consider briefly the features of an "ideal" system where all national markets are tied into a single, integrated global one.

We can imagine a food commodity such as wheat or rice which is consumed in practically every country and produced in many countries. A global regime, through various institutional incentives, necessarily determines exactly how much of the commodity will be produced and consumed in each country. Such a system could take two "pure" forms: all incentives could be determined by governmental controls, or a system of free exchange with market incentives could exist. Although some mix of these two extreme forms nearly always exists in reality, let us look at the situation in the absence of government controls, where some form of market would emerge. Suppose the market among countries has the following properties:

(1) *Non-domination.* The numbers of buyers and sellers are sufficient to prevent any single one (or group in case of attempted collusion) from dictating the prices and other terms of transactions.

(2) *No-separation.* No country of any quantitative significance makes a distinction between its consumers and consumers abroad; likewise, domestic producers are undifferentiated from producers abroad.

(3) *Open-pricing.* A free and generous flow of information exists to make production and consumption decisions, and to carry out transactions.

Under these three circumstances, all national markets would be part of one global market. The same price would prevail everywhere at any moment for *comparable* transactions (e.g., same in quality, grade and delivery date). Price disparities from one location to another derive only from transportation costs. If the commodity is expensive to transport (because it is bulky and perishable), the differences may be large. Potatoes, for instance, seldom move long distances unless an exceptional deficit occurs as happened in Western Europe in 1976, making imports from the United States economical.

Significantly, for such a global market to exist, the institutional arrangements and commercial practices need not be standardized. It does not need to meet the extreme concept of a competitive market with thousands of individual buyers and sellers. For instance, one agency could serve as the sole procurement agent for a country's imports (or the sole marketing agent for its exports) if it was not in a position to dictate external prices (the non-domination property) and did not elect to dictate internal prices (the no-separation property). Prices could be established in a centralized and public way, as in an auction market, or they could be set by bilateral transactions as long as they were generally known (the open-pricing property).

From the standpoint of encouraging efficiency in production, that is, bringing a given amount of food to consumers at the lowest average cost, such a global market would rank high. This is the chief argument in favor of basically free markets: they automatically provide the incentives to produce where it can be done for the least use of resources. By producing at the lowest cost, the system would also result in more production than if regulations were added which raised costs. Any significant government intervention that would modify production and trade flows would reduce performance. For instance, a country that placed quotas on grain imports would simply substitute its own higher cost production for lower cost imports, as Japan does for rice.

This global market system would also rank high in terms of price stability because any temporary shocks (bad crops in South Asia) would be diffused through the whole system, and government interventions for whatever reason which isolate their own markets from outside shocks would increase instabilty.[5] Such a system, however, would not guarantee supply stability itself, nor would it provide food security to very poor countries when they suffer setbacks in their own food production. Still, it would spread shocks evenly as regards price and it would give all countries equal access, assuming they had the resources to buy food.

How would the global market rank from an equity standpoint? If equity is measured by the ability of producers and consumers to obtain food on comparable price terms, it would rank high. However, if receiving reasonably equal amounts of nutrients is the standard of equity, we would judge the market's performance adversely, for unless everyone had fairly equal incomes and a similar propensity to purchase nutritious food, nutritional disparities would be probable. Sweden's high income would place her in a most favored position from a food adequacy standpoint today. The poorest countries would be (and obviously are) the least favored.[6]

Regulation and markets

Real world markets have significant government regulation so that the properties of the hypothetical global market are seldom fully met.[7] In practice, transac-

---

[5]The argument in favor of government grain reserves depends largely on the fact that there is not a global grain market; government regulation causes national markets to be separate from one another. Although the more actual grain markets deviate from a single global market, the greater the justification for government reserves. This does not, in my view, mean there is a strong case for extensive government reserves even under the existing non-global grain markets. For one reason, one of the presumed costs of instability is overstated. It is argued that instability reduces efficiency by increasing risks. However, risk results from divergence between anticipated outcomes and actual outcomes, not from fluctuations in actual outcomes per se. The futures markets provide one important way to remove divergence for producers, merchants, and consumers by hedging.

[6]Any attempts to improve equity toward the extreme goal of equalizing food received by everyone would have to take account of their impact on the cost of producing food. Redistribution measures within the food system usually also raise average production costs, resulting in less *total* food availability. Provision of food-aid is an example. Pure redistribution measures include general and unrestricted foreign aid which operates outside the food system itself. Technical assistance provided to food-deficient countries, if effectively administered, would be a measure that would improve equity and presumably also improve efficiency.

[7]I am using the word regulation loosely to mean both a policy and the means of implementing the policy. A more precise meaning would be only the "means of implementing." In matters of domestic agricultural policy, the means-of-implementing has traditionally been called programs. Regulation usually has referred to a subset of programs, e.g., regulation of meat inspection, or regulation of commodity futures trading, or regulation of chemical food additives. I shall use regulation in a more general way.

tions for various food commodities reflect a mixture of market-type approaches by some countries and more control-oriented ones by others. In addition, rather than being integrated, the global market has been partitioned into segments. To accomplish other objectives such as self-sufficiency (for national economic and military security), or to better achieve the three food performance objectives domestically, most nations have adopted regulations that insulate themselves somewhat from the global system. Paarlberg has demonstrated this rather emphatically by describing some extreme cases. The result is a world food system composed of national markets which, though linked together, rarely form an integrated whole. Thus, the "international market" for a particular commodity that moves among nations is in most cases a residual market which reflects the total global forces of supply and demand only partially and often in a distorted form. The extent to which the international market for each commodity meets the properties set out for a "pure" global market will depend on a case-by-case evaluation.

It must be understood from the beginning that there is in fact very little *international regulation* of international commodity markets, largely because no international authorities are entrusted to make and enforce such regulations. Other authors in this volume attempt to explain the weaknesses and meeknesses of international authority. For the moment however, the important point is that regulations affecting international markets are in overwhelming measure national regulations applied to domestic markets largely for domestic purposes.

National regulation

The sources and features of national regulation have been addressed earlier in this volume. Typically a distinction can be made between domestic regulation (e.g., price supports or ceilings, acreage allotments, storage program) and foreign trade regulation (e.g., import restrictions and export subsidies). While the significance of this distinction should not be pushed too far, it should be emphasized that domestic regulation has important effects on international markets in two respects.

First, most food never enters international channels; the bulk of what is produced is consumed principally within the nations that produce it. Government regulation affects the extent to which this occurs, and the net result is that, on balance, a smaller proportion of total food production moves among nations than would be the case if a global market prevailed. However, even if a global market obtained, nations would still be predominantly self-sufficient because the advantages of economic specialization would not outweigh the transportation costs associated with high ratios of trade. Table 1 shows the degree of self-sufficiency attained by various countries during a recent three-year period. These figures are based upon the estimated caloric content of food, admittedly a crude measure. Table 2 gives estimates based upon grain tonnages and shows, as one would expect, that nations have greater dependency on grain trade than on food trade altogether.

Second, nationally imposed trade regulations are usually the consequences of programs of domestic regulation for domestic ends. Controlling international trade

Table 1 Caloric self-sufficiency ratios and related data, 1973/74–1975/76 average, selected regions and countries

PERCENT OF WORLD

Region/country	Self-sufficiency ratio	Food production	Food consumption[1]	Population
Developed countries	110	34.0	30.9	18.8
Importers
Japan	55	1.5	2.7[2]	2.8
Western Europe	91	11.0	12.1	8.8
Exporters
United States	127	17.4	13.7	5.5
Centrally Planned	96	34.4	35.7	30.7
USSR	97	14.5	15.0	6.5
People's Republic of China	99	11.6	11.7	20.9
Less Developed Countries	95	31.7	33.2	50.5
Importers
India	96	8.2	8.5	15.8
Brazil	97	3.4	3.5	2.7
Exporters
Thailand	121	1.0	.9	1.1

1. Includes cereals, starchy foods, sugar, pulses, nuts, seeds, vegetables, fruits, meat, eggs, milk and edible fats and oils.

2. Inclusion of fish products raises Japanese food consumption to roughly 2.9 percent as compared to the 2.7 percent shown.

Note: Self-sufficiency calcuated as food calories produced as a percent of food calories consumed. Tables 1 and 2 are calculated on the basis of a net food trade measure. (I.e., food calories minus food calories exported equals net food calories imported or exported.) Such a calculation can understate the volume of food entering the world market. The extent of the understatement, however, is not large enough in most cases to change the self-sufficiency ratios shown above.

Note: No adjustment made to reflect the use of grain and other food products as feed for livestock.

Source: *Economic Research Service,* US Department of Agriculture.

Table 2   Grain self-sufficiency ratios and related data, 1973/74–1975/76 averages, selected regions and countries

PERCENT OF WORLD

Region/country	Self-sufficiency ratio	Grain production	Grain consumption	Population
Developed Countries	116	37.8	32.7	18.8
Importers				
Japan	39	1.0	2.6	2.8
Western Europe	88	11.7	13.4	8.8
Exporters				
United States	145	19.7	13.6	5.5
Centrally Planned	95	35.2	37.3	30.7
USSR	94	14.8	15.8	6.5
People's Republic of China	97	13.0	13.4	20.9
Less Developed Countries	90	26.5	29.4	50.5
Importers				
India	95	8.1	8.6	15.8
Brazil	95	2.0	2.2	2.7
Exporters				
Thailand	108	1.0	.9	1.1

Note: Self-sufficiency calculated as total grain produced divided by total grain consumed; no adjustments have been made for livestock feed. See note at end of Table 1.
Source: Economic Research Service, US Department of Agriculture.

is rarely an end itself. For example, a price-support program for wheat will often necessitate import restrictions to prevent foreign supplies from undermining the support level. Or imports may be highly regulated to achieve a domestic price-support goal, as was the case with sugar in the United States when the Sugar Program was in effect (until 1974). In the first example, regulation through trade policy is a complement of domestic policy, and in the latter case it is a substitute to achieve a domestic target.

Actually, the distinction between domestic and trade policy is somewhat arbitrary since their political motivations, as well as many of their economic effects, are often the same. Both are part of the same overall package, and it is the package as a whole which counts. This package includes not only domestic and trade regulation for food but also other policies including transportation, health and financial regulation.[8] A nation's regulation of foreign exchange, for instance, will have a major influence on its food situation. The US devaluation in 1971 was obviously an

[8] Health regulations are an important form of national food regulation. One can distinguish between legitimate regulations (i.e., intended to protect domestic animal, plant, or human health) and regulations established for the purpose of discriminating against foreign products. The impact on food markets can be significant in either case. For instance, the US prohibits imports of fresh meat from Argentina to prevent the spread of hoof and mouth disease. As a consequence, Argentina exports large quantities of meat to Western Europe, some of which would otherwise flow to the United States.

important factor in the expansion of foreign demand for US agricultural products, which became cheaper to foreign customers.[9]

The World Food Council (WFC) has called particular attention to the distortion of trade caused by domestic and trade policies of major developed countries. Because domestic production in these countries has been subsidized, certain foods have had lower ''real'' costs in international markets. This has resulted in reduced incentives for production by many poor countries. Estimates published by the Food and Agriculture Organization (FAO) suggest that the magnitude of such ''subsidization'' has been upwards of $20 billion per year in the past. Those policies have been criticized by the WFC and FAO as well as most economists as distorting long-term adjustments and reducing production efficiency.[10]

Regulation from abroad

Each nation's regulation of its food market is conditioned and influenced by the collective regulation of all other nations. In complex fashion, it is the composite result of national regulations worldwide that influences conditions in international markets. This then feeds back into each nation's policy making, which reacts with new regulations intended to obtain national goals in the light of international conditions. In turn, this yields another set of international conditions, with further feedbacks into national policy making. Nations such as the centrally-planned countries, which follow a strategy of thoroughly insulating their domestic markets, will be less affected by regulation from abroad than those nations which follow open trade strategies. Those nations that go the farthest toward integrating their domestic markets with the international market, either as exporters or importers, are most directly affected by international conditions altered by others' regulations.

Johnson and Schnittker[11] have divided countries into three groups with respect to their food strategies:

Self-sufficient Nations. Such nations attempt to protect and encourage agricultural production through price guarantees and import restrictions. The EC (both before and after its enlargement to nine members), Russia, China, and India are important examples of countries aiming at self-sufficiency. Well over half the world's population lives in such countries.

---

[9]The influence of exchange-rate regulating is demonstrated by the recent US experience. As the dollar became progressively over-valued prior to the depreciation that began in August 1971, US food exports were indirectly regulated because they were priced artificially high abroad. Likewise, food imports into the United States were stimulated by an indirect subsidy. It seems clear that the dollar's depreciation has played a role in altering and tightening the US food situation since 1972. For an analysis of the consequences, see G. Edward Schuh, ''The Exchange Rate and US Agriculture,'' *American Journal of Agricultural Economics,* Vol. 56, No. 1 (February 1974): 1–13. It is less clear, however, to what extent the dollar's rather abrupt depreciation contributed to the essentially concurrent worldwide tight situation, as compared with USSR purchases, crop shortfalls and business cycles.

[10]See World Food Council, ''Food Trade, Report by the Executive Director,'' Paper No. 42 (Rome: March 30, 1977), p. 14.

[11]D. Gale Johnson and John A. Schnittker, *US Agriculture in a World Context: Policies and Approaches for the Next Decade* (New York: Praeger Publishers, 1974), pp. 1–5.

Net Importers. Such nations import a large percentage of their food requirements as a matter of policy. The United Kingdom was the classical food importer until it joined the closed EC system in 1973. Japan and a few smaller countries are the best examples of countries that, for reasons of economic efficiency or because they lack sufficient arable land, are major agricultural importers. These contain a small percentage of the world's population.

Net Exporters. These nations exceed their basic food requirements and pursue agricultural development and pricing policies to promote exports. The major cases are the United States, Canada, Australia, Argentina, and New Zealand. Brazil and Pakistan may obtain this status in the future.

Pursuing these various strategies results in regulations that cause the world system to deviate substantially from the system that a global market model would produce. Currently, governments participate directly as well as indirectly in food markets. Sometimes government agencies purchase or sell food. ExportKhleb, for instance, is the sole USSR buyer of grain imports; Ghana and Nigeria have marketing boards which buy their cocoa crops and conduct all marketing functions through resale in the export market. Governments establish ceilings and floors for prices (usually within their own markets, but with effects in international markets) and they control trade flows. The United States puts quotas on meat imports and for years attached subsidies to wheat exports. Argentina has used quotas on grain exports to maintain internal supplies. These are examples of direct regulation with a direct impact on international food markets. Much other regulation, from subsidized credit to environmental controls, is primarily for internal purposes but can have indirect impacts on international food markets.

International regulation

International regulatory arrangements also affect each nation's food system and the international market, but, as noted, such regulation is of minor significance at present.[12] International commodity agreements are the only noteworthy instances. Such agreements take many forms. Current agreements for wheat and olive oil provide a forum for information exchange but they are not regulatory schemes. Two commodity agreements (cocoa and coffee) have price-regulation provisions and qualify as multilateral regulation. All four of these agreements include both producing and consuming countries. The recent proposals for a New International Economic Order,[13] especially the common fund designed to establish multilateral buffer

---

[12]I would classify regional trading blocs such as the European Community as a modification of national rather than multilateral regulation. In 1974, trade among members of the EC, the Latin American Free Trade Association and among centrally-planned economies accounted for 14.7 percent of total agricultural trade.

[13]The proposals for NIEO are discussed in Branislav Gosovic and John G. Ruggie, "On the Creation of a New International Economic Order," *International Organization,* Vol. 30, No. 2 (Spring 1976): 309–39.

stocks, would, if implemented, go a step beyond current international collaboration. The food commodities to be covered by the proposal at the 1976 UNCTAD Conference are noted in Table 3.

Table 3 Exports of major food commodities from the United States and world total, 1972–74 average

Commodity	United States	World total	U.S. share (percent)
	BILLION DOLLARS		
Grains (including flour)	$7.3	$16.9	43
Oilseeds[b]	2.8	4.7	60
Soybeans	2.6	3.1	84
Vegetable and Animal Oils[b]	0.9	4.5	20
Animal Products			
Meat[b]	0.4	8.7	5
Dairy	a	4.6	a
Sugar[b]	a	5.6	a
Coffee and Tea[b]	a	4.8	a
Cocoa[b]	a	1.1	a
Fruits and Vegetables	0.8	4.5	18
Bananas[b]	a	0.6	a

[a]Zero or nominal.

[b]These seven commodities are included on the initial list of commodities to be included in the integrated program for commodities adopted at UNCTAD IV Conference, May 1976.

Source: Economic Research Service, U.S. Department of Agriculture.

The concept of commodity cartels, newly attractive due to the successful operation of OPEC, differs from conventional commodity agreements, including those proposed by UNCTAD. Cartels are organized by producing countries and are intended explicitly to improve prices of their export commodities. If the objective of producer cartels is to increase commodity earnings, the economic circumstances under which they could succeed are very limited. For instance, in 1974 countries controlling about two-thirds of the world banana market attempted to raise earnings by imposing a large tax; favorable economic conditions did not exist, however, and the effort quickly floundered. For most commodities, prospects for effective and sustained producer cartels appear to be quite limited,[14] particularly with respect to food. Although Australia, the US, and Canada (especially the latter two), played a predominant role in the world wheat market in the 1960s, as Edward Martin notes, they could not exercise the prerogatives of a cartel by maintaining artificially high prices to consuming nations.[15]

[14]The pros and cons of this conclusion have been discussed by C. Fred Bergsten, Stephen D. Krasner, and others in *Foreign Affairs* during 1974. Also, see the following for a derivation of economic conditions and the application to selected commodities. Carl Van Dyne "Commodity Cartels and the Theory of Derived Demand," *KYKLOS*, vol. 28 (1975): 597–611.

[15]Edwin M. Martin, comments, in Don Wallace, Jr. and Helga Escobar, eds., *The Future of International Economic Organization* (New York: Praeger, 1976).

Regulation in overview

The coordination of food flows among countries results from the joint workings of national regulations and market incentives. To talk of *the* world food market for any commodity is to discuss something that does not exist; reality differs from the abstract ''global market'' outlined earlier. For each commodity there are differing degrees of a single market. The typical food commodity moves internationally as follows: nearly every nation has its own market in the sense that government regulation provides a degree of separation from the outside market. The ''outside'' market is a composite residual of regulations and economic forces arising from all other markets. Except for instances of joint regulation by a few countries (e.g., the EEC), there is relatively little regulation initiated beyond the national level. Commodity agreements presently have limited use because they seldom work when under pressure. Their record shows them ineffectual as multilateral regulatory tools, and often opposed by leading industrialized nations and major private business interests. The United States, for example, rejected two proposals by importers to negotiate grain commodity trade agreements during 1977.

The most important conclusion is that flows of food among countries are determined primarily in a residual market which I have referred to as the ''international market'' in contrast to a (hypothetical) global market or the broader structural features of the actual world food system. Quantitatively, the international market is a small fraction of the world total. International prices usually are more volatile than domestic prices and, in this sense, prices play a significant role in international markets. The major reason why prices are more volatile is that national or regional regulation reduces short-term price movements in domestic markets (as Paarlberg describes for the European Community) thereby diverting more of the adjustments to the residual international market. Thus, a relatively small shift in production often has had a much larger ''international'' impact than would be the case otherwise.

A second conclusion concerns how well actual world systems perform in relation to three objectives: efficiency, stability and equity. Compared with the global market (one meeting the three criteria above), current world food systems probably are less efficient and less stable. Whether they are less secure from the standpoint of poor nations depends on special arrangements that nations could make to cushion temporary food setbacks. It is difficult to determine whether the current systems are more or less equitable than a global market. A global market would not preclude concessionary financing of food imports for the neediest states, but it might eliminate domestic political support for such transfers as the US PL 480 or food aid program.

Third, when there is significant separation among markets and the residual international market is small, there will be greater opportunity for firms and government agencies dealing in the international market to engage in collusive practices. The size of the market within which they operate has been reduced. This may best be illustrated by looking at a highly integrated world system, such as the international soybean trade. Nearly all soybean exports originate in the United States and a few firms account for a high fraction of overseas sales. However, the international soybean market incorporates the entire domestic US market. This market includes dozens of private firms and producer cooperatives engaged in marketing and, therefore, the major trading firms do not have a dominant position. If the United States were to separate its domestic market through export quotas, the nation as a whole would be in a much stronger position to exercise influence over international transactions. Conceivably, the major trading firms also could utilize their position in the smaller international market, although for them to do so would require some form of collusion, or a "weeding out" to only two or three firms.

My final conclusion is that unless significant reform of national systems is assumed, the international market should be judged not against a hypothetical ideal model but in terms of how well it performs given the world within which it operates. This is particularly applicable in the case of grains, which, because of their importance in food trade, I have singled out for special treatment below.

The case of grains

Although the world food system includes a great diversity of commodities, grains are the most basic of food ingredients. They are by far the most heavily used source of nutrition produced in most of the world and can be used as inputs in the production of a number of other products. Furthermore, since they are not highly perishable they can easily be traded. Grains are also one of the cheapest sources of food calories available in the world. In recent years, grain exports have averaged about one-fifth of the value of international trade in agricultural commodities; the corresponding figure for the United States has been nearly one-half (Table 3). The shift from (relative) food surplus to scarcity in 1972/73 was most dramatic for grains. World trade in grains averaged 12.9 percent of global grain production in 1972–75 (155 million metric tons) compared with 10.4 percent of production in the three-year period prior to 1972 (115 million metric tons). Yet since the major exporters of grains are wealthy industrialized countries, UNCTAD efforts to stabilize commodity prices have not focused on grains but on those commodities in which less developed states have a larger share of total exports.

The world grain system and the international grain market

How well does the world grain system conform to the global market model? Does the system meet the no-separation, non-domination and open-pricing properties? Quite clearly regulation is a major factor, since at least half of the world's grain production and consumption fails to meet the test of no significant separation. In addition to the USSR, mainland China and the Eastern European countries, many third world countries insulate their domestic grain markets from outside forces to a significant degree. The insulation of internal European Community grain markets and Japanese foodgrain markets is well described by Paarlberg.[16]

Because the separation criterion is not met in the world grain system, the domination and open-pricing criteria are only relevant to the (residual) international grain market.

Is domination prevalent?

Although monopoly elements are present on the export side, grain exporting comes reasonably close to meeting the criterion that no single country is exercising monopoly influence. This is because the United States is a competitive seller whose market is *not* dominated and *not* separated from the international market (the role of grain-trading companies will be discussed below).[17] Of the next seven largest exporting countries which, together with the United States, accounted for some 85 percent of the world's 1973/74–1975/76 export total, four used marketing boards (Canada, Australia, South Africa and Argentina) and one employed a state-trading corporation (USSR). These tools give them full control over grain exports. But these countries accounted for only about one-third of world exports and their selling must compete with the other countries as well as with each other. In Thailand, state and private trade were mixed but state-trading dominated. France, the other country among the top eight, should not be viewed as being a single seller in terms of its activity in the international grain market. France functions as an integral part of a grain-deficit European Community with international trade (imports and exports) in grains heavily regulated. About one-half of total exports moved from free-trading countries—primarily the United States—in which any part of the entire domestic supply eventually consumed was potentially available to foreign importers competing for purchases with domestic consumers. In all, the number of potential competitors was sufficiently high to make domination improbable, at least in the 1970s.[18]

Grain imports are subject to either direct or indirect government control in the majority of the nations making purchases on the international market. However, there are 120 countries that make regular purchases on the international market. Of the 40 nations that account for about three-fourths of total imports, 24 enforced state-trading monopolies either indirectly through regulation or directly through state-trading corporations. The 24 included the centrally-planned nations (including the USSR, PRC, North Korea, Cuba, and all the countries of Eastern Europe) and a number of somewhat more market-oriented economies (including India, Egypt,

---

[16]In periods when either consumers or producers are "protected," separation regulations retard achievement of the low-cost (efficiency) production objective. When stability is a problem, the same regulations shift "shocks" to those without separation regulations. In either case there are costs. When international grain prices rose above internal EC prices in 1973–74, they were no longer interfering with efficiency but their actions to maintain internal stability compounded instability elsewhere.

[17]Based upon information from Foreign Demand and Competition Division, Economic Research Service, US Department of Agriculture.

[18]This was not necessarily true in the past when surplus stocks were present. For a discussion of wheat pricing during an earlier period, see Alex F. McCalla, "A Duopoly Model of World Wheat Pricing," *Journal of Farm Economics*, Vol. 48 (August 1966): 711–29.

Mexico, Brazil, Algeria, Morocco, Sri Lanka, Indonesia, Pakistan, Peru, Portugal and Chile). Some form of government approval (e.g., licenses) was required in eight of the remaining countries (Iran, Greece, Philippines, Spain, South Korea, Venezuela, Taiwan and Israel). In virtually all the LDCs, whether included in the state-trading group or the "approval" group, grain imports were essentially controlled through costly and complicated tender, inspection, and reporting procedures which have been characteristic of developing nations. In instances where private traders were allowed to import, it was often under procedures that constrained their competitive incentive or discriminated against them by imposing "costs" above those incurred by state-trading corporations. In the remaining eight nations (the UK, Netherlands, West Germany, Belgium-Luxembourg, Switzerland, Ireland and Denmark), trade-restrictive import taxes or variable levies were used to control imports of grain. Private companies, however, did purchase the bulk of the grains imported without any further government intervention. Japan followed a mixed system with state monopolies, licensing procedures, and free private trade functioning together: the government enforced a state monopoly on foreign purchases of wheat, rice and barley; a stand-by licensing system existed for feed corn, but imports of corn as well as sorghum have been left to the private trade. The imports of these 40 countries indicate that roughly half of world imports over the 1973/74– 1975/76 period were controlled indirectly through licensing and "approval" schemes, and some 30 percent were affected by trade-restrictive duties. Because of the large number of countries involved, however, even if every country had acted as a single entity (with no sub-national, "private" market activity), the potential for monopoly pricing would have been minimal. The obvious qualification is that the USSR is singly large enough to exercise some degree of monopoly power by withholding information on its intentions. Otherwise, the import side of the international grain market also seems to be free of domination.

Although dominance is not significant in the international grain market, the bilateral agreements signed in the mid-1970s between the United States and several countries (USSR, Poland, Japan, Israel) introduce an element of separation into the market. Canada and Australia have used agreements with the USSR and China to provide a multi-year framework within which annual purchases occurred. They permitted considerable year-to-year flexibility in quantities purchased and prices. For the most part, the recent bilateral agreements by the United States are nonbinding. However, if bilateral dealings came to contain rigid and enforceable limits on either prices or quantities, they would reduce the effective size of the residual market and further impair the market benefits of world grain trading.

Is international pricing open and competitive?

International grain transactions are consummated in four ways, depending largely on the strategy used by buyers.[19]

---

[19]*Improving the Export Capability of Grain Cooperatives,* Farmer Cooperative Service Research Report 34, US Department of Agriculture, June 1976, pp. 22–23.

(1) *Open market*. Grains may be priced in an open market in which export firms make continuous offers and import firms react to those offers and make bids themselves.[20] In addition to US grain markets, the London, Rotterdam, and Hamburg markets represent this form of pricing. The continuous flow of offers and bids together with unrestricted access makes this a competitive market and a safety-valve to prevent manipulative pricing in other transactions. Prices in these markets are directly linked to each other and to prices established in various futures markets for grains. While reliable data are not publicly available, one-third or more of international grain trade probably is priced directly in these open markets. Although private firms are the primary users of this transaction form, nothing prevents government agencies from using such markets, as they do on occasion.

(2) *Public tenders*. Under this procedure buyers initiate transactions by announcing in trade channels their intentions to buy (issue tenders) which carry explicit terms and deadlines for the submission of sell offers. Typically, importing nations with monopoly-procurement agencies buy in this way, as do most nations that obtain grain under PL 480 sales agreements.[21] Roughly speaking, about one-fourth of international grain trade is priced through public tender.

The public tender market is becoming more important as government procurement increases in importance. Tenders are more adaptable to the specific requirements of importers, and they are more conducive to forward-buying. In recent years, most US wheat exports have been sold by private exporters in the public tender market.

(3) *Private tenders*. This method of pricing is similar to public tenders except private importing firms issue the tenders which are sent directly to prospective sellers. It is most commonly used by local flour mills in Central America, Africa

---

[20]The price may be set when the sale is initially made. These fixed-price sales normally account for a majority of US exports. Under a typical fixed-price sale, an exporting firm might sell 200,000 tons of corn to an importer for $2.85 per bushel delivered at a Gulf port in 90 days. The exporter might obtain price protection (i.e., hedge) by buying corn futures at the Chicago Board of Trade. Then when the exporter purchased actual corn for this shipment, the hedge would be removed by selling corn futures. However, in many sales, the price is not established when the transaction is consummated. Instead, provisions are made for fixing a price at a later date. In sales where an absolute price is not set, the price usually is based upon a particular month's price on a futures exchange in Chicago, Minneapolis, or Kansas City. This is called "basis pricing." For example, a Japanese firm may have agreed to buy 200,000 tons of wheat from a US exporter (with specified grade, quality, and delivery provisions) at $.10 per bushel over the December futures price in Kansas City. The Japanese firm then would have the option of requesting a price at its convenience. At this time, the US firm typically would buy futures contracts, thereby hedging itself against subsequent changes in cash wheat prices. When it bought wheat for this shipment, the firm would sell futures (lift its hedge). The Japanese importer has selected its time to price, and the US exporter has used the futures market to reduce risks of price changes between the time it has a fixed-price sale and when it purchases wheat for this shipment. Actually, each side has several other choices.

[21]Most P.L. 480 "sales" are handled just like commercial sales once the US government and the recipient country have reached a financial agreement. This agreement covers the commodity to be purchased, the total dollar amount to be provided, and the repayment terms. Usually a quantity to be purchased is stated in the agreement but this presumes a specific price. It is the total dollar figure which is binding and the recipient country has an incentive to get the best possible deal. American food-aid thereby is a transfer mechanism of dollar commitments (to be spent to purchase food); the actual food is transferred like commercial sales. Responsibility for effective and low-cost procurement rests with the recipient country.

and Southern Asia. About one-tenth of international grain trade moves in this way.

(4) *Negotiated trades.* Purchases by countries with centrally-planned economies, most notably the USSR, fall in this last category. They engage in bilateral negotiations involving much larger quantities than are normally transacted in any one purchase in the other three markets. Little is known about the precise strategies they follow, or the calculations of sellers, whether private trading companies or exporting agencies such as the Canadian Wheat Board. Practically all USSR grain purchases to date have been at specific prices, rather than according to a formula which permits gradual pricing over a period of time. Procurement agencies for China, India and Iran also purchase on a negotiated basis instead of issuing public tenders. Occasionally, when prices change the buyer will cancel a trade contract and reimburse the seller for his costs. China did this in 1976 as prices fell.

Exporting nations with marketing boards may deal in any of the ways discussed above. They also have another alternative: they may and do sell to the grain trading firms who in turn resell into one of the four markets.

What is the role of "futures"?

Futures markets are contracts to buy and sell at specified prices and dates. They have become extremely important in tying these four marketing avenues together and facilitating transactions. They have also become a barometer for grain prices worldwide. A high proportion of grain in the international market is, in effect, priced in relation to the futures markets. That is, futures quotations are used to specify the price at which actual grain will be sold. As the tender markets and negotiated sales have increased in significance, the futures markets have become even more important. They bring relevant market information together promptly and cheaply, and being quasi-public institutions, they assure full and prompt dissemination so that all buyers and sellers can be simultaneously informed. The effect of the futures markets, particularly those located in Chicago, Kansas City and Minneapolis, is to insure that the open-pricing feature of the international grain market is realized. For either buyers or sellers to accept a non-competitive grain price in today's market would be more the result of negligence or inexperience than from lack of openly-determined price.[22]

[22]In addition to providing the function of competitive price discovery for the market as a whole, a properly-operating futures market provides a risk-transfer mechanism. This function reduces costs of handling and merchandising the commodity. Futures markets provide economic benefits but they also are subject to distortions and manipulations which interfere with the pricing and risk-transfer function. The primary justification for their regulation has been to ensure that futures prices accurately reflect anticipated supply and demand at that time. The economic benefits and operation of futures markets are poorly understood. For example, while 14.6 billion bushels of soybeans were traded at the Chicago Board of Trade in 1974–75 crop year futures, only 33.2 million bushels were delivered on these contracts (less than one percent of the total traded). The total deliveries equaled 2.7 percent of the US 1974–75 soybean crop—though in many cases the same soybeans may have been delivered more than once, and all of them subsequently were sold for commercial end use. The futures market is not intended or used as a separate cash commodity market. Rather, the futures market is auxiliary to the cash market and helps the cash market operate more efficiently. The possibility of delivery is, however, an absolute necessity to insure a linkage between cash and futures prices; otherwise futures could become a separate and artificial market and serve no economic purpose. In certain cases, "selling" or "buying" in the futures markets is the most suitable marketing channel.

The role of multinational business firms

Aside from nations, the principal participants in international markets are multinational firms, especially grain trading firms. Along with governments and individual producers, multinational agribusiness firms play a significant role in the global food system, and hence in shaping the context within which the international market operates.

Multinational agriculture and food firms can be divided into three types (although some firms belong in more than one category). These are input suppliers, producers and processors, and traders. While some firms own large plantations, the great bulk of world food production is not directly controlled by multinational or even by large firms. Through supplying inputs (such as fertilizers and tractors), managing farm operations, processing food, marketing and distributing it, providing storage and transport and making investment decisions, such firms have helped spread farming and food handling innovations. They have also facilitated the integration of the international markets. Considerable debate has occurred regarding the value of their contribution to the global food system as a whole, especially their effect on food security and equity (see the essay by Christensen). Certainly these firms are large: it has been estimated that the combined sales of the 72 largest US food processing firms (in 1975) was $94 billion or 11 percent of total revenue of the country's top 500 manufacturing firms.[23] Input suppliers—such as W. R. Grace (fertilizer), Pfizer (pharmaceuticals and pesticides), John Deere (implements), De-Kalb (seeds), and FMC Corporation (land and processing developers)—accounted for about $12 billion in the same year. The largest grain-trading firms—Cargill, Inc., Continental Grain, Bunge, Cook Industries and Louis Dreyus, Inc.—have sales estimated at around $20 billion.[24] Other countries host major multinationals as well, such as Nestlé (Switzerland) and Brooke Bond (UK). While the total role of such firms in the politics and economics of the world food system is substantial, my analysis of international marketing is limited to the large grain-trading firms.

The multinational grain-trading firms have been subject to frequent criticism in recent years. Two reasons seem to be important. First, four of the five largest firms are privately-held and little is known about their business operations.[25] Second, the major trading firms account for a very large share of the total international movement of grain. Even though over 50 firms are engaged in the US grain export business, the five largest account for some 85 percent of all grain exported from the United States, or about one-half of total international trade (Table 4). They also do much of the business from other export sources. If being responsible for movement of grain could lead to domination, the major trading firms could be in a position to

[23]See Ray A. Goldberg and James E. Austin, "Multinational Agribusiness and Global Food Problems," paper presented to the meetings of the American Political Science Association (Chicago: September 2, 1976), pp. 6–8.

[24]Ibid.

[25]See *Improving the Export Capability of Grain Cooperatives* (pp. 17–19) for brief description of each firm. The only publicly-held firm is Cook Industries, Inc., which entered the grain business about a decade ago, and in 1977 ran into serious financial difficulties and began to curtail its grain business.

Table 4   Estimated share of world wheat and feedgrain imports supplied from the United States by major grain trading firms, 1972/73 and 1973/74[a]

	Wheat	*Feedgrains*
	PERCENTAGE	
1972–73	40.3	52.8
1973–74	41.9	58.5

[a]These estimates derived from a variety of sources. Estimates are not available for subsequent years, or for the share of world exports accounted for by the major trading firms.
Source: *Improving the Export Capability of Grain Cooperatives,* Farmer Cooperative Service Research Report 34, U.S. Department of Agriculture, June 1976. Appendix Tables 4 and 5.

dominate and hence influence the international grain market to their advantage. If they could *substantially* affect transport costs, they would indirectly affect the size and direction of trade flows. However, there is little evidence that the shipping market is subject to domination. The Baltic Exchange in London, which handles many cargo arrangements, is not subject to government regulation but is considered a competitive market. Thus the large grain trading firms primarily act as intermediaries in the world grain trade.

The ability of trading firms to dominate the international grain market is also weakened by the fact that at any one time, these firms own only a small fraction of total supply. Furthermore, there are other checks on the exercise of monopoly influence which include: competitive rivalry among the major firms; potential expansion of smaller competing firms; entry of new firms; and potential new government controls. Competition is evidenced in the rivalry and secrecy of operations, as discussed by Destler with regard to dealings between the grain-trading firms and Soviet representatives in 1972. Expansion, and hence competitiveness in the industry, is well illustrated by the example of Cook Industries. Until the 1960s, the firm traded mainly cotton; by 1973 it had become the third largest grain-trading firm in the world, although its grain activities were sharply curtailed in 1977. It would seem that the link between the US and the international market enables smaller firms to keep the larger ones competitive since there is always the potential for entry into world trading. As for government controls, and the limits they can enforce against market abuse, 1975–76 scandals associated with grain handling at US Gulf ports are a good case in point. Government regulation to correct and prevent such abuses, and the ever-present threat of government intervention, should add to the integrity and competitive environment for grain trading.

Grain-trading firms enjoyed several very profitable years after 1972. But such profits can be justified on strict economic grounds. Periods of favorable returns are normal in cyclical, high risk industries and in this case the abrupt increase in grain exports raised the demand for the marketing function the traders perform. This raised returns at each marketing stage and thus profits to the major firms. These returns provided the incentive for expanded export capacity which, as it has become available, brought returns back down. Entry into the exporting business requires large, lumpy investments in new physical facilities, such as grain elevators and ships. Further, construction of such facilities is time-consuming. Moreover, extensive market knowledge and a global network of sales offices are necessary for successful international grain operations. The large firms have an accumulation of knowledge, as well as of business contacts and reputations, that serves as a deterrent to new entrants. In these respects, they have an advantage over potential competitors (a degree of control) but it is over but a very small fraction—around five percent—of all grain consumed in the world. The few majors may dominate the market for grain-trading skills, but that is quite different from controlling the international market, let alone the pricing or trading patterns found around the world. If there were any evidence of collusion among the majors, the case for domination by the trading firms would be much stronger.

Evaluation and conclusion

How well does the international grain market perform? My tentative answer is, "favorably, on balance." However, the question cannot be answered easily or conclusively, and an evaluation from almost any viewpoint would be subject to change over time.

Compared to the ideal global market, some recent trends are discouraging. The tendency toward bilateralism may lead to elements of separation in the international market, over and above the separation of national units prevalent in the current total pattern of world grain production and distribution. With respect to dominance, the USSR's huge purchases and its buying procedures have had obvious adverse consequences. However, Russian purchases have been regularized to a degree and their destabilizing activity is being gradually corrected, albeit at the cost of bilateral separation in the international market. Beyond the USSR, dominance does not appear to be a factor. In terms of open-pricing, information on grain transactions and on likely production is more open and easily acquired than for most other international transactions, mainly due to an active futures market and to improved information gathering and dissemination. However, the provision of more information on sales would be an improvement. The mandatory export-commitment reporting system instituted by the United States in 1974 was an advance, although early reports were difficult to interpret and gave misleading signals. This could occur again, but it should not. A statistical series on *export* prices (including those in negotiated transactions) for wheat, corn and soybeans is needed.

The role of the grain trading firms in the international food system is frequently misunderstood. Their behavior should be evaluated in relation to how well they perform the functions associated with *marketing* grain. Are they performed at low cost? Do bottlenecks develop that cause delays, spoilage or waste? Is the current marketing system flexible and responsive to unforeseen developments and shifting needs?

The criticism that the major grain trading firms determine the international distribution of food seems, as I argued above, very dubious. But if they do not, then who does? My answer is that no single entity does. Final distribution results from complex interactions. Ability and willingness to pay has much to do with final distribution and consumption. This is modified by concessional national and international food-aid distribution. The criticism that LDCs are shortchanged by the market system is true in the sense that they are poor, and if they do not receive assistance, they consume less food per capita because of this fact. From an equity standpoint, the international grain system has responded positively to the growing import needs of LDCs. During the 1971–1974 period, LDCs imported 75 percent of their grain from industrialized countries, compared with only 67 percent in 1966–70. They paid higher prices to be sure, but the profits that resulted sparked further production, and this led to the turnaround by 1977 resulting in lower grain prices and easier credit for LDC grain imports. While there was increased provision of grain to LDCs, LDCs have also become more dependent on the industrialized nations to meet their food needs.

As regards the role of the United States, the performance of the international grain market analyzed here was predicated upon the continued inclusion of the US market as a subset. Not only because of its size but also because the domestic US grain market is highly competitive (i.e., it meets the separation, domination and open-pricing properties), its conduct and regulation are major determinants of performance in the international grain market. Moreover, US policy, which enables its domestic market to be essentially fully integrated with the international market, provides, in effect, derivative and collective benefits to all those served by the current international market.

This extends to institutional arrangements within the United States. For instance, the US grain futures markets, by providing a mechanism for hedging (i.e., using futures markets to reduce price risks associated with production, processing and distributing commodities) and for competitive price discovery for the domestic market, also provide the same economic functions for the international grain market. US regulation, in this case designed to enhance the market system by fostering the economic openness and reliability of futures trading, becomes international regulation since there is no significant futures trading in grains outside the United States. Unless other futures markets develop, making regulation of US markets an international function instead of a national function would add nothing to performance and might decrease the reliability of regulation, given the capacity of formal international bodies to enforce regulation.

The legislation enacted by Congress in 1976 to increase federal supervision of inspection and weighing of grain moving into export channels is another example of US regulation with potentially beneficial effects in the international market. Relatively formalized arbitration procedures for resolving domestic and international disputes are a form of self-regulation by the grain trade that appears to have worked reasonably well. For instance, defaults on international sales, such as those by Korea and China in 1975, have been settled to the satisfaction of the grain trading firms. In general, any regulation which improves performance of these criteria in US domestic markets will have secondary benefits by also advancing international market performance, subject to the proviso that US policy permits continued integration between its own market and the international market.

A basic premise of my analysis is that markets which are integrated (free of domination and provide adequate information) will serve the three broad goals of efficiency, stability and equity. Recall that the world food system is made up of many national producers and consumers, joined in separate markets for numerous food commodities. In general, improvements that would integrate these national markets to a greater extent would improve the system's performance, at least with respect to efficiency and stability. However, to reduce regulations which separate markets and thus encourage freer trade would require major institutional and political changes. Little in food diplomacy or multilateral organization presently suggests that much change is likely. In the meantime, international flows of food, reflecting residual supply and demand, occur primarily through conventional markets. Markets perform best when they are fully informed, when regulation that exists is stable and durable rather than discretionary (or *ad hoc*) and sporadic, and when pricing mechanisms are open and public.

An alleged deficiency of current international food markets is their instability as evidenced by price volatility, and insecurity, manifested in the drop in consumption experienced by people in some poor importing countries during 1973–75. A regulatory way to deal with this deficiency is to enforce stability on the entire market through new international arrangements. This entails increased regulation and new transfer mechanisms and is discussed elsewhere in this volume (see the essays by Austin and by Hopkins and Puchala). An alternative to international regulation which imposes marketwide price stability is to create mechanisms which permit individual nations to stabilize their respective situations without imposing stability on the entire system (see the essay by Johnson).

The distinction between marketwide stability and providing mechanisms for individual market participants to reduce the effects caused by it is an important one. Organized commodity futures markets provide such a mechanism. In commodities where there is a viable futures market, private firms routinely are able to deal with price instability on an individual basis. More firms have started utilizing the futures market during the 1970s and foreign government agencies recently have begun to recognize this possibility. Producers of commodities can adopt marketing strategies that reduce the variability of revenues from their commodities, although such strategies normally would also reduce the chances for exceptionally large revenues as well as for exceptionally low revenues. Likewise, consumers of food commodities can adopt purchasing strategies that reduce the variability of their expenditures for the commodity. Like producers, consumers would find their expenditures more stable from year to year, but in some years they would be disadvantaged as compared with simply buying on the open market while in other years their costs would be lower. For both producers and consumers, viable futures markets afford individual market participants a way to alleviate instability arising from fluctuating market prices.

But US futures markets as presently organized have limitations. For some food commodities (e.g., rice) viable futures markets simply do not exist; for others the current contracts are not suitable for trading commodities produced and consumed outside the United States. Also, futures markets have a connotation of being "private" rather than public entities, which is contrary to the ideological and regulatory stances of many national governments. Nevertheless, the distinction between programs to impose marketwide stability with their attendant costs and the development of institutional mechanisms is a concept worth pursuing.

When current formalized futures markets do not provide this mechanism, it may be feasible for governments to cooperate in establishing mechanisms that would give producing and consuming nations more flexibility and choice in the forward pricing of their food imports and exports. Nations which are now locked into taking the going "spot price" when their crop is ready for market might be able to price separately on some moving average basis throughout the year. Nations which now believe they are locked into pricing import needs under a uniform consumption pattern (thereby facing uncertain foreign exchange requirements for the year ahead) might be able to lock-in their food import costs (at a satisfactory price) a year in advance. To a major extent, such options are already available and probably are quite widely utilized. However, if the US, in collaboration with other states, increased governmental supervision to make them more credible, this could enhance their use and provide an alternative based on greater rather than less reliance on markets.

Effective markets diffuse economic power. In so doing they prevent states or firms from gaining a dominant position by which they could reap unfair advantages. Public markets such as futures markets, in particular, minimize the effect of "private" information or control over a large share of what is traded by one firm or country and thereby provide better signals to all market participants. As such, they serve the social goals of efficiency and stability. No market can insure that poor people will always have adequate nourishment because that is a general problem of income distribution and one that is not improved by moving further from the features of effective markets. In short, a move toward a more global market would not necessarily serve the goal of equity, but neither would it harm it. Most assuredly it would enhance efficiency, price stability and security of access.

6

World Hunger:
A Structural Approach

Cheryl Christensen

Chronic hunger is rooted in poverty and radically unequal distributions of income and assets, within and across countries. In market or quasi-market systems, the distribution of income and assets structures both food consumption patterns and food production systems. Radical inequality leads to structures which make it difficult to eliminate hunger, both because they increase the quantity of food needed to do so and because they support production structures in which the poor are "marginalized." The effect of radical inequality is to severely limit the usefulness of "market mechanisms" as efficient instruments for reducing hunger. Marginal adjustments of existing food markets are unlikely to make any real progress in ending chronic hunger. Broadly based development and/or changes in the structuring mechanisms supported by market economies are necessary.

In many parts of the world, hunger is pervasive and chronic, persisting even when weather is good and global agricultural production is adequate. Those who are undernourished in "normal" times are overwhelmingly the poor in the "developing market economies" of Asia, Africa, Latin America and the Near East.[1] For these people hunger is fundamentally a reflection of poverty embedded in unequal distributions of wealth, income and power within their societies and among nations.[2] The tight link between hunger and poverty is widely acknowledged; it is spelled out in James Austin's essay, and it is the starting point of the analysis below. It is not yet clearly understood that the hunger-poverty linkage under conditions of radical inequality has important implications for attempts to define and solve "world food

Cheryl Christensen is Assistant Professor of Political Science at the University of Maryland.

[1] 94 percent of the people with insufficient calorie or protein intake lived in the developing countries of Asia (excluding the planned economies), Africa, the Middle East, and Latin America. See the UN *Preliminary Assessment of the World Situation* (Rome, 1974).

[2] Cf. National Academy of Sciences (Committee on World Food), *Population and Food: Critical Issues* (Washington D.C.: 1975) which stresses the role of economic and political variables, as do most of the articles in the special food issue of *Scientific American* (September, 1976). Francis Moore Lappe and Joseph Collins present an argument for the primacy of economic and political relations in establishing the

problems.'' In particular, inequalities in income and wealth tend to negate the effectiveness of so-called ''market'' solutions to hunger—not necessarily because of malevolence, but due to the logic and laws of the market itself. The thrust of this essay is to explain the shortcomings of conventional market-oriented analyses of food problems and related prescriptions for solution.

In one important way, hunger is quite different from the other ''world food problems'' discussed in the introduction to this volume.[3] It can be argued that global food shortages (defined as shortages vis à vis international effective demand), price instability and import crises are relatively new phenomena in the postwar global food system. Their recent occurrence may in fact signal fundamental changes in that system or in the regime that governs it, as Hopkins and Puchala suggest. On the other hand, there is certainly nothing new about hunger and poverty in the less developed countries (LDCs). Widespread, chronic hunger in the Third World characterized the postwar global food system even at the height of the ''surplus era.''[4]

Alleviating such hunger calls for measures that go beyond returning the world food system to its pre-1972 status. While market shortages, import crises and price instability certainly hold potential for exacerbating hunger, it is difficult to argue (as Seevers appears to in his essay), that ''stabilizing'' or ''normalizing'' the international food system on pre-1972 terms would significantly reduce it. To understand why, it is necessary to go beyond conventional analyses of the supply and demand for food, and examine the structure of food production and consumption patterns.

The argument of this essay is that radical inequality of income and wealth is reflected directly in the structure of food consumption and production, both nation-

---

poverty which produces hunger in ''Food Self-Reliance'' (mimeo), Institute for Food and Development Studies, 1975, and in their book, *Food First: Beyond the Myth of Scarcity* (Boston: Houghton-Mifflin, 1977). Keith Griffin presents links between poverty and socio-economic structures in his books, *The Political Economy of Agrarian Change* (Cambridge, Mass.: Harvard University Press, 1974) and *Land Concentration and Rural Poverty* (New York: Holmes and Meier, 1976). Radha Sinha, *Food and Poverty* (New York: Holmes and Meier, 1976), explores both issues jointly. The Bariloche model attempts to demonstrate some alternate economic structures, capable of meeting minimal food needs, when more egalitarian distributions of wealth are posited. See Amilcar O. Herrera, et al., *Catastrophe or New Society? A Latin American World Model* (Ottawa, Canada: International Development Research Centre, nd).

[3]The problems, in order of discussion, are global food shortages, instability, food imports by LDCs, low productivity and poverty, and malnutrition. See the introduction to this volume by Raymond Hopkins and Donald Puchala.

[4]Through most of the post-war period, until 1972, food supplies were generally in excess both of effective international demand and global ''reserve requirements.'' Prices for grains were extremely stable, and international prices were below the support prices for American agriculture—requiring export subsidies through most of the 1950s and 1960s. Importers were advantaged, both by concessional sales (primarily for LDCs) and by the competition among major exporting countries in offering attractive credit. For a discussion of the problems of coordinating action to avoid further depressing prices and prohibiting ''unfair'' market development efforts, see Robert L. Bard, *Food Aid and International Agricultural Trade: A Study in Legal and Administrative Control* (Lexington, Mass: Lexington Books, 1972).

ally and internationally. That is, income and wealth distribution explain the functioning of the global food system in a rather fundamental way. Moreover, the effects of inequality limit severely the capability of market or quasi-market economies to eliminate or even significantly reduce world hunger. The essay will argue that *if* reducing hunger (within the shortest possible time given resource constraints) is a primary policy goal, market mechanisms are inefficient ways of achieving this outcome. Moreover, a global food system which simply stabilizes the inadequate consumption of the past would not, in any real sense, provide the undernourished with food security. Finally, there are implications from this argument for wider issues of development strategy, technology choice and basic human needs. Concluding sections will examine some of these.

Hunger and poverty

The relationship between hunger and poverty has been apparent for some time in micro studies of consumption and case studies of famine.[5] However, it was only recently that an attempt was made explicitly to consider income distribution within countries in making aggregate estimates of global undernutrition.[6] In their pathbreaking study, Reutlinger and Selowsky estimated that in 1975 895 million people (over 40 percent of the population of the developing world) fell short of minimal daily caloric requirements by 250 calories or more; some 1.3 billion people (two-thirds of the population of the developing world) were to some extent undernourished.[7] Latin America and the Middle East fared best, with about one-third of the population undernourished, while in Africa 60 percent of the population had inadequate caloric consumption, and in Asia over 80 percent of the population were underfed.[8]

Hunger on such a scale should provoke a rethinking of the appropriateness of the criteria for "food security" and "efficiency" suggested in the discussion of global food markets. In his essay in this volume, Seevers suggests that food stability and security would be achieved "when no significant group of people is threatened with reduced food supplies."[9] But is this a sufficient definition when we know that

[5]See, for example, F. James Levinson, *Morinda: An Economic Analysis of Malnutrition Among Children in Rural India* (Cambridge, Mass: International Nutrition Policy Series, 1974), which also provides some discussion of the nutrition literature. For a good case study of the economic and political dimensions of one particular famine, see R. Robbins, *Famine in Russia 1891–92* (New York: Columbia University Press, 1975).

[6]Shlomo Reutlinger and Marcelo Selowsky, *Malnutrition and Poverty: Magnitude and Policy Options* (Baltimore: Johns Hopkins for the World Bank, 1976).

[7]Reutlinger and Selowsky project 1975 levels from a 1965 data base. The estimate in the text assumes a calorie income elasticity of 0.15, and the following rates of annual per capita growth in income (operating over the 1965–75 period): Latin America—3 percent, Asia—2 percent, Middle East—6 percent, and Africa—2 percent. Cf. pp. 26–32.

[8]Ibid. pp. 30–1. For a fuller discussion of undernutrition, see Austin's essay in this volume.

[9]Seevers, in this volume.

in the recent past millions of people were chronically hungry? Minimal world food security, as the term is used here, implies that no significant group of people consumes too little food to meet basic nutritional needs, and that global consumption patterns are sustainable over most weather and price fluctuations.[10] This implies either that price gyrations are not excessive or that mechanisms exist to sustain basic consumption when prices rise. Similarly, sensitivity to the pervasiveness of undernutrition suggests the need to examine more carefully the domain of standard definitions of "efficient" food systems. Conventionally, *efficiency* implies that "the production of food and its distribution to ultimate consumers be accomplished with the least possible use of resources."[11] This assumes, of course, that consumers in a market context have sufficient resources to purchase desired goods or services. However, when a significant portion of the population is too poor to purchase enough to meet nutritional needs, technical market efficiency is too narrow a concept upon which to base discussions of alternative food systems. Hence, I suggest a broader concept of a socially efficient food system, one in which the production and distribution of (at least basic staple) food to a total population is accomplished with the smallest possible use of resources.

The links between poverty and undernutrition (also discussed in Austin's essay) are examined in a growing literature, and will only be summarized here.[12] For the rural population in LDCs, in a position to grow food directly, the ability to produce adequate quantities of food depends on the amount and quality of land available, the availability and use of yield-increasing inputs, agricultural practices, and of course, the number of people who must be supported by the available natural, economic, and human resources. Hunger in rural areas stems either from underproduction or from farmers' inabilities to retain proportions of their harvests large enough adequately to feed their families, or both. As often as not these constraints on rural production and consumption continue because farmers are poor and consequently powerless in their societies. In many instances, access to capital

---

[10]The literature on reserves suggests the meaning of "over most weather and price fluctuations." Based upon historical patterns of shortfall (by implication in the present system price increases), one can calculate the quantity of grain needed to cover some desired percentage of deviation from trend. Many people writing on reserves argue for coverage of about 95 percent. See, for example, David Easton, W. Scott Steele, Jared L. Cohen, and Charles S. ReVelle, "A Method to Size World Grain Reserves: Initial Results," in *Analysis of Grain Reserves,* (Washington, D.C., USDA/ERS, August, 1976). The grain could be physically stored (e.g., standard reserve proposals) or come from changes in the consumption of wealthier customers (e.g., the reallocation of grain from livestock sectors of market-oriented exporters in 1973/4). Mechanisms for insuring the transfer can include price (with import insurance and subsidization for poorer LDCs) or pre-established release rules. See D. Gale Johnson and Daniel Sumner, "An Optimization Approach to Grain Reverves for Developing Countries" in *Analysis of Grain Reserves,* pp. 56–76.

[11]Seevers, in this volume.

[12]For a general discussion of the factors affecting nutritional adequacy, see Levinson, especially pp. 1–12. Griffin, *Political Economy,* discusses the general economic factors affecting poverty and production in rural areas. Recognition of underemployment (rural and urban) as a basic cause of hunger, albeit from a different perspective, is found in John Mellor, *The New Economics of Growth* (Ithaca, N.Y.: Cornell University Press, 1976). A discussion of the obstacles to helping the bottom 40 percent in agricultural projects is found in Uma Lele, *Design for Rural Development* (Baltimore: Johns Hopkins for the World Bank, 1975).

and other yield-increasing inputs mirrors rural economic and political hierarchies, making it more difficult for smaller, poorer farmers to increase their production. Whether rural producers can directly consume the food they produce depends on wider social, economic and political arrangements. These include land tenure and land use policies, as well as state taxation and agricultural procurement policies. Sharecropping or tenancy arrangements may require a farmer to give up a substantial portion of the food that he grows, irrespective of whether or not the family has enough food. Land oriented toward the production of export crops (e.g., cocoa, coffee, tea, sugar, oilseeds, rubber, cotton, tropical fruits) may limit the ability to grow food for local consumption on prime agricultural land.[13] Taxation policies may require small farmers to give up part of their produce directly or sell it to obtain cash for taxes, while government procurement policies may require farmers to market a certain portion of their crop through government-established marketing agencies at unattractive prices.[14] Less discussed than population growth, agricultural technologies and inputs, these wider socio-political factors may interact with them and constitute serious, immediate causes of hunger.

When people are not in a position to grow their own food, what and how much they eat depends primarily on their income (generally their wage rate and whether they are employed), the price of food, and the facilities through which food is transported to them. Poor people, rural or urban, who depend on wages often have the most acute nutritional problems.[15] These people, like rural producers, find their ability to get enough to eat conditioned by wider social, economic and political factors. If a country is following a capital intensive development program during a period of rapid population growth, unemployment or underemployment is likely. This implies that many people may not have enough purchasing power to meet the nutritional needs of themselves and their families. As critical, but more subtle, is the way in which a skewed income distribution structures food consumption and food processing and marketing over time.

Recognizing hunger as a reflection of poverty, and hence of the level and distribution of wealth within countries, has important implications for accepted judgments about the role increased food production can play in alleviating chronic hunger. The bulk of the literature on world food problems and indeed most of the

[13]Lele, ibid., pp. 28–32, discusses situations in which greater emphasis on export production (without increases in the efficiency of food production) leads to decreased local food supplies. A sharper, more polemical, criticism is contained in Robert J. Ledogar, *Hungry for Profits: US Food and Drug Multinationals in Latin America* (New York: International Documentation, 1976).

[14]For a discussion of the possible consequences of pricing and marketing policies on production, see US Department of State, Agency for International Development, *Providing Economic Incentives to Farmers: Increases in Food Production in Developing Countries,* a Report to the Congress by the Comptroller General of the United States (Washington, D.C.: Government Printing Office, May 13, 1976). For a general discussion of disincentive producing policies in LDCs, see Government Accounting Office (GAO), *Disincentives to Agricultural Production* (Washington, D.C.: US Government Printing Office, 1976).

[15]Cf. the analysis of Hollis Chenery et al., *Redistribution With Growth* (Oxford: Oxford University Press for the World Bank and the Institute for Development Studies, 1974), esp. pp. 113–156.

analysis offered in this volume emphasize the need to increase food production as rapidly as possible (especially in ''food deficit'' LDCs), with the tacit or explicit assumption that increased production will benefit the hungry.[16] Only a few scholars have challenged the benevolence of this emphasis on production, arguing that *if* processes for increasing food production further impoverish the already under-nourished poor, more aggregate production may lead to increased hunger.[17] Yet the clear implication of even a brief analysis of the position of the poor in wider economic and political structures suggests that greater impoverishment as a result of efforts to rapidly increase production is a real possibility. *Analyses of world hunger, therefore, should deal simultaneously with questions of how to increase food production and questions of how to increase the consumption of the undernourished poor.*

The development literature offers three general perspectives which may be adapted to address production and consumption issues together. First, the *market* approach suggests that food production and the consumption of the undernourished poor are to a significant extent separable concerns. The task of an efficient food system is to produce at minimum cost for the market. The problem of chronic hunger is one of market expansion, thus increasing the ability of the poor to operate within the market environment. Increased purchasing power for the undernourished poor can result either from wider economic growth and development patterns or from public programs to subsidize the consumption of the needy, or both. Whichever path is taken to expand purchasing power, it will be to the benefit of the hungry (as well as the wider society) to have food produced as quickly and efficiently as possible.[18]

A second perspective stresses incremental, *joint maximization* of the increases in food production and increases in the consumption of the undernourished.[19] This

---

[16]For a perspective that is pessimistic about the possibility of such a strategy, see Lester Brown and Erik Eckholm, *By Bread Alone* (New York: Praeger, 1975) and Erik Eckholm, *Losing Ground* (New York: Norton, 1976). The focus on production is pervasive in the policy orientation of food-oriented agencies. See, for example, Economic Research Service, US Department of Agriculture, *The World Food Situation and Prospects to 1985,* FAER #98 (Washington, D.C., December, 1974) and International Food Policy Research Institute (IFPRI), *Meeting Food Needs in the Developing World: The Location and Magnitude of the Task in the Next Decade* (Washington, D.C.: IFPRI, February, 1976).

[17]Cf. Lappe and Collins, *Food First* and Ledogar, *Hungry for Profits.*

[18]This is essentially the position taken by Mellor, who differs from advocates of a capital-intensive, industrialization-oriented development strategy in his emphasis on labor-intensive production and agriculture as a ''leading sector,'' but nonetheless argues that deep problems in the rural areas cannot be solved in the agricultural *production* sector. Hence, he argues for a big push toward increasing production (to the benefit of large and medium size farmers) and a labor-intensive attempt to meet their new consumption needs, thus creating employment for the poor. This is, at root, a new ''trickle down'' theory which relies on changes in other sectors to alleviate undernutrition and poverty.

[19]For discussion see E. F. Schumacher, *Small is Beautiful: Economics As If People Mattered* (New York: Harper and Row, 1973). This is basically the position implied by the emphasis current in the World Bank on assisting the ''bottom 40 percent,'' as presented in Chenery et al. A review of this literature is presented by Harry T. Oshima, ''New Directions in Development Strategies,'' *Economic Development and Cultural Change* 25:3 (April, 1977) pp. 555–77.

perspective stresses the possibility that certain production decisions (e.g., selective strategies which allocate resources disproportionately to regions or producers with greatest immediate production potential) may increase both the costs of providing food to the poor (e.g., marketing, delivery, subsidization) and the number of hungry poor requiring such assistance (e.g., *via* dislocation from land, less demand for relatively unskilled labor). Hence, social efficiency will be improved if production strategies are devised which place a greater quantity of *new* food production in the hands of the undernourished, even if this implies a smaller increment of new production or a slower rate of growth in overall production.

The third perspective stresses the need for significant *structural change* prior to attempts to increase food production. There are strategies for increasing production compatible with a normative commitment to meeting basic food needs, but they are possible only after significant changes have been made in existing economic and political structures, including patterns of land ownership, wealth concentration, consumption patterns, and political power. The claim is that existing structures act as impediments to *both* greater productivity and minimal food security.[20] Structural changes open new production frontiers; changes in political interests and institutions make possible a readjustment of consumption patterns which relate more directly to the needs of the undernourished. Structural change is thus a prerequisite for attempts to increase food production not only because unreformed structures may limit the application of improved techniques, but more importantly because greater production will generate a wide range of "perverse effects"—including greater relative and absolute impoverishment of economically marginal groups, more polarized structures for the generation and control of wealth, and reinforced links between economic elites and political control.[21]

These alternative perspectives raise a number of salient questions, which will be examined in the next sections of the paper. First, is the problem of chronic undernutrition basically a problem of market expansion? Second, if changes in either consumption or production structures are necessary to provide minimal food security, can such changes be made as incremental adjustments in *growth* patterns, or must such changes redistribute existing consumption or production inputs? Third, can more optimal uses of resources (with respect to the criteria of minimal food security and socially efficient food systems) be achieved by changing existing structures to open new production or consumption frontiers? Finally, to what extent would major changes in structure imply changes in, or disengagement from, portions of the global food system?

---

[20]This is the claim of Lappe and Collins, and is discussed sympathetically in Griffin. Especially regarding land reform, authors unwilling to call for a thorough-going restructuring of society have argued for change in rural land-holding patterns. Cf., for example, Anthony Y. Koo, "An Economic Justification for Land Reformism," *Economic Development and Cultural Change* 25:3 (April, 1977), 523–38.

[21]See, for example, the discussion of India's adoption of high yielding varieties in F. R. Frankel, *India's Green Revolution: Economic Gains and Political Costs* (Princeton: Princeton University Press, 1971).

Income inequality and the structure of food consumption

Agricultural economists recognize two general relationships between the level of income and food consumption patterns. The first, Engles' Law, is that the portion of income spent on food falls as per capita income rises.[22] For all but the severely undernourished poor, the aggregate income elasticity of demand for food is less than 1, and the elasticity falls as income rises. Engles' Law is simple, but has important implications. First, allocating the same quantity of money to rich or poor people will have different economic consequences. Allocating it to the poor means that a greater share of the money will be spent for food. Less will then be used to purchase industrial goods or services. In addition, agricultural economists have reasoned that increases in the income of the poor would stimulate inflation unless there were substantial growth in per capita food production. Hence, it has been argued that mediocre food production is a serious constraint to income redistribution, or even differential allocation of new income growth, unless extra-market steps are taken to affect consumption patterns.[23] Furthermore, because a greater share of their income is spent for food, the poor are more vulnerable to real increases in food prices.[24] They will suffer in times of higher prices because only a relatively small share of their relatively small incomes can be reallocated to "compete" for food in the market. Third, and by contrast, very rapidly increasing production, *in the context of a market composed of relatively wealthy consumers,* may generate "surplus" and downward pressure on prices. This has been the experience of the US vis à vis its domestic market for the last fifty years. If prices fall below the cost of production, food production will, *ceteris paribus,* decline even though potential demand for it, among poor people, exists.

The second general principle to note is that changes in income produce changes in the kinds of food which compose an individual's diet. In general, increasing income produces a shift away from the direct consumption of grains and starchy staples toward the consumption of animal protein (dairy products, eggs, poultry and meat), fruits and vegetables.[25] Naturally, the composition of consumption will be different for high and low income individuals. Consequently, the most "profitable" items of production will be different given different distributions of income. As income rises, for example, it may be much more profitable to use grain to feed cattle and sell the meat to an emerging group of wealthier consumers than it would be to try to "capture" a greater share of the market for direct grain consumption by poorer consumers. At still higher income levels, greatest profit will be made in

[22]John Mellor, *The Economics of Agricultural Development* (Ithaca, N.Y.: Cornell University Press, 1966), pp. 57–66.

[23]Mellor, *New Economics,* reviews the literature on this topic.

[24]See Lyle Schertz, "World Food Prices and the Poor," *Foreign Affairs* 52:3 (April, 1974), 511–37.

[25]For detailed descriptions of the consumption patterns for most LDCs, making this pattern clear, see the food balance sheets in FAO, *Agricultural Commodity Projections, 1970–1980,* volume II, pp. 85–407.

providing convenience and diversity, as is presently the case for the US domestic food market.[26]

These two principles, taken together, suggest ways in which income distribution will be reflected in the structure of societal consumption patterns. An income distribution skewed enough to exclude a significant portion of the population from the market may result in quite different ''price signals'' from those of a market which includes the entire population on a more egalitarian basis. Shifts away from using staples for direct human consumption will occur too early (before most basic consumption needs have been met) partly because of the greater purchasing power of wealthier consumers and partly because the price at which grain could be purchased for direct consumption by the poor may be too low to make its production profitable. As will be demonstrated shortly, this effect is important within developing countries. But it is equally dramatic internationally, since the bulk of international food transactions occur to provide greater quality, diversity or convenience to people whose diets are clearly above basic minimal nutritional requirements.

What this line of reasoning points to is that without significant changes in income distribution in underdeveloped areas, it is unlikely that unaided market forces will make more than token reductions in undernutrition. Rather dramatically, but quite logically, Reutlinger and Selowsky show that if per capita income grows at roughly the same rate as in the past two decades, and food production expands to meet the growth in effective demand (at constant real prices), there will be virtually no change in the portion of the population undernourished in LDCs over the next decade.[27] Furthermore, because they assumed that all groups would have equal shares of income growth, and that all groups would experience the average rate of population growth, this scenario is probably too optimistic to constitute a forecast. It would be a fairer test of the results of a policy which *equally distributed new growth,* something which numerous studies indicate is highly unlikely in the next decade.[28]

The portion of the population undernourished remains relatively constant primarily because the increments to the income of the poor implied by even this optimistic extension of historical patterns are too small to make dramatic changes in the availability of food. Even so, production constraints appear. Having enough food to meet even this limited increase in effective demand would require annual increases in per capita food production between 0.2 percent and 0.5 percent.[29] At

[26]In 1975, over 65 percent of consumer expenditures on food were accounted for by the processing and marketing of foods. USDA, *Handbook of Agricultural Charts,* Agricultural Handbook #504, October, 1976, p. 30.

[27]Reutlinger and Selowsky, pp. 28–31.

[28]There are now numerous indications that certainly greater inequality, and perhaps absolute declines in living standards, are the consequences development has for the poorer people in LDCs. Cf. Irma Adelman and Cynthia Morris, *Economic Growth and Social Equity in Developing Countries* (Stanford: Stanford University Press, 1973), Felix Paukert, ''Income Distribution at Different Levels of Development'' in *International Labour Review* (Aug-Sept. 1973), Keith Griffin and Azizur, ''Rural Poverty: Trends and Explanation'' (mimeo) and Griffin's *Poverty and Landlessness in Rural Asia* (New York: Universe, 1976).

[29]Reutlinger and Selowsky, pp. 26–9.

the global level, there is clearly no difficulty in exceeding these growth rates, if historical growth trends are sustained. During the 1960s, world production grew by an average of 3 percent per year while population grew by an average of 2 percent, leaving an average per capita increase in food production of 1 percent.[30] However, the progress was uneven. Developed countries increased per capita production by an average of 1.5 percent per year (even though major grain exporters were trying to curtail production) while the LDCs as a group achieved a 0.4 percent increase. Notably, over 40 percent of the population of the less developed countries lived in nations whose recent production record (1972–4) could not have supported even the minimal increase in effective demand hypothesized by Reutlinger and Selowsky.[31]

In addition to providing inadequate additional income to enable the poor to meet minimal nutritional needs, equal distribution of new growth leaves the market-structuring role of wealthier consumers untouched. This is of crucial importance. New purchasing power, spread equally across all income groups, not only makes it possible for the undernourished to purchase more food, but it also enables people with nutritionally adequate diets to shift away from the direct consumption of grain toward meat, poultry and dairy products. Since producing these products requires substantial input of grain, wealthier people consume larger quantities of grain indirectly,[32] and the diet shift of wealthier consumers means that more food resources will be used to meet their consumption preferences. Changing consumption patterns by adequately nourished people may divert a disproportionate share of new food resources to upgrading already adequate diets, and structure production toward providing ''luxury'' commodities rather than expanding the supply of staple foods.

An attempt was made to estimate the effect a skewed income distribution supporting different dietary patterns would have on the allocation of the new grain produced in response to the growth pattern projected by Reutlinger and Selowksy. The allocation of grain to different income groups was estimated on the basis of direct and indirect consumption, with indirect consumption reflecting only grain used to produce meat.[33] As Table 1 shows, growth in the context of an unequal distribution of income and associated dietary preferences did not allocate new food resources effectively to the needy. In both the Middle East and Latin America, adequately nourished people accounted for most new consumption, although undernourished people were the bulk of the population. Latin America was a particularly stark case, for the 46 percent of the population undernourished in the base year

[30]USDA/ERS, World Food, p. 17.

[31]See the definition of food production and the statistical evidence in FAO, *The State of Food and Agriculture, 1975* (Rome, 1976), p.x.

[32]For the quantities of grain required to produce a pound of different kinds of animal protein, see Francis Moore Lappe, *Diet for a Small Planet* (New York: Ballantine for Friends of the Earth, 1973).

[33]USDA, ERS, *Growth in World Demand for Feed Grains Related to Meat and Livestock Products and Human Consumption of Grain* (Washington, D.C.: July, 1970) presents estimates of the grain/meat ratios at different levels of per capita income—essentially reflecting the extent to which livestock are grain fed. These ratios, rather than the current American ratio, were used in estimating the indirect consumption of LDC regions.

consumed only 25 percent of new grain resources; after a decade of such growth, significant undernutrition would persist (36 percent of the population) but the undernourished would get an even smaller share of new grain production. In the Middle East, the undernourished were 63 percent of the population, but received only 29 percent of new grain resources. While their situation improved, even after a decade the undernourished (51 percent of the population) would consume less than their share based on population. The implication is clear. *If market forces were to dictate the allocation of new grain production, most of it would go to feed adequately nourished people.* Undernutrition would persist because of the low purchasing power of the hungry and the market-structuring tastes of the more adequately fed.

Table 1   Percent of new direct and indirect grain consumption accounted for by the undernourished

	FIRST YEAR OF GROWTH		TENTH YEAR OF GROWTH	
Region	*Percent of new grain consumed by the under- nourished*	*Percent of the population undernourished*	*Percent of new grain consumed by the under- nourished*	*Percent of the population undernourished*
Latin America	25 percent	46 percent	16 percent	36 percent
Asia	83 percent	82 percent	84 percent	82 percent
Africa	75 percent	77 percent	76 percent	77 percent
Near East	29 percent	63 percent	40 percent	51 percent

Source: Computed from statistics on income distribution and calorie consumption presented in Reutlinger and Selowsky, *Malnutrition and Poverty,* pp. 28–30, 76 and elasticities and grain/meat ratios presented in USDA, ERS, *Growth in World Demand for Feed Grains Related to Meat and Livestock Products and Human Consumption of Grain* (Washington, DC: July, 1970), p. 113.

As regions, Asia and Africa present a different picture. The bulk of the population in both areas consists of very poor people. For this reason, equal distribution of income growth would generate a distribution of new food resources which allocates most new food to the undernourished. The major problem is that even equal distribution of new income and consumption will not reduce undernutrition at the low per capita growth rates anticipated on the basis of past performance. More growth, in both wealth and food production, is clearly necessary to alleviate chronic hunger.

Unequal growth in the future with lower rates of growth for the economically marginal poor may be a more realistic expectation based on past experience. Indeed, there is growing evidence that the poorest within LDCs may have experienced an absolute decline in their standard of living—implying negative growth. Clearly, uneven distributions of new growth would further reduce the already low portion of new food resources purchased by the poor in Latin America and the Middle East. The result in Africa and Asia would be to encourage a structuring of the food market which would center more heavily on diet upgrading for the adequately nourished, implying greater inequality over time. As Table 2 indicates, a situation in which the incomes of the undernourished grew by one percent per year less than those of adequately nourished people would significantly change the food distribution pattern. The proportion of undernourished people in the total population would remain the same, but their share of new food consumption would be smaller. In Africa, the 77 percent of the population that are undernourished would consume only 62 percent of new food resources after a decade of unequal growth; the undernourished in Asia (82 percent of the population) would consume only 60 percent of new food resources.

Table 2   Portion of the population undernourished after a decade of unequal growth, and their food share

Region	Percent of population undernourished	Percent of new food resources consumed by the undernourished
Asia	82 percent	69 percent
Africa	77 percent	62 percent

Source: Computed from statistics in sources detailed in Table 1.

It could be argued on the basis of this information that addressing chronic hunger is essentially a problem of market expansion, but that historical growth rates were simply too low (or maldistributed) to increase the purchasing power of the poor. This argument deserves closer examination, particularly in light of recent debate about the potential limitations on global food production.

Distributing food directly to the malnourished (and only to the malnourished) would eliminate hunger with the smallest possible expenditure of *food*. While it is certainly unrealistic to expect such a program to operate without substantial ''slippage,'' it is useful to examine the quantity of food it would require to carry out such an effort since this quantity will, in essence, represent the minimum amount of food needed to eliminate world hunger. Reutlinger and Selowsky estimated that 36.5 million metric tons of grain, distributed directly to the malnourished, would achieve minimal food security.[34] This quantity is not small in relation to the production of LDCs. It amounts to 9.1 percent of their 1974 cereal production.[35] In relation to world production, however, the quantity is small—2.7 percent of 1974 world cereal production.

Much larger quantities of grain would be required to end malnutrition if it were to be achieved simply by raising income across the board until the poor could afford to purchase what they need. While such a program of growth would be attractive to those who seek to avoid the disruption inherent in redistributive strategies, it is more

[34]Reutlinger and Selowsky, p. 25.
[35]Production figures are taken from FAO *Production Yearbook,* vol. 28-1 (1974), p. 42.

costly in terms of agricultural resources since increased income for the already adequately nourished will be used, in part, to change consumption patterns. Lyle Schertz estimated that raising income in developing areas across the board to levels which would reduce malnutrition to Latin American proportions would require between 86 and 258 million metric tons of grain.[36] The wide variation reflects alternative assumptions about the grain-intensiveness of livestock production. Sustaining such growth in grain consumption from their own resources would imply increasing LDC cereal production by 22–66 percent. Generating such quantities would involve increasing global grain production by 6.4–19 percent.

The magnitude of these figures suggests some of the problems in present market-oriented approaches to world hunger. On the one hand, as we have seen, incremental increases in the income of poor people (in the context of existing income distributions) will do very little to reduce hunger. On the other hand, greatly increasing the ability of the poor to purchase food (in the context of the established lifestyles of richer consumers) would require extraordinary increases in resources and production to meet the overall demand for food. *If,* as market orientations suggest, the problem is one of expanding the market, *then* doing so through growth and "trickle down," whether large or small, creates serious problems. In such situation, hunger and production choices are not separable.

Wealth inequality and the structure of international food markets

The effects of unequal wealth distributions are not limited to structuring food patterns within developing countries. There are also biases in production and distribution inherent in the international arena. The explanations for these biases lie primarily in historical patterns of economic "specialization," reinforced by present patterns of wealth, consumption and economic control. The purpose of this section is to identify these biases, suggest the reasons for them, and demonstrate their implications for attempts to reduce world hunger.

Throughout the global food system, food transactions occur *primarily* to enhance the diets of already adequately fed people. This includes food transfers from LDCs, which reflect historical specializations in export commodities such as coffee, tea, sugar, cocoa, and newer transactions which essentially involve upgrading the protein in European, Japanese and recently Soviet diets. A large portion of international grain sales flow from developed exporters to developed importers for diet improvement. In the period 1956–60, developing countries imported 32.1 percent of total world grain imports, developed market economies 54.1 percent and centrally planned economies 13.6 percent.[37] Between 1972–6, developing countries imported 30.5 percent of total world grain imports, developed market economies

---

[36]Lyle Schertz, "World Needs: Shall the Hungry Be With Us Always?" in Peter Brown and Henry Shuh, *Food Policy: The Responsibility of the United States in the Life and Death Choices* (New York, Free Press, 1977).
[37]ERS/USDA, *World Food,* p. 20.

44.8 percent, and planned economies, 22.4 percent. During 1972–3, under admittedly unusual circumstances, the USSR's net imports of grain were equal to 88 percent of the imports to all LDCs combined.[38]

For both Western Europe and Japan, the international grain trade no longer supplies staple grains for direct human consumption. Dietary patterns and agricultural policies have shifted enough so that both Japan and the European Community are able to produce their own supply of traditional primary consumption grains.[39] The crucial role of trade now is expanding the variety and protein content of diets, in the latter case by assuring adequate feed for expanding animal protein industries. Here the role of trade is impressive. The European Community imports from the United States almost 60 percent of its protein requirements for animal feed, with additional imports from Canada and Australia. Japan imports nearly 80 percent of its feed requirements.[40] Considering the importance of relatively affluent nations in Europe and Japan as grain importers, and the fact that Soviet and Eastern Europe purchases reflect attempts to provide more meat for citizens' diets, it becomes clear that the thrust of most international grain transfers is to expand and sustain the diets of comparatively wealthy societies.

The agricultural exports of LDCs also flow to relatively wealthy nations to enhance the variety of already adequate diets. To a significant extent, poorer LDCs remain "one crop" or "few crop" economies—exporting agricultural products to wealthier regions as a primary means of earning needed foreign exchange. For fifty LDCs, an agricultural commodity is the leading export, frequently accounting for a third or more of foreign exchange earnings.[41] Because the export pattern of LDCs has been structured by the purchasing power and tastes of wealthier countries (and historically by their political and military power as well), the commodities produced for export are frequently supplements to dietary staples. This has a number of important consequences. First, many export products such as sugar, tea, coffee, cocoa and sisal, have limited nutritional value, and hence cannot be directly "diverted" from the international marketplace to meet pressing domestic needs. Second, there are limited internal markets for most traditional export crops, and larger domestic markets are unlikely to develop until income increases. To the extent that internal markets develop, they are most likely to reflect the tastes of the wealthier portions of the domestic population. Such patterns of export agriculture can easily

[38]Computed from data printout provided by Economic Research Service/Foreign Agricultural Service, United States Department of Agriculture (Sept. 1976).

[39]Indeed, both countries now have "surpluses" in several major commodities—the EC in dairy products and soft wheat, Japan in rice. In part, this reflects Engles' law and decreasing direct cereal consumption. In part, it reflects policies to subsidize agriculture. See OECD, *Agricultural Policy in the European Economic Community* (Paris: OECD, 1974) and OECD, *Agricultural Policy in Japan* (Paris: OECD, 1976).

[40]See the OECD studies on the EEC (p. 34) and on Japan (p. 46).

[41]Computed from David McNicol, *Commodity Agreements and the New International Economic Order*, Social Science Working Paper #144, California Institute of Technology, November, 1976, pp. 52–5.

lead to a sharp and direct tradeoff between foreign exchange earnings (whose general benefit depends on political-economic structures and development plans) and the production of basic foodstuffs.

In many LDCs where there is significant chronic undernutrition, substantial portions of prime agricultural land (and in most instances fertilizer and other modern inputs) are allocated to export production. Table 3 presents data on one facet of this problem—the acreage tradeoff between traditional export sectors and cereal production. As the table indicates, fifteen LDCs devote more land to export crops than to cereals, and another fifteen devote at least one-third of the amount of land devoted to cereals to export crops. Where land and other inputs are plentiful, the impact of export crop production on domestic food production may be minor, as appears to have been the case in instances where export crops were planted on land not needed for food production.[42] However, if population increases and productivity does not rise proportionately, greater production of export crops translates directly into diminished local food supplies.[43] In addition, because export earnings often do not "trickle down" to people whose subsistence cultivation is displaced, the aggregate benefits LDCs allegedly gain from exports do not work to reduce chronic hunger.

It is within the context of international and domestic LDC consumption patterns that the importance of a few grain exporting countries for "global food security" must be assessed. Much attention has been paid to the fact that a relatively small number of countries provide most of the world's grain exports. The American predominance in export markets did not simply occur because other areas of the world could not produce enough basic foodstuffs. On the contrary, it reflects the operation of Engles' Law within the United States, the political reaction to the agricultural imbalances thus produced, and the ways in which the domestic agricultural adjustments of the major grain exporters worked to reinforce traditional export patterns in LDCs.

The greatest increases in agricultural productivity in the United States came when the bulk of the American people were spending a declining share of their income on direct grain consumption. Despite the development of grain-intensive livestock production (e.g., feedlots), the US has produced far more grain than could be consumed, directly or indirectly, by its population. In addition, except for immediate post-war shortages, American grain exports faced an international milieu in which the effective demand for food grew too slowly to absorb US production "surpluses." Agricultural policies were unable to sufficiently decrease production, and there was strong political resistance to allowing too many technologically efficient farmers to go out of business in response to the market's price signals.

[42]Examples of such a "vent for surplus" can be found, e.g., Nigeria and Ghana in early cocoa export development and the Ivory Coast during the 1950s. Cf. S. Berry, *Cocoa, Custom, and Socio-Economic Change in Rural Western Nigeria* (Oxford, 1975) and Samir Amin, *Neo-colonialism in West Africa* (New York: Monthly Review, 1973).
[43]Lele (cited, fn. 12), pp. 28–33.

Table 3 Land devoted to cereal and export crops in major LDC agricultural commodity exporters (1975)

Countries devoting more land to export crops than to cereals

Barbados	sugar	Ghana	cocoa
Belize	sugar	Guinea Bissau	cocoa
Costa Rica	coffee, bananas	Ivory Coast	coffee
Dominican Republic	sugar, coffee, cocoa	Mauritius	sugar
Guadaloupe	sugar	Reunion	sugar
Panama	bananas	Togo	cocoa, coffee
Central African Republic	coffee, cotton	Uganda	cotton, coffee, tea
Gabon	cotton		

Countries devoting one-third or more of cereal acreage to export crops

Brazil	coffee, cotton, sugar, cocoa	Angola	coffee
Colombia	coffee	Cameroon	coffee, cotton
El Salvador	coffee, cotton	Egypt	cotton
Guatemala	coffee, cotton	Liberia	rubber
Haiti	sisal, coffee	Tanzania	cotton, sisal, coffee
Honduras	coffee, bananas	Indonesia	rubber, coffee, sugar, tea, oil, palms, coconut
Nicaragua	cotton, coffee	Sri Lanka	tea
Peru	cotton, coffee, sugar		

Countries with less than one-third of cereal acreage in export crops

Ecuador	bananas	Malawi	tea, tobacco
Mexico	cotton, coffee	Mali	cotton
Burundi	coffee	Rwanda	coffee
Chad	cotton	Sudan	cotton
Ethiopia	coffee	Upper Volta	cotton
Guinea	coffee, bananas	Bangladesh	jute, tea
Kenya	coffee, tea		

Hence export promotion programs, special credit arrangements, market development efforts, and especially concessional transfers became important means of maintaining, and attempting to increase, the American share of world grain exports. While accomplishing this, Americans (and other exporters as well) also accomplished a structuring of international food trade and aid which assigned roles as "producers," "consumers," "sellers," "buyers," "donors" and "recipients" that became relatively immutable over time. Most looked upon this structure as benign, but a few were prompted to ask about constraints that the structure imposed on LDCs while it offered opportunities to Americans.

American efforts to dispose of surplus internationally had several important effects on LDC policy options. First, the efforts tended to lock agricultural commodity exporting LDCs into traditional export patterns. US domestic markets were heavily protected against agricultural imports that would compete with American "surplus" commodities, and with the emergence of the Common Agricultural Policy, the same became true for the European Community. Hence, expanding grain production with a view toward penetrating lucrative markets in developed countries seemed unattractive. For agricultural commodity exporting LDCs, the best chance of access to those markets remained in "traditional export" sectors. Expanding these sectors to increase exchange earnings had the effect of putting LDCs into competition with each other, in products where oversupply was difficult to control, and where there were no beneficial "spillover" effects in domestic nutrition. There were similar problems in attempting to diversify into grain for export to other LDCs. New, poorer exporters would not have been able to compete with the credit terms offered by the United States, and to some extent, Canada and Australia. Indeed, even established third-world exporters, such as Argentina and Thailand, repeatedly claimed that soft US terms were making it difficult for them to maintain their international markets.[44]

Second, American efforts to dispose of agricultural surplus in some cases served as a disincentive to food production for domestic LDC markets. Whether substantial disincentive effects occurred appears to depend primarily on whether concessional food imports were sold on the domestic market in competition with domestic production, or were distributed through special channels to people who would otherwise be unable to enter the market. Colombia, with the open, single market experienced substantial disincentive effects, while India, with its more discriminating Fair Price shops, experienced negligible direct disincentive effects.[45]

[44]Bard (cited, fn. 4), pp. 35–44.

[45]For a discussion of the Colombian case, see L. Dudley and R. J. Sandilands, "The Side Effects of Foreign Aid: The Case of PL 480 Wheat in Colombia" *Economic Development and Cultural Change* 23:1 (January, 1975); 325–36. A good discussion of the general literature on disincentive effects, and an excellent estimation of the disincentive effects in India taking into account the Fair Price shop market is Uma Srivastava, Earl Heady, Keith Rogers and Leo Mayer, *Food Aid and International Economic Growth* (Ames, Iowa: Iowa State University Press, 1975). An attempt to put together case studies and infer the conditions under which disincentive effects occur is Paul Isenman and H. W. Singer, "Food Aid: Disincentive Effects and Their Policy Implications," *Economic Development and Cultural Change* 25:2 (January, 1977): 205–37.

The skewed distribution of income within LDCs, and development policies which depended on low food prices in industrial centers, may have had more important disincentive effects than concessional imports, although the two are clearly not independent.[46]

Third, as Destler has indicated in his essay, American efforts to dispose of surplus abroad were made primarily through Title 1, and as such were often more oriented toward providing general political and economic benefits to governments than they were toward reaching and assisting the undernourished.[47] Local elites could gain revenue through the sale of P.L. 480 commodities in domestic markets and loans or grants of "soft currencies" which the United States received in payment for food imports.[48] Such funds could provide additional revenue for governments faced with serious financial problems, or too unpopular to raise additional revenue domestically. In addition, until 1973, counterpart funds could be used for a variety of purposes, including military expenditures, as was the case in Cambodia and Vietnam. The availability of cheap imports also made it possible for some political leaders to placate important groups within the country. In Indonesia, for example, civil servants and the military were at one time paid in rice rations to insulate them from the effects of inflation.[49] The low prices were necessary if providing food was not to become an intolerable drain on the national budget; imports were used because it was difficult to procure grain domestically at such low prices.

Fourth, American concessional sales contributed to the expansion of private firms involved in marketing, and in the export of American agribusiness technology. Government contracts for overseas delivery of grain (first to Europe, later to LDCs under P.L. 480) provided companies such as Cargill with their first entries into international marketing. In addition, the volume of shipments and flexible rules about swapping different grains of comparable quality between government storage and company inventories helped major grain companies vertically integrate. Finally, because concessional sales were as profitable as commercial sales to private firms, they provided a relatively secure profit source.

The export of American agribusiness technology was facilitated by the Foreign Agricultural Service's program to link government and private interests in an attempt to increase American agricultural exports. Producers, distributors and pro-

---

[46]The effect of a skewed income distribution is in part borne out by the fact that attempts to increase production which are successful often create "local surpluses" which in turn depress production—primarily because the region does not have enough purchasing power and the chance to ship to other areas is inhibited by pricing policies, acquisition policies or transportation facilities. Cf. Lele, pp. 101–15. Under conditions where the export of grain internationally was very unattractive to LDCs, it is likely that the same principle operated at a national level.

[47]Less than 20 percent of total PL 480 shipments 1954–74 were under Title II (nutritionally oriented). *Annual Report*.

[48]For a discussion of the PL 480 program, and detailed description of the options available under Title I sales, see O. H. Goolsby, G. R. Kruer and C. Santmyer, *PL 480 Concessional Sales: History, Procedures, Negotiating and Implementing,* FAER #65 (Washington, D.C.: USDA/ERS, September, 1970).

[49]C. Peter Timmer, "The Political Economy of Rice in Asia: Indonesia." *Food Research Institute Studies* XIV:3 (1975): 197–232.

cessors of agricultural commodities formed non-profit organizations to work with FAS officials in promoting foreign sales. About 40 such market development cooperators work on a regular basis with FAS, including the American Soybean Association, Great Plains Wheat Inc., Western Wheat Associates, and the Egg and Poultry Institute of America.[50] In all, over 1500 cooperatives and 7,000 processors are represented in cooperator organizations. The program provides a way of linking business and government by establishing plans for exporting American agricultural products, often integrating the exports into new business ventures in the foreign country. As USDA notes:

> Contributing to the development of the plan are those people who are concerned with all phases of market development. Included are cooperator staff, both US and foreign nationals, organizations in foreign markets that stand to benefit from successful completion of market development activity, and sometimes members of foreign governments.... Considerable financing of the program comes from the "foreign or third party cooperators" who will benefit from the program.[51]

As will become clearer in later analysis, the FAS cooperator market development programs are important vehicles for transferring American agriculture technology and patterns of production by *developing new kinds of agricultural markets* in which US exports will then be important. These markets, and associated technologies, often are not beneficial to the poorest, chronically undernourished members of LDC societies.

The point here is not to denigrate American farmers or make a scapegoat of the commercial sector. What really comes into question, in light of the foregoing analysis, is the overall effectiveness of food distribution via international market mechanisms when a goal of distribution is to alleviate hunger. The experience with international food transactions suggests that there are very real limits to automatic food "trickle down" once the consumption of wealthier people tapers off and Engles' Law becomes a constraint on additional profitable production. National policies to protect agricultural producers prevented a decline in food production, and resulted in surplus (vis à vis the paying market). This could have supported a massive assault on hunger, but concessional sales were by and large not directed toward meeting the immediate nutritional needs of the hungry. The possibility of export earnings through sales of "complementary" agricultural products to wealthier countries, coupled with internal income distributions which made production of foodstuffs for internal consumption less lucrative, encouraged allocation of land and inputs in LDCs which essentially benefitted consumers in Western industrial societies. This suggests an alternate scenario to the neo-Malthusian vision of physi-

---

[50]Darwin Stolte, "Team Effort Boosts US Farm Exports," *Foreign Agriculture* XIII:21 (May 26, 1975), provides a list of cooperator organizations from which these examples are drawn.
[51]Ibid., p. 8.

cal scarcities of food: misallocation of productive resources which leaves millions chronically undernourished while constraining the revenue of agricultural exporters in developed and less developed countries alike. The impetus to the realization of such a scenario would likely be growing inequality in income distribution within and among societies.

Asset inequality and the structure of food production

Accepting the judgment that increasing food production would be necessary to all but the most radical redistributive programs for consumption, it then becomes important to consider the possible effects different patterns of food production may have on chronic hunger. Not surprisingly, how and where food is produced affect employment and income, and thus help to account for the quantity and quality of food consumption. Ironically, producing *more* food, the *wrong way,* or in the *wrong place,* can cause hunger. Since the chronically hungry in the world are in large part the "bottom 40 percent" in the LDCs, the interest in examining the effects of alternate production systems on chronic undernutrition converges with the growing literature on assessing the implications of different development models. Important among questions in this assessment is the issue of impact upon the poorest people. While the final verdict is by no means in, there is increasing evidence that conventional industrial development models tend to increase income inequality in developing countries, and that in some cases they may produce an absolute decline in the standard of living of the poor. Studies reporting these results point to inequality in the distribution of assets, and therefore of economic opportunities as a major reason for deteriorating standards of living.[52] For this reason, it is important to examine the role that asset inequality may have in structuring food production and causing undernutrition.

Within the framework of market-oriented perspectives, such concerns can be interpreted as queries about factor structures. The existence and competitiveness of markets for factors of agricultural production determine the "price signals" which govern economic decisions about alternative mixes of productive resources. Within agriculture, factor markets affect the allocation of resources, the methods of production adopted, the readiness to innovate, and the distribution of returns. What is significant here is that a variety of studies have found highly imperfect local markets for capital, technological inputs, and land, especially within LDCs. To a notable extent the market is differently structured for different participants, especially for large and small farmers, landlords and tenants. The purpose of this section is to indicate the direction of the bias introduced by such market imperfections, and their

---

[52]Irma Adelman, Cynthia Morris, and Sherman Robinson, "The One-Shot Attack!" *Cerces* 9:5 (Sept-Oct., 1976) pp. 17–20, summarizes findings of studies—including simulation efforts—indicating that attempts to change income distribution without changing asset distribution have relatively little enduring impact.

implications for policies which emphasize increasing production as rapidly as possible within LDCs.[53]

Griffin has argued that inequality in the distribution of land and/or unequal access to credit in rural areas will establish structures in which both small farmers with little access to credit and large farmers with preferential access to capital arrive at combinations of inputs which are not socially optimal.[54] Larger landholders often receive key factors of production at less than their social opportunity cost, reflecting their initial stock of land, easy access to credit, preferential access to infrastructure (e.g., irrigation) and foreign exchange policies biased in favor of mechanization. Small farmers, on the other hand, tend to pay more than the social opportunity cost for land and capital. Allocative inefficiency (in comparison with the socially optimal combination of inputs) results. Because for large landholders land and capital tend to be cheap relative to labor, they adopt techniques of production which maximize their own profit—i.e., those with high land/labor and capital/labor ratios. Such production patterns depress employment opportunities for landless rural laborers, one of the poorest, most undernourished, groups in most LDCs.[55] On the other hand, small farmers adopt techniques with very high labor/land and labor/capital ratios, but because of the small size of their holdings and the restricted capital, this generates little paid employment. This pattern, presented here as an ideal type, explains the widespread finding that small farmers get higher returns per acre of land, but larger farmers have greater production per employee.[56] Where such structures exist, total output could be increased if factors were redistributed.[57]

The distortion of relative factor prices reflects not only physical characteristics (e.g., lack of transportation and communication facilities) but also the political and social structure. Griffin argues from case studies:

> There are many explanations for the high degree of market imperfection in rural areas. Resources are immobile, means of communication are poor, accurate information is scarce. Probably the two most important explanations, however, are government policies which are systematically biased in favor of certain groups, and the monopoly power possessed by the relatively wealthy and prosperous members of the farming community .... Inequalities may persist indefinitely because the local monopolist may be aware of his market power and knows that if he sells land he will drive the price down against himself. Moreover ... the control of land gives the landowner ease of access to other resources as well.[58]

[53]Griffin, *Political Economy*, op. cit., pp. 16–55, develops factor structure analysis much more completely than can be summarized in this paper. The interested reader is referred to this work.
[54]Ibid., pp. 36–37.
[55]Cf. data in Chenery et al., op. cit., pp. 113–35.
[56]For summary treatment of these findings, see L. Reynolds, *Agriculture in Development Theory* (New Haven: Yale University Press, 1975).
[57]Griffin, *Political Economy*, op. cit., pp. 36–37.
[58]Ibid., pp. 17–18, 22.

Where this is the case, structural change is likely to be a prerequisite to even adequate functioning of rural market mechanisms.

The wider social implications of attempts to introduce production-increasing technologies in the context of distorted factor markets depend heavily on the type of technology which is introduced. An ultra-superior technology is one which will increase output for all producers given the relative factor prices they face. Such a technology could be profitably adopted by all producers, although the size of the benefits would vary. A selectively superior technology, on the other hand, is economically profitable to some producers (e.g., those practicing extensive agriculture) but economically irrelevant to others (e.g., those engaging in intensive agriculture). Introducing selectively superior technologies implies that some classes of producers will benefit, while others will gain nothing and over the longer term, may even lose.

Policies which emphasize the need for as rapid an increase in production as possible, then, will have different social consequences depending upon the type of technology available for rapidly increasing production (ultra-superior or selectively superior) and the pattern used to disperse new technologies. With the possible exception of new "intermediate technologies," none of the yield-increasing technologies have been biased in favor of the peasants' and small farmers' mix of relative factor prices.[59] Green Revolution technologies are either ultra-superior or selectively superior in ways which benefit larger landholders. While there is theoretical evidence that the Green Revolution technologies perform as well on small intensively cultivated plots, in practice, strategies for introducing the Green Revolution technology have brought differential benefits. Where new seeds and fertilizer were provided first to large farmers (sometimes for political reasons, sometimes because they were easier to reach and once reached promised greater increases in aggregate production because of their larger holdings) smaller farmers suffered. The greater production in local areas reduced prices, leaving larger farmers better off because of the volume of their marketings, but decreasing the income of smaller farmers who could not make up for lower prices by selling more. Reduced revenue, plus the increased wealth of larger farmers, in some cases led to smaller farmers being displaced from their land, thus increasing land concentration. Eviction of tenant farmers, reduced opportunities for rural employment, and the curtailment of traditional gleaning rights by producers who benefitted from the new technologies also contributed to increased local poverty. In such cases, it appears that the emphasis on *rapid* increases in *aggregate* production, more than an emphasis on production per se or the inherent nature of new technologies, was responsible for eroding the economic well-being of the poor and for increasing hunger.

To take another example, the agribusiness technology developed in the United States, and exported through commercial channels and American market development programs, seems even more genuinely selectively superior. Emphasizing mechanization, production techniques designed to achieve economies of scale at

---

[59]Ibid., pp. 49–50. "Ultra-superior" is Griffin's term.

high initial capitalization costs, and vertical integration, agribusiness techniques frequently cannot be profitably adopted by small operators (as the heavy concentration in American livestock and poultry industries suggests).[60] Yet serious efforts have been made to export these technologies, as a statement by the US Feedgrains Council (working with FAS in the market development program described earlier) indicates:

> ...designs and demonstrates technological systems to boost usage of US feedgrains by overseas livestock and poultry industries. Tailoring these integrated packages to conditions in each respective country, USFGC (US Feedgrains Council) nonetheless emphasizes feeding of US high energy rations. During fiscal 1975, USFGC conducted programs in Austria, Denmark, France, Germany, Greece, Ireland, Italy, Japan, Korea, the Netherlands, Norway, the Philippines, Poland, Portugal, Spain, Switzerland, Taiwan, the United Kingdom, and Yugoslavia.[61]

Because the greatest advances have come in the feedgrains-livestock-poultry nexus—products consumed by relatively affluent consumers more than the chronically undernourished—the adaptation of these technologies may also be selectively advantageous to wealthier consumers.

While the impact of Green Revolution technologies has been widely studied, very little has been written about the impact of new agribusiness technologies.[62] Some of the social implications of their adaptation are suggested by a series of studies (done as training guides for agribusiness students) in the Philippines. In an attempt to reduce imports of processed meat (consumed almost exclusively by the wealthiest 3 percent of the population) the Manila government encouraged experiments with larger ranches, feedlots, and processing plants.[63] The thrust of the attempt makes clear some of the likely social consequences. There is hope that large-scale cattle raising can be integrated with plantation crops—such as sugar cane and pineapple—with wastes from the primary crops being used to supplement animal feed.[64] This would be economically efficient for large plantation holders. On the other hand it would reduce the viability of smaller "backyard producers" who produced 58 percent of national beef production in 1968.

---

[60]See USDA/ERS, *Market Structure of Food Industries,* Marketing Research Report #971 (Washington, D.C., September, 1972).

[61]Stolte (cited. fn. 50), p. 9.

[62]The technology has been criticized for its operation within the United States, e.g., Jim Hightower, *Eat Your Heart Out* (NY: Crown, 1975). Specific examples (generally illustrating negative effects) are found in Ledogar (cited, fn. 13) and in M. Jacobson and C. Lerza, *Food for People Not Profit* (NY: Ballentine, 1975).

[63]P. M. Villegas, "Notes on the Philippine Beef Cattle Industry" in J. D. Drilon (ed.) *Agribusiness Management Resource Materials,* vol. II (Tokyo: Asia Productivity Organization, 1968), pp. 3-25.

[64]Cf. R. X. Barker and N. M. Nyberg, "Coconut-Cattle Enterprises in the Philippines," *Philippine Agriculturist* 52 (1), 49-60.

The larger ranches have been oriented primarily toward supplying demand in more lucrative urban areas (especially greater Manila), and new marketing and processing technologies have given differential advantages to large suppliers, even making possible some vertical integration. For example, the attempt to develop feedlots near the capital, both to produce marbled beef and to serve as feeders to modern processing facilities, is economically profitable only to those able to guarantee a dependable supply of cattle in large enough quantities to make possible the economies of scale upon which feedlots depend.[65] Feedlot operations have relied primarily upon large ranches for their supply of cattle, partly because of the number of cattle they can supply and partly because these ranches can ship enough cattle to make investment in transportation facilities profitable. Similarly, large modern processing facilities, which must have a steady supply of cattle to operate at enough capacity to be profitable, reinforce the advantages of larger ranches,[66] and, of course, exacerbate the disadvantages of smaller operations.

The ability to operate such a network profitably depends in addition on a substantial demand for the final product. The most successful marketing of beef produced by the new methods occurred in areas where the population:

> ...were from well-to-do homes and possessed some fundamental knowledge concerning beef. However, only about 10 percent appeared to know the fine points concerning various cuts of beef, such as ageing or marbling. *About 10–15 percent of the firm's patrons were non-Filipinos (mostly Americans).*[67]

A major task of the new commercial establishments then became "educating" wealthier consumers into taste patterns which would make them willing to pay more for meat which had undergone additional, more expensive, processing.

The attempt to develop a feed industry to supply both new livestock and new poultry industries also favored larger farmers. Feed manufacturers, using modern techniques to blend feeds, required both local supplies of corn and imported feed constituents. The production of corn for processing into feed was done primarily by larger farmers (who could guarantee supplies and afford to transport the grain). In providing corn for feed processors, they sometimes diverted supplies from *less profitable ventures which supplied corn for human consumption.*[68] Even more dramatic impacts occurred in the development of the Venezuelan feed industry, where monopolistic control by multinational feed companies and the availability of cheap imports under P.L. 480 contributed to reducing (1) the income of small farmers, (2)

---

[65]Ralph Sorenson, "Los Arenas Marketing Corporation" in Drilon (cited. fn. 63), p. 31.

[66]Cattle ranching results are discussed in P. M. Villegas, "Delta Manufacturing Corporation" in Drilon, pp. 51–68. Most generally the bias of those sectors toward concentration is documented in United States agricultural history. Cf. USDA/ERS, *Market Structure,* op. cit., and Federal Trade Commission, *The Structure of Food Manufacturing,* Technical Report #8 of the National Commission on Food Marketing (Washington, D.C.: June, 1966).

[67]Sorenson, p. 31.

[68]P. M. Villegas, "Wonder Feeds Incorporated" in Drilon, op. cit., pp. 119–41.

the supply available for human consumption, and (3) total corn production. Imports rose.[69]

It should be clear, then, that one cannot *assume* that an emphasis on rapid increases in aggregate food production will work to the benefit of the undernourished, especially in the context of distorted factor markets and consumption patterns created by skewed income distributions. Production technologies developed for commercial markets in major grain exporting countries, especially the United States, emerged in a milieu in which ''surplus'' grain encouraged feed-intensive methods of producing animal protein. Concurrently, cheap energy encouraged heavy mechanization and extensive agriculture, and the availability of capital made possible large initial investments in processing and production which became profitable as economies of scale. But adopting such technologies in LDCs may be detrimental to the chronically undernourished; this is clearly the case where development does not work to create employment for laborers and cultivators displaced from the rural sector. Furthermore, more neutral technologies (e.g., Green Revolution) remain very sensitive to the *timing* of their introduction, and to policies on infrastructure. The internal advantages of wealthier people in LDCs may easily be reinforced by international transactions and technology transfers designed to facilitate production increases. These can turn out to be disadvantageous to the poor and hungry.

Food policies and wider development strategies

While food can certainly be discussed as a single issue, the implications of findings on production structures are very sensitive to wider development strategies. For example, displacing rural labor and marginal cultivators may not be bad if more lucrative employment which makes better use of societal resources is being created in other sectors (industry, services). Similarly, an emphasis on increasing the production of large farmers may be justifiable, and necessary, if programs to alleviate urban undernutrition require that the government be able to procure more grain (directly or through the market). Thus, it is necessary at least briefly to discuss the possible roles agriculture may play in development strategies before attempting to evaluate production and consumption policies.

Authors stressing the importance of alleviating rural poverty and increasing the food intake of the poorest rural classes have advocated introducing labor-intensive agriculture in conjunction with intermediate technologies which could increase the efficiency of cultivation.[70] Such an approach assumes that it is necessary to promote

---

[69]Polly Wright, ''Multinational Power: Agribusiness in a Developing Country,'' Department of Agriculture and Resource Economics, University of Maryland, (mimeo, May, 1977), pp. 16–8.

[70]There is at present no evidence known to the author which establishes even a rough idea of what productivity increases might be expected. Mellor, *New Economics,* argues that such technologies will be inadequate, but without detailed discussion of productivity potential.

rural development, both to stop the influx of people to urban areas where jobs are not available, and to increase domestic food production in concert with attempts to build an industrial sector. Success rests on increasing the productivity of small farmers and generating employment in agriculture, thus making increased consumption possible. This strategy seems in principle most appropriate for a nation where the undernourished are primarily rural people, and where a significant portion of these are marginal farmers. Successful implementation would be more difficult where the number of landless laborers greatly exceeds the number of farmers capable of adopting labor intensive methods. With numerous small holdings, it seems unlikely that paid employment can be generated for a population much in excess of the population on labor-intensive farms.[71] In addition, even with double cropping, the demand for labor will be seasonal. Implementation difficulties are also likely in countries where poor farmers are tenant farmers or sharecroppers. Under such conditions, increases in productivity may not provide cultivators with much additional food. This would depend upon the share of production taken directly or indirectly by the landowner. Where tenancy arrangements place the burden and risk of innovation on the cultivator, even modest investments in appropriate technologies may be unprofitable unless they result in very high increases in productivity.[72] Finally, such a strategy may be less desirable in areas where population pressure and/or land use policy have brought about the exploitation of ecologically marginal land. Attempting to increase the intensity of cultivation under such conditions could be disastrous in the long run.[73]

The situation is clearly more complicated when a significant share of the chronically undernourished live in urban areas. Here attempts to alleviate hunger must depend upon subsidizing the consumption of the poor. Reutlinger and Selowsky have shown that under most circumstances, selectively subsidizing the hungry is more cost-effective than policies which depress the price of staple grains for the entire urban population.[74] However, implementing such policies depends on the government's ability to procure food for urban areas and the cost of subsidizing consumption. Both of these, in turn, depend to some extent on decisions made about agricultural production. It is well known that larger farmers market a higher portion of their production than small farmers. Indeed, one of the alleged advantages of large holdings and/or tenancy arrangements is that they increase the quantity of food which enters the market, and hence become available for consumption outside the area in which it is produced.[75] If increased food production by small farmers is

[71]This depends on the assumption that small holdings (under 2.5 hectares) will experience diminishing returns to labor quickly.

[72]Lele presents data on an extreme case (Ethiopia) where the combination of sharecropping requirements and tenant assumption of risk would require a 60 percent increase in productivity to make high yielding varieites economically profitable. See Lele (cited, fn. 12), pp. 87–8.

[73]In many cases, exploitation of marginal land occurs as a combination of population pressure and the poverty of rural people forces expansion into areas previously recognized by the local inhabitants as unsuited for cultivation. While the ''long term'' effects may sometimes be realized, short term imperatives pervail. Cf. Eckholm, cited (fn. 16).

[74]Reutlinger and Selowsky (cited, fn. 6) pp. 39–45.

[75]Griffin, *Political Economy* (cited, fn. 2), pp. 52–3.

largely consumed in rural areas (directly by cultivators and by some landless laborers earning wages in agriculture), it may be harder to obtain food for urban consumers. Difficulty in procuring food was, in fact, one of the factors which entered into both the Soviet and the Chinese decisions to replace the relatively small farms which resulted after land reform with larger collectively owned farms.

Where procurement problems arise, attempts to alleviate urban hunger can easily become too expensive or self defeating. As noted earlier, inflation created by inadequate food supplies will most strongly affect the poor. If income supplements are used to subsidize their consumption, and food supplies do not rise to meet the new demand, inflation will erode the benefits of the program. If, on the other hand, the government either provides direct rations to the poor or makes it possible for them to purchase food at special low prices, the cost of the program will increase if procurement problems arise.[76] In addition, ''leakage'' will increase if the difference betwen the subsidized price and the market price becomes more substantial due to rising commercial prices. Within this milieu, reducing urban hunger may require changing urban consumption patterns—e.g., through rationing or placing high ''taxes'' on certain types of food.

How difficult it would be to meet the needs of both urban and rural undernourished from increases in domestic food production depends very crucially on *how much more food* can be produced by labor-intensive ''appropriate technologies'' and a bias toward smaller farmers in the distribution of Green Revolution technologies. If production grows enough to meet minimal consumption needs and provide a marketable surplus, then the tradeoff is less acute, and becomes essentially a matter of pricing and acquisition policy. If, on the other hand, increases are too small to provide a voluntary ''marketable surplus,'' or in the worst case too small even to meet basic needs among producers and laborers, the case for changing land use patterns, production strategy and/or consumption patterns becomes stronger. Unfortunately, there is very little empirical evidence on what production increases can be realistically expected.

It is important, however, to remember that sharp trade-offs arising from limitations in food production are not unique to production strategies which emphasize increasing the productivity of small farmers. Indeed, unless the number of rural malnourished is extremely small, and the difference between the quantity which could be produced under alternative strategies and the small farmer strategy is very large, an emphasis on labor-intensive, peasant-biased growth will reduce the overall cost of a national program to achieve minimal food security. Reducing the number of chronically undernourished people in rural areas would significantly decrease the cost of selective consumption subsidies. Reutlinger and Selowsky demonstrate that the cost of delivering a unit of additional food to some target population generally exceeds the unit price of the food.[77] Their calculations are for urban programs. The

---

[76]This has been a major reason for reliance on imports to subsidize consumption—as in the case of Sri Lanka and India. Until 1972–3, these prices were low and stable.

[77]See pp. 46–52.

cost for similar rural programs would be higher, and the program more difficult to implement, because of the additional difficulty involved in identifying and servicing the undernourished. Hence, increased local production, effective in reducing chronic hunger, would reduce the size of the target group most difficult to locate and expensive to reach.

Achieving the substantial production increases necessary to make minimal food security posible without redistribution implies shifting the allocation of new capital away from larger farmers and toward small and marginal farmers. Because the national stock of capital is not touched, it is reasonable to expect capital availability to be limited, and further to expect its actual delivery to be slowed by the need to make changes in administrative structures and political coalitions.[78] Yet, since more land is not made available to the poor, increases in production will depend primarily on increasing productivity, which, in turn, rests on investment in and adoption of yield-increasing inputs.

Constraints imposed by the *ceteris paribus* conditions of the status quo are likely to be more significant in limiting the success of marginalist attempts to link increases in production and increases in nutritional well-being than actual physical production constraints. Although the quantity of grain needed under the ideal assumption that it went only to the hungry was high (34.5 million metric tons), such growth in physical yield is not beyond the increases associated with many of the new high-yielding varieties—which to a large extent remain unadopted in many LDCs.[79] Removing the constraints to wider adoption by small farmers, however, depends on making capital available, and removing major distortions in factor markets, introducing once again limitations imposed by the assumption that changes in resource allocation must occur at the margin.

The issue of whether marginalist strategies are so constrained that food security within a decade becomes unrealizable has not been systematically explored. But recent attempts at simulating alternative development strategies suggest that this may be the case. A joint study by the World Bank and the Institute of Development Studies (Sussex) simulated alternative development strategies for LDCs over a 40-year period. Their findings suggest that redistributing GNP simply to increase the consumption of the poor (without making productive resources available to them) left them worse off than did growth policies biased in favor of increasing capital accumulation of the rich. A scenario which allocated two per cent of GNP each year to public investment to build up the capital stock of the poor did increase the economic standing of the poor, but slowly, at a rate of about 0.5 per cent per year.[80]

Redistribution of existing income and assets produces more dramatic benefits for the poor and changes growth patterns. William Cline argued that a redistribution

[78]For difficulties in delivering credit to the poor, see Lele, pp. 81–99; for more generalized difficulties associated with wider rural development efforts, see ibid., pp. 118–61.

[79]See Dana Dalrymple, *Development and Spread of High Yielding Varieties of Wheat and Rice in the Less Developed Countries* (Washington, D.C.: USDA, 1974).

[80]Chenery et al. (cited, fn. 15), pp. 209–35.

of income which reduced inequality in Argentina, Brazil and Mexico to roughly British levels would reduce aggregate growth, but increase the well-being of the bottom 70 per cent significantly. Without such a distribution, a comparable economic improvement would occur only after 34–56 years of growth.[81] The Bariloche model, which examines the implications of explicitly seeking to achieve egalitarian consumption patterns which meet basic human needs, finds that this goal can be accomplished within 10 to 30 years if regional resources are reallocated. This is the case even for Asia, although it is unable to achieve Bariloche consumption standards without very optimistic assumptions about productivity increases.[82]

These studies, of course, are only suggestive. Nevertheless, redistributive approaches seem clearly advantageous (from the perspective of the poor) because they affect *both* the quantity of productive resources available for meeting their needs and the societal consumption patterns. Affecting consumption patterns, both initially and in terms of expectations about future consumption, makes it possible to escape the difficulties discussed earlier. None of this, however, speaks to the political feasibility of redistributing assets.

Conclusion

Some analysts focusing on the inter-related problems of poverty, inequality, and hunger conclude that market mechanisms per se impede the resolution of these fundamental problems. This is too strong. However, where there is gross inequality, the prospects for alleviating chronic hunger are extremely small. Distributions of income, wealth and power are reflected so pervasively in the structure of food consumption and production that "price signals" must be seen as tacit reflections of these distributions.

There is a fundamental tension between the goal of reducing hunger as quickly and as permanently as possible, and the desire to make at most marginal changes in consumption and production patterns. Leaving very inegalitarian consumption untouched while trying to relieve hunger through market mechanisms will require much more food than the hungry themselves will consume. Leaving very unequal asset patterns unchanged increases the need for "supplementary" nutrition programs and increases the risk that they will become relatively permanent subsidies for people with few prospects of being central to the economies in which they live.

Being sensitive to the consequences of radical inequality may stimulate a rethinking of several "conventional" prescriptions. First, unconditional exhortations to increase rapidly aggregate production need to be tempered by a knowledge of conditions within even "food deficit" countries. Where the emphasis on *rapid* production increases tolerance for policies directed toward larger farmers or exces-

[81]William R. Cline, *Potential Effects of Income Distribution on Economic Growth:* Latin American Cases (New York: Praeger, 1972).
[82]Herrera et al. (cited, fn. 2), pp. 87–95.

sively capital intensive technologies which displace rural labor, such policies may increase hunger while aggregate production grows. Second, ignoring the possibility of changing consumption patterns may place an excessive burden on agriculture, and increase the pressure to do "what is necessary" to increase production quickly. Third, the idea that increased production or productivity provides more resources to marshal against hunger may be misleading. While it is certainly true that the poor and hungry suffer when food supplies are short vis à vis the paying market, a "surplus" is not always easy to redirect toward the hungry. This is apparent from the history of American "food aid" programs. There may be similarly difficult problems in trying to "stimulate" food production or "procure" commodities in market systems where there is no strong economic demand for it.

There are, of course, various options for "working around" specific consequences of radical inequality. Nutrition intervention programs, selective increases in purchasing power, reallocation of new resources at the margin, and global "insurance programs" will all help to counter some of the effects of inequality. However, such programs are inherently limited in scope, and are difficult to apply when the hungry are a significant portion of the population. Furthermore, such programs cannot touch *either* the mechanisms by which wealth structures production and consumption *or* the underlying distribution of income and assets. In the end, at least one of these must be dramatically changed if chronic hunger is to be eliminated.

7

The Diplomacy of World Food: Goals, Capabilities, Issues, and Arenas

Henry R. Nau

Food is a factor in international diplomacy as a direct instrument of policy and as a condition underlying policy. Grain trade is particularly important. For most of the postwar period, principal grain exporting countries pursued policies designed to support domestic prices, using foreign agricultural policy to dispose of accumulated surpluses and to pursue broader non-food (political and economic) objectives. Grain importing countries came to rely on cheap food supplies in international markets, neglecting incentives to stimulate domestic production. Worldwide food shortages in 1973–74 made clear the need to consider international as well as domestic food requirements. Food considerations acquired a foreign policy dimension, while foreign policy considerations sparked a debate about the use of food for power. A return to surplus conditions in world food markets reduces the opportunities for the exercise of food power, while creating the conditions to meet historically unattainable food goals. To accomplish this, a system of international coordination and review of separate national food policies may be needed. Such a system would ensure greater accountability of private groups to governments and governments to one another without relying excessively on either automatic market forces or a centralized world food authority.

Food is an old factor in world diplomacy. It has been considered a source of strength, as well as an important influence on diplomatic behavior, since the origins of the modern state. In the 15th and 16th centuries, according to Immanuel Wallerstein, "food needs dictated the geographical expansion of Europe."[1] In the 18th century, David Hume cited a public granary of corn, along with a magazine of arms and storehouse of cloth, as evidence of "real riches and strength in any state."[2] In

Henry R. Nau is Associate Professor of Political Science at George Washington University. He wishes to express his appreciation to the editors of this volume, Ernst Haas and Robert Keohane, for helpful comments on earlier drafts of this paper. He particularly thanks I. M. Destler, with whom he began this enterprise and whose counsel and criticisms were valuable throughout.

[1] See *The Modern World-System: Capitalist Agriculture and the Origins of the European World-Economy in the Sixteenth Century* (New York: Academic Press, 1974), p. 42.

[2] See his essay, "Of Commerce," in *Essays: Moral, Political and Literary*, Vol. 1 (London: Longmans, Green and Co., 1912), p. 294. I am indebted to Nannerl Keohane for drawing this reference to my attention.

the present century, food resources played an important role in two world wars. Lloyd George contended, for example, that "food . . . decided the issue of [the first world] war," being "directly responsible for the downfall of Russia" and "the element that led to the collapse of Austria and Germany."[3] Meanwhile, food relief shipments continued throughout the war to the Belgian and French populations in German-occupied territory. Altogether, these shipments directed by Herbert Hoover provided some $5.2 billion of food to war-ravaged Europe.[4] During World War II, the Allies blockaded all food and other shipments to Nazi-occupied Europe. Renewed shipments after the war became a critical part of European reconstruction. Under the Marshall Plan, the United States supplied some $3 billion for import of foodstuffs in Europe.[5] After 1954 and the inauguration of the Food for Peace program, US food aid shifted to developing countries, totaling by 1975 some $25 billion.[6]

While food is not a new factor in international diplomacy, the revolution in storage and transportation facilities enabled food markets to become global for the first time only in this century (see the essay by Seevers). This process of physical integration, however, was not accompanied by global policy coordination. In the early 1950s, the member countries of the General Agreement on Tariffs and Trade (GATT), led by the United States, deliberately excluded agriculture from international economic negotiations. Most of these countries pursued food policies based on domestic support of farm groups, employing a wide range of trade restrictions to maintain high domestic prices. In the 1960s, the high costs and inefficiencies of such policies, particularly in the United States, contributed to the search for greater liberalization of food trade in the Kennedy Round negotiation. Still, the issue of freer agricultural trade was largely confined to North America and Western Europe. In the 1970s, however, serious world food shortages affected nearly every region and country of the world, revealing the underlying globalization of food markets that had been taking place during the postwar period. Governments, as well as international organizations, showed a growing awareness of the international, as well as domestic, implications of food policies. Whether they are able to convert this awareness into global policies that constructively coordinate domestic and international interests remains to be seen. An opportunity to give new emphasis to world (as opposed to domestic) food requirements may hang in the balance.

This essay looks at the recent history and current prospects of nation-state diplomacy in shaping international food markets and the global food regime. It

[3]From *War Memoirs of Lloyd George,* Vol. III (Boston: Little Brown, 1934), cited in Dan Caldwell, *Food Crises and World Politics* (Sage Professional Papers in International Studies, 1977). Caldwell offers an interesting comparative discussion of the role of food in World Wars I and II.

[4]Frank M. Surface and Raymond L. Bland, *American Food in the World War and Reconstruction Period* (Stanford University Press), 1931, p. 9.

[5]Murray R. Benedict, *Farm Policies of the United States, 1790–1950* (New York: The Twentieth Century Fund, 1953), pp. 443, 501.

[6]USDA/ERS, *Foreign Agricultural Trade of the United States* (hereafter FATUS), (December 1975), p. 16.

examines the role of high-level, national government officials who have the primary responsibility for integrating domestic and international interests in food.[7] After exploring the goals and capabilites of major food exporters and importers, the discussion focuses on the principal issues and arenas of world food diplomacy. It then reviews the current diplomatic situation, in which food is once again in surplus in the world system, and evaluates the prospects that food diplomacy might be managed in the future to meet newer, broader objectives of world food security.

Goals of food diplomacy

In a broad sense, governments may use food resources in international diplomacy for two purposes: 1) to influence international food markets, and 2) to influence international economic and political relationships going beyond food markets.[8] The first involves goals associated with the functional and structural aspects of what we call in this volume the global food system—production, consumption, distribution and reliance on public vs. private transactions. These goals may have to do with the efficiency (production), equity (consumption), predictability (prices) or degree of interdependence (trade) in global food markets. They reflect a commitment to find mutually acceptable standards for global food supply and consumption. On the supply side, for example, more efficient production might be sought; or, on the demand side, the achievement of minimum levels of food consumption by all the peoples of the world, as well as the reduction of disparities beyond these levels between wealthy and poorer consuming countries, might be emphasized. A government may seek to achieve these international food goals by supply and demand competition through the market place (expand production and export of domestic farm products as the United States did under the Nixon administration, or increase domestic consumption and import of food as the Soviet Union did through world grain purchases in 1972 and 1975) or by directly negotiating international agreements or taking unilateral national action (e.g. the European Economic Community's preference to maintain high world prices to ease the costs of its internal price support policies, or Japan's policies since 1973 to reduce its food trade dependence—see Paarlberg).

The use of food resources to influence international relationships beyond food

[7]Other essays in this volume deal more directly with the role of private and lower level public actors in world food relations.

[8]In this essay, the focus is on the international or foreign policy goals of governments in food relations. Obviously, foreign policy goals reflect a mix of domestic and international factors. Indeed, one of the interesting questions is how this mix changes over time and objectives regarded primarily as domestic in one period (e.g., domestic stabilization programs for food in most industrialized countries) become international in another (e.g., interest today in an international stabilization program or grain reserve). Nevertheless, foreign policy goals may be distinguished analytically as those goals that emerge in relationships *among* countries rather than *within* countries. Thus, in the case of export controls, the foreign policy goal is to protect domestic consumers from *foreign* buyers; the domestic goal is to prevent (reduce) rising prices between domestic consumers and domestic producers.

markets is more diffuse and open-ended. Non-food goals in this category might include the use of food shipments to affect the general balance of payments position and broad economic policy of a foreign country. More obviously, it may involve the desire to influence general political relations abroad, as in US food aid to Syria or Soviet wheat shipments to India. Food may also be used to promote multilateral and global objectives (institutional and economic), as in the potential role of certain food commodities in the new international economic order proposed by developing countries.

In reality, food and non-food goals may not be strictly separable. Food flows, like resource flows more generally, occur in a political, social and environmental setting in which broader consequences result whether or not consciously intended or easily measured. Even the use of food for the most exemplary purposes—to relieve famine or chronic malnutrition—involves environmental consequences (relieving pressure to increase local production), institutional requirements (storage and transportation facilities) and social and political change (mobilizing a passive rural populace).[9] All uses of food, therefore, entail non-food or larger social and economic consequences. The debate about food power deals with only a limited aspect of this reality, namely the conscious or purposive use of food by governments for non-food purposes.[10] Another aspect has to do with the power implications of food flows motivated by food goals (e.g. humanitarian programs) or initiated by other actors (e.g., private companies or lower-level public bureaucrats).

The key issue, therefore, may have less to do with whether food is used for power purposes or has power consequences than with increasing the visibility of the purposes and consequences of food flows and holding those involved in these flows more accountable both for the purposes they intend and for the consequences they unintentionally cause.[11] Is, for example, food policy being exercised, as in the past, primarily to serve the interests of domestic farm groups? Or does this policy seek to achieve some international goals as well, such as acceptable levels of efficiency, equity, predictability, and interdependence in world food markets? Finally, does the use of food resources in international diplomacy contribute to a broader consensus on global economic and political objectives?

Capabilities of food diplomacy

As governmental decisions affecting global food relations become more explicit, conflicts and bargains among governments will define the limits, tasks and

---

[9]For a stimulating, though perhaps overly pessimistic, view of the role of politics in famine relief, see Donald F. McHenry and Kai Bird, "Food Bungle in Bangladesh," *Foreign Policy* (Summer 1977) pp. 72–88. Politics is cited in this essay as the problem, which it often is, but not recognized also as the solution, which it inevitably must be.

[10]For an evaluation of food power from this narrowly defined perspective, see Robert L. Paarlberg, "The Failure of Food Power," paper prepared for the 1977 Agricultural Policy Symposium, Washington, D. C., July 25, 1977.

[11]Visibility alone is not enough, because as choices and consequences are made more explicit, opportunities arise for harmful as well as helpful uses of food.

Table 1   Shares of world grain[a] production and consumption

(percentages)

| | 1960/61–62/63 | | 1969/70–71/72 | | 1973/74–76/77 | |
	Prod.	Cons.	Prod.	Cons.	Prod.	Cons.
Developed Countries	37.3	35.4	36.1	33.5	35.7	31.2
United States	19.8	16.4	18.7	15.0	18.8	12.9
Canada	2.7	1.8	3.0	2.0	3.0	1.8
European Economic Community (9)	8.4	10.8	8.4	9.9	8.1	9.5
Japan	1.8	2.5	1.1	2.5	.9	2.5
Oceania	1.3	.5	1.3	.6	1.4	.5
Centrally Planned Countries	34.6	35.0	35.8	36.9	36.4	38.2
Soviet Union	14.8	14.0	15.0	15.2	14.9	15.6
China	13.0	13.5	14.1	14.3	14.3	14.8
Developing Countries	27.4	28.6	27.5	28.8	27.2	29.7
Brazil	1.7	1.9	1.8	2.0	2.0	2.0
Argentina	1.5	1.0	1.7	1.0	1.9	1.0
South Asia[b]	10.8	11.4	10.6	10.9	10.4	11.2
North Africa/Middle East	3.8	4.4	3.6	4.4	3.6	4.7
Total of Sub-entries	79.6	78.2	79.2	77.8	79.3	76.5
Total of Regions (Developed, Centrally Planned and Developing)	99.3	99.0	99.4	99.2	99.3	99.1

[a]Includes wheat, milled rice and coarse grains.
[b]Bangladesh, India and Pakistan.
Source: Percentages calculated from data in USDA/ERS, *World Agricultural Situation,* WAS-12, December 1976, Table 8, p. 18.

rules of acceptable global food management. Countries differ, of course, in their interest in and capability for participating in such management. These differences are, in part, a function of the configuration of the world food economy and each country's position within that economy.

Food, beverages and tobacco comprise about 13 percent of total world trade by value. Grains (or cereals) make up about 20 percent of this amount.[12] By value, grains are the most important product traded in international markets next to oil.[13] The rest of our discussion, therefore, focuses principally on grain markets and diplomacy.

Though second to oil, the proportion of grain moving in international markets is considerably smaller. This follows from the more even distribution of grain production and consumption around the world. As Seevers notes, most countries are or nearly are self-reliant in grains (and food more generally). Table 1 shows that, since 1960, the United States, Soviet Union, China, South Asia, the European

[12]Figures are averages for 1970 to 1974 and are taken from United Nations, *Yearbook of International Trade Statistics 1975,* Vol. I, Trade by Country, Special Table G, p. 86. Cereals include wheat, rice and coarse grains and represent by far the largest source of human food energy intake, about 56 percent. Other principal sources of food include root crops and animal products (meats, dairy products, etc.). See Lester R. Brown with Erik P. Eckholm, *By Bread Alone* (New York: Praeger, 1975), p. 24.
[13]Mineral fuels and related materials constituted in 1974 20 percent of total trade, while grains represented in the same year about 3 percent.

Community, and Canada have been the principal grain producing areas in that order, accounting for roughly 70 percent of total world grain output. These same areas, however, as Table 1 further shows, also account for about the same percentage of world grain consumption. This concentration of grain production and consumption in the same areas means that during the 1950s, only about 6–7 percent of total world grain production was traded. This percentage rose to 8–10 percent during the 1960s and then jumped dramatically to 12 percent in 1972–74. With large harvests in 1976–77, the proportion is expected to fall back to 10 percent.[14] By contrast, 50 percent of all oil produced is traded internationally. Grain also differs from oil in that capacity to expand production to alleviate dependence on international markets is fairly widely distributed among regions and countries of the world. Whereas 60 percent of all proven oil reserves exist in the Middle East, all regions of the world have substantial capacity to expand grain production. Some of these areas may be pushing against the limits of arable land (e.g., Europe, Near East, North West Africa, and Asia), but all of them could achieve significant increases through higher yields.[15]

Taken together, these data suggest that grain markets may be too "thin" to invite the kind of diplomatic bargaining and manipulation that has characterized oil markets. While this overall observation is generally true, it masks two important trends. First, as Table 1 indicates, grain production and consumption have become increasingly skewed in recent years by region. From 1960 to 1976 the margin of production over consumption in developed countries widened from 1.9 to 4.5 percentage points. During the same period, the margin of consumption over production in developing countries widened from 1.2 to 2.7 percentage points. Meanwhile, centrally planned countries shifted from rough self-sufficiency in production and consumption to a margin of consumption over production of 1.8 percentage points. If these shifts continue, more and more grain may be traded internationally to maintain nutrition and support rising consumption in developing and centrally planned countries. Second, while the proportion of world grain production that is traded has doubled from the 1950s to 1970s (6 percent in early 1950s to 12 percent in 1972–74), two countries, the United States and Canada, continue to dominate this trade. According to Table 2, these two countries accounted for 63 percent of all grain exports in 1948/49–1951/52 and about 65 percent in 1972/73–1973/74.[16]

---

[14]The figure 1976/77 is an estimate from documents prepared for the Third Session of the World Food Council, Manila, June 20–24, 1977. See United Nations, WFC, *Assessment of the World Food Situation and Outlook,* WFC 34, March 30, 1977, pp. 5 and 9. Other figures calculated from United Nations, FAO, *Production Yearbook* and *Trade Yearbook,* 1975 and earlier years.

[15]United Nations, FAO, *Provisional Indicative World Plan for Agricultural Development,* Vol. 1, p. 49.

[16]These percentages are even higher if France is included in an EEC grouping in both the earlier and later periods. This is due to the fact that a larger share of French exports than either US or Canadian exports go to other EEC countries, thereby reducing France's share and raising the US and Canadian share of world exports outside the EEC.

Table 2 Shares of world grain[a] exports[b]

(percentages)

	1948/49 *–51/52*	*1958/59* *–61/62*	*1968/69* *–71/72*	*1972/73* *–73/74*
North America	63.2	62.6	52.0	64.8
United States	41.2	45.9	37.7	52.3
Canada	22.0	16.7	14.4	12.6
Western Europe	3.7	9.9	19.5	18.0
France	1.6	4.4	12.4	12.3
Netherlands	.1	.3	1.4	1.5
Centrally Planned	6.9	4.3	2.4	1.0
Soviet Union	5.2	3.2	1.3[c]	.7[c]
China	—	—	.09[d]	.07[e]
Oceania	9.6	8.6	10.1	5.3
Australia	9.6	8.6	10.1	5.3
South America	9.8	9.5	10.3	6.5
Argentina	9.2	9.3	9.1	6.3
Total of Sub-entries	88.9	88.4	86.5	91.1
Total of Regions	93.2	94.9	94.3	95.6

[a]Includes wheat and wheat flour, rye, barley, oats, maize, sorghum and millets [excludes rice which from 1963–64 to 1973–74 fluctuated around a level of 7 m. metric tons while exports of all grains increased from 100 to 150 m. tons, rice representing therefore 7 percent or less of total grain exports during this period. See Note 2, p. 6 of Philip H. Trezise, *Rebuilding Grain Reserves* (Washington: Brookings Institution, 1976)].

[b]Does not include trade among the centrally planned countries (E. Europe, China and Soviet Union).

[c]Reflects Soviet crop failures.

[d]For 1971/72 only.

[e]For 1973/74 only, share is .09 percent.

Sources: 1948/49–51/52, United Nations, FAO, *World Grain Trade Statistics 1958/59,* Tables 31–38, pp. 54–72. 1958/59–61/62, United Nations, FAO, *World Grain Trade Statistics 1963/64,* Tables 27–34, pp. 48–72. 1968/69–71/72 and 1972/73–73/74, United Nations, FAO, *World Grain Trade Statistics 1973/74,* Tables 1, 2, and 29–36, p. 16 and pp. 52–75.

While supplier dominance has been maintained, however, the number and importance of grain importers have shifted. Table 3 shows that Western European countries accounted for nearly two-thirds of all grain imports in 1950 but take up only one-third today. On the other hand, Japan, the Soviet Union and China absorbed less than 7 percent in 1950 but import more than 30 percent today. In addition, many less developed countries are net importers in the current period.

The continuing concentration among exporters and more recent spread among importers suggest enhanced opportunities for influence and diplomacy in contemporary world grain markets.[17] This depends, of course, on the relative importance of grain trade in the exporting and importing countries and the comparative capabilities of these countries to control this trade for diplomatic purposes (food and non-food).

[17]All else being equal, the advantages should go to exporters since they acquire a larger number of alternative markets while importers remain dependent on a few suppliers. For a general and pathbreaking discussion of influence in international trade relations, see Albert O. Hirschman, *National Power and the Structure of Foreign Trade* (Berkeley: University of California Press, 1945).

Table 3   Shares of world grain[a] imports[b]

(percentages)

	1948/49 –51/52	1958/59 –61/62	1968/69 –71/72	1972/73 –73/74
Western Europe	61.9	52.9	42.3	33.9
Belgium/Luxembourg	4.5	3.4	3.9	3.1
Italy	4.8	5.0	7.7	6.3
West Germany	12.2	9.6	7.9	6.0
United Kingdom	18.7	16.2	9.4	5.9
Spain	.9	1.6	2.7	2.6
Netherlands	4.2	6.1	4.6	4.6
France	3.7	1.3	.9	.5
Austria	2.1	1.1	.2	.1
Centrally Planned	.8	2.6	5.8	14.4
Soviet Union	—	.2	2.7	11.8
China	—	—	4.1	5.1
Asia	19.7	23.7	31.9	28.7
India	8.1	6.0	2.9	2.3
Bangladesh	—	—	—	1.5
Japan	6.2	7.6	15.3	13.7
South Korea	—	—	2.1	1.9
Pakistan	.07	1.5	1.3	1.0
Israel	.7	1.1	1.2	1.0
South America	5.0	5.9	5.7	5.9
Brazil	3.2	2.0	2.2	2.0
Chile	—	.2	.7	1.0
Peru	.6	.7	.7	.8
Venezuela	—	.6	1.0	1.0
Central America	2.7	2.1	2.3	3.0
Africa	5.0	6.5	6.7	6.5
Egypt	2.3	2.6	2.4	2.4

[a]See Note a of Table 2.

[b]See Note b of Table 2.

Sources: 1968/69–71/72 and 1972/73–73/74, United Nations, FAO, *World Grain Trade Statistics 1973/74,* Tables 1, 3 and 29–36, pp. 52–75. 1958/59–61/62, United Nations, FAO, *World Grain Trade Statistics 1963/64,* Tables 27–34, pp. 48–72. 1948/49–51/52, United Nations, FAO, *World Grain Trade Statistics 1958/59,* Tables 31–38, pp. 54–72.

Tables 4 and 5 offer two rough measures of the relative importance of grain trade to major exporters and importers. The first measure in each table indicates something about the sensitivity of major exporters and importers to the price and volume of grain trade; the second measure suggests the vulnerability of these countries to cutoff of this trade.[18]

For all exporters, grain trade as a percentage of total exports is less important than grain exports as a percentage of total domestic production (Table 4). Taken by itself, this fact suggests that the need to export grain is less urgent in terms of foreign exchange or foreign economic policy than in terms of domestic farm pol-

[18]On these concepts of sensitivity and vulnerability, see Robert O. Keohane and Joseph S. Nye, *Power and Interdependence* (Boston: Little Brown, 1977). especially chapter 1.

Table 4 Stake of major exporters in grain trade

Major exporters	(by value) Cereals exports as % total merchandise exports (1969–74 avg.)	(by weight) Cereals exports as % total cereals production (1973–75 avg.)
United States	8.5	33.1
Canada	6.5	43.2
France	5.6	39.2
Australia	10.6	51.5
Argentina	28.8	41.3

Sources: United Nations, FAO, *Production Yearbook 1975,* Vol. 29, Table 12. United Nations, FAO, *Trade Yearbook 1975,* Vol. 29, Table 35 and assorted country tables 134–192.

Table 5 Stake of major importers in grain trade

Major importers	(by value) Cereals imports as % of total merchandise exports (1970–74 avg.)	(by weight) Cereals imports as % of total cereals consumption (1973–75 avg.)
Japan	5.2	53.5
Soviet Union	4.3[a]	8.6
Italy	3.8	33.6
West Germany	1.5	27.4
United Kingdom	3.1	34.8
China[c]	—	—
Netherlands	3.0	142.4[d]
Belgium/Luxembourg	2.7	89.6
Spain	7.0	24.3
India	21.0	4.5
Egypt	25.1	27.6
Brazil	5.8	9.9
South Korea	16.8	26.8
Bangladesh	60.5[b]	16.3

[a] This percentage would be considerably higher if the denominator were for exports to dollar areas only.
[b] In 1973 and 1974, cereals imports were more than total merchandise exports.
[c] No data available.
[d] Imports as a percentage of consumption overstates the nutritional vulnerability of a few countries such as the Netherlands (to a lesser extent, Belgium/Luxembourg) which reexport a sizeable portion of their imports. Cutoff of these imports does nevertheless represent a commercial vulnerability.
Sources: United Nations, FAO *Production Yearbook, 1975,* Vol. 29, Table 12. United Nations, FAO, *Trade Yearbook 1975,* Vol. 29, Table 35 and assorted country tables 134–192.

icy.[19] This is especially true for the *principal* grain exporters—the United States, Canada and France—and it suggests one of the reasons why the food diplomacy of these countries in the past has been largely a derivative of their domestic farm support programs (see following discussion).

Table 5 suggests four principal classes of importers in terms of relative importance of grain trade. First, there are the wealthy grain importers for whom imports are a much larger percentage of total consumption than of total exports—Japan, Italy, West Germany, United Kingdom, the Benelux countries and Spain. More recently several Middle East members of the Organization of Petroleum Exporting Countries (OPEC)—notably Iran and Saudi Arabia—have joined this group.[20] These countries can pay for their grain imports but remain highly vulnerable to cutoff of these imports. Since most of them import primarily feedgrains (85 percent of total imports for Japan and Western Europe) and already enjoy relatively high per capita grain consumption rates, however, cutoff would not be as serious to them in terms of nutrition standards as it would be to many developing countries.[21] A second class of importers includes countries such as India and Bangladesh whose food imports represent a much larger share of their annual foreign exchange earnings than of their total domestic consumption. While these countries in some sense are more vulnerable to price than cutoff of food imports, the margins they import, given their already low levels of per capita grain consumption, are extremely critical to overall food and nutrition needs. A third group of importers includes the Soviet Union and Brazil for whom both price sensitivity and cutoff vulnerability are *relatively* low (Brazil being more vulnerable because of lower existing per capita consumption levels). And a fourth class of importers is represented by countries such as South Korea and Egypt for whom both price sensitivity and cutoff vulnerability are *relatively* high (South Korea being better off than Egypt because of its greater ability to pay). Thus, while world grain markets are important to all of these importers, the second group and some countries in the fourth group, such as Egypt, are most vulnerable and therefore most likely to count international food diplomacy as an important aspect, and not just an adjunct, of domestic food policy. Ironically, however, these countries are among the least important importers of world grain (Table 3) and hence have the least influence over the international market or politically negotiated outcomes in grain diplomacy.

In addition to their varying dependencies on grain trade, countries also differ in their respective capabilities to control grain flows. Such control is usually a function

---

[19]The importance of grain trade for foreign exchange purposes, of course, is also a function of the overall balance of payments. If a country is in deficit, as the US has been for much of the past two decades, a large surplus from grain trade can be very important in offsetting deficits in other areas (for the US, for example, in the capital account).

[20]The OPEC states are not included in Tables 3 and 5 since their imports have increased only recently. For some data on recent OPEC imports, see note 71; also see Paarlberg, in this volume, for details on advanced country importers.

[21]For example, reducing the European Community's per capita consumption by one-half would still leave it well above per capita consumption in Central and East Africa, and South and East Asia. See USDA/ERS, *World Agricultural Situation,* WAS-12, December 1976, Table 12.

of national policies, institutions and information sources.[22] Historically, national policies have dictated intervention in the agricultural sector for all major exporters and many importers as well. The determination of governments to protect the integrity of their farm programs has produced an array of import and export restrictions. In the mid-sixties, both the United States and Canada began to reexamine these traditional agricultural policies. Dissatisfied with the high costs of supporting farm incomes and stockpiling grain surpluses, they sought to place more emphasis on production controls, foreign sales and the liberalization of import restrictions. These policy changes were a factor leading to depleted world grain reserves in 1973–74, and they undoubtedly contributed to a reluctance on the part of the world's most important grain exporters to reconsider the need for reserves once conditions of heightened uncertainty and, in the opinion of some, chronic shortages began to characterize world grain markets.

All of the major grain exporters except the United States operate through centralized boards for grain trade.[23] In Canada, Australia and Argentina, these institutions are the sole authority for wheat and certain feed grain sales. In the EEC, exports are controlled through licensing and subsidy policies set by the Commission and implemented by national authorities. In the United States, grain sales are subject to export control legislation and since 1973 to stricter export reporting requirements. For the most part, however, grain trade in the United States takes place in the private market (see Seevers), and is carried out by multinational grain companies. The six largest grain companies—Cargill, Continental, Cook, Bunge, Dreyfus, and Garnac—dominate this trade, handling in 1970–1975 as much as 96 percent of US wheat exports, 95 percent of US corn exports, 90 percent of US oats exports and 80 percent of US sorghum exports. At the same time, these companies also managed 90 percent of wheat and corn exports from the EEC, and most of the grain exports of Canada, Australia and Argentina that are traded outside of government-to-government agreements.[24]

Major importing countries also centralize grain trade. In Japan, an import agency monopolizes grain purchases. In the Soviet Union and China, state trading agencies dominate. The EEC import levies and export subsidies act in a similar fashion, being set by the Community and administered by national government authorities. India, Bangladesh and many other developing countries also employ

[22]For a detailed and insightful comparative analysis of the objectives and institutions of advanced countries in general foreign economic policy areas, see Peter J. Katzenstein, "Between Power and Plenty: Foreign Economic Policies of Advanced Industrialized States," *International Organization,* Vol. 31, No. 4 (Autumn 1977).

[23]For information on grain trading institutions in major exporting and importing countries, see inter alia, General Accounting Office (hereafter GAO), "Grain Marketing Systems in Argentina, Australia, Canada, and the European Community; Soybean Marketing System in Brazil," May 28, 1976; Vernon L. Sorenson, *International Trade Policy: Agriculture and Development* (East Lansing: Michigan State University International Business and Economic Studies, 1975), chapter 5.

[24]See US Senate, Committee on Foreign Relations, Subcommittee on Multinational Corporations, *Hearings on International Grain Companies,* Second Session, June 18, 23, and 24, 1976, Part 16 (Washington: GPO, 1977), p. 2.

central trading organizations.[25] Thus, with the partial exception of the United States, major exporters and importers maintain fairly heavy government control over their grain trade.

Information is the final resource affecting capabilities to participate in world grain market management. Here the dominance of multinational grain companies and US government agencies is unchallenged. According to Richard Caves, information is a principal advantage of grain companies, and scale economies to be derived in coordinating information and risk offer one explanation for high concentration in the grain export business.[26] The large grain companies are chief suppliers of price and other relevant grain market information to other exporting country governments, no less than the US government. Simultaneously, the US Department of Agriculture (USDA) and Central Intelligence Agency dominate information about grain production. Thus, while the United States government is in a weaker position to utilize information about grain trade (relying as it does on private grain companies rather than government marketing boards), it has the best sources of such information.

Issues and arenas of food diplomacy

The issues involved in international grain diplomacy cannot be reduced to the functional dimensions of the global food system alone.[27] Nor because of their diversity and mix do they lend themselves easily to classification on the basis of broader dimensions. Yet, historically the issues in world food diplomacy have shifted, sometimes rapidly, from concerns with production increases to concerns with production surpluses, from questions of food aid to debates about food embargoes. Under these circumstances it seems necessary (even if risky) to try to identify some of the principal variables affecting the definition and discussion of food issues on the diplomatic agenda. Table 6 suggests at least two such variables: 1) the foreign policy goals of the participants in world food diplomacy and whether these goals relate to specific food or broader non-food (economic or political) objectives, and 2) the physical conditions of surplus or shortage prevailing at the time in world food markets.[28]

---

[25]For a brief description of grain trading policies and organizations in various countries, see United Nations, FAO, *National Grain Policies 1975*.

[26]See *Organization, Scale and Performance in the Grain Trading Industry* (Cambridge: Harvard Institute of Economic Research, Discussion Paper #546, April 1977).

[27]For a discussion of the flaws in analyzing international economic and technological issues from a purely functional or systemic view, see Ernst B. Haas, "Is There a Hole in the Whole?" *International Organization*, Vol. 29, No. 3 (Summer 1975), pp. 827–877.

[28]The two axes of Table 7 are independent to the extent that nature may intervene to increase or reduce food harvests. They are dependent to the extent that countries may adopt domestic or foreign policy goals that actually seek to create surplus or shortage conditions. See Emma Rothschild, "Food Politics," *Foreign Affairs*, Vol. 54 (January 1976), pp. 285–308.

Table 6 Food issues

MARKET CONDITIONS

FOREIGN POLICY GOALS[a]	Surplus	Shortage
FOOD	Price Stabilization (Grain Reserves) Food Aid-Chronic Malnutrition	Production Increases Food Aid-Famine Relief Trade Intervention: 1. Bilateral Purchase Agreements 2. Negotiated Trade Commitments 3. Preferential Access for Less Developed Countries
NON-FOOD	Food Disposal (Aid): 1. Economic Purposes: Balance of Payments or Agricultural-led Growth 2. Political Purposes: Influence Domestic or Foreign Policies in Non-Economic Areas Trade Liberalization	Food Export Controls/Embargoes: 1. Economic Purposes: Protect Domestic Consumers from Foreign Buyers 2. Political Purposes: Influence Domestic or Foreign Policies in Non-Economic Areas

[a]See Note 8 for definition. The Table treats only international goals. For example, price stabilization here refers to global price stabilization. Obviously, the latter may also be a domestic goal.

Depending on the particular combination of these variables, certain food issues seem more likely to emerge than others. Similarly, some issues will have a better chance of being resolved than others (e.g. stockpiling issues under surplus conditions). The actual issues that emerge, of course, will be a function of the individual and collective judgment of participants (i.e. what their goals are), acts of nature (weather, etc.), and other relationships in which states find themselves. Table 6 deals only with food relationships.

When surplus conditions and non-food foreign policy goals prevail (lower left hand section), exporters will be looking for ways to use surpluses to affect foreign economic or political aims. To do so, they may offer food on concessional terms. The economic purposes of such food disposal (it is only secondarily aid since the primary motivation is disposal) may be short-term, buttressing the balance of payments of the exporting country through foreign market development (market access) or providing general balance of payments support for the importing country; or these purposes might be long-term, promoting agricultural-led economic growth at home or seeking to do the same in the recipient country abroad. Political purposes may also be involved, that is, the desire to influence the domestic or foreign policies of the recipient country in areas other than strictly economic ones.[29] Importers gener-

---

[29]Such political issues may include institutional questions in economic areas such as those involved in the debate concerning the new international economic order.

ally will seek to avoid such influence, confident that surplus pressures will cause exporters to sustain high levels of food shipments without economic or political preconditions. Ignoring international food goals no less than exporters, importers may also build up a dangerous dependence on global food markets. To the extent that they seek to limit or reduce such dependence for whatever reasons (e.g., to protect their own producers as in the EEC in the 1960s), trade liberalization may become an issue between exporters and importers.

While importers may benefit in the short-run from food disposal patterns, they become vulnerable in the longer-run to a shift to shortage conditions. In times of shortage and the prevalence of non-food foreign policy goals (lower right-hand section), importers are likely to find access to food supplies limited either because of higher prices or because of export controls. Rather than promoting exports to meet global food needs, exporters may restrict shipments both to protect domestic prices against foreign buying pressures and to extract greater compliance from food recipients in non-food areas. Food aid becomes a key issue for importers, but it is unlikely to be an issue that can be resolved until food shortages end or participant goals shift to more specific food concerns. Pressure grows on importers to pay more attention to international food goals, particularly long-term increases in food production or, in the face of interim or chronic shortages, more predictable trade relationships, such as those reflected in multiple-year purchase agreements or negotiated trade commitments swapping stable supply for market-access guarantees.

To the extent that exporters also emphasize food goals under shortage conditions (upper right-hand section), food aid may be made available in amounts sufficient at least to provide relief from famine. Priority attention in both exporting and importing countries, however, is likely to center on eliminating shortage through longer-term production increases. This may be done both through enhanced investment in technical development in the most developed food producing states and by increased technical assistance to the least developed food producing states. Where the latter require export markets to achieve efficient production, preferential access to advanced country markets may become an issue.

The conditions for stable and balanced investment and development of worldwide food production, however, are unlikely to be fully achieved until prices are stabilized at some mutually acceptable level for both producers and consumers. This becomes possible only when surpluses reemerge sufficient to permit the building up of reserves and buffer stocks to stabilize price. Thus, with food goals and surplus conditions prevailing (upper left-hand section), grain reserves become an issue. Food aid may also be increased to attack chronic malnutrition, going beyond mere famine relief.

While all the issues in Table 6 have characterized postwar food discussions, some have been more apparent in certain periods than others. Before the worldwide shortage in 1972–74, surplus conditions and non-food foreign policy goals of many participants (especially in the 1950s) put primary attention on disposal issues. In the immediate aftermath of shortages a continued emphasis on non-food foreign policy goals shifted the focus to export control issues (e.g., in summer 1973, soybean embargo in the United States and export taxes in the EEC). About

Table 7   Matrix of world grain trade

Exporting regions \ Importing regions	Developed	Developing	Centrally planned	World
	PERCENT DISTRIBUTION			
Developed				
1956–60	40.6	18.2	2.3	61.3
1966–70	41.7	22.3	8.3	72.3
1971–72	43.7	23.2	11.2	78.1
Developing				
1956–60	10.2	11.9	0.7	22.8
1966–70	7.8	7.9	2.0	17.7
1971–72	6.2	6.4	0.8	13.4
Centrally Planned				
1956–60	3.3	2.0	10.6	15.9
1966–70	1.9	3.0	5.1	10.0
1971–72	1.0	2.0	5.5	8.5
World				
1956–60	54.1	32.1	13.6	100
1966–70	51.4	33.2	15.4	100
1971–72	50.9	31.6	17.5	100

Note: The columns denote importing regions while the rows are the exporting regions. Thus, by reading down one obtains imports for the region listed and by reading across exports for that region.
Adapted from USDA/ERS, ''The World Food Situation and Prospects to 1985,'' December 1974, p. 20.

the same time, however, growing concern for specific global food needs led to the World Food Conference and the subsequent emphasis through the World Food Council and the International Fund for Agricultural Development on production increases, enhanced development assistance and food aid for immediate famine relief. The World Food Conference also stimulated new initiatives toward setting up a grain reserve, both to stabilize price and to attack chronic conditions of malnutrition in food deficit countries. With the emergence of surplus conditions in 1975–76, the establishment of reserves became an actual possibility, and, in the views of those preparing for the Third Session of the World Food Council in June 1977, the overriding food issue before the world community.[30]

Just as food issues vary by circumstance, food flows vary by geographic region. Current international grain trade is concentrated in three geographic arenas. The most important in terms of proportion of world grain trade is the arena of advanced industrial nations (the members of the Organization of Economic Cooperation and Development—OECD), which includes most of the major grain exporting *and* importing states. As Table 7 shows, about 44 percent of total world grain exports in 1971–72 moved among these countries alone.

[30]See United Nations, WFC, *International System of Food Security,* WFC/37, March 26, 1977. By contrast, as surpluses have reemerged, some decline in emphasis on production increases may be evident. Preliminary estimates suggest that in 1976 external resources for expanding food production did not increase and may have actually declined for the first time in four years. See United Nations, WFC, *Progress Toward Increasing Food Production in Developing Countries,* WFC/36, March 25, 1977, p. ii.

The second major arena is between OECD nations and the centrally planned countries, principally China, the Soviet Union, and Eastern European states. In 1971-72, OECD sales to these countries represented 11.2 percent of total grain exports, while sales by these countries to the OECD accounted for 1 percent (largely within Central Europe). The percentage of world grain trade moving within this arena over the postwar period has varied widely, creating the principal instability in postwar grain markets. The third arena is between OECD and developing countries, which embraced in 1971-72 about 29.4 percent of total world grain trade (23.2 percent from OECD to developing states and 6.2 percent from developing states to the OECD).

While grain trade in each of these arenas has increased in significance during the postwar period, trade in other arenas—among developing countries, among centrally planned countries and between centrally planned and developing countries—has proportionately declined (among developing countries, for example, from 11.9 to 6.4 percent). The following discussion, therefore, treats only the principal arenas. In addition, only the United States and Canada enjoy a relatively even spread of grain exports to the principal arenas. In 1973-74, for example, these countries shipped somewhat less than half of their exports to OECD countries, about a quarter to centrally planned countries, and from a quarter to one-third to developing countries. By contrast, France and Argentina concentrated over two-thirds of their exports in OECD countries (mostly EEC countries in the case of France), while Australia shipped half of its exports to Asia and another quarter to Japan alone.[31] Canada and the United States, therefore, have the primary stake in *world* grain trade.

As the following discussion suggests, the character of international transactions in each of the principal geographic arenas varies considerably. Transactions within the OECD arena are all commercial, while trade with the centrally planned countries is mostly commercial, the principal exception being Poland which has received US food aid. By contrast, the OECD—developing country arena reflects a mixed character of transactions, including sizeable amounts of both concessional and commercial shipments.

OECD arena

Until recently, agricultural policies in the individual OECD countries served primarily domestic goals of farm income support. The primary objectives of these policies in the EEC, North America, and Japan, one source notes, were "remarkably alike... (namely) to increase the return to farmers and to narrow disparities between farm and non-farm incomes."[32] Foreign policies in agriculture were de-

---

[31] Figures are taken from United Nations, FAO, *World Grain Trade Statistics 1973/74*, Tables 11 and 14-18, pp. 30-31 and 36-42.

[32] "Toward the Integration of World Agriculture," a tripartite report by fourteen experts from North America, the European Community, and Japan, Brookings Institution, 1973, p. 12. For a comprehensive analysis of OECD agricultural policy issues, see also D. Gale Johnson, *World Agriculture in Disarray* (New York: Macmillan, 1973), and John O. Coppock, *Atlantic Agriculture Unity: Is It Possible?* (New York: McGraw-Hill for the Council of Foreign Relations, 1966).

signed primarily to deal with the consequences of domestic objectives and programs. Each country sought to transfer the costs of domestic policies to foreign markets. The United States and Canada wanted Europe to absorb more of their productive capacity, thereby reducing costly payments for acreage limitation and farm income support. The EEC tried to gain acceptance of higher prices worldwide, shifting the costs of subsidizing EEC exports from the Community to foreign buyers. Japan supported domestic rice producers at the expense of more efficient foreign producers, while in other grains it exploited low world prices to replace domestic grain production with sharply increasing foreign imports.[33]

These conflicts came to a head at the time of the Kennedy Round negotiations from 1962–67. The negotiations focused principally on US and Canadian access to U.K. and EEC markets; access to Japanese markets was thought to be satisfactory since Japan had little potential to increase production and was rapidly expanding consumption.[34] With the elaboration and implementation of the Common Agricultural Policy (CAP) in 1962–67, the United States and Canada had both experienced a serious reduction in grain exports to the EEC. From 1965–66 to 1968–69, for example, total US agricultural exports to the EEC (of which grains represent about one-third) dropped by 19 percent while exports to which CAP levies applied directly (which included grains) dropped nearly 40 percent.[35] From 1965–66 on, Canada lost half of its British and European grain markets.[36] Both the United States and Canada were determined to crack the highly protectionist barriers within the EEC, secure an increase in the minimum floor price for wheat under the 1962 International Wheat Agreement, and compel other grain producers and consumers to share more responsibility for food aid.

France, the principal beneficiary of CAP, the United Kingdom and the EEC Commission were equally determined to resist these demands. The negotiations, as a result, were both inconclusive and misdirected. No liberalization of CAP occured; a new International Grains Agreement (IGA) was concluded but the higher price floor was ignored in the absence of effective means to control production; and a Food Aid Convention was signed as part of the IGA, assigning proportional responsibility to major trading countries for food aid (US and Canada still accounting for more than 50 percent). The entire negotiations may be said to have been misdirected because little attention was given to reserves which existed only because of stockpiling policies in the United States and Canada.[37] Moreover, no one considered suffi-

---

[33]From 1961–71, as Paarlberg notes, grain production in Japan decreased by 2.2 percent annually, while grain consumption increased by 3.3 percent annually. The difference was made·up by imports.

[34]See Irwin R. Hedges, "Kennedy Round Agricultural Negotiations and the World Grain Agreement," *Journal of Farm Economics*, Vol. 49 (December 1967), pp. 133–34.

[35]F. O. Grogan, *International Trade in Temperate Zone Products* (Edinburgh: Oliver and Boyd, 1972), p. 46.

[36]GAO, "Grain Marketing Systems . . . ," p. ii.

[37]The 1962 International Wheat Agreement worked only because the United States and Canada maintained firm selling and stockpiling policies. By 1965–66, however, these stocks were largely liquidated through large requirements in the centrally planned countries (China and the Soviet Union) and several developing states (Pakistan and India). They were built up again after 1966, and Canada supported (through stockpiling) the minimum price floor in the 1967 Agreement long after others, including the United States, abandoned it. Nevertheless, production limitations after the mid-1960s sharply reduced the levels of reserves held by North American exporters over what they might have been otherwise.

ciently the consequences of subsidizing disposal of grain surpluses on world markets. Japan, many developing countries, and even, in the short-term, China and the Soviet Union, came to rely increasingly on artifically cheap grain imports. These demands eventually overloaded the system, especially after US and Canadian stockpiling policies changed. Ironically, one of the outcomes of the Kennedy Round agricultural negotiations may have been renewed determination by the major grain exporters, if others would not share stockpiling costs, to cut down on surpluses and withhold acreage from production. Policies to this effect in the United States, Canada and Australia subsequently brought world grain markets to the edge of minimum resource requirements.[38]

When the Tokyo Round of trade negotiations opened in September 1973, conditions had shifted from surplus to shortage. Nevertheless, initial positions among the major OECD grain trade players were surprisingly similar to earlier ones. In the face of stock depletion and growing shortages, the United States had lifted acreage limitations and was rapidly increasing production and exports.[39] Access to foreign markets, particularly in Europe, remained a high priority. The EEC, on the other hand, had just completed the difficult negotiations for UK membership in CAP. Moreover, in the summer of 1973, CAP had proved itself useful not only in times of surplus but also in times of shortage; export taxes helped to stem the outflow of grain and reduce domestic inflation. Neither of the two principal protagonists in OECD grain diplomacy, therefore, seemed inclined to alter its traditional stance.

There were other issues that afflicted the new agricultural talks. Worldwide food shortages and accelerating pressures from the developing countries had politicized commodity, including food, issues, raising questions of the relationship between grain reserve negotiations and negotiations on other commodities. Moreover, demands from developing countries for improved and indeed preferential access to manufacturing markets in the OECD countries had mobilized domestic protectionist forces, reducing in particular US leverage to trade off greater access to US industrial markets for enhanced US access to European agricultural markets (a tactic of US diplomacy also in the Kennedy Round). Not only was agricultural trade becoming enmeshed internationally in broader trade issues (in contrast to its separation from these issues in the 1950s) but agriculture was also being viewed domestically as an increasingly vital part of overall foreign economic policy and performance. Amidst the array of interventionist policies in agriculture, however, few standards existed either to measure comparative advantage in agriculture or to understand fully the contribution of agriculture to domestic economic growth (or recession).

---

[38]See comments on cartel-like collaboration among the United States, Canada and Australia by Edwin M. Martin in Don Wallace, Jr. and Helga Escobar (eds.), *The Future of International Economic Organization* (New York: Praeger, 1976), p. 33.

[39]U.S. agricultural exports have more than tripled in this decade to an estimated $24 billion in fiscal 1977.

While making trade and diplomacy more complex, the increasing interrelation of agriculture with broader international and domestic issues also began to prompt some reevaluation of traditional positions among principal grain negotiators. The United States was experiencing first hand the consequences of open-ended access to US grain markets. Soviet purchases in the private market in 1972 sent US food prices skyrocketing and contributed to the ill-advised soybean embargo in June 1973.[40] The latter episode, in particular, delivered a serious shock to Japan, a major US soybean customer, and led to the conclusion by USDA of an informal US-Japanese bilateral agreement (in which the United States agreed to sell and Japan agreed to buy 14 m. tons of grain per year) as well as an intensive Japanese search for alternative suppliers (e.g., Brazil). The EEC, despite the advantages and enlargement of CAP, was smarting under increasingly heavy support costs borne in largest measure by a less and less compliant Germany.[41] Finally, the coalition of developing countries known as the Group of 77 had made clear at the Third United Nations Conference on Trade and Development (UNCTAD III) in 1972 and again at the VI Special Session of the United Nations in April 1974 that stalemate in trade negotiations among the OCED countries could no longer be allowed to delay treatment of the pressing problems facing the poorer countries in the wake of the food and energy crises.

The World Food Conference was convened in November 1974 to impart global impetus to the historically and geographically fragmented agricultural issue. One result was a meeting of principal grain exporters in February 1975 to discuss the possibility of establishing a global food reserve. In September the United States put forward a new proposal for such a reserve. A tortured compromise among US government agencies, worked out in a troubled time of domestic recession and inflation, the proposal called for quantitative triggers to control stocks. This provision fell short of the EEC interest in price triggers. Moreover, the proposal was tabled at the International Wheat Council where the Soviet Union is a member while the EEC wanted all commodity issues to be discussed at Geneva (where the Tokyo Round trade discussions moved in 1974). Although the discussions deadlocked as US elections and a change-over in the EEC Commision took place in 1976, the politicizing of the reserve issue in global forums after 1973 may have played an important role in insuring that this issue would be seriously considered once supplies again became sufficient (see subsequent discussion).

OECD–centrally planned country arena

Historically, the Soviet Union and most other centrally planned countries have also pursued agricultural policies based largely on domestic goals. In this case,

---

[40]For details of these events, see the article in this volume by I. M. Destler.
[41]EEC expenditures for support and stockpile programs are much higher for non-cereals (butter, dried milk, etc.) than cereals. Nevertheless, in 1973, expenditures for cereals alone amounted to $1 billion (out of a total cost of $3.7 billion).

however, goals favored the consumer rather than the farmer. Policies sought to maintain low food prices to feed an urban-based population. An inevitable consequence was low incentives for increased food production. In the last 15 years this has led many centrally planned states to rely increasingly upon international markets for required imports. Eastern Europe and China have been fairly consistent importers, averaging respectively 5–8 million and 4–6 million tons of grain annually over the period 1961–1975.[42] The Soviet Union, on the other hand, despite major efforts to increase agricultural supplies, has been the principal element of instability in world grain markets. Production shortfalls in the Soviet Union in 1963, 1965 and 1972 led to major grain imports. In other years, Soviet purchases have been small or negligible.[43] Moreover, in 1972, the Soviet Union imported far more grain than was needed to cover production shortfalls and even reexported some to India while offering to do the same to the United States.[44] These patterns of Soviet purchases contributed to sharp market fluctuations for grains, accounting in 1960–1973 for 80 percent of the deviation from trend in world wheat imports.[45]

Until 1972, instability of Soviet purchases was a factor principally affecting Canadian and Australian exporters. These countries consistently exported to the centrally planned states, eschewing political controls. By contrast, the United States, except for one sale to the Soviet Union in 1963 (1.8 million tons of grain), maintained special restrictions on such exports by means of "cold war" legislation introduced in the late 1940s. This was reinforced by the requirement imposed at the behest of maritime unions that fifty percent of grain sold to these countries be carried in "US bottoms." In 1971–72, however, US policy shifted. In the onrush of detente, export control regulations eased, the 50 percent US bottoms requirement was lifted, and the Secretary of Agriculture was dispatched to Moscow to negotiate a credit agreement. As a result, the United States sold 13.7 m. metric tons of grain to the Soviet Union in 1972–73 (including 9.5 million metric tons of wheat, about one quarter of the entire wheat harvest that year) and increased agricultural exports to China as well.[46]

The grain sale to the Soviet Union revealed a new side to the bargaining over world grain trade. Commercial cooperation was a high priority in both Washington and Moscow. In May 1972, the Soviet Minister of Foreign Trade came to

[42]USDA/ERS, *World Agricultural Situation*, WAS-12, December 1976, p. 18. See also Brown, "The Politics and Responsibility of the North American Breadbasket," Worldwatch Paper 2, October 1975, p. 15.

[43]For example, Soviet wheat purchases from Canada reached 200 million bushels a year in 1966 and then dropped to nearly zero in 1968. GAO, "Grain Marketing Systems . . . ," p. 44.

[44]The offer was at a much higher price than they paid for grain in the United States, of course. See Paarlberg.

[45]USDA/ERS, *The World Food Situation and Prospects to 1985*, Foreign Agricultural Economic Report No. 98, p. 42.

[46]See USDA/ERS, *USSR Agricultural Situation: Review of 1976 and Outlook for 1977*, Foreign Agricultural Economic Report No. 132, April 1972, Table 25, p. 43. US agricultural exports to China rose from $200 million in fiscal year 1973 to $838 million in fiscal year 1974 and back to $328 million in fiscal year 1975. See USDA/ERS, *FATUS*, December 1975, pp. 36, 33. In 1976–77, however, China imported no agricultural commodities from the United States.

Washington to discuss grain and other purchases, and in October, a full trade agreement was signed.[47] Perceptions were still influenced by surplus conditions and non-food goals. There was little doubt that the grain sale, no less than the trade agreement, was meant to be an important symbol of superpower rapprochement. The Soviets, however, with their centralized state trading agencies, were able to exploit the fragmented private market in the United States. They not only made their purchases quickly and secretly, avoiding the price effects of their massive interventions, but also benefited from USDA subsidies (as did US grain companies) which were still paid on commercial grain exports to help reduce US surpluses.[48] If the United States continued to promote free markets in world grain trade, it was clear that other countries (and not only the centrally planned ones) had greater capabilities to manipulate and exploit these markets.

When the full price effects of the so-called "great grain robbery"[49] became apparent, US officials moved to gain greater control over US private grain activities. At first clumsily through export controls (on soybeans) and then through a system of export monitoring and bilateral negotiations, US policy makers attempted to establish a more predictable system of interaction with the Soviet Union (as well as other major importers, such as Japan). Not surprisingly, the effort met with mixed success. Farmers and their champion, Secretary of Agriculture Earl Butz, bitterly opposed restraints on exports. On the other hand, consumers and opponents of detente increasingly criticized policies which appeared to purchase Soviet good will at the expense of American pocketbooks. On the basis of an uneasy balance between these conflicting interests, a bilateral agreement was concluded with the Soviet Union in October 1975. Additional and in some cases informal agreements were also concluded with Japan, Poland and most recently East Germany.[50]

The conclusion of bilateral agreements raises some issues for the larger diplomacy and management of world grain markets. The purpose in reaching the US-Soviet agreement was to stabilize grain purchases by the most volatile buyer in world grain markets. By limiting Soviet purchases to 8 million tons and requiring purchases of 6 m. tons even when the Soviet Union may not need it, the agreement encourages the Soviet Union to build up its own stocks against larger production shortfalls. A Soviet reserve would act to reduce the requirement for a multilateral

[47]The priority of the commercial objectives is suggested by a comment made by the Soviet Trade Minister in May. After being informed about the US mining of Haiphong and bombing of Hanoi, he turned to his negotiating partner, Secretary of Commerce Peter Peterson, and said: "Well, let's get back to business." *Wall Street Journal,* October 20, 1972. Cited in Dan Caldwell, "Appraising Detente," paper presented at International Studies Association Convention, St. Louis, March 16–20, 1977. For details on the Soviet purchase, see Marshall Goldman, *Detente and Dollars* (New York: Basic Books, 1975), chapter 7.

[48]See GAO, "Russian Wheat Sales and Weaknesses in Agriculture's Management of Wheat Export Subsidy Program," July 9, 1973, p. 22.

[49]See the book with this title: James Trager, *The Great Grain Robbery* (New York: Ballantine, 1975).

[50]The US-Soviet agreement covers a five-year period and requires the United States to sell at least 6 m. tons of wheat and corn to the Soviet Union each year and the Soviet Union to purchase no more than 8 m. tons per year. The agreement however, is not self-executing and calls only for consultation when the limits are reached.

grain reserve. From one perspective, therefore, concluding the bilateral agreement dilutes the US rationale for holding reserve discussions at the IWC (since the Soviets now may not need to be involved), as well as shifts the purpose of the reserve from price stabilization and world food security (which would be less urgent if the Soviets stockpiled) to price support, an objective much closer to the interests of the EEC.

A primary Soviet motivation in concluding the agreement may have been to secure guaranteed access to US grain supplies without having to participate in a multilateral reserve arrangement. While the bilateral agreement may achieve this purpose for the Soviet Union, it is unlikely to substitute for multilateral price stabilization and security for other countries.[51] First, it does not constrain Soviet purchases from other exporters and Soviet purchases therefore could still have the same aggregate effect on world prices. Second, the Soviets could always make the minimum purchase and reexport to Eastern Europe or buy the maximum amount and reduce exports to Eastern Europe. The latter countries could then turn to international markets with the same net impact on world prices. Third, the agreement encourages similar bilateral accords with other importers; and unless such agreements are multilaterally coordinated, wealthy and politically important states will be taken care of first, while residual markets, where poor countries have to go, will become even thinner and more volatile. Fourth, a system of bilateral agreements is unlikely to hold without stronger commitments than those contained in the US-Soviet agreement, and multilateral agreement may be necessary to get Congressional approval in the United States as well as to hold private interest groups to the terms of the accord.

In sum, as Phillip Trezise has noted, "this issue of a stabilization undertaking on a broad international basis . . . will arise anyway, bilateral agreements or not."[52] The US-Soviet agreement may diminish Soviet incentive to participate in a multilateral reserve system, since it guarantees a certain market access outside such a system. But, the negotiation of a multilateral reserve will have to be coordinated in any case with commitments to the Soviet Union, since rules for dealing with non-participants will be an essential part of any such reserve.

OECD–developing country arena

Developing countries, at least since gaining independence, have also subordinated food diplomacy to domestic goals.[53] Beginning in the 1950s, most of these countries embarked on development programs emphasizing industrialization and urban needs rather than agriculture and rural advance. Where agriculture was sup-

---

[51]For a similar argument, see Paarlberg's essay in this volume.

[52]See *Rebuilding Grain Reserves: Toward an International System* (Washington: The Brookings Institution, 1976), p. 34.

[53]Prior to independence, as Christensen notes in her article in this volume, agriculture in developing countries was often organized to serve foreign interests. See also Frances Moore Lappé and Joseph Collins, *Food First: Beyond the Myth of Scarcity* (Boston: Houghton Mifflin, 1977).

ported, it was done more often to produce cash crops for export. The foreign exchange earnings were then used to help finance capital equipment and other imports for broad-scale industrialization. Otherwise, domestic food policies sought to maintain stable and relatively low grain prices for politically important urban populations, while providing few incentives for domestic agriculture. Although food production in developing countries grew from 1961 to 1975 by 2.7 percent annually, per capita food production increased by only .1 percent per annum.[54]

The policies of OECD countries and international organizations generally supported these development orientations of developing countries. As we noted earlier, the major producers had grain supplies to spare and subsidized the disposal of these supplies to create artificially low world grain prices. Food was cheaper to provide than money, and it was also easier to support politically, particularly in the United States, the principal food donor. As a result, bilateral and multilateral food aid in 1965, 95 percent of which came from the United States, totaled $1.3 billion, while all other aid commitments from OECD countries for economic development as a whole totaled $9.7 billion.[55] As one source notes, "even international institutions created during this period, such as the World Food Program, were often primarily an attempt to deal with the North American agricultural problem of surplus capacity."[56]

The vast majority of food aid went for non-food purposes, both economic and political. The availability of such aid provided budgetary support for governing elites but by depressing local prices did little to encourage local agriculture or the development of domestic infrastructure to improve the distribution of food outside urban areas.[57]

Greater interest in agricultural development began to emerge in the 1960s. Changes in US legislation sought to tie food aid more effectively to agricultural development objectives.[58] Persistent US pressure to get other OECD countries to

[54]United Nations, WFC, *Progress Toward Increasing Food Production in Developing Countries,* WFC/36, March 25, 1977, p. 5. For more on developing-country policies toward agriculture, see Nicholson and Esseks in this volume.

[55]See OECD, Development Assistance Committee, *Development Cooperation: 1976 Review,* November 1976 and previous annual reviews. The basic US legislation for food aid is Public Law 480 (PL480) passed in 1954 to facilitate marketing of "surplus" American commodities to countries on terms more favorable than those in commercial markets. About 70 percent of PL480 shipments is sales at subsidized rates (Title I); the rest is donations for disasters, regular nutrition programs, etc. (Title II).

[56]See David Kay, "The Behavior of International Organizations in the World Food Arena," in Giulo Pontecorvo (ed.), *The Management of Food Policy,* (New York: Arno Press, 1976), p. 126.

[57]See McHenry and Bird, "Food Bungle. . . ." For an extensive analysis of the multiple impacts of food aid on agricultural development, see Paul J. Iseman and H. W. Singer, "Food Aid: Disincentive Effects and Their Policy Implications," *Economic Development and Cultural Change,* January 1977, pp. 205–237.

[58]The Food for Peace Act of 1966 formalized the link between PL480 and local agricultural development, requiring that each Title I sales agreement contain a "self-help" statement by the recipient country concerning the program to be followed in expanding its food production. The Act further stipulated that PL480 could be terminated if such a program were insufficiently implemented. In practice, the impact these "self-help" provisions had on development goals was probably marginal, both because surplus conditions ensured ultimate disposal and because the United States continued to have strong non-food reasons for making PL480 shipments.

share more of the burdens of food aid led to the conclusion of the Food Aid Convention (see earlier discussion) and to a reduction in the US share of overall food aid. Most importantly, international organizations, principally the World Bank group, began to give higher priority to agriculture and the needs of the poorest countries, as well as of the poorest rural elements in these countries. In 1962 the World Bank group invested only 7.8 percent of its total disbursements to less developed countries in agricultural projects; by 1971, this figure had risen to 17 percent and by 1975 had reached 31.5 percent.[59]

It took the dramatic swing from surplus to shortage conditions and the politicization of the food issue through the World Food Conference, however, to confirm the emphasis on expanded development assistance and food production in developing countries. International organization and civil servants played an important role in this process.[60] The Secretary-General of the World Food Conference, Sayed Marei, and his deputy, Sartaj Aziz, stressed the need to establish "a high-level, nonbureaucratic, political committee to keep food concerns and commitments before the international community. . . ."[61] While the World Food Authority (WFA) they proposed did not win approval, "the two most important institutional frameworks to emerge from the World Food Conference—the International Fund for Agricultural Development and the World Food Council—actually represented the rationale and even the language" of the WFA.[62] What is more, the new institutions brought added attention to the key problem of food production in the developing countries. The World Food Council (WFC) at its first session in June 1975 made the expansion of food production in developing countries its first priority, and the negotiation and establishment of the International Fund for Agricultural Development (IFAD) in 1976 set aside major new resources for this purpose.[63] In 1973–75, assistance for agricultural development more than doubled ($2.1 billion to $5.5 billion) and agriculture made up 21.6 percent of all aid in 1975 compared to 16.1 percent in 1973.[64] Almost two-thirds of this aid went to countries with per capita incomes less than $450. Food aid also increased by 75 percent (in value) over the 1965–74 average ($2.1 billion compared to $1.2 billion) but was increasingly viewed as a "transitional" measure which required periodic assessments and forward planning to minimize disincentive effects on local agricultural development. Moreover, the US share of food aid dropped sharply from 94 percent in 1965 to 59 percent in 1975, while the EEC, Canada and Australia increased their share. Japan

[59]See Martin Kriesberg, *International Organizations and Agricultural Development,* Foreign Agricultural Economic Report No. 131, USDA/ERS, May 1977, p. 66.

[60]See Thomas G. Weiss and Robert S. Jordan, "Bureaucratic Politics and the World Food Conference: The International Policy Process," *World Politics,* Vol. XXVIII (April 1976), pp. 422–440.

[61]Ibid., p. 435.

[62]Ibid., pp. 433–34.

[63]Total pledges for IFAD now equal $1.022 b.—$567.3 m. from developed countries, $435.5 m. from OPEC-developing donors, and $9 m. in convertible and $10.3 m. in nonconvertible currencies from developing recipient countries. Operation of this fund will add some $300 m. per year to external agricultural assistance.

[64]United Nations, WFC, *Progress Toward Increasing Food Production in Developing Countries,* WFC/36, March 25, 1977, pp. 13–14.

and the Soviet Union continued to contribute far below their capabilities to the concessional food aid system.[65]

The increased availability of aid for agricultural development reflected a greater emphasis in the foreign aid policies of developed countries on agricultural modernization (as opposed to earlier industrialization strategies based on import substitution). This has been accompanied by increasing stress on agriculture in the developing countries themselves where food shortages in 1973–74 had their most serious impact. As an OECD report notes, "one of the positive results of the World Food Conference was to create a greater awareness among developing countries' policy-makers and officials responsible for development planning that agriculture needs to be given a higher priority."[66] Some of these countries, notably Senegal, Sudan, Honduras and Bangladesh, are working closely with the Consultative Group for Food Production and Investment, an affiliate of the World Bank established by the World Food Conference, to formulate investment strategies for increasing domestic food production. From 1974–76, agricultural production in developing countries expanded by 4 percent per annum compared to 2.6 percent for the entire period from 1970–76.[67]

If the food production potential of developing countries is to be fully achieved, enhanced access to OECD markets will also be required. Many developing countries depend on exports in non-cereal products to offset cereal imports.[68] This is especially true for the second class of importing countries we identified earlier for whom cereal imports represent a sizeable percentage of total exports—India, Bangladesh, and Egypt. For these three countries, for example, products included in the integrated commodity program of UNCTAD represented in 1974 25, 35 and 55 percent respectively of total export earnings. Increases in these earnings through further exports to developed countries could significantly enhance the ability of these countries to pay for needed grain imports.[69] Negotiations on these issues are going on in UNCTAD and GATT. While progress remains slow, the Lomé Convention concluded in 1975 by the EEC with forty-six African, Caribbean and Pacific developing countries establishes some interesting potential precedents for OECD–developing country relations in this area.[70]

---

[65]OECD, *Development Cooperation: 1976 Review,* pp. 148–149. See Paarlberg in this volume for further details of EEC, Japanese and Soviet contributions.

[66]Ibid., p. 134.

[67]See WFC/36, pp. 18–19; and WFC/34, p. 2.

[68]From 1970–75, for example, the agricultural trade balance of developing countries improved by $5.1 b. (from $8.3 b. to $13.4 b.), but this increase was completely erased by a rise in cereal imports of $6.4 b. (from $1.7 b. to $8.1 b., excluding OPEC).

[69]United Nations, WFC, *Food Trade,* WFC/42, March 30, 1977, pp. 12–13.

[70]The Lomé Convention granted non-reciprocal access to EEC markets (earlier association agreements provided for reciprocal access of EEC exports to developing country markets) and included most agricultural products covered under CAP (which had been excluded from earlier association agreements). Except for sugar, which is dealt with in a separate protocol, 99.2 percent of all imports from developing country signatories now enter the EEC free of duty and other restrictions. The Convention also establishes a fund to stabilize developing country earnings in the event of export shortfalls. See Isebill V. Gruhn, "The Lomé Convention: Inching Toward Interdependence," *International Organization,* Vol. 30 (Spring 1976), 241–263.

Prospects of food diplomacy

Non-food goals

While shortage conditions increased the emphasis on food goals, they also created the prerequisites for enhanced "food power" or the use of food by exporters to achieve non-food objectives. Accordingly, discussions of food diplomacy in 1974–75, particularly in the United States, turned to questions of linkage between food trade and other issues, principally oil. Arab states, it was noted, represented a new class of developing countries capable of paying for US agricultural exports. From 1971 to 1976, each of three leading OPEC agricultural importers (Iran, Iraq and Saudi Arabia) increased the value of its farm imports by 400 percent, from below $250 million to an estimated $1 billion.[71] The US share of these imports fluctuates, but reached as high as 75 percent in fiscal year 1975 for Iran and ranges around 15 percent for Iraq and Saudi Arabia. Moreover, in the near term, it is expected that "mideast OPEC members will become increasingly dependent on food imports until their massive agricultural development projects show results in the late 1970s."[72] Why then, it was asked, could not the United States exploit its food leverage over these states, just as they had exploited their oil leverage over the United States? Similarly, if the Soviet Union needed US grain, as it did in 1972 and again in 1974–75, why could not the US demand something in return that it needed, like Soviet oil?

These speculations went beyond oil and dealt with US leverage to use food more broadly for diplomatic purposes. *Business Week* wondered whether "US food power" might not prove the "ultimate weapon in world politics,"[73] and the Central Intelligence Agency's Office of Political Research speculated that, if the world food situation took a very sharp turn for the worse, "the US might regain the primacy in world affairs it held in the immediate post-World War II era."[74]

The soybean embargo in 1973, the temporary grain moratorium and the agreement with the Soviet Union in 1975 (which contained a letter of intent to negotiate oil purchases from the Soviet Union), and the use of American food aid in the Middle East after 1973, all demonstrated that the US government could influence the magnitude and direction of American food exports, and how it did so mattered to other governments. For some governments, like the Soviet Union, the value of US food was largely a function of the costs of other options (e.g., belt-tightening as in

---

[71]From 1971 to 1976 (estimated), total agricultural imports in Iran increased from $250 m. to $1,020 m., in Iraq from $220 m. to $1,025 m. and in Saudi Arabia from $225 m. to $1,030 m. See Table 1 in John B. Parker, Jr., "Agricultural Imports by Major Developing Countries," Foreign Demand and Competition Division, USDA/ERS, August 1976.

[72]*FATUS*, March 1975, However, these imports decreased in fiscal year 1975 when Iran, benefiting from record grain harvests, cut back her US food purchases from $757 million to $148 million.

[73]December 15, 1975, p. 54.

[74]CIA, Office of Political Research, "Potential Implications of Trends in World Population, Food Production, and Climate," August 1974, p. 3.

1965 or purchases from non-US suppliers as in 1975–76 when the Soviet Union imported the same amount as in 1972 but not as much from the United States).[75] For others, like developing countries which have fewer options, the value may be more immediate.[76]

The use of food for broader diplomatic purposes, however, reflects not only the increased value of US food under conditions of world shortage but also the relative decline of US power in more traditional areas of diplomacy. As long as the United States was able to achieve its foreign policy purposes through security or prestige instruments, economic policies were not used directly to influence political outcomes. For much of the postwar period when the United States dominated the Western alliance, it carefully separated economic relations from political bargaining.[77] At times, it even risked relative economic losses to sustain political objectives—discrimination against the dollar under the Organization for European Economic Cooperation (OEEC), support for European economic integration. As US power began to recede in the late 1960s, however, the United States became more aware of such costs, which also increased (as in the case of the overvalued dollar). In a number of areas, as Emma Rothschild notes, US policy sounded "a retreat from the arduous costs of world power in economic policy as well as in foreign policy more generally."[78] Through unilateral economic policy measures (for example the dollar devaluation and import surcharge of 1971), the United States sought to shift some of the costs of international system maintenance to other countries, particularly its wealthy allies—Germany and Japan.[79]

Thus, while in a broad sense US political and diplomatic power sufficed in the early postwar years to shape economic relations,[80] economic power came to be used in later periods to affect political outcomes. For example, one interpretation of US post-1973 energy policies, widely circulated in Europe, accused the United States of using the less vulnerable position of the US in international oil markets to reassert

---

[75]If such options are limited, the Soviet Union may indeed refrain from political actions that could jeopardize US-Soviet grain trade. Secretary of Agriculture Earl Butz clearly believed that "food power" had this effect in 1974: "I couldn't prove it if my life depended on it. But I think everybody agrees that the Soviets could have stopped the Sinai agreement that Secretary Kissinger worked out between Egypt and Israel. They sat on the sidelines . . . I am convinced that they knew they had to come into our market for more grain. This is no time to rock the boat." See his testimony before Senate Agriculture Committee, "Who's Making Foreign Agricultural Policy," January 1976, p. 19.

[76]For example, PL480 agreements with Egypt and Syria helped Henry Kissinger in his Mideast diplomacy in 1974, just as more food aid enabled the US to extract concessions from South Korea on textiles in 1971. On the latter, see GAO, "Economic and Foreign Policy Effects of Voluntary Restraint Agreements on Textiles and Steel," March 21, 1974, p. 29; and *Washington Post,* May 20, 1976.

[77]This resulted in what Richard Cooper described as a "two-track" system. See "Trade Policy Is Foreign Policy," *Foreign Policy,* Number 9 (Winter 1972-73), pp. 18-36.

[78]"Food Politics," p. 290.

[79]The same motivation exists in US policy toward an international grain reserve—to get others like the Soviet Union and Japan to bear some of the costs of maintaining reserves.

[80]For such an argument, see Robert Gilpin, "The Politics of Transnational Economic Relations," in Robert O. Keohane and Joseph S. Nye, Jr., (eds.), *Transnational Relations and World Politics* (Cambridge: Harvard University Press, 1972), pp. 48-70.

US political leadership vis-à-vis Europe and Japan.[81] It was argued that the US had attempted and failed to achieve this same objective through more traditional means in the "Year of Europe" exercise of 1973. Similarly, it could be argued, discussions in 1974–75 linking food and oil issues sought to achieve through food instruments what traditional diplomacy had been unable to achieve up to then, namely a lowering of oil prices. Viewed from this perspective, then, the focus on "food power" seems a symbol of both new strength *and* new weakness in US diplomacy.

But food diplomacy raises not only questions of strength and weakness but also of priority among moral or humanitarian and other goals. For some, the moral issue is joined immediately by considering food as an instrument of diplomacy, like any other, to achieve political purposes. They point out that food, especially under conditions of shortage, ought not be viewed as an instrument; it is instead a right for every individual and should not be manipulated, with good intentions or cynically, for other ends. If it is accepted, however, that food under some circumstances may be used to pursue non-food objectives, then the issue becomes one of what objectives. If US food helps build a stable relationship with the Soviet Union, if "diversion" of food aid to Egypt, Israel, or Syria helps bring peace to the Middle East, then such use of food power could be very moral indeed. Conversely, it may be quite moral for the Third World countries to exploit world food forums to press broader redistribution initiatives. The judgement in each case must rest on the desirability of the goals and the practicality of this means of advancing them.

In all of these cases, however, the precise value of food transfers in diplomatic bargaining will depend upon conditions in world grain markets and the underlying ability of key supplier countries to discriminate among purchasers in line with non-food, foreign policy objectives. Conditions in world grain markets are rapidly shifting once again from shortage to surplus. Under such circumstances, as the experience of the International Wheat Agreement suggests, suppliers compete vigorously for markets, and cooperation is difficult to sustain for economic, let alone more politically-charged, foreign policy reasons. Without supplier cooperation, buying countries that have the hard currency to pay for food can choose to whom they will give their business and, if faced with actual or threatened cutoff, can shift their purchases to other suppliers.[82] Buyers that cannot pay for food may be more influenced by who can finance, as well as provide, the required food shipment. The major grain suppliers, principally the United States, no longer dominate concessional finance today as they did in the 1940s. Concessional terms covered

---

[81]See discussion in V. H. Oppenheim, "Why Oil Prices Go Up, (1), The Past: We Pushed Them," *Foreign Policy* (Winter 1976–77), pp. 50–51.

[82]For example, as a recent Agriculture Department study noted, "The cancellation of US soybean contracts in 1973 at least partially caused Japan's negotiating in 1974 a contract with Brazil for the production and purchase of soybeans." Charles E. Hanrahan and Richard M. Kennedy, "International Considerations in the Development of Domestic Agricultural and Food Policy," in USDA/ERS, *Agricultural-Food Policy Review,* January 1977, p. 132.

only 6 percent of US food exports in the fiscal year 1975 compared to 33 percent in fiscal year 1959. In fiscal year 1975, on the other hand, "large financial flows and investments from various OPEC countries . . . helped India increase its commercial imports" of US farm products to a record $548 million.[83] Finally, the use of food for non-food goals is limited by the ability of major exporters to control food trade. The strength of farm interests in the United States and other exporting countries may have declined somewhat in recent times, but it nevertheless remains quite important. Moreover, the grain companies exercise a dominant influence in the US market and provide invaluable export services to other grain exporters. The political costs of imposing new controls on these companies are high (though perhaps not as high as in the case of farmers) even in times of crisis; these costs escalate rapidly as crisis conditions ease and the operation of market forces becomes more tolerable.

In sum, it is unlikely that food can be used in the years ahead as a major instrument for significant diplomatic gain. The market conditions for denying food as a means of influence will probably not exist, while supplier cooperation to provide food on the basis of certain political terms is more likely with developing countries than with wealthy importing countries (Soviet Union, Japan) where commercial stakes are so much higher. Yet the developing countries are not the principal actors in international politics from whom one would seek to extract important political benefits through the use of food.

Food goals

The world grain situation today is again one of surplus. Supply-demand balances reported as of July 1977 suggested a 1976–77 world grain carryover in excess of 185 million tons, making year end stocks the largest in six years.[84] This shift from shortage to surplus conditions creates new opportunities as well as old problems for a world diplomacy that seeks to shape the global food system. The experience of shortages is still fresh in the minds of the world community. In all countries, developed and developing alike, there is greater awareness of the mutual requirements and benefits of an improved world food system. At a minimum, all states appear willing to recognize that food is not a domestic issue only, the consequences of which may be merely dumped on international markets. As one analyst notes, "food has clearly taken on an additional dimension, namely that of playing a major role in foreign policy."[85] It is not yet clear, however, whether foreign policy

---

[83]*FATUS,* December 1975, p. 13. In fiscal years 1955 through 1973, India imported $5.5 billion in US agricultural commodities; $5.06 billion of this was financed by US government programs, mainly PL480. (USDA/ ERS, *US Agricultural Exports Under Public Law 480,* October 1974, p. 216.) In 1975, notwithstanding the resumption of PL480 wheat imports, India imported $544 million commercially, and just $215 million with government financing. For fiscal 1976, the figures were $647 million commercial and $93 million concessional. For LDCs taken as a whole, the figures for fiscal 1976 were $5,828 million and $852 million, respectively. (USDA/ERS, *Foreign Agricultural Trade Statistical Report, Fiscal Year 1976,* September 1976, pp. 24–25.)

[84]USDA/ERS, *World Agricultural Situation,* WAS-13, July 1977, p. 8.

[85]See J. Dawson Ahalt, "Agricultural and Food Policy: An Insiders View," in Pontecorvo (ed.), *The Management of Food Policy,* p. 253.

concerns of major participants in world grain diplomacy will focus on food or non-food goals. The World Food Conference and the recent emphasis of international organizations on agriculture and the rural poor have given new importance to specific food goals such as minimum nutrition levels and conditions for price stabilization and more equitable distribution of food production and consumption around the world. Is it possible that these goals will weigh more heavily in the foreign policies of participants in world grain diplomacy, or will new surpluses trigger policies aimed at the domestic food and foreign policy non-food goals of the past (such as production cutbacks to protect domestic farm prices or surplus disposal of excess production abroad)?

Timing in diplomacy is often critical. The present conjunction of new surpluses and lingering memories of shortage may provide the right occasion to use grain surpluses to achieve international food goals. Food issues, as suggested by Table 6, have a tendency to shift under varying circumstances. As these shifts occur, bargaining advantage changes between exporter and importer. In times of surplus, importers have the advantage. They feel little pressure to contribute to grain reserves or to give more emphasis to their own agricultural production. They are confident that grain exporters will be led by self-interests of their own to hold reserves or to dump surpluses on the world market, probably under subsidy. Yet, in the present world situation, one could hope that importers are not too far away from the experience of shortages to realize that this advantage is often short-lived. Moreover, the longer they enjoy the advantage and the more they get used to cheap foreign imports, the worse they will suffer when markets shift once again to shortage (as they inevitably must given the vagaries of weather, not to mention the lack of foresight of men). Similarly, grain exporters should be close enough to their experience with domestic inflation and the limits of foreign ''food power'' to recognize that their presumed advantage in times of shortage is also ephemeral and, in the long-run, counter-productive. If they fail to protect against future shortages, the costs to them of another serious dose of world food inflation may be serious. Indeed, one might wonder if these costs, which would be avoided by wiser price stabilization policies, are ever deducted from the estimated costs of maintaining reserves. The presumed high costs of such reserves persist as a principal obstacle among exporters to establishing these reserves.

If the lessons of recent food shortages are not to be lost, therefore, the need to stockpile present surpluses against future shortage may be urgent. As the WFC Secretariat recommended in preparations for the third session of the Council, ''it is imperative that the World Food Council seize the opportunity provided by the unique circumstances which exist now and exert its maximum influence with governments and with international fora to create a grain reserve this year which will ensure against any repetition of the disaster of 1972-74.''[86]

During the first half of 1977, the principal grain exporters, the United States and Canada, showed greater interest in reserves. Both are concerned about the need

[86]United Nations, WFC, *International System of Food Security,* WFC/37, March 26, 1977, p. iii.

to prop up falling grain prices.[87] The United States however, is unwilling to stockpile unilaterally again at enormous cost. In February 1977, the Carter administration proposed a new farm bill which called for a privately-held wheat reserve of 8 m. metric tons (compared to an estimated world reserve requirement of 30 million tons). At the same time, President Carter warned that the United States could not afford large outlays for farm support, especially if it was serious about the desire to balance the federal budget by 1981. During the summer of 1977, large crop surpluses generated pressures once again for production cutbacks (first such cutbacks since 1973). In August, the Administration came forward with a revised plan, calling for a 20 percent reduction in wheat acreage for 1978 (a 10 percent set-aside of feed grain acreage was also considered) and enlarging the privately-held wheat reserves to include 17–19 m. metric tons of feed grain. In addition and as part of a compromise to insure against future world shortages and another round of price inflation, the Administration proposed to establish a new international emergency grain reserve of 6 m. tons. These US steps alone, of course, are not enough, but a US proposal that balances domestic and international requirements may go a long way toward encouraging other participants to contribute their share to the establishment of world food reserves.

Reserves, however, do not provide the whole answer to world food management. Other programs and institutions are required to maintain production incentives, meet emergencies, encourage long-term agricultural reform, and relate food requirements to larger development objectives.

Alternatives for dealing with world food problems may be grouped into three categories, taken in order of the increasing intervention required by *centralized* institutions and regulations: 1) liberalization of agricultural trade; 2) coordination or harmonization of national agricultural policies; 3) integration of institutions and policies for food. These alternatives may be applied bilaterally (as in the case of coordination of US-Soviet grain trade policies under the 1975 bilateral agreement), regionally (as in the case of integration of agriculture in the EEC), or globally (as in the internationally-coordinated national grain reserve proposal originally put forward by FAO).

In evaluating these various alternatives, there is an inevitable trade-off between efficiency and flexibility, at one extreme, and predictability and greater accountability, at the other. As we argued at the outset of this essay, all food flows involve consequences for political, economic and social relationships, whether intentional or not. Diplomacy cannot avoid these consequences. Instead it should seek to make the power that is inherent in such trade more visible and accountable. Making power more visible, of course, risks politicizing the global food system. Ideally one might hope that such a system would operate without frequent centralized intervention through a global food regime setting out agreed international rules, norms and practices. Market solutions have the virtue of removing food issues from the daily

---

[87]The wheat price in summer 1977 of $2.40 per bushel was much lower than the 1971 price relative to production costs. Ibid., p. 5.

intrusion of interstate politics; they rely, however, on the familiar and, in the opinion of many, inadequate "invisible hand" to ensure accountability. Centralized interstate management, on the other hand, ensures day-to-day accountability but subjects world food trade to the rigidity of bureaucracy and the constant threat of political manipulation. Accountability need not imply, however, answering to a single authority or a single set of rules. It can involve continuous review of multiple practices by multiple authorities. Since, as we have argued, world food problems may require multiple solutions, a flexible, more decentralized system of account-ability somewhere between a world food authority and the free market may be most desirable. For these as well as practical reasons limiting the extent to which food can be dealt with globally on food terms alone (see conclusion), a global food regime based on coordination and review of national government policies recommends itself. This outcome seems to offer the possibility of greater accountability of private interests to governments and of governments to one another without relying excessively on either private or authoritarian processes.

(1) *Liberalize global agricultural trade.* This has been the thrust of US domes-tic policy in recent years and is the basic position of the US in the multilateral trade negotiations (MTN). To pursue it consistently, of course, the US would have to ease quotas on those products (meat, dairy) which it continues to protect. Additional liberalization of agricultural trade, if implemented, would ease world food problems in two major ways. It would expand markets and therefore incentives for the most efficient producers on a worldwide basis, lowering the average cost of food worldwide. And as D. Gale Johnson emphasizes, it would distribute adjustments to price changes more evenly throughout the world, thereby reducing market instabil-ity.[88]

Free market policies, however, suffer several drawbacks under contemporary conditions. If governments have considered agriculture in the past to be too impor-tant to leave to free market forces *at home* where the benefits remain in the same country, they are likely to consider it too important to leave to free markets *abroad* where benefits are shared with other countries. This is probably true over the longer run even for the United States, which seems determined to avoid the disproportion-ate costs borne in the past from unilateral management of world agriculture. Experi-ence suggests that free market policies cannot survive surplus accumulation without production controls, which are costly to exporters and anathema to importers, or without stockpiling, which is again costly to exporters unless the burden is shared through some kind of non-market arrangements. Furthermore, after the Soviet grain purchases in 1972, everyone, expecially the United States, is likely to insist on closer surpervision and regulation of the multinational grain companies. If these

[88] With some markets protected, adjustment falls unevenly on unprotected markets, exaggerating fluctu-ations in these markets. Johnson notes, for example, that, under liberalized conditions, the EEC would have borne a greater measure of price adjustment in 1972–74 rather than most of this adjustment being absorbed by the United States. See Johnson's *World Food Problems and Prospects,* American Enterprise Institute for Public Policy Research, June 1975, pp. 33–34. See also the article by Seevers in this issue.

companies, in addition to conducting grain trade, are to have new responsibilities for holding grain reserves (as called for in US grain reserve proposals), they will have to be accountable for their actions to more than just the market forces of competition. This may be necessary for no other reason than to protect the grain companies themselves against an increasingly aroused inflation-weary public.

Finally, pushing liberalization much further seems impractical in the face of European determination to preserve the CAP, though negotiation to reduce the level of protection CAP offers may be possible. The deadlock caused by US-EEC differences has delayed decisions on world food issues for too long already. As Paarlberg notes in this volume, not all EEC policies are harmful to stabilizing world food supplies, providing as they do greater geographic balance in grain production and consumption (a corrective to the growing imbalance indicated in Table 1). On the other hand, the EEC must recognize that it is not even in its own interest to continue to spend billions supporting marginal farmers, highly inefficient production, and recurrent excessive food stockpiles. Greater flexibility among trade diplomats in both Europe and the United States might pave the way toward less dogmatic solutions such as greater coordination of national agricultural policies involving different mixes of private and public mechanisms.

(2) *Coordinate or harmonize national agricultural policies.* This alternative underlines the International Undertaking on World Food Security approved by the World Food Conference and recent US proposals at the IWC. These proposals call for a food reserve system based on coordinated management of national stockpiles. Such a system would discriminate against non-members but seek to pool costs and benefits among members, rather than simply dumping the consequences of domestic policies onto the international food system. Production controls as well as stockpiling responsibilities would be worked out and shared among both importers and exporters. Moreover, stocks would be built up and held on a decentralized basis, encouraging more self-reliance and local market production and stability. Flexibility would exist both in the choice of arrangements adopted by individual governments to coordinate with private interests (in the United States, for example, stocks would be privately held) and in alternative arrangements among governments (for example, bilateral commitments with the Soviet Union could be meshed with multilateral reserve rules for dealing with non-participants). The system strikes a balance between the risks and uncertainties of global production and distribution systems, on the one hand, and the inefficiencies of greater independence from international markets, on the other. Least costs are traded off for greater security.

This alternative places heavy emphasis on enhanced local production, as well as storage, of food. As the editors of this volume point out, international food markets may have great difficulty meeting projected deficits in developing countries over the next decade. Greater self-sufficiency is one way to meet absolute food requirements, as well as to reduce sensitivity to fluctuating prices of food obtained through international markets. Coordination of national policies builds in some necessary redundancy in the world food system.

Building up productive capabilities in food-deficit countries takes time. Interim food needs will continue to be a cause of concern. Grain exporters might consider assuring, either early within a crop year or on a multiple-year basis, that a certain minimum volume of grain will be available for food aid to poor developing countries.[89] Such a step would transform food aid from its domestic purposes of the past, i.e., as a residual or swing factor in domestic markets available in times of plenty when developing countries least need it, to international goals of feeding the world's poor when they most need it, i.e. when supplies are tight.

(3) *Integrate global policies and institutions for food.* This approach represents the thrust of EEC policies. It was also the basis of original proposals (not adopted) for a World Food Authority at the World Food Confrence.[90] Proposals to implement this approach call for market stabilization schemes to set agricultural prices and to ensure long-term investments and development in agriculture.

This solution might expect too much from contemporary interstate diplomacy and offer too little to those who seek greater fairness and accountability in the distribution of world food. To be effective, an integrated regime would have to be strong enough to control national bureaucratic as well as farm and food marketing interests. If this were not the case, centralization of world food management might reduce accountability below that which exists today. Powerful farm and marketing interests might be able to influence weak international institutions more effectively than current national institutions. In addition, while such an approach might fit the "ideology" of the less developed countries (see the essay by Nicholson and Esseks), it has been shown by most mainstream Western economists to be highly inefficient (see Johnson's article in this issue) and may, as we have argued, be vulnerable to political manipulation as well. In any case, it is not clear that such a system would benefit those most in need in the developing countries. Domestic food policies have tended to benefit efficient and large producers or wealthy and urban consumers. If these policies are seen as reflections of prevailing interests, centralized policies are unlikely to be much different. Moreover, centralized policies are likely to force a choice among the interest groups involved in the world food system, while coordination of decentralized policies allows different choices to be made in different countries and ensures through continuous review some balancing between the interests of producers and consumers, exporters and importers, efficient and inefficient producers, and urban and rural consumers.

---

[89]By the end of 1976, only Canada, the EEC and Sweden had adopted medium term (three years) indicative planning for food aid commitments.

[90]The proposal put forward by the World Food Conference Secretariat "spelled out comprehensive institutional alterations complete with organizational flowcharts, designed to integrate all the UN's activities relating to food and agricultural matters and to solicit more adequate funding for them." The proposal was subsequently dropped by the Secretariat when opposition proved to be too strong. See Weiss and Jordan, "Bureaucratic Politics and the World Food Conference," p. 433.

Conclusion

This discussion of world food diplomacy does not suggest any ready panacea for global food problems. Food has been and will continue to be an issue characterized by multiple goals, both food and non-food, changing climate, and varying linkages to other issues. It is symptomatic of interdependence in contemporary world affairs that at the same time agricultural issues have emerged as foreign policy and not just domestic problems, they have also become increasingly integrated with other domestic economic issues (growth, inflation, etc.) and with other international issues (non-food commodities, oil, reform of international institutions, etc.). In such a complex setting, it is not possible nor perhaps even desirable that food be dealt with only on its own terms. The proportion of food production traded internationally is not large enough to prescribe the rules of food systems overall (although the amounts traded are often marginally critical). Achieving the best food system possible in terms only of food goals (absolute nutrition levels, significant decreases in food consumption disparities) will draw limited resources from other worthwhile objectives. Nevertheless, in comparison to what has been emphasized in food diplomacy in the past, there is ample room for major world food participants to give more attention to specific international food needs and to be more aware at least of the food costs involved in seeking to satisfy non-food international goals. As noted in the beginning of our discussion, the global food system has been gradually integrated in this century through the spread of physical communication, transportation, and storage facilities. The real test ahead is whether diplomatic perceptions and policies can recognize this new situation and exploit the opportunity it presents to satisfy world food needs that were historically outside the reach of food diplomacy.

8

Institutional Dimensions
of the Malnutrition Problem

James E. Austin

The roots of malnutrition are found in economics. education. agriculture. and health. This
multiple etiology requires that approaches to the problem engage many different institutions.
These organizations can be viewed as constituting an International Nutrition Institutional Network. The functions of this system are collection and dissemination of information. provision
of goods and services. financing. and coordination. Significant problems. however. have been
identified in the performance of these functions. These are organizational: poor coordination.
vague responsibility delineation. inadequate evaluation. people limitations. and international-
national relationships. They are also political: policy vacuum. knowledge gaps. and priority
conflicts. Unless these are rectified. the Network's effectiveness will remain severely limited.

As the introductory essay of this volume indicates, widespread, though regionally-
and class-concentrated malnutrition is a prime aspect of the world food problem. It
is the *qualitative* dimension, and perhaps the most defiant one since it is not to be
overcome by simply raising food production. If malnutrition is to be analyzed as a
distortion of the global food system, it is fundamentally a distortion of the distributive functioning of that system. Many consumers in many places and strata continually receive too few nutrients to sustain energy, health, and sometimes life.

The distributive distortion of the global system that produces malnutrition
reflects in part the playing out of some of the norms of the global food regime. It has
been the implicit norm that matters of nutrition are not to be treated as very important questions in food diplomacy, especially when raising them would tend to
generate further questions about domestic distributions of food. Low priorities
accorded nutrition in food diplomacy led to low funding for programs of international research and intervention, low capacity in international institutions assigned
nutritional roles, and consequently low performance from these institutions.

James E. Austin is Associate Professor of Business Administration at the Harvard Business School and
Lecturer in Nutrition Policy at the Harvard School of Public Health. He has served as a Special White
House Adviser on Food Policy and as a consultant to The World Bank and other international development
organizations.

There is currently some evidence that international indifference to malnutrition and its causes is changing, as for example in the United Nations Economic and Social Council's (ECOSOC) designation, "Organizational Arrangements for Nutrition," as a major agenda item of its summer 1977 meetings and The World Food Council's (WFC) decision to include nutrition planning and interventions as the major items for its June 1978 annual meeting. But even if there is new interest, new action will probably require institutional overhaul. After taking stock of the magnitude of global malnutrition, this essay critically examines the structure and capacity of existing international nutrition institutions. Concluding comments focus on prospects for improved institutional efforts.

Global malnutrition

The magnitude of global malnutrition

More than 1.3 billion people, over two-thirds of the developing nations' population, are suffering from some degree of caloric undernutrition. As can be seen from Table 1, the problem is most acute in Asia, the Far East, and Africa. The

Table 1   Population with calorie intake below requirements (1975)

Region	Millions of people	% of Total population
Asia and Far East	924	82
Africa	243	77
Near East	112	51
Latin America	94	36
	1,373	71

Source: Shlomo Reutlinger, Marcelo Selowsky, I.B.R.D., Working Paper No. 202, December 1975.

global daily shortage of calories of the undernourished population is 444 billion calories, which is equivalent to 127,000 metric tons of grain. This means that on an annual basis there is a global calories shortfall equivalent to 46 million metric tons of grain, which is about one-third of all grain traded internationally.[1]

[1] The International Food Policy Research Institute estimated that 1974–75 cereal shortfall at 45 million tons, rising to 98–105 million tons in 1985: *Meeting Food Needs in the Developing World: The Location and Magnitude of the Task in the Next Decade,* Research Report No. 1, February 1976, p. 2. This is not to suggest, however, that the best way to meet nutritional needs is necessarily through grain trade or international food donations.

Even if one takes a narrower view of the problem and only focuses on those with daily caloric deficits greater than 250 calories (10 percent), the numbers are, unfortunately, still very large. As Table 2 reveals, the total number of people suffering from these more severe caloric deficits amounts to over 900 million or almost 50 percent of the developing countries' population.

Table 2   Population with daily deficits in excess of 250 calories

Region	Millions of people	% of Total population
Asia and Far East	707	63
Africa	93	61
Near East	61	33
Latin America	71	23
	932	48

Source: Shlomo Reutlinger, Marcelo Selowsky, I.B.R.D., Working Paper No. 202, December 1975.

Calorie energy deficiencies are pervasive and primary and almost always signify accompanying protein shortages which reduce the body's growth capacity and disease resistance. The protein deficits are particularly devastating for young children, as the high infant mortality rates in developing countries reveal. Beyond calories and proteins, mineral and vitamin deficiencies affect even larger numbers.

The magnitude of these deficits and the human suffering they inflict clearly make global malnutrition one of the most pressing social problems confronting the world today. It will also be extremely costly to alleviate. The costs of meeting the calorie deficits cited above are estimated at $19 billion.[2] The size of the problem means that large resources must be mobilized and that will require significant assistance from international development agencies if the immediacy of the problem is to be addressed. It will also require sizable allocations from the developing countries' scarce internal resources, creating pressures among the various national agencies and development programs which compete for their pieces of the governments' modest budgets.

[2] J. E. Austin et al., *Urban Malnutrition: Problem Assessment and Intervention Guidelines,* Harvard University, Report Submitted to International Bank for Reconstruction and Development, September 1976. The calculation assumes a cost of $263 per ton including delivery system costs and the need to distribute 72 million tons to meet the calorie deficit, including 30 million tons which get drained off through leakages such as storage, consumption by nontarget group individuals, etc.

Nature of the malnutrition problem

Scarcity of resources is but a reflection of the fundamental causes of malnutrition: poverty, poor nations, and poor people. National incomes are low and what little there is is maldistributed. Table 3 reveals that on a world basis two billion people in 95 countries exist on an average per capita national income of less than 60¢ per day; 60 percent of the population controls only 10 percent of the world's GNP while almost 80 percent of the global GNP is in the hands of only 25 percent of the population.

Table 3 Global income and population distribution—1973

Per capita GNP income grouping	Average GNP per capita	Number of countries	POPULATION		TOTAL GNP	
			Millions	%	Billions	%
Below $200	$ 120	43	1,151	30.1	$ 136	2.9
$200–$ 499	280	52	1,184	30.9	332	7.0
$500–$1,999	1,000	53	531	13.8	530	11.0
$2,000–$4,999	2,800	28	654	17.0	1,871	39.3
Over $5,000	2,970	12	316	8.2	1,896	39.7

Source: *World Bank Atlas*, World Bank 1975.

Specific country data reveal further the poverty-malnutrition link and also illustrate the particularly precarious nutritional state of the urban poor in most developing countries. Brazil has a national per capita average calorie intake above the recommended daily adult allowance of 2500 calories, but when one disaggregates this average by income strata the adverse nutritional reality of the poor emerges. Calorie intakes of the poorest 20 percent of the households in the Northeast, East, and South are about 40 percent less than those of the highest 20 percent. In all instances the caloric intake of the poorest urban households was less than that of their rural counterparts. Nutritional data for Rio de Janeiro show that this inverse income deficiency correlation tends to hold for other nutrients as well as calories. In India, as well, the urban poor are in the worst nutritional situation. Anthropometric and biochemical indicators also show this urban-rural nutrition pattern. The urban malnourished are fewer in numbers but appear to experience more severe deficiencies.

These income and nutritional intake figures raise the basic issue of equitable income distribution. Malnutrition now results not so much from absolute total food shortages as from the uneven distribution of food supplies. China and Cuba had 1974 per capita annual income levels ($300 and $490, respectively) much below Brazil ($900), but the income redistribution in those two poorer countries reportedly has dramatically reduced malnutrition there while it still prevails in the richer country. The problem is one of inequity, not just poverty. Malnutrition mirrors income maldistribution. Consequently, effective nutrition intervention programs require resource transfers which begin to shift the distribution pattern.

Income redistribution is a politically sensitive issue in most nations, and, therefore, nutrition programs run the risk of jangling the nerves of politically significant power blocs. For example, increased taxes on industrialists to pay for government nutrition programs in Colombia and Costa Rica met (but overcame) considerable resistance; similarly, fortification programs of salt in Nicaragua and sugar in Guatemala encountered opposition from processors. Nutrition intervention is almost inevitably political intervention, which practically ensures institutional resistance on one front or another. Nevertheless, in some countries, e.g., India and Chile, nutrition has been used as part of redistribution-oriented political campaigns. Feeding is highly visible and therefore can be a political asset; its basic humanitarian nature may in fact make it a more politically palatable way to effect redistribution than, say, land reform. Thus, nutrition programs find themselves in the ironic position of being blocked by redistribution opponents or being supported by them as a palliation to obviate more fundamental structural changes.

The fact that malnutrition is enmeshed in the poverty web means that it is both a contributor to and consequence of the multiple strands that stifle development. To understand fully the malnutrition problem one should also identify the noneconomic strands and how they are entwined. Malnutrition stems from insufficient food intake in quantitative and qualitative terms, and many factors can lead to inadequate intake other than just low incomes. Four such factors are:

(1) Food beliefs, e.g., certain protein foods are not to be eaten during pregnancy;
(2) health concepts, e.g., food is withheld from sick children;
(3) cooking practices, e.g., nutrient leaching due to excess boiling of rice and discarding of the water; and
(4) intrafamilial food distribution patterns, e.g., the male head of household receives priority in family food allocation, often to the detriment of the small children who are more nutritionally vulnerable.

In addition to the sociological factors, deficiencies in the food production and delivery system itself can constrain intake. Several countries (e.g., Sahelian Africa) simply may not have the natural resources to produce adequate supplies of food imports which often must be limited to less than the needed amounts due to foreign exchange scarcity. Even where the natural agronomic resources do exist, their exploitation is often hampered by lack of the necessary physical infrastructure or institutional mechanisms to realize the food production potential. These inadequacies mean that either output remains low or sizable food losses occur during the seed-to-consumer flow. The net result is the same: lower supplies, higher prices, reduced intake, nutritional deficits.

Malnutrition impinges adversely on overall health status, particularly of young children, through its interaction with infection. Simplistically stated, undernourishment reduces the body's resistance to disease such that an infection, like measles, which would be relatively harmless to a healthy child, can be fatal to a malnourished child. Or, conversely, a healthy child can be pushed into a malnourished state by reduced nutrient intake or retention due to the advent of sickness. Consequently, improved sanitation and water supply along with other health care measures are important in alleviating disease and malnutrition incidence.

. From the foregoing, the multiple etiology of malnutrition is evident. Its roots are found in economics, education, agriculture, and health. This multiple causality indicates the need for a multi-sectoral approach to the problem of combating malnutrition. Such an approach carries very significant institutional ramifications: it requires that multiple institutions—i.e., national and international, public and private, formal and informal groups, programs and organizations—and professionals from different disciplines and sectors with different resources and inputs all direct their energies toward the common problem. For most existing institutions actively working against world hunger, nutrition has been a largely neglected focal point, usually an orphan to simpler and more obvious concerns about state to state movements of quantities of food. Nutrition interventions can take many different forms: supplementary feeding programs, food fortification, nutrition education, formulated, nutrient-dense foods, agricultural technology, ration shops. Such programs address specific nutritional deficiencies and particular nutritionally vulnerable groups. They go beyond simple food production. With nutrition now beginning to appear on organizational agendas, the newness and unfamiliarity with the problem area is creating both trepidation and institutional resistance. Complicating the situation even further is the requirement for multi-institutional interaction for effective programming. Always difficult in any event, problems of organizational coordination and intergration can attain paralyzing proportions at the international level.

The international nutrition institutional network

In one way the "international nutrition institutional network" is coextensive with the "UN Food Network." The cluster of public international institutions generally mandated to deal with global food problems is also assigned the general task of enhancing nutrition. Technically, participants in the nutrition network are really a subcluster of groups, programs, committees, and the like—organizations within organizations—specifically charged with nutrition-enhancing assignments. Typical international nutrition groups would include the FAO/WHO Protein-Calorie Advisory Group, UNICEF's Child Feeding Program, FAO's Nutrition Division, teams at the regional research centers at work on enriching the protein content of maize, potatoes, etc. In its most extensive definition, the nutrition institutional network interlinks not only personnel associated with public international organizations but also counterparts within national governments and private organizations. To gain proper perspective, the reader should note that this global network of nutrition institutions is extensive, but it is not large in terms of either the number of professionals it includes (hardly more than a few thousand globally) or in terms of the resources it commands and dispenses (a small fraction of resources allocated to food aid). In addition, there is some danger that the term "network" may be a bit overworked here; to lend the impression of a tightly linked set of institutions bound by a common purpose would be misleading. Actually, the institutional links are often tenuous, and the orientations are diverse. Nonetheless, the organizations are all in the nutrition business in some form. All are directing their efforts toward the alleviation of malnutrition, and all interact with one another.

Beyond the nutrition-targeted institutions are organizations and programs whose activities carry nutritional implications even though their main focus is broader than just nutrition, e.g., agricultural or rural development. These are secondary rather than primary institutions in the nutrition network, but they still must be considered in an overall examination.

The purpose of this section is neither to present an exhaustive institutional shopping list, nor to detail the work of specific nutrition groups. Analysis here is rather directed toward identifying the principal functions that organizations perform in the international nutrition field and illustrating these with brief descriptions of the activities of some of the major actors in the network.

Collection and dissemination of information

A fundamental ingredient of most institutional systems is an information flow. For nutrition such an information function encompasses basic and applied research as well as the generation of more operational data such as nutrient supply and nutritional status statistics.

On the research side there exist several institutes which are viewed as international nutrition information centers. Among these are the Institute of Nutrition for Central America and Panama (INCAP), the Caribbean Food and Nutrition Institute (CFNI), the Indian National Institute of Nutrition (ININ) and various universities and research institutes within the United States and other developed nations, including the newly launched United Nations University which has hunger as one of its main research areas. At the World Food Conference, Resolution V gave the World Health Organization (WHO), United Nations Children's Fund (UNICEF), and the Food and Agriculture Organization (FAO) the responsibility for arranging an internationally coordinated program in applied nutrition research. This effort is designed to increase and improve these and other institutions' ongoing research. At an October 1975 interagency meeting in Rome, it was proposed that the Protein-Calorie Advisory Group (PAG) should initiate coordination of applied nutrition research. Subsequently, the Administrative Committee on Coordination (ACC), the UN system's highest coordinating body, under pressure from the line agencies, reversed the Rome decision and stated that no interagency consultative machinery should be established to coordinate nutrition research as a whole. Additionally, there are several international agricultural research centers (CIMMYT, IRRI, CIAT) carrying out research on basic grain production, with modest emphasis on nutritional aspects. Despite these ongoing efforts, significant nutrition knowledge gaps exist concerning the nature of malnutrition and the means to alleviate it most effectively. Continual probing is needed to provide a sturdier base for directing international efforts.

On the operating data side the FAO and the USDA have traditionally been the major assemblers and disseminators of food production and trade data. Recently the International Food Policy Research Institute (IFPRI) was formed with support from several sources, including the Rockefeller and Ford Foundations, the World Bank, and the Canadian International Development Agency. IFPRI seeks to carry out policy-oriented research that leads to improved food intake by developing country populations; it has a mandate from its Board to give explicit attention to nutrition policy and programs. The World Bank and bilateral agencies play significant roles in shaping and disseminating the research results funded under their auspices or carried out by their own staffs. The World Food Conference also recommended that WHO, FAO, and UNICEF establish a global nutrition surveillance system to monitor the food and nutrition conditions of the disadvantaged groups. WHO is the lead organization, working with the UN agencies as well as other international institutions. This system presumably will be related to the Global Information and Early Warning System established in 1974 under the aegis of the FAO (unfortunately without the participation of the USSR or China). Without reasonably accurate and timely information on food availability and nutritional status, program planning will take place in a vacuum or be based on shaky data foundations. In either case, the effectiveness of international efforts will be diluted.

Provision of goods and services

Information provides the basis for action and international nutrition action takes the form of supplying needed food, supplies, or technical assistance. International food aid flows through bilateral and multilateral arrangements. Of the former, the largest currently and historically has been the US P.L. 480 Food for Peace Program, which sold on concessional terms or donated over $1 billion worth of food in 1976. This food is shipped by the international grain companies, with voluntary agencies such as CARE, Catholic Relief Services, and the Church World Services frequently administering the in-country donated food feeding programs. The major multilateral food aid effort is the World Food Program (WFP) which is operated under the joint auspices of FAO and ECOSOC. As noted in the previous chapter, the WFP budget for the 1976–77 biennium is $750 million, of which the US has pledged $188 million with the balance coming from other developed nation donors and the oil-rich developing nations.

During emergency famine or disaster situations other organizations are involved in the food relief operations, for example, the United Nations Disaster Relief Office (UNDRO), the League of Red Cross Societies, OXFAM, and other voluntary agencies. Emerging from the World Food Conference was a Committee on World Food Security (CWFS) which was given responsibility for developing an international grain reserve system to handle food emergencies as well as designing other measures to insure greater food security to developing nations. While progress in this direction has been minimal, as Destler explains, the emergence of an international reserve system would be a major step toward reducing the world's nutritional vulnerability.

The fertilizer problem has begun to be addressed institutionally. In 1974 the FAO established the International Fertilizer Supply Scheme (IFS), through which

73,000 tons of fertilizer had been placed as of June 1975 in 30 of the most seriously affected importing nations. This amount is still far less than that financed through bilateral aid. Also, the International Fertilizer Development (IFDC) has been established to carry out research and provide advice. This latter entity perhaps will enable a smoothing out of the traditionally marked peaks and troughs in fertilizer prices and investments, which are due in part to the technology which leads to lumpy investments, and in part to inadequate effective demand data.

The development institutions provide considerable amounts of technical assistance in various areas. One area that has received particular attention has been national food and nutrition planning, which entails assessing nutritional status and designing viable, multi-sector nutrition programs to improve nutritional well-being. A.I.D.'s Office of Nutrition has centered much of its technical assistance activities in this area, accompanied by several other countries' development agencies—particularly those in Canada, Sweden, the UK, Germany, Norway, and the Netherlands. Also. the FAO was designated after the World Food Conference as the lead agency in promoting the strengthening of national nutrition planning capacities.[3]

The Consultative Group on Food Production and Investment (CGFPI), established in 1975 by the World Bank, the FAO, and the UN Development Programme (UNDP), also stress to governments the importance of planning. Its technical assistance role, however, is somewhat different. The CGFPI Chairman, Ambassador Edwin Martin, described it as follows: "Unlike the World Bank, we have no money to give or lend; we make no decisions like FAO. All we can do is encourage people and organizations to do the right thing by offering what we think is sound advice. In this sense then, our role is one of catalyst or facilitator."[4] The CGPI assembles donor countries, developing nations, and public and private agricultural investors and attempts to stimulate investments which would increase food supplies to the most nutritionally disadvantaged. In effect, the CGPI is an institutional matchmaker using technical advice and institutional prestige as the uniting mechanisms.

Financing

The tab for the research, information dissemination, planning, food donations, agricultural production, and technical assistance activities of the international institutions is picked up by several organizations. The funds for nutrition research come from foundations, national and international development agencies, and the United Nations. It is estimated that world expenditures on nutrition research related to developing country malnutrition, excluding funds for agricultural research, are $20 to $40 million per year. The expenditures for food aid amounted to approximately $2 billion in 1976.

The bulk of international financing goes to food production efforts rather than specific nutrition projects. The 1975 AID appropriation for food and nutrition was

---

[3]For further discussion see "The United States, FAO and World Food Politics: US Relations with an International Food Organization," Staff Report of the Senate Select Committee on Nutrition and Human Needs, June 1976, Washington, D.C.

[4]Interview, August 1976.

$300 million.[5] UNICEF's child nutrition expenditures in 1975 were $15.1 million.[6] The World Bank, Inter-American Development Bank (IDB), and the Asian Development Bank (ADB), destined, in 1976, $2.5 billion for agricultural production. The FAO and UNDP accounted for another $300 million. The newly established International Agricultural Development Fund (IADF) is expected to have a capitalization of about $900 million. The IADF was one of the most financially significant institutional developments emerging from the World Food Conference but its thrust is toward food production rather than nutrition per se. Although food aid and nutrition expenditures are sizable, they are small compared to the previously cited $19-billion short-run expenditures that would be needed to remove the current nutritional deficits. Resources are scarce and therefore a premium exists on their efficient use.

Coordination

A prerequisite to efficient and effective use of allocated resources is the coordination of international efforts. When world attention was drawn to the global food crisis by the dramatic crop shortfalls of the early seventies, considerable international institutional activity was generated which gave rise to a host of new coordinating bodies and activities. The World Food Conference, for example, created several institutional coordinating vehicles, primary among these the World Food Council. As the highest political body of the UN system dealing exclusively with food, the council set forth the following as its main functions: "(a) to monitor the world food situation in all its aspects, including what international organizations and governments are doing to develop short-term and long-term solutions to food problems; (b) to look at the total food picture and determine in its coordinating role whether the world food strategy as a whole made sense; (c) to identify malfunctions, gaps, and problem areas; and (d) to exert its influence, through moral persuasion, to get any necessary improvements made."[7] Given these functions, the World Food Council, in one sense, could be viewed as the general manager of the UN food network performing the overall coordinating role of interlinking the various food and nutrition institutions. In fact, in the Council's June 1977 meeting, nutrition planning and programs were designated as priority items for Council study in preparation for the 1978 meeting.

Other UN entities are serving as the subcoordinators in different areas, for example, WHO for global nutritional status surveillance and FAO for applied nutrition research and nutrition planning. The old Intergovernmental Committee of the World Food Program was reconstituted as a 30-member Committee on Food Aid Policies and Programs (CFAPP) to serve as a forum for consultations and coordination on food aid policies and operations. An International Group for Agricultural Development in Latin America (IGAD/LA) is being organized by the Inter-American Development Bank to coordinate efforts in removing agricultural production constraints and in reducing malnutrition in the hemisphere.

[5]The authorization was $500 million but was reduced by the Appropriations Committee.
[6]"General Progress Report of the Executive Director," UNICEF, E/ICEF/6422, 1976, p. 16; an additional $43.7 million was spent on child health (medical care, water supply and family planning).
[7]"Report of the World Food Council," United Nations General Assembly, Thirtieth Session, New York, 1975.

Other coordinating bodies that existed prior to the World Food Conference have expanded their activities. The Consultative Group on International Agricultural Research (CGIAR), which has been coordinating the activities of the international agricultural research centers since 1971, almost doubled its budget from $34 million to $64 million between 1974 and 1976. The International Wheat Council (IWC), as Destler reports in his essay, has been the forum for international grain reserve discussions.

Coordination is essential and clearly there is considerable movement in this direction. Its effectiveness, however, is not so clear and will be discussed in a moment. As a means of recapping this section, Table 4 presents a summary profile of the institutional roles of the various main food and nutrition groups discussed thus far.

Table 4   International nutrition system: institutional roles

Institutions	*Collection & dissemination of information*	*Provision of goods & services*	*Financing*	*Coordination*
Primary Nutrition Institutions:				
INCAP	x			
CFNI	x			
ININ	x			
PAG	x	x		
Food for Peace Program		x		
WFP		x		
Voluntary Agencies		x		
CWFS				x
IFS		x		
CFAPP	x			x
WFC		x		x
Secondary Nutrition Institutions:				
Universities and Research Institutes, etc.	x			
WHO	x	x	x	x
UNICEF	x	x	x	x
FAO	x	x	x	x
Ag Research Centers	x			
CGIAR	x			
USDA	x			
IFPRI	x			
UNDRO		x		
Red Cross		x		
IFDC	x	x		
IWC	x			x
National Development Agencies (A.I.D., SIDA, etc.)		x	x	
CGFPI				x
UNDP		x		
World Bank	x		x	
IDB			x	
ADB			x	
IADF			x	

A final addition to this inventory: the most important institution in the nutrition system is the malnourished family. If the entire hierarchy of nutrition institutions and the focus on macro policies and programs fail to understand and meet the needs of the target families, then even the neatest, most logical, well-coordinated network is meaningless. Thus one should remember the critical importance of designing structures and procedures to overcome barriers to implementation that keep nutrition delivery systems from reaching needy groups. Christensen argues in her essay that such barriers are numerous and formidable, especially at the national level.

Institutional problems and prospects

Despite this multitude of international institutions involved in nutrition, the progress made toward alleviating malnutrition has been far from dramatic. In fact, the numbers of malnourished have increased; we have not even been able to keep up with the geometry of population demography and the erosion of global impoverishment. Although the task is large and the resources scarce, few leaders in the international nutrition community are satisfied with performance to date. The spectre of even worse malnutrition looms ominously on the horizon; thus it is critical that the international nutrition community examine why its performance has not been more effective and try to delineate ways to strengthen its future efforts.

From an examination of published documents and discussions with functionaries from many of the international nutrition organizations, several institutional problems emerge as major areas of concern for the international nutrition system. These concerns fall into two broad categories: organizational and political.

Organizational concerns

Good intentions and financial resources can be readily squandered by organizational deficiencies. The international nutrition community cannot afford the luxury of ineffectual organization. There appear to be five areas of organizational concern: poor coordination, vague responsibility delineation, inadequate review and evaluation, people limitations, and international-national relationships.

Poor coordination

A major organizational problem is with inter-institutional coordination. A recent study of the World Food Conference and the UN's role concluded that "Even with the myriad of specialized agencies and bodies of the UN there is as yet no capacity to anticipate and plan responses to new global exigencies or ones that overlap the mandates of several organizations."[8] Furthermore, the authors raise the "central and long-standing question as to whether ECOSOC can achieve a central

---

[8]Thomas G. Weiss and Robert S. Jordan, *The World Food Conference and Global Problem Solving* (New York: Praeger, 1976), p. 143.

coordinating role in human welfare within the system of international organizations.''[9] Other outside observers have come to similar conclusions: "We are seriously concerned that the UN system . . . has no effective mechanism for coordinating and managing the tremendous resources made available to it for carrying out economic and social activities in the world community.''[10] The problem is also recognized by the UN officials themselves who have to deal with it directly. One put it this way: "I am myself very much concerned with the present situation of interagency coordination which, to say the least, is in my opinion very unsatisfactory, and the programmes and the countries we are trying to serve are the ones who suffer.''[11] Exacerbating this problem further is a reported lack of communication among institutions it is rather difficult to coordinate if one does not even know what there is to coordinate.

Coordination problems are certainly not unique to the UN system. Bilateral development agencies have only recently begun to communicate about their respective nutrition activities and have not yet begun significantly to coordinate their substantive field activities. Even less progress has been made on the interface between bilateral and multilateral institutions.

These interinstitutional problems appear to be generic to food- and nutrition-related institutions at the national level and across political systems. The author sat in the office of the Director of Nutrition of a socialist East African nation and listened to the same lament about the difficulty of attaining coordination among ministries of agriculture, education, health, and finances that he had heard a week earlier in the office of the US Senate Select Committee on Nutrition and Human Needs. In one Latin American nation the inability of the Planning Ministry to achieve adequate coordination with and among the various implementing ministries led a major multilateral development organization to refuse to finance a national nutrition program.

The coordination problem is not just inter-institutional but also within organizations. Most development institutions involved in nutrition also are concerned about other development areas, too. Those activities, e.g., health, water systems, industrialization, do not have nutrition as their central focus, but do have nutritional implications. People carrying out these operations frequently lack the appreciation for, or knowledge of, nutrition to coordinate effectively their efforts with the institutions' nutrition programs. Significant nutrition awareness and know-how has not yet permeated the ranks of loan officers, project managers, and country analysts that constitute the bulk of the professional staffs of the national and international development agencies. Even within institutions specializing in nutrition, particularly universities and research organizations, professionals become prisoners of their particular disciplines and fail to interact with their in-house colleagues from other departments.

Poor coordination is an easy target for organizational critics. Such criticism is frequently responded to by institutional shuffling in the form of new committees and

[9]Ibid.
[10]Senate Select Committee Staff Report, p. 11.
[11]Personal communication, August 1976.

more meetings. As one UN Director put it: "For institutional reasons coordination already receives an undue amount of discussion in UN circles."[12] Too often coordination can simply become a guise for inaction, a meaningless part of the bureaucratic ritual. Coordination requires time and resources; clear benefits must be forthcoming to justify the investment. It is not sufficient simply to point out coordination problems; more often than not they are simply symptoms of other underlying organizational problems.

Vague delineation of responsibility

Some point to inadequate leadership as the source of the coordination problem:

—The one major resolution of the World Food Conference on which no institutional follow-up arrangements have been put in place is that on nutrition. The UN family still has divided responsibility with no single, dynamic source of leadership for all of us.[13]

—The running battle going on between UN agencies about who has jurisdiction and who should be doing what and who should be in charge of whom is a good example of the leadership vacuum at the international level.[14]

—My personal experience with each of these agencies suggests that a considerable amount of time is spent in conflict with each other.[15]

The failure clearly to delineate institutional responsibilities fosters agency rivalries that have been extremely counterproductive. The experience of the evolving role of the Protein-Calorie Advisory Group is illustrative. During the 1960s, the PAG basically concerned itself with providing technical guidelines by drawing on experts from the international scientific nutrition community. By the 1970s many countries had developed their own technical capacity and the era of viewing nutrition as a "technology problem" was passing. As nutrition became more of a development issue other disciplines became involved and the PAG Board was reconstituted to reflect this change. The new function of the PAG was then to advise the heads of the UN agencies on where emphasis should be placed in their nutrition activities. This role encountered resistance from other UN entities, particularly the FAO. The PAG's new role was viewed as an encroachment on the sphere of influence of others. When an institutions's boundaries have been trespassed, a not unusual bureaucratic reaction is to counterattack. The UN's Administrative Committee on Coordination (ACC) proposed a Nutrition Subcommittee at the Secretariat level as the new focal point for UN agencies and bilateral agencies and nongovernmental organizations. As an adjunct to the Subcommittee, the ACC also proposed a Nutrition Advisory Panel to replace the PAG, with the new group having

[12]Personal correspondence, October 1976.
[13]Edwin M. Martin, "Nutrition Problems of the World," The Johns Hopkins University Centennial Symposium on Nutrition and Public Health, November 11, 1976.
[14]Interview, July 1976.
[15]Personal correspondence, November 1976.

a broader scope. This proposal, in turn, met vigorous opposition and action was deferred by ECOSOC until its 1977 Summer meeting.

Another example occurred with the World Food Conference follow-up activities in the area of food and nutrition planning. FAO was the designated lead agency in this area and initially proceeded in isolation, presenting its plan to the other UN and bilateral agencies as a fait accompli. FAO's self-image of being the expert in this aspect conflicted with the perception of the other institutions which also felt capable of contributing significantly to this field. Considerable resentment was generated by the perceived imposition of a plan and the presumption of institutional dominance in the planning area. The plan was rejected, to be replaced by a document incorporating all the institutions' viewpoints.

This vagueness in the delineation of responsibility, with the resultant inter-institutional conflicts, is probably due both to the complex nature of the problems being addressed and the institutions' historical emergence as somewhat ad hoc responses to particular problems or pressures. In this regard McKitterick observed that, "These branches of the United Nations have constituted since their inception a kind of world community, attacking its social and economic problems across a broad front and in a largely uncoordinated way."[16] Malnutrition, as one of several socioeconomic problems, is especially complex and multifaceted. Consequently, the problem of where to draw institutional dividing lines is particularly difficult. WHO was given the mandate in health and FAO in food, but nutrition is both a health and food problem. Consequently, both have claim to the nutrition turf. Whereas WHO and FAO were organized with a sector orientation, UNICEF was formed with a target group focus. Given that children are an especially nutritionally at-risk group, UNICEF stakes an additional claim to the nutrition ground. The sectoral vs. the target group focus creates an organizational inconsistency which will inevitably lead to overlap. Additionally, the traditional sectoral definitions simply are inconsistent with the multi-sectoral nature of the malnutrition problem. These UN inter-institutional problems mirror similar rivalries at the country level between ministries of agriculture, health, and welfare. Institutional friction and poor coordination will inevitably continue unless responsibilities and authority are more clearly delineated, operating activities integrated, and a superior arbitrator mechanism created to reconcile turf disputes. Such delineation, integration, and arbitration is not readily forthcoming under the current UN setup and similar organizational voids exist within individual countries. A further reflection of, and in part a contribution to, this vacuum are deficiencies in the review and evaluation processes.

Inadequate review and evaluation

Resistance to evaluation is commonplace among institutions: they are threatening, particularly when they come from outside entities. In international agencies in-house reviews often are exercises carried out more to generate the information

---

[16]Nathaniel M. McKitterick, "US Diplomacy in the Development Agencies of the United Nations," planning pamphlet No. 122, National Planning Association, Washington, D.C., July 1965 p. 13.

needed to produce an annual report than to provide a critical assessment of activities. Among the UN nutrition institutions, UNICEF has on several occasions used outside organizations to review both the managerial and strategic aspects of its operations. Perhaps its target group orientation forces it to take a more eclectic and open view. In any case, such frank introspection has been more the exception than the rule in the UN.

Because of the vagueness of nutrition programming responsibilities and because these are often secondary activities for many of the implementing organizations, nutrition operations are particularly at risk of becoming nobody's responsibility. Consequently, nutrition is especially in need of an effectively functioning review and evaluation system. Such review procedures should cut across implementing organizations rather than be just within each entity. Furthermore, they should be conducted by a group which does not have a vested interest in the individual organizations and can, therefore, take an objective view. With this approach, program reviews can serve as an oversight net and as an inter-institutional coordinating mechanism.

People limitations

A fourth organizational concern is one of personnel. A problem common to both international and national nutrition efforts is the staff perspective and limited understanding of nutrition. For example, Dr. Doris Calloway, Professor of Nutrition at the University of California, Berkeley, and FAO consultant, has criticized the FAO for the absence of sufficient qualified nutrition staff and for viewing malnutrition as largely a "food-supply gap" to be remedied by greater output and higher incomes coming from rising GNPs.[17] The international agricultural research centers have been similarly criticized for being fixated on a "grow more" philosophy neglecting the economic, sociological, and distributional aspects of malnutrition. Expanding the professional staffs' nutrition vision and knowledge is a basic task facing the whole gamut of international nutrition institutions from the FAO to the World Bank to Harvard University to the National Ministry of Planning. Nutrition education begins at home.

The other people limitation concerns a bureaucratic affliction reportedly acutely present within the UN system. The highly politicized nature of the institution results in personnel selection too often based on political rather than technical criteria. The net effect is professional mediocrity which is a disservice to the member nations. After a recent six-month sabbatical at FAO, Professor Vincent H. Malstrom commented on the work environment: "There were many evidences that FAO was grossly overstaffed. With no clocks to punch, no real boss to crack the whip, and no fear of being fired, most employees of FAO had found themselves an apparently 'ideal' situation—a well-paid job with little or no work."[18] Viewing the

---

[17]Senate Select Committee Staff Report, p. 26.

[18]Vincent H. Malstrom, "Roman Holiday: An Inside Look at the UN Food and Agriculture Organization," *Middlebury College Newsletter* (Spring 1975), p. 31.

UN as a patronage basket only serves to discourage the many competent professionals in the organization and results in poor service to its constituency. The depoliticization of personnel selection is a prerequisite to achieving institutional credibility as a true development force. Strict professional hiring standards and a staff development program seem in order. Without good people even the best organizational design will not work.

International-national relationships

Another organizational dimension can create serious barriers to effective action, namely, the unwritten rules of conduct that govern relations between international institutions and the countries with which they deal. The tragedy of the Ethiopian drought as documented by Jack Shepherd illustrates the extreme case. Between April and November of 1973 more than 100,000 Ethiopians starved to death. The need for food aid was known by the international agencies but they did not act. "Their reason—their only excuse—was diplomatic tradition and practice. For in the international community, no aid is given or even offered, regardless of consequences, without the specific request and cooperation of the recipient country....Behind the protective curtain of respect for local sovereignty the second coverup went along with the Imperial Ethiopian Government's own coverup and involved every major international relief agency, most donor nations, and many African leaders. All kept quiet as the Selassie government requested. One authoritative voice might have saved thousands; their silence condemned tens of thousands.[19]

It can be contended that to speak out would be interfering in the internal affairs of a country. The international community does have a standard of conduct other than the diplomatic code and that is the Declaration of Human Rights. It speaks out against the torture of political prisoners; starvation is simply a different form of the same. At an operational level, however, one can contend that an international organization can only operate if it has the trust of the host country. To receive confidential information from the government and then use it against them would destroy the working relationships. Trust and confidentiality are important elements to preserving a relationship, but there are times when the cost of maintaining a relationship clearly exceeds the benefits.

In normal situations, however, the task is more one of fostering a meaningful relationship rather than terminating one. In nutrition, as in some other development areas, three aspects of the interface between the international organizations and the country governments are of concern. First, international organizations have frequently tended to "sell" certain types of nutrition intervention programs (e.g., high protein foods) that their research or judgements lead them to consider optimal. This frequently results in lender or donor needs (rather then country needs) dictating nutrition strategy. The financial and information leverage of these international

---

[19]Jack Shepherd, *The Politics of Starvation* (Carnegie Endowment for International Peace, New York, 1975), p. x.

agencies puts the recipient countries in an dependent position with no outside institutional vehicle to which they can turn to verify the desirabiltiy of the proposed course of action. The second problem arises because the various lender, donor, or technical assistance agencies frequently give conflicting advice or espouse very different approaches. Such fragmentation only confuses the development process, erodes the credibility of the international institutions, and strains institutional relations. The poor coordination among bilateral and multilateral agencies carries a very real cost in decreased effectiveness at the country level.

Action options

There are two basic reorganization options: change institutional process or change institutional structure. It was precisely these alternatives that the World Food Conference Resolution XXII focused on when it requested ECOSOC to urgently consider "whether or not rearrangements in the United Nations' system or new institutional bodies may be justified in order to ensure effective follow-up on Conference Resolution V on nutrition."

The Administrative Committee on Coordination opted for the process alternative. After studying the situation it concluded that "The existing arrangements for ensuring appropriate planning, implementation and assessment of nutrition-related activities were not adequate . . . the system required an action-orientation based on common policies and approaches to nutrition improvement . . . the rearrangements required were more in the nature of new mechanisms for cooperation and common action than new institutions or bodies."[20]

Given the nature of the organizational concerns identified above, it is far from clear whether this prescription is appropriate. It may be that a bandaid is proposed where surgery is in order. Keeping the old institutions and adjusting their roles is not an easy task. The old roles emerged in a different food and nutrition environment and are often inconsistent with the new needs which are more action oriented. One is confronted with a situation of new roles being imposed on old institutional structures–square pegs and round holes. This role-structure incongruity requires resolution. The new Director General of the FAO found that 80 percent of FAO's regular budget was "destined to pay for a gigantic centralized bureaucracy in Rome, 11 percent to put out publications that no one reads and the remaining 9 percent to holding meetings and for travel expenses that are largely unnecessary."[21] He has apparently decided to attack the problem through structural and process change via a vigorous decentralization program. This is desirable and is consistent with a more action-oriented country level assistance role for the FAO, but it will undoubtedly generate great internal turmoil and backlash from the affected bureaucrats. It is not clear, however, how nutrition activities will be affected or affect this reorganization. Changing long-standing institutional structures is a tough business. Nonetheless, merely fine tuning existing international nutrition institutions may not suffice to clear away the static or lack of coordination.

[20]UNICEF, p. 9.
[21]*The New York Times,* April 25, 1976, sec. 1, p. 7; note that the FAO budget also supports the country and regional field offices.

Institutional structure has also begun to change through the recent proliferation of food and nutrition institutions. The emergence of new entities from the World Food Conference probably indicates a belief on the part of the developing nations that the existing institutions were not adequate for their needs. However, as Asher argued some time ago, proliferation most likely reflects a tactical maneuver designed to achieve greater political control than was possible through the traditional institutions.[22] Still, not all of the new institutions were prompted by urging from the developing countries. The CGFPI was a US initiative and the IFAD was an OPEC-sponsored scheme. The new organizations may be very useful if they permit the international community to escape the clutches of those bureaucracies still clinging to an unproductive status quo. The concomitant risk, however, is that this multiplication of bureaucracies will only add to the already cumbersome burden of institutional coordination without making any net positive contribution against malnutrition.

The potentially most significant addition to the structure of the international nutrition network is the World Food Council. The WFC provides the system with an institutional focal point that had previously been missing. It provides the logical pivot around which structural changes can be carried out. However, the track record of the WFC has been less than satisfactory. The WFC has encountered active resistance from the other UN agencies which feel their jurisdictional power threatened by the Council; the lines of responsibility and authority remain cloudy and confusing. Furthermore, the participation of non-UN entities remains restricted. Consequently, without basic organizational changes the World Food Council's full potential may well remain unrealized. Under such a reorganization two operating committees could (and should) be established: the Technical Coordinating Committee (TCC) and the Overview Committee (OC).

The TCC would be divided into two subcommittees. One would be concerned with food and nutrition research activities and the other with operational programs. The subcommittees would be chaired by the professional staff of the WFC, supported by a group of outside expert TCC-affiliated consultants, and constituted by the member UN food and nutrition agencies (FAO, WHO, UNICEF, WEP, etc.), bilateral agencies (USAID, SIDA, etc.), and nongovernmental entities (IFPRI, CARE, etc.). The UN system must open up because most of the money and action in food and nutrition are really outside the system. Co-opting and broadly representing the whole international nutrition network within the UN framework is therefore critical to framing UN strategies and executing global-level undertakings. Concurrent with, and perhaps stemming from, this broadened participation must be a concerted effort to depoliticize the operations of the WFC. A high level of professionalism is a prerequisite to credibility and support from the broader nutrition community. If this is garnered, then the WFC could draw on and help channel more efficiently and effectively the significant technical, human, and financial resources existing in the previously described international nutrition network.

[22]See Robert E. Asher, "International Agencies and Economic Development," *International Organization,* Vol. 22, No. 1 (Winter 1968).

Figure 1. U.N. nutrition reorganization option

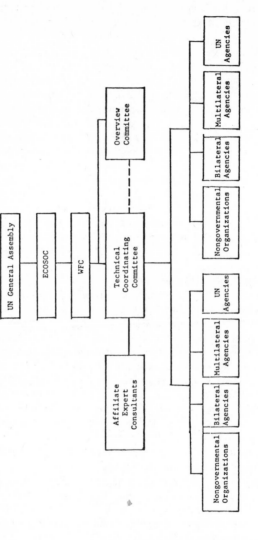

The functions of the TCC would be as follows:

(1) To provide a common forum to reach a consensus on problem diagnosis and desired action areas both in research and operations;
(2) Formulate a multi-institutional assistance strategy, including action priorities, for approval by the full Council;
(3) Pinpoint institutional gaps, delineate areas of implementation responsibility and clarify institutional roles;
(4) Integrate the programmatic endeavors of multiple institutions via the formation of multi-institutional task forces aimed at specific food and nutrition problems (e.g., vitamin A deficiencies, food reserves, infection-nutrition interaction, etc.);
(5) Serve as a central nutrition information collection and dissemination vehicle for the international institutions and for individual countries.

The OC, which would consist of a multidisciplinary professional staff, would perform the needed review and evaluation function that was identified earlier as a problem area. The Committee would review the activities of the member institutions of the TCC subcommittee to see if proposed actions were implemented and with what effects. The results would serve as constructive feedback to the TCC and its members for strategy reformulation. Each UN agency would be requested to submit to the OC a nutritional impact statement designating the expected effects of each project they sponsor. The purpose of this would be to heighten nutritional awareness among personnel and to operationalize nutritional accountability.

This reorganization option (see Figure 1) implies more than minor structural and process changes. It would vest considerable power in the WFC in terms of advising, planning, coordinating, arbitrating, communicating, and reviewing. The PAG's functions would largely be absorbed and expanded through the TCC and the OC. The other UN agencies' nutrition activities would come under the TCC auspices. The WFC would be the ultimate nutrition authority within the UN system and nominally within the entire international nutrition system. This implies cutting across multiple institutions in a difficult-to-manage matrix organization. But you have to step over bureaucratic lines if you want to get over bureaucratic barriers. However, for the WFC to carry out this expanded role successfully and for the reorganized international nutrition system to make an increased impact will require the resolution of several political concerns.

Political concerns

Oiling the organizational machinery is not enough. More development resources are needed as well as a higher priority for nutrition in the allocation of existing development resources. Changing allocations and priorities require political action both internationally and domestically. There appear to be three barriers to more effective political action: policy vacuum, knowledge gaps, and priority conflicts.

Policy vacuum

Political action requires the delineation of an overall strategy including the specification of priorities. Such systematic planning has generally been absent at both the international and national level. The United States is in the particularly ironic and inexcusable position of aggressively pushing for formal food and nutrition planning in developing nations while being unable to do the same itself. This internal policy vacuum leads to inadequacies in policies vis-à-vis the other international organizations and encourages similar vagueness in their policies. For example, the Senate study of US-FAO relationships concluded that "A coherent, rational and explicit policy consisting of goals, objectives, and priorities for FAO and for the United States as a member of FAO does not exist. What does exist are fragments of policies . . . US policy tends to be 'situation-or-issue-specific.' These policies tend to be negative and reactive rather than positive and creative."[23]

As can be seen from Table 5 only a handful of developing nations have actually adopted an integrated national food and nutrition policy. For most countries nutrition programs have been launched on a rather ad hoc basis rather than being an integral part of an overall development program. Unless nutrition programming becomes systematized it will likely not receive significant attention in the national planning process and will not get a meaningful piece of the national budget. The organizational problems indicated in the previous section hamper this planning process but inadequate knowledge about the problem and the options also hamper action.

Table 5   Food and nutrition planning in developing countries[a]

Planning/policy status	Number of countries
1. Extensive nutrition interventions but not on a coordinated intersectoral basis.	36
2. Steps being taken toward intersectoral food and nutrition plan/policy.	41
3. Intersectoral food and nutrition plan/policy adopted.	6

[a]Where UNICEF has projects.
Source: UNICEF, "General Progress Report of the Executive Director," p. 55, E/ICEF/642, 1976.

Knowledge gaps

Nutrition is a relatively young science and nutrition interventions a relatively recent addition to the development program portfolio. Consequently, several key questions remain unanswered on both the biological research and field application sides.

For example, it is not clear how critical it is in terms of physical and mental functional performance whether 60 percent, 70 percent, 80 percent, or 90 percent of recommended allowances of various nutrients are consumed and when, and for how long. Such a lack of understanding of the functional significance of nutritional status

[23]Senate Select Committee Staff Report, p. 2.

clearly hampers decisions on the quantity, timing, and direction of nutrition resource allocation. There is also a gap in understanding the relative effectiveness and true costs of alternative interventions, e.g., nutrition education vs. feeding programs vs. price subsidies vs. fortification vs. agricultural production vs. health care. The recent launching of major national food and nutrition programs by a South American country was delayed considerably by the lack of hard data on which nutrition programs would make best use of its scarce resources. Even as finally formulated the effect is still almost "flying blind." This increases the risk of failures and exposes the program to attacks from its abundant critics who are lurking in the wings waiting to pounce. Furthermore, little systematic research has been done on the nutritional impact of government policies dealing with the production, processing, and distribution of food.

These questions have remained unanswered either because of the technical difficulty of the research or the failure to allocate sufficient research funds. A higher priority for research must accompany organizational changes in the international nutrition system if programmatic action is to accelerate. Policy makers need a clearer picture of their options and the expected costs and benefits. This will also require a more systematic collection and dissemination of research results and field experience in a form usable to country planners. Today much of the existing knowledge is not readily accessible to decision makers on an international basis. The WFC could serve an important function here.

Priority conflicts

Removing the nutrition knowledge gaps will enhance policy formation but policies remain hollow unless they are given a high political priority. Nutrition has not traditionally ranked high on the priority agenda. Within the UN system it has, until recently, received relatively modest resource allocations[24] and has been terribly underrepresented in terms of staff.[25] Nutrition has fared no better in other multilateral institutions; the World Bank has spoken often of the need to confront the malnutrition problem, but to date the level of the Bank's nutrition lending as a percent of its total portfolio verges on tokenism.[26] In developing countries nutrition projects more often than not have consisted of small efforts hidden away in the Health Ministry or feeding programs supported by international food donations and run by international voluntary agencies.

Conclusion

Political inaction in nutrition has been due to the knowledge and policy vacuums as well as organizational weaknesses. It should also be recognized that mal-

[24]For example, UNICEF spent $5.9 million on child nutrition in 1971 and $15.1 million in 1975.
[25]For example, the Nutrition Unit at WHO Headquarters consists of only about five professionals.
[26]In 1976, nutrition loans or nutrition components of other loans were less than 4 percent of total annual agriculture and rural development lending.

nutrition is rooted in poverty and the economic roots of poverty are embedded in politics, as Christensen makes amply clear. Alleviating malnutrition will require increased and reoriented resource mobilization and this takes political commitment. Attaining and maintaining sufficiently high priority among policy makers for food and nutrition problems is a major political concern facing the international nutrition system.

The World Food Conference generally receives high marks from the nutrition community[27] for effectively drawing political attention to the world food problem:

> "· · · It was as good a step forward as was possible at that time. I think the main benefit was a focusing of attention on the problem. Until that time there were many groups in many places talking but no central focus. I think the World Food Conference centralized discussion and attention and in that sense I would rate it a success."

> "· · · The World Food Conference was good as far as it went. Of course one's expectations have to be tempered by realities of world organizations but I still believe the Conference was important in that it called attention to the size and kind of problem we are facing."

> "· · · The major contribution of the Conference was that it identified the idea that coordination and cooperation are imperative if we are ever going to have any kind of world food security program."

The Rome Conference did reach reasonable consensus which is more than the earlier Bucharest World Population Conference achieved.[28]

The marks are not so high, however, for the Post-Conference results, but to expect instant breakthroughs is politically naive. Nonetheless, there is considerable concern[29] about the apparent loss of political momentum in this post-Conference period:

> "· · · If you try to evaluate the Conference in terms of commitments, I cannot be so positive."

> "· · · The Conference generated more bureaucracy, and I have seen little evidence of any real gains made by the new organizations that were created."

> "· · · It is too early to evaluate the success or failure of the Conference, but I am concerned with the lack of follow-up with respect to some of the organizations that were set up."

> "· · · We are going through a kind of no-growth period in hunger problems. The heyday of loose money for food programs is over—we are in a period of consolidation and tend to look at projects in a much more reserved light. Unfortunate as it may seem, human well-being by itself is not sufficient to justify a commitment of development funds."

[27]Interviews, July and August 1976.
[28]This is not to suggest that consensus is to be equated with success; the disagreements at Bucharest probably provided the dissonance to force a needed rethinking of approaches to the population issue. Nonetheless, post-Conference follow-up was complicated by the lack of consensus.
[29]Interviews, July and August 1976.

"· · · We are losing momentum in facing the problem. The worst thing that could happen to any kind of world food movement is two good crop years. Attention would shift to other matters and we should have lost the force generated by the Conference. The sense of urgency has diminished which is most unfortunate."

The international nutrition community finds itself in the ironic position of viewing more food as undesirable from a political perspective.[30] The global political system may be in the lamentable situation that more crisis and starvation are the prerequisites to developing the necessary political will to deal with hunger.

This reactive posture perhaps can be averted if the current leadership vacuum is filled. The World Food Council is a significant institutional step toward removing that vacuum. To be effective, however, the WFC's leadership role must be further legitimized and strengthened. A basic impediment to the WFC's aggressive leadership role in the international nutrition network is the tenuous nature of its authority. It is in the difficult position of being a manager with great responsibility but without commensurate authority. Within the UN system the proposed reorganization, especially if accompanied with concomitant budgetary allocations, would create needed authority. In effect, a new leadership strategy requires a new organizational structure. Organizational change becomes a prerequisite to legitimizing the new role of the WFC. An international body cannot readily prevail against the sovereign will of the countries it serves. Thus externally, the WFC's legitimacy comes from the countries' perception of its utility. This perceived utility will be stronger to the extent that countries share Kurt Waldheim's perception that "Our global interdependence as people, and the constantly growing interrelationship between political, economic, social, ecological, and population factors, will make it increasingly difficult for any of us to discuss major world issues except as against the background of commonly agreed goals established by the world community working in concert."[31]

The ultimate viability of the WFC will depend on support from the major international political forces. More specifically, it is the US and the USSR, because of their dominant roles in the world food system and international politics, who could make the WFC and global food system management a reality. The support of the Group of 77 is already present. It is the American and Russian political and economic commitment to the WFC that is needed. This implies the need for a clear delineation of their own national food and nutrition objectives and policies and a further extension of their existing joint efforts in the food area. Political rhetoric must be translated into institutional capacity. This will entail a delegation of food authority and responsibility to a multilateral entity. The need for this joint leadership

---

[30]There are likely few in the nutrition community who would opt for the food shortfall, but the realities of the political process do create a discouraging dilemma.

[31]Kurt Waldheim, "Keynote Address," *The World Food and Energy Crisis: The Role of International Organizations,* Richard N. Gardner, ed. (Rensselaerville, New York: Institute on Science and Man, 1974), p. 4.

effort appears clear, the political costs relatively low, and the international benefits large. History, however, makes one somewhat pessimistic about its realization.

Leadership is needed not only on the macro level but also within nutrition institutions throughout the network. Such leadership implies political involvement because food is politics. Jelliffe put it this way: "One of the biggest blocks to implementation is the lack of appreciation by the research workers that—without becoming politicians—they have to develop some homespun wisdom as advocates and presenters of their results. The idea that communication by means of a research report is sufficient to get something done is wrong. Advocacy is needed as well."[32]

The leadership and advocacy needs boil down ultimately to individuals. To be an effective nutrition leader and advocate, one's fundamental responsibility must be seen as being to the people, not to institutions or to governments. In one sense the acceptance of that perspective by decision makers throughout the nutrition system is the most basic political challenge. It is also the most difficult to achieve.

In 1963 President Kennedy told the First World Food Conference:

> We have the means, we have the capacity, to eliminate hunger from the face of the earth in our lifetimes. We need only the will.

In 1974, Secretary of State Kissinger told the World Food Conference:

> All governments should accept the removal of the scourge of hunger and malnutrition . . . as the objective of the international community as a whole, and accept the goal that within a decade no child will go to bed hungry, that no family will fear for its next day's bread, and that no human being's future and capacities will be stunted by malnutrition.

In 1985 will someone again have to step forward and urge the world to feed its hungry?

---

[32]D. Jelliffe, "Comments on Bottlenecks in Implementation: Some Aspects of the Scandinavian Experience," W. Eide, M. Jul and O. Mellander, *Human Rights in Health* (Ciba Foundation Symposium Amsterdam, N. Y.) 1974, p. 269.

IV. Considerations for Future Policy

9
World Food Institutions:
A "Liberal" View

D. Gale Johnson

World food institutions include the whole range of policies and programs that affect the production and distribution of food, including national programs as well as those of an international nature. Trade liberalization, both international and intranational, can contribute significantly to the expansion of food production. Unfortunately, recent suggestions, such as the Integrated Programme for Commodities, will result in increased trade barriers, a reduction in specialization of production and increased price instability. If there are appropriate policies—adequate incentives for farmers, increased support for research and available supplies of modern farm inputs—food production in the developing economies can be increased more rapidly than population. Food security in the developing countries could be increased significantly by a grain insurance program that supplied grain to meet all production shortfalls below trend level production. Such a program should be the major source of food aid to the developing countries in order to avoid disincentives to local farmers.

I have been asked to discuss desirable policies for addressing world food problems from a "liberal" perspective. While the contemporary global food system is regarded as flawed by virtually every analyst, quite diverse prescriptions are put forward by such analysts to alleviate these flaws. It is impossible to detail every positive step I would recommend to alter institutional practices of what the writers in this volume refer to as a global food regime. In what follows, therefore, I will attempt to clarify my position as a "liberal" economist and to suggest some policy steps which would address recurrent world food problems without adding to existing problems or creating new ones.

D. Gale Johnson is the Eliakim Hastings Moore Distinguished Service Professor of Economics and Provost, The University of Chicago.

While I assume that it would soon be evident what meaning I attach to the word liberal, let me remove any doubts at once. During the past century liberal has been used to describe a wide range of views, so wide that it can and does encompass almost all notions of social, economic, and political philosophy except the extremes of anarchy and Communism.

As a general concept liberal means to me primarily the following: a firm belief in the worth of the individual; confidence in the ability of individuals to think and act rationally in terms of their own interests; and the view that individual freedom and choice should be cherished and nourished.

It is something of a hopeful sign, at least in terms of the subject matter of this essay, that in discussions of commerce and traffic among nations liberal still retains a reasonably restricted meaning and the word freedom still means the right of unimpeded transit, passage, and access. The "double think" concept of freedom as including the power to do something as well as the absence of restraints that would prevent an individual from undertaking an act if he so desired has gained little currency in discussions of trading relations among nations.

Introduction

Why are we interested in world food institutions? Our interest, I assume, is that these institutions can have and do have positive and negative effects upon the availability, price and distribution of food. I am also assuming that our concern is primarily with the effects of institutions, defined very broadly, upon the food and nutrition available to the poorer peoples of the world.

World food institutions include not only the actions of groups of nations but also the policies and programs followed by individual nations. The marketing boards in the developing countries that expropriate a large fraction of the earnings from palm oil or peanuts are as much a part of world food institutions as is the Food and Agriculture Organization of the United Nations. In terms of impact upon production the marketing boards are undoubtedly of much greater significance than FAO. Similarly the agricultural trade and pricing policies of the European Community, of the Soviet Union and of the United States are world food institutions.

This essay can deal only with a limited range of world food institutions. I have selected three broad topics to illustrate what the policy perspectives from the liberal view might be. Other topics could be approached from the same viewpoint but it is not my wish merely to provide a catalog of institutions and appropriate policies. My objective, quite frankly, is to convince; it is to provide evidence that liberal policies have the highest probability of achieving a significant improvement in the food and nutrition of the poorer people of the world in this century.

The essay will consider three closely related policy areas: (1) reducing the barriers to trade in agricultural products, both within and between countries; (2) increasing food production in the developing countries; and (3) improving food security for the poorer people of the world. It is hoped that it can be shown that these are related areas and that progress in one depends upon and reinforces progress in the other two.

Reducing barriers to trade

Trade in agricultural products, both international and intranational, is encumbered by a myriad of regulations and interferences. India has a national policy of expanding food production, yet she has effectively held the price of rice received by her farmers substantially below the world price even when the world price was very low by historical standards. The European Community has an interest in and concern for the economic development of the poorer countries, yet virtually excludes such countries from exporting beef to Europe and imposes very high taxes on the importation of cereals. Almost all industrial nations heavily subsidize the production of sugar and regulate its importation and exportation even though this is a product that is peculiarly adapted to the climatic conditions of many developing countries.

As a group the industrial countries are substantial net importers of agricultural products, in spite of the innumerable efforts to reduce such imports. Among the industrial countries only the United States, Australia, France, and Canada are significant net exporters of agricultural products (see Paarlberg, Nau, and Destler). The developing countries are important net exporters of agricultural products and for many of the developing countries agricultural exports account for 50 to 90 percent of their export earnings.

A more liberal trade regime for agricultural products would result in a number of benefits to the developing countries. These include increased export earnings and increased certainty of an outlet for expanded production for low cost producers among them. More liberal trade would add stability to prices in international markets which would have a favorable impact upon expansion of production and food security, as Seevers argues.

The effects of the agricultural trade and price policies of the industrial countries upon the alternatives reasonably available to the developing countries have given legitimacy to the efforts of the developing countries to try to change the rules of the food regime. Two of the major objectives of the so-called New International Economic Order as it is applied to agriculture through "An Integrated Programme for Commodities" are to achieve access to markets for the products of the developing countries and to reduce the variability of prices in transactions among countries. The interrelationships between these two objectives are much more adequately recognized in the documents prepared by the UNCTAD secretariat than in the specific proposals that have been made.

The UNCTAD secretariat recognizes that access to markets, in the face of domestic programs that significantly interfere with the operation of the price system, is both complex and necessary if significant price stability is to be achieved.

Since their discussion of this point is exactly what one "liberal" economist has been emphasizing for some time,[1] I quote it at some length:

> In this way, a buffer stock would take care to a large extent of one aspect of the problem of security of export outlets for exporting countries. This problem, however, has another aspect, which is that of the assurance of access to export markets on fair terms. If world import demand for a commodity decreases, or if export supplies are increased as a result of an expansion of production under protection or subsidy, this will naturally tend to depress the world price of the commodity and hence also the price at which a buffer stock could undertake to purchase all the surplus export supplies offered to it. Conversely, reductions in protected or subsidized production would have the opposite effect. Policies of protection and subsidization of commodity production therefore work to the disadvantage of competitive exporting countries and cause misallocation of productive resources, although they may benefit consumers in countries which import the commodity at artificially depressed world prices.
>
> Moreover, if rates of protection and subsidy increase when the world price of a commodity falls, and decrease when the world price rises, as is usually the case, the instability of the world market is intensified.
>
> *It is clear, therefore, that no international stabilization arrangement for commodities produced to a large extent under protection or subsidy can provide security of export outlets to competitive exporting countries unless they contain provisions for abolishing, reducing or, at the very least, limiting protection.* A buffer stock would be able to iron out excessive short-term fluctuations in the world price, but even if it was supported by a system of export quotas, it would not be able to solve the problem posed for competitive exporting countries by the fact that an expansion of production under protection or subsidy obliged them to accept either a slower rate of growth (or even perhaps an absolute decline) in the volume of their exports or a fall in the price obtained for them.[2]

There is little that I can add to the above. When price instability is due to policies of governments that control trade to meet domestic price objectives rather than to fluctuating consumer demands or production variability, little can be done to achieve increased price stability without modifying those policies. And it is not only the industrial countries that pursue policies that add to international price instability; developing countries also contribute to the problem.

Yet the Integrated Programme for Commodities has very little to say about such modifications. In fact, much of the Integrated Programme would involve measures

---

[1]D. Gale Johnson, "World Agriculture, Commodity Policy, and Price Variability," *American Journal of Agricultural Economics,* Vol. 57, No. 5 (December 1975): 823–27; "Are High Farm Prices Here to Stay?" *The Morgan Guaranty Survey,* (August 1974) pp. 9–14; *World Agriculture in Disarray* (London and New York: Macmillan, 1973), especially Chapters 11, 12, and 13.

[2]United Nations Conference on Trade and Development (UNCTAD), "An Integrated Programme for Commodities: International arrangements for individual commodities with an integrated programme; Report by the UNCTAD secretariat," TD/B/C.1/188, July 8, 1975, p. 9 [italics added for emphasis]. The footnote included in the original was "Rates of Protection may even become negative, which is what happens when export of a commodity is prohibited or restricted."

that are inimical to trade liberalization—export quotas, export taxes and commitments to import (import quotas?). These measures, when combined with possible supply management schemes by producers and buffer stock programs, are expected "to achieve the objective of maintaining prices at adequate levels in real terms."[3] In a footnote that has further ominous implications for the liberalization of trade it is stated: "It is this objective, defined rigidly, which 'direct indexation' would seek to achieve."[4] It is hard to believe that it was possible to learn so few lessons from the numerous experiments in agricultural measures that have been conducted over the past half century. If anything has been learned it is that even the most powerful of treasuries have not been able to afford fixing the prices of agricultural products in real terms and that the efforts to do so, which have uniformly failed, have led to pervasive interference with international trade and the restriction of markets.

I have emphasized the Integrated Programme for Commodities not to be critical of UNCTAD, since their proposals represent little or nothing that is new, but to emphasize that trade liberalization is the only approach that offers any significant opportunity to the developing countries and the developed countries that export raw products for both higher and more stable international market prices.

If there were trade liberalization of a significant magnitude, then it is possible that a properly managed buffer stock program could provide some additional price stability. Even under relatively free trade there are variations in final consumer demand and in supply that result in significant price variability. But if a buffer stock program were to be viable for products such as cocoa, coffee, sugar and tea, it is essential that both producers and importers refrain from significant interferences with supply and demand. Supply interventions, such as loans on favorable and subsidized terms for investment in the production of a particular product, can disrupt a buffer stock program just as quickly as a new barrier to imports.

An important consideration in trade liberalization is that the seemingly innocuous protection provided to the processing of raw materials in the importing countries, where such exists, should be eliminated. A fairly common tariff structure is one that has a zero duty on the raw product, a seemingly modest level of duty on the semi-processed product (say 10 percent) and a somewhat higher duty on the product as generally sold to consumers. When these seemingly modest duties are related to the value added in the first or early processing it is found that the effective protection of the activity in the importing country can be 50 to 100 percent or more. Thus it is virtually impossible for the country producing the raw material to engage in even relatively simple processing operations.[5]

While there are factors other than tariff structures of the importing countries that affect the processing of raw materials at the source, such as costs of transporting and storing the primary product compared to the processed products, it is clearly reasonable for the developing countries to push for the elimination of the discrimina-

[3]UNCTAD, An Integrated Programme for Commodities: Specified proposals for decision and action by governments; Report by the Secretary-General of UNCTAD," TD/B/C.1/193, October 28, 1975, p. 10.
[4]Ibid.
[5]Harry G. Johnson, *Economic Policies Toward Less Developed Countries* (Washington: Brookings, 1967; London: George Allen & Unwin, 1967), especially Chapter 2.

tion against their processing of the raw products that they produce. The very high effective rates of protection of processing in importing countries have largely gone unnoticed until quite recently. It is important that the current round of trade negotiations recognizes the full implications of those tariff structures that escalate duties as the degree of processing increases.

The sad aspect of the agricultural policies followed by many of the industrial countries is that viewed solely in terms of their domestic effects the benefits are modest and the costs have been exceedingly high. It is true that the costs represent primarily income transfers from consumers and taxpayers, on the one hand, to producers of agricultural products, on the other hand. The real costs in terms of resources are relatively low; perhaps only 2 or 3 percent of the income transfers involved.[6]

But what useful social purpose has been served by the very large income transfers to agricultural producers? The answer is hardly any. Very briefly, in the United States, Canada and Western Europe a significant part of the transfers has been from relatively low income consumers to relatively high income farm operators and land owners. In fact, in the long run, the only significant improvement in the income of farm families has been through the effects of higher land prices.[7]

One of the primary arguments for the agricultural price policies of the industrial countries has been to maintain a larger and more viable farm segment of the economy and society. It is not at all clear that this objective has been met. One rather consistent aspect of the price policies that has been followed is an emphasis on high prices (or payments) for farm products that are land and capital intensive (the grains and certain other crop products) and the penalizing of other farm products that are relatively labor intensive (livestock products, with dairy products representing an exception).

The pricing policy of the European Community illustrates this situation, though other examples are possible.[8] The relative prices of grains have been kept very high. Prior to the price increases for grains that started in 1972, the internal prices for grains in the EC were from 50 to 100 percent higher than international market prices. Livestock prices, except for dairy products, were above world market levels but by hardly more than what was required to pay for feed costs substantially above those paid by meat producers in North America or Australia. Consequently the production of meat products was restricted by high consumer prices that kept consumption below what it would have been if grain prices had been nearer to world market levels. Thus it is not clear that the price policy actually followed increased the demand for farm workers and thus not clear whether the actual policy resulted in more farm employment in 1972 than there would have been if internal prices had been more attuned to world market prices.

[6]D. Gale Johnson, *World Agriculture in Disarray,* Chapter 11.
[7]Ibid., Chapter 9.
[8]Ibid., pp. 144–48.

There are those who may be surprised by the discussion of the high costs and modest benefits of the farm programs of the industrial countries when food and farm prices are believed to be relatively high. In fact, if one accounts for the effects of inflation, neither food nor farm prices can now be said to be relatively high. Retail food prices as of mid-1977 were only 6 or 7 percent higher compared to all other items in the US consumer price index than during the late 1960s or the first two years of this decade. And prices received by farmers in mid-1977, after deflation for the general increase in prices, were below the levels of 1970 and 1971 by at least 5 percent.

It must also be noted that the United States and Canada have reintroduced commodity programs providing returns to farmers significantly above the prices at which supply and demand would be equated. In an effort to more nearly equate demand and supply at politically acceptable prices, the United States Government has announced that farmers will be required to set aside 20 percent of their wheat area in 1978 and there will probably be a set-aside for the feed grains as well. The variable levies on grain imposed by the European Economic Community have recently returned to the same high relative levels that prevailed for several years prior to 1972. The EC variable levy on both wheat and corn in mid-1977 were greater than the farm prices of these grains in the United States. Thus, so far as the EC is concerned, farm price policies are once again very costly.

If the highly protectionist policies inherent in the agricultural policies of Western Europe and Japan and in the Soviet Union are maintained, the markets for the products of the developing countries will be severely restricted in the future as in the past. For the moment the United States has relatively few protectionist sins. With the abolition of a highly protective sugar program at the end of 1974 and a significant modification of our rice program, we are left mainly with a peanut program which has made us a high cost producer and the world's largest exporter of peanuts, import quotas on milk products, and restraints on the importation of beef. We also have some significant restraints on the importation of vegetables and fruits, especially during domestic peak marketing seasons. But I have fears for the future and doubt that our commitment to liberal trade will be strong enough to prevent the return of deficiency payments and, perhaps, of export subsidies.

The agricultural policies of these industrial states constitute much of what exists in terms of rules that govern the world food system combined with the national policies of the other more than 100 governments of the world. These policies, unless they are changed significantly, constitute a major limitation on the potentialities for growth of exports of agricultural products by the developing countries and a major source of price variability that exists in international markets. Creating new institutions, such as buffer stocks or commodity agreements, without modification of national policies will do little to benefit the developing countries and may only minimize what chance there may be for trade liberalization for agricultural products.

The strongest argument against the Integrated Programme for Agricultural Commodities is that it diverts interest and concern from the significant real barriers to the development and expansion of agricultural trade. By giving lip service and even a little money to support the Integrated Programme the industrial countries will be permitted to continue along their present paths. When the Integrated Programme fails, as it will if any significant part of it is ever implemented, the industrial countries can say they gave it their support and cannot be blamed for the failure.

I will close this part of the paper by recalling a small bit of recent but generally ignored history. One of the criticisms of the functioning of private markets is that such markets fail to reflect real ''need,'' whatever that term may mean (see the essay by Christensen). One meaning of a failure to reflect real need is that in times of a reduction in supply the market does not provide supplies for those to whom a shortfall would create the greatest hardship. During 1973 and 1974 the policies followed by the United States, which were to rely upon the market plus modest food aid shipments to distribute the available supply of grains, were severely criticized for lack of concern for the poorer people of the world. Yet compared to all other industrial countries of the world, except Canada and Australia, the policies of the United States resulted in the only significant contribution to the food supply and welfare of the poorer people of the world.

In 1974–75 world grain production was 50 million tons or approximately 4 percent below 1973–74. The decline in grain production in the United States was 33 million tons over 14 percent of the previous year's production.[9] Given the policies followed by the other industrial countries of the world, the reaction to the sharp decline in US grain production would have been a nearly equal decline in grain exports. Given the limited foreign exchange resources of most developing countries, these countries would have suffered a major decline in grain imports and in their food supply. At the beginning of the 1974–75 crop year US grain stocks were minimal—at or near the working stock level. Yet grain exports in 1974–75 at 55.0 million tons were only 2.3 million tons below those of 1973–74 though production had declined by 33 million tons. How was this accomplished? Very simply— through the functioning of the price system. Feeding of grain to livestock declined by 37 million tons or by 25 percent.[10] Does anyone imagine that such a major reduction in feed use of grain could have been managed by governmental controls?

The reduced levels of grain feeding of livestock continued into 1975–76 in the United States. If the 1973–74 level of grain use in the United States had continued through the next two years our use of grain would have been 356 million tons; actual use was 298 million tons. Thus the operation of the market released for export during these two years a total of 58 million tons of grain or 5 percent of the world's annual grain production. Canada, which also permitted internal feed grain prices

---

[9]Economic Research Service, US Dept. of Agriculture, *World Agricultural Situation,* WAS-10, July 1976, p. 15.

[10]Ibid., p. 21. In the rest of the world grain fed to livestock decreased by only 1 million tons between 1973–74 and 1974–75. Since the feed use of grain in Canada and Oceania combined decreased by 3.4 million tons (16 percent of the 1973/74 feeding levels) the rest of the world actually increased grain fed to livestock. Prices do have beneficial effects, when they are permitted to play a role.

(though not wheat prices) to reflect world market conditions reduced its grain use by 4 million tons and Australia by 2 million tons. If these adjustments in grain use in the major exporting countries had not occurred, the net grain imports of the market of developing countries (excluding Argentina) would have declined after 1973–74 instead of increasing by almost 7 million tons in 1974–75 over the prior year. Americans, instead of condemning our policies for insensitivity, should take pride in a system and set of policies that prevented serious hunger for tens of millions of the poorer people of the world. Can the citizens of the Soviet Union or of Western European countries have a similar pride in their governments' reactions to the same circumstances? I think the answer is a clear and definite negative.[11]

In a time of potential crisis in world food supplies, systems based on liberal principles responded. Those based on governmental management and control did not.

Increasing food production in the developing countries

If there is to be a significant or noticeable improvement in per capita food consumption in the developing countries, it must come through increasing the rate of growth of food production and/or reducing the rate of population growth. Since even a substantial decline in birth rates will have little effect on population growth rates for the next decade,[12] in that time span virtually all of the improvement in nutrition must come from increasing the rate of growth of food production.

Apart from increasing the rate of growth of food production in the developing countries there is only one other alternative for improving the nutrition of the poorer people of the world. This alternative is that of redistribution of the available food supplies of the world. There are those who divide the world's total food production by the number of persons and arrive at the conclusion that the world's food problem is not total production but maldistribution of the available food supply. It is factually correct that there could be a significant improvement in the nutrition of the world's poorest billion people if the food consumption of the relatively well-to-do (the billion or so that are best fed) were reduced and the excess were transferred to the poorest people. But this is true *only* if world food production were not affected by the transfer.

I know of no reputable scholar of the world's food problems who now claims

---

[11]Between 1973–74 and 1974–75 grain feeding in the Soviet Union is estimated to have increased by 2 million tons. Grain fed to livestock in the European Community did decrease by 1.5 million tons—an insignificant reduction of 2 percent. See WAS-10, p. 21.

[12]Whatever factors that may induce a reduction in the birth rate are highly likely to further reduce death rates. While there has been a remarkable decline in death rates in the developing countries since 1950, in the near term a significant part of any decline in birth rates will be offset by further declines in death rates. As a rough guess, it seems reasonable that perhaps half of any decline in birth rates during the next decade will be offset by further reductions in the death rate.

that such an approach represents a reasonable solution to the problems of the poorest people. The critical assumption of such an approach is that world food production is independent of methods used to price and distribute that food. I speak here not solely of the implications to countries such as the United States, Canada, and France but also to recipient countries, such as India, Indonesia, or Botswana. Another assumption is that it is somehow ethical and desirable that many nations and hundreds of millions of people should become dependent upon the generosity of other people and nations for a major fraction of their food supply.

Nevertheless, while there is no expectation that the kind of equalization of food availability implied by a significant redistribution of the world's current food output is practical, there remains for many concerned observers a considerable faith in the benefits of significant food aid transfers. The World Food Conference called for a minimum annual food aid commitment of 10 million tons of cereal, a call repeated by the World Food Council in June 1977. As I shall argue later, I think that there is a useful role that can be served by some types of food aid. But I strongly believe that it is a mistake to leave the impression, either implicit or explicit, that food aid shipments of 10 million tons, two times that or five times that, will make a positive contribution to the longer-term improvement of the food situation.[13]

There is a significant potential for increasing the rate of growth of food production in the developing countries. The requirements for doing so have been outlined in numerous other places and will not be dealt with in detail here.[14] I only wish to make a few points that are often overlooked, even in more systematic discussions.

One important point is that the developing countries as a group have been increasing their food production at a significant annual rate for the past quarter century. What is required is to increase the rate of growth, from something on the order of 2.7 or 2.8 percent annually to perhaps 3.5 percent. It is true that during the early 1970s some of the modest gain in per capita food production in the developing countries was lost due to near stagnation of food production and continuing population growth. But except for Africa, 1975–76 and 1976–77 were relatively good years for grain production, and food production may well have returned to its long-term growth path.

Another important point is that the poorer people of the world, say the poorest third, are almost certainly better fed and more secure in their food supplies than at any time in the past two centuries. The incidence of famine in the last quarter century has been much less than during the later part of the 19th century or the first part of the 20th century. Life expectancy in the developing countries has increased more rapidly during the last quarter century than it ever did during a comparable span of time in Western Europe, Japan, or North America. It has now reached the level attained by the United States at the beginning of this century and by Japan as late as the 1930s.[15]

[13]T. W. Schultz, "Value of U.S. Farm Surplus to Underdeveloped Countries," *Journal of Farm Economics,* Vol. 42 (December 1960): 1031–42.

[14]D. Gale Johnson, *World Food Problems and Prospects* (Washington: American Enterprise Institute, 1975), Chapter 7, and citations therein.

[15]Ibid., Chapter 2.

But the main point that I want to make is that most of the increase in food production must come from the resources of the developing countries themselves. The industrial countries can make limited but important contributions, primarily through research and development, some forms of technical assistance, and trade liberalization. But of critical importance are policies and resources which the developing countries control themselves. Developing countries must follow policies that provide adequate incentives for farmers to produce. A recent report by the US Government Accounting Office catalogs and describes a wide variety of measures that have disincentive effects upon agricultural production.[16] The measures include export taxes, controlled producer prices, and exchange rates that discourage exports of agricultural products and encourage food imports and relatively high prices for certain key inputs, such as fertilizer.

Let me provide just two examples of the pricing policies that have had adverse effects upon production. During 1968 through 1972, the first five years when the high yielding varieties of rice were available, the wholesale price of rice in India averaged $136 per ton, if the official rate of exchange is used. During the same five-year period the average import value of rice was $175 per ton. The Indian farmer received approximately 78 percent of the import price. If a more realistic rate of exchange between the rupee and the dollar is used, the price received by the Indian farmer per ton of rice was $91, approximately 52 percent of the import price.

On the other hand, wheat was priced more reasonably. At the official rate of exchange the average wholesale price of wheat was $123 per ton for 1968–72 compared to an import cost of $78 per ton. At a more realistic rate of exchange, the price of wheat in India was $82, very nearly the same as the import cost. While other factors were in operation, the differential price treatment was clearly responsible for some of the difference in the rates of adoption of the high yielding varieties of wheat and rice in India during the period,[17] and explains, in part, the success Nicholson and Esseks find in Indian wheat production efforts.

For nearly two decades the Government of Thailand has had what is euphemistically called a "rice premium"; this is a nice sounding name for an export tax on rice. The major objective of the export tax has been to provide foreign exchange to the government and to hold down the price of rice for consumers. As is so often the case, the beneficiaries of policies of low food prices are urban consumers who, on the average, have significantly higher real incomes than the farmers who produce the food product. Chung Ming Wong has investigated the effect of the export tax on rice production in Thailand for the period 1966–70. His results are striking. The production of rice was reduced by as much as 1.5 million tons or by nearly 15 percent of the actual production during the period. In addition, he found that Thailand probably suffered an average annual loss of foreign exchange earnings of about $250 million for 1966–70. The loss of foreign exchange earnings was approx-

[16]Comptroller General of the United States, *Disincentives to Agricultural Production in Developing Countries,* Washington: GAO, ID-76-2, November 26, 1975.
[17]Vasant A. Sukhatme, "The Utilization of High-Yielding Rice and Wheat Varieties in India: An Economic Assessment," unpublished Ph.D. dissertation, Department of Economics, The University of Chicago, 1976, Chapters 4 and 5.

imately five percent of national income.[18] For a nation with a major comparative advantage in the production of agricultural products, the loss in foreign exchange earnings was a very large and apparently unrecognized cost of the export tax on rice.

In most developing countries farmers or marketing agents are not free to sell farm products in international markets. As a consequence, when production is favorable domestic prices fall to very low levels. This has occurred in India during the past year. Instead of permitting grain to be exported, India is attempting to store substantially larger quantities of wheat and rice than it has adequate storage facilities for. Consequently significant amounts of grain will be wasted, farmers will produce less in the future than would have been the case if prices had been maintained by exporting some of the grain, and while consumers will have gained for a period, they will later be faced with higher grain prices.

Resources, including knowledge gained through research, are important requisites for increasing production of food in the developing countries. But those of us who are interested in increased food production in the developing countries have for far too long been silent or talked too softly about the adverse effects of national agricultural and trade policies. Two examples of efforts to measure the adverse effect on food production of the policies followed by developing countries have been given. Many other examples remain to be investigated. Unfortunately, most of the proposals that are now being made for restructuring food policies or the international economic order do little or nothing to correct the disincentive effects of existing policies. In fact, all too many of the proposals would buttress and support such policies and perhaps add a few new ones. Only a move toward liberalization of both domestic and trade policies offers any real hope of reducing or eliminating the current policies that have negative effects upon food production in the developing countries.

Improving food security

As indicated above, most food aid contributes very little, if anything, to the long run improvement of per capita food supplies. I can see no general argument for food aid that differs from the general case for aid. It is highly likely that with some minor exceptions food aid has contributed significantly less to the welfare of recipient countries than most other forms of aid.

I do hold that food aid in case of emergencies has a significant value. I refer, in the first instance, to emergencies that grow out of natural catastrophes such as earthquakes, floods, and storms. It is frequently easier, cheaper and quicker to bring food to stricken areas from another country, such as the United States, than it is to mobilize domestic resources. These types of aid, which depend as much or more on delivery capacities as on available food supplies in one or more of the industrial countries, do make the world a somewhat safer place for poor people.

I believe that there is another type of food aid for which the benefits may be

---

[18]Chung Ming Wong, "A Model of the Rice Economy of Thailand," unpublished Ph.D. dissertation, Department of Economics, The University of Chicago, 1976. Production loss estimate derived from Table 9, p. 53.

comparable to those from aid provided in the form of money. This aid is also related to primarily natural events, namely the fluctuations in the production of grain. Recall that for most of the developing countries with nutrition problems grain accounts for a high fraction of the total caloric intake—up to 70 percent or more in many low income countries. Furthermore, in the developing countries almost all of the grain is used either for seed or human consumption; less than ten percent is used for livestock feed (see the essay by Austin). In the developed countries more than half of the grain is used for livestock feed. Consequently fluctuations in grain production in the developed countries are primarily an inconvenience; there is no reasonable prospect that a very poor grain crop could result in starvation or a serious deterioration in the nutritional status of most people. Reductions in grain production can be absorbed by reducing the quantities fed to livestock, and adequate resources are available to increase imports to offset part or all of the grain shortfall.

However, in the developing countries a sharp decline in grain production can result in significant hardship. For people whose average food supply just about meets the minimum caloric requirements for ordinary activities, a reduction in the grain production of a few percent can be a serious matter for a significant part of the population.

I believe that the United States, and any other country that wished to participate, should undertake an insurance program for developing countries that would provide for meeting any shortfall of grain production below a given percentage of trend production. This program should constitute the primary or major form of food aid provided by the United States.[19]

My proposal for a food aid program, which I have called a grain insurance program, is a very simple one. The United States would offer to any developing country that wished to participate a pledge to meet all annual shortfalls in grain production from trend in excess of a given percentage. Except for the limited forms of emergency food aid described earlier, this program would be the primary form of food aid that we should provide. The cost would not be beyond our means. If we covered all shortfalls below trend production for grain in excess of six percent for each developing country the average annual payment would be approximately five million tons. If a developing country held even very modest stocks of grain or reserved foreign exchange to import limited amounts of grain, the largest annual shortfall in grain consumption could be held to three percent or less. The six percent criterion is admittedly quite arbitrary, though not entirely so. The selection of the percentage criterion should reflect two considerations—the incentive to hold some grain reserves in the developing country and the effect of the insurance payments on the output behavior of the local producers. If the percentage were very low, say between one and two percent, there would be no economic incentive for holding reserves. Furthermore if such small departures from trend were met, the magnitude of the grain transfers would be large enough to reduce significantly the average

[19]I have presented this program in greater detail in "International Food Security: Issues and Alternatives," in U.S. Department of Agriculture, *International Food Policy Issues, A Proceeding,* For. Agri. Econ. Rpr. No. 143, January 1978, pp. 81–90.

Table 1   Effects of carryover program on available supply based on actual production, 6 percent insurance policy, India and Africa, 1968–1975

(million tons)

Year	Actual production	Optimal carryover	Insurance payment	Available supply
		India		
1968	81.6	0.5	0.0	81.1
1969	85.1	1.5	0.0	84.1
1970	91.7	5.0	0.0	88.2
1971	90.2	4.0	0.0	91.2
1972	86.6	0.0	0.0	90.2
1973	95.4	1.0	0.0	94.4
1974	86.7	0.0	4.3	92.0
1975		at probability levels		
		Carryover $< \dfrac{.5}{1.0} \quad \dfrac{.75}{2.0} \quad \dfrac{.95}{4.0}$		
		Africa		
1968	40.5	2.5	0.0	39.5
1969	41.3	3.0	0.0	40.8
1970	40.2	2.0	0.0	41.2
1971	40.9	1.0	0.0	41.9
1972	44.4	2.0	0.0	43.4
1973	37.1	0.0	4.2	43.3
1974	42.2	0.0	1.2	43.4
1975		at probability level		
		Carryover $< \dfrac{0.5}{0.5} \quad \dfrac{0.75}{1.0} \quad \dfrac{0.95}{2.0}$		

expected returns to the local producers and thus lower the rate of growth of domestic grain production.

The examples that I have worked out with colleagues indicate that with modest resource commitments by the developing countries annual shortfalls in grain consumption could be held to very low levels with a program that met all production shortfalls in excess of six percent. For example, between 1968 and 1974 if India had had an optimal grain storage program and had stored during that period 12 million ton-years of grain, consumption would have fallen below trend in only two years—by 1 million tons in 1972 and by 4.9 million tons in 1974. The latter shortfall was approximately 5 percent and could have been reduced to 3 percent by importing 2 million tons of grain. A similar exercise was undertaken for Africa and similar results were obtained even though grain crops were poor in both 1973 and 1974. The total grain transfer for the seven years would have been 4.3 million tons for India and 5.4 million tons for Africa.

The results summarized in the previous paragraphs are given in Table 1, which provides estimates of annual production, optimal carryover, insurance payment and available supply for each year from 1968 through 1974 for India and Africa. The optimal carryover is defined as the amount of grain that if stored from the available

Table 2   Effects of carryover program on available supply based on actual production, India and Africa, 1968–1975

(million tons)

Year	Actual production	Optimal carryover	Aailable supply	Trend
		India		
1968	81.6	3.0	78.6	80.7
1969	85.1	5.0	83.1	83.2
1970	91.7	10.0	86.7	85.8
1971	90.2	10.0	90.2	88.5
1972	86.6	5.5	91.1	91.2
1973	95.4	7.0	93.9	94.0
1974	86.7	1.0	92.7	96.9
1975		at probability level		99.9

$$\text{Carryover} < : \frac{0.5}{4.0} \quad \frac{0.75}{4.5} \quad \frac{0.95}{6.5}$$

Year	Actual production	Optimal carryover	Aailable supply	Trend
		Africa		
1967		(1.0)		
1968	40.5	2.5	39.0	38.2
1969	41.3	3.0	40.8	39.3
1970	40.2	2.0	41.2	40.4
1971	40.9	1.0	41.9	41.5
1972	44.4	2.0	43.4	42.7
1973	37.1	0.0	39.1	43.9
1974	42.2	0.0	42.2	45.1
1975		at probability level		46.4

$$\text{Carryover} < \frac{0.5}{1.0} \quad \frac{0.75}{1.5} \quad \frac{0.95}{3.0}$$

supply (production plus carryin) would have an expected return equal to the expected cost. The expected cost includes the cost of storing grain, including interest on the value of the grain. In the examples in the tables, the cost of storage is assumed to be $7.50 per ton and the real interest rate is 5 percent. While the expected return is measured in terms of the change in the total area under the demand curve due to transferring consumption from the current year to some future year, a simpler explanation is that if a ton of grain is added to stocks it is expected that the increase in the future price per ton will equal the current price plus the per ton costs of storage, including interest on the investment. It should be noted that storage is undertaken in response to an expected return and that there is no guarantee that storage undertaken in any given year will result in the coverage of the total storage costs. Since the gain from storage results from random fluctuations of production (around the production trend), it is highly likely that most storage decisions will result in either a financial loss or a financial gain and very few storage decisions would result in just covering the costs of storage, including interest costs. The optimal storage rules provide for approximate equality of gains and costs only in the very long run.

Table 2 provides estimates similar to those in Table 1 except that it assumes that in India and in Africa an optimal carryover program had been in operation from 1968 through 1974 without the insurance program.[20] The results given for India, with no insurance program, indicate that for India with two relatively poor crop years since 1967 (1972 and 1974) an optimal carryover program would have resulted in relatively small deviations of available supply around the trend, which is given in the last column of Table 2. The available supply in 1972 would have been almost exactly at the trend level, while in 1974 with production approximately 11 percent below trend, consumption would have been 4.2 million tons or approximately 4.3 percent below trend. With a price elasticity of demand for grains of -0.1 grain prices in 1974 would have been approximately 40 percent above those in 1973. Added imports of grain of 2 million tons would have held the price increase to approximately 20 percent.

The probabilistic aspect of optimal carryovers—any carryover program for that matter—is illustrated by the grain availabilities for India in 1974 under the assumptions in Tables 1 and 2. The combination of optimal carryovers and the grain insurance program covering all shortfalls of production below trend in excess of six percent would have resulted in 0.7 million tons less grain in 1974 than would have an optimal carryover program without the insurance program. The insurance program would have encouraged higher levels of grain consumption from 1969 through 1973 and very low levels of carryover at the end of 1973. 1974 results were due to the ''accidents'' of the production levels in the years immediately prior to 1974.

The bottom part of each table gives similar calculations for Africa. In this case there are no surprises—the insurance program would have provided increased stability of available supplies. The major contribution of the insurance program would have been to increase supplies substantially in 1973 when an optimal carryover program alone would have resulted in an available supply of 4.8 million tons below trend or a shortfall of 11 percent. With the insurance program the shortfall below trend would have been only 0.6 million tons.[21]

For the seven-year period the insurance program would have reduced carryovers in India to 12 million ton-years from 41.5 million ton-years for a national

[20]An important assumption that underlies both of the tables should be noted. In calculating optimal carryovers it was assumed that international trade in grains remained at a ''normal'' or average level. In other words, variations in net trade were not permitted to offset any part of the year-to-year production variations. If such variations in trade were permitted, the level of optimal carryovers would be reduced. For further discussion of the model and the results, see D. Gale Johnson and Daniel Sumner, ''An Optimization Approach to Grain Reserves for Developing Countries,'' in David J. Eaton and W. Scott Steele, eds., *Analyses of Grain Reserves, A Proceedings,* US Department of Agriculture, Economic Research Service Report No. 634, Washington: August 1976, pp. 39–55.

[21]It should be noted that one of the assumptions made in the tables was that there was free trade in grain among the countries of Africa. This, of course, is not true. Thus both optimal carryovers and the size of the insurance payments for Africa would be larger if the analyses had been carried out for each country. One of the important points made by the author and Sumner (ibid., pp. 67–68) is that policy barriers limiting or preventing trade in grain among countries greatly increase the size of reserves required to achieve increased stability of grain availability. Much of the need for grain reserves is the result of policy decisions and is not due to production variability. For example, our analyses indicate that if there were free trade in grain among all the developing countries, with no variation in annual grain trade with the industrial countries, the optimal grain carryovers would be approximately the same (for a given level of probability) as for India alone (ibid., p. 77).

optimal carryover program. The savings in interest and storage costs to India would have been approximately $450 million if the price of grain in India were $150 per ton. This saving would have required the delivery in insurance aid of 4.3 million tons of grain with a value of $650 million, including transport costs. If one assumes that the net gain to the Indian economy was four million tons of grain and that the insurance program had no noticeable effect upon domestic production, the net gain from the insurance program to India would have been approximately $1 billion.

For Africa the insurance program would not have reduced the optimal carryover by a significant amount since production variability prior to 1973 implied a very low probability of a production shortfall greater than six percent. The insurance program would have reduced optimal carryovers from 10.5 to 8.5 million ton-years and the savings in storage cost would have been $30 million. However, the insurance program would have made a major contribution to the available supply of grain in 1973 and 1974.

The illustrations presented here, as well as others, indicate that developing countries, assisted by the modest insurance proposal, could achieve a high degree of stability of domestic grain, and thus food, supplies at relatively low cost. It would not be difficult or costly to limit supply shortfalls to three percent or less. The expected average annual cost to the United States would be in the range of four to six million tons of grain.

I have said that the grain insurance proposal was a simple one. Obviously there would be complications. Grain production estimates for many developing countries leave much to be desired in terms of accuracy. Some have argued that the existence of such a program would induce governments to falsify their production data. This is obviously a potential problem with all food aid programs. But since the insurance payment is related to trend production, lowering grain production estimates would affect future payments. Unfortunately this attribute would not be of overwhelming importance to a government that had a relatively short life expectancy, as is the case in numerous developing countries. But one of the conditions of the insurance program could be that outside observers would be permitted to evaluate the accuracy of the grain production estimates, a practice that could benefit the global information system as well.

The grain insurance program represents a means by which a limited form of economic aid could be provided to the developing countries. With reasonable management of domestic supplies of grain by the developing countries the insurance program should eliminate most of the under-nutrition and hardship associated with grain production variability. Admittedly, the program would contribute very little to the long run problems of inadequate food supplies for the poorer people to create productive national agricultural research systems; if the developing countries do not think any food aid program, even a massive one, can contribute to long run improvement in the food supplies of the poorer people of the world. Such people are going to have better diets only as economic growth occurs and food production expands.

What can be said for the insurance program is that it would not interfere significantly with efforts of the developing countries to expand their own food supplies. The negative incentive effects, both upon governments who have in the past relied upon massive food aid as an alternative to measures to expand domestic production and upon farmers who have been adversely affected by previous food aid programs, would be very small. But I believe the grain insurance program is responsive to an important problem that exists in many, if not most, developing countries and it would make the world a somewhat more secure place for millions of poor people.

Conclusion

If the nutritional status of the poorer people of the world is to be improved significantly during the remainder of this century, a prime requirement is the major modification of existing global food regime rules rather than the creation of new institutions or organizations. Far too many of our existing food practices interfere with the effective use of the world's resources in achieving increased food production in the developing countries. And far too many of the suggestions for new international institutional arrangements would result in new barriers to the expansion of food production. This is not to say that there are no new institutions that would assist in the efforts to expand food production at a more rapid rate. Clearly improved information systems would be desirable, if nothing more than for their effects in improving the functioning of markets. More could be done to assist the developing countries to create productive national agricultural research systems; if this is to be accomplished new arrangements must be devised.

Still the major determinants of the global food regime are the national agricultural and trade policies of the industrial and developing countries. It is these policies that require modification if the developing countries are to have reasonable access to markets for their exports of agricultural products and if there is to be a significant reduction of price instability in the international markets. But the developing countries could contribute to the expansion of their own agricultural production, either for domestic use or export, through modifications of policies. All too many developing countries follow price and trade policies that create disincentives for farm production.

Unfortunately it is not at all obvious that there is the political incentive for those in power to modify national agricultural and trade policies in order to make more effective use of the world's agricultural resources and thus to improve the nutrition of the poorer people of the world. The consequences of the failure to act are clear. There will be less progress in improving the nutrition of the poor people of the world than the available resources could make possible. And it is highly probable that some time during the next decade the world will witness a "food crisis" similar to that of 1973 and 1974. There have been no changes in policies, nor are any likely, that would prevent such an occurrence if for two years in three world grain production fell moderately short of trend level. In a technical sense, it would be easy to avoid such a future event. In a political sense, it is unlikely that anything will be done to prevent it.

10

Toward Innovation
in the Global Food Regime

Donald J. Puchala and Raymond F. Hopkins

The market-oriented focus of the global food regime, as it functioned from the late 1940s to the early 1970s, has proved inadequate. Preoccupation with perfecting markets led food policy makers to underemphasize the need for increased production in the Third World. It also led them to exaggerated attention to short-term surplus disposal and too little concern about scarcity. The regime emerged from a context in which unilateral actions and domestic considerations prevailed. This resulted in regime pathologies in which mutually beneficial international food solutions were not reached and multilateral coordination to analyze and solve food problems was discouraged. Such regime inadequacies cumulated over time; while they did not cause the food "crisis" of 1973–74, they blunted international responses to it. Reform of the global food regime is needed to (1) raise priorities accorded to rural modernization in Third World countries, (2) increase attention to malnutrition and chronic hunger, (3) provide resources for development, and (4) structure and stabilize the market so as to provide security of supply and income. The legitimacy of multilateral forums and processes also must be enhanced.

In the course of preparing this volume, the editors and authors joined together along with 37 others at a conference to explore issues of global food interdependence.[1] Participants at this conference represented a cross-section of the American food policy community—government and international organization officials, academic specialists, foundation officers, agribusinessmen, lobbyists, and missionaries. While our primary goal was to evaluate global food problems and the

[1] The "Conference on Global Food Interdependence" was held at Airlie House in Virginia, April 7–9, 1977, with help from the Rockefeller Foundation grant that partially supported this volume, and with principal sponsorship by the Department of State's Office of External Research. For a synopsis of the conference, see, "Global Food Interdependence: Issues and Answers," External Research Study, INR/XRS-15, July 27, 1977.

American response to them, the primary result of the conference was tension. This resulted less from differences of philosophy and viewpoint among participants (although there were these differences) than from prevailing uncertainties in the food policy community. With regard to American foreign agricultural policy in particular, no policy was proposed as having confidently predictable effects. In most cases, unilateral American actions were seen to lack credibility because key cause-effect relationships in the global food system were beyond unilateral control. Multilateral actions, however, lacked appeal, mainly because they were multilateral and hence thought to be less likely to serve American and liberal trade interests.

Sensitive readers will be aware that similar tensions are present in this volume. Successive authors accept the gravity of current and foreseeable world food problems, although different ones assign varying relevance and priority to them and to conditions in the global situation from which they arise. With respect to improving the world food system, the varying positions and recommendations of the authors generate a lively and useful debate. At issue are the promise of "market" solutions and their justice versus the advisability of increased public intervention, national versus international responsibility for food security, the utility of unilateral initiatives and bilateral dealings versus the need for multilateral regulations, the effects and desirability of food aid and the wisdom in separate nations' striving for self-sufficiency. Beyond disagreements on these issues, however, there is a collective consensus among contributors: *to cope with predictable crises of global food scarcity, deteriorating nutritional conditions and economic instability in coming years, public and private participants in the global food system must accomplish a fundamental rethinking of principles behind national agricultural policies, and an equally fundamental reformulation of priorities in international food diplomacy.* Executing this recommendation would amount to a reform of the global food regime. While various contributors agree that this should be done, they do not agree altogether on the manner of reform, or on whether it can be done, whether it will be done in time to solve problems, or whether it will be done at all. Some of us are more sanguine than others about men's capacities to meet great challenges with enlightened responses, and this injects tension into our dialogues.

In the first chapter of this volume we introduced the concept "global food regime," defined as the "set of rules, norms or institutional expectations" that govern participants' behavior in the global food system. We hypothesized that this resulted in identifiable normative parameters ("rules of the game") that prescribe certain kinds of transactions, proscribe others, and generally condition the process of public and private diplomacy among actors in international food affairs. Discussion throughout this volume has sufficiently convinced us not only that the regime concept has proven analytically useful, but also that the sketch of the existing regime in our introduction was accurate. In summary, the norms of the global food regime[2] of the postwar era were (1) supportive of international trade to the extent

---

[2]Recall that the norms of the regime are myriad, ranging from fairly universal mutual expectations as to which countries and groups stood ready to provide food in disasters in particular regions, to fairly narrow

that they evoked constant behavior directed toward preserving and perfecting markets, (2) permissive of concessional dealing, but only within limits, (3) supportive of decentralized adjustment, and permissive of a pre-eminent American role in this process, (4) encouraging to the dissemination of agronomic information, (5) supportive of behavior directed toward famine relief and other collective responses to acute hunger, (6) unsupportive of behavior directed toward alleviating malnutrition and chronic hunger, (7) unencouraging to rural modernization in the Third World and (8) inhospitable to challenges to national sovereignty either in the form of international interference in domestic affairs, or in the form of supranational regulation.

The regime norms producing these characteristics largely emanated *de facto* as emergent properties of national policies. In other words, what has been ''normal'' in the global food system, and established as such, is a set of patterns of behavior that reflect recurrent actions and interactions of participants pluralistically pursuing individual interests. Rules and norms to sustain these patterns were internalized by individuals responsible for maintaining the regime largely because they were rewarding. This was especially so for those elites who played roles as large traders, lenders, donors and recipients. Formal coordination, multilateral action and international organization are notably weak in the global food system, and supranational authority and regulation are largely absent. Orthodox behavior according to regime norms therefore tends to be either self-enforced by participants who anticipate costs or penalties from deviance, or bilaterally enforced via sanctions available to those who control disproportionate shares of resources. The postwar food system, conditioned by the existing regime, embodied many of the attributes of a liberal world order guided by seemingly ''invisible hands''—e.g., apparently automatic adjustment mechanisms sensitive to shifting production and consumption conditions, minimal demands upon participants' communication and coordination capacities, minimal needs to allocate resources toward the overhead costs of running the system, minimal constraints on most participants' autonomy, and relative price and market share stability provided as a collective good, primarily as an outcome of domestic policies and paid for by those most committed to the system.[3]

But what is most important in our estimation is that this regime, created from the confluence of participants' self-interested pursuits in the 1950s and 1960s, has proven inadequate in the face of global crisis in food and agriculture in the 1970s. At least three inadequacies have, over time, proven serious enough to bring tenets of the global regime into question in recent years.

---

understandings among officials in major grain exporting states as to what constituted ''unfair'' competition. American archival records document a number of such expectations and norms, as do interviews of current officials. For an account of the 1950s and 1960s, see Trudy Peterson, ''Sales, Surpluses and the Soviets,'' paper read at the Agricultural Policy Symposium, Washington, D.C., July 25, 1977, and for the 1970s see the article by Destler in this volume.

[3]Some countries such as the Soviet Union and China, by placing minimal demands on the system, reduced the need for international adjustment. Others, particularly the United States, bore much of the adjustment costs of stability by holding large reserves available for use in international trade. Both those most committed and those least committed to the postwar regime acted to support it principally in pursuing domestic policy objectives.

First, while there is a good deal to be said about the desirability of market solutions, both pro and con as various authors would have it, the inadequacy of the postwar global food regime has been much less in the international food markets it created and supported than in the "market orientation" it promoted. With only slight exaggeration it can be said that the preoccupation of both managers and analysts of the current regime has been with selling and buying considerations to the almost total exclusion of other concerns. As a consequence there has been a prevailing obliviousness to global food developments outside international markets unless these had fairly immediate effects upon them. There has also been a prevailing tendency to evaluate the performance of the international food system in terms of monetarized values, or things priced and counted in normal social exchange. The market, its division, its problems and its perfection were the agenda for food diplomacy from the late 1940s to the early 1970s. Issues of aid, research and information were considered in the *context* of desired commercial market performance; issues of hunger, the effects of malnourishment on the quality of life, and the costs of hunger-related political instability arose only when acute famine threatened.

Meanwhile, as the international relations of food focused on strict market economics, food production in key Third World countries remained isolated from the benefits of the international economy. Production features in many countries were conditioned by internal policies frequently geared toward goals that had little to do with increased returns to farmers, increased food production and better distribution, and for various political and domestic economic reasons such policies were often directly intended to insulate national agricultures from the international market.[4] One immediate result of this is that many Third World farmers, denied the price incentives of international trade (or sometimes any price incentives) and often restrained by grossly unequal land tenure practices and credit access have remained unmoved to increase production by innovating technologically or otherwise. Coupled with increasingly unfavorable soil and climate conditions in some regions,[5] the aggregate result of this is that Third World agriculture lags by technological centuries, and the food security of millions of people remains in or is slipping towards extreme jeopardy—all of this while food diplomacy has focused on marketing matters of marginal concern to most Third World producers.

A second and related inadequacy of the postwar food regime has been the overemphasis upon managing surpluses. Combined with the regime's indifference to rural modernization in poor countries this overemphasis on surpluses helped to produce global panic in the early 1970s. The regime's failure here was rooted in myopia: participants and analysts assumed that huge North American surpluses were perennial and that *the* international challenge was to reduce and channel these without disrupting or depressing the market. As a result, several norms institutionalized between 1950 and 1972 legitimized and reinforced actions intended

---

[4]Abdullah A. Saleh, "Disincentives to Agricultural Production in Developing Countries: A Policy Survey," *Foreign Agricultural Supplement* (Washington: GAO, March, 1975).

[5]See Eric P. Eckholm, *Losing Ground* (New York: W. W. Norton, 1976).

to meet the perceived challenge. North American domestic adjustments came to be the internationally expected, and hence "normal," responses to market gluts; concessional dealings for "surplus disposal" were legitimized as mechanisms to sell cheaply without depressing prices except for poor country recipients; famine relief became a principle that everyone could accept. Yet, the astonishing paradox in all of this was that many of the norms arising from global market surpluses abetted behavior that neglected or even exacerbated what was the more fundamental, but unacknowledged, problem of the period: lagging food production in the Third World. Industrialized countries protected their farmers from the competition abroad; economic assistance was forbidden for use in programs that would improve rural modernization in crops that could compete with donor country exports. Thus, not only did the regime of the fifties and sixties accomplish little by way of encouraging rural modernization, but through priority given to norms enchancing the selling, bartering, or giving away of surpluses produced in North America, food diplomacy probably actually discouraged agricultural progress in poor countries.

Finally, the global food regime of the postwar era has proven inadequate because it failed to legitimize processes or institutions for the multilateral regulation of the international food system. As noted, the regime has emerged *de facto* from the customary behavior of its participants, with each pursuing self-interest, guarding autonomy and steadfastly rejecting authority beyond the nation-state. Indeed, that the international food system *should* be a residual of domestic oriented food policies became itself a principle of the global food regime. Therefore, no effective authority has managed the system in the interest of global welfare or toward the definition and pursuit of collective values. Furthermore, it has been deemed illegitimate for international agencies to penetrate uninvited into states' sovereign jurisdictions, for example by pointing to a famine, as in Ethiopia in 1973.

This reverence for sovereignty, as legitimized by the existing regime, produces pathologies in behavior. Not only is optimum functioning of the system inhibited, but individual participant's behavior is perversely affected. Among pathologies of global practice under the existing regime, five in particular can be cited.

First, the effective absence of international authorities or mechanisms to coordinate the interests and policies of major national participants renders the global food system prone to "irrational" production outcomes. That is, imposing or relaxing domestic production controls may appear to be rational responses to market cues from the individual points of view of national governments. But when similar and simultaneous—yet isolated and uncoordinated—national production decisions are made, the aggregate result is frequently highly irrational from the global or systemic point of view.[6] The food system fluctuates between crises of overproduction and underproduction, prices abruptly rise or dramatically fall, farm incomes swing between boom and bust, and consumers are erratically rewarded and punished. Not only are there no effective multilateral means available to avoid such aggregate

[6]This dilemma requiring collaboration for resolution is roughly equivalent to the structural paradox in the "Prisoner's Dilemma" of game theory. Without communication (at least implicitly) and trust, the prisoners are doomed to worse outcomes or higher costs than they could achieve through cooperation. A good statement of this mathematically formulated paradox may be found in Anatol Rapoport, *Fights, Games and Debates* (Ann Arbor: University of Michigan Press, 1960), pp. 173–179.

inefficiencies, but neither are there any international means available to buffer resulting price and income instabilities.

Second, the absence of legitimized multilateral regulation under the existing regime renders the global food system prone to agricultural trade wars that are mutually disadvantageous to all participants. These become particularly likely during periods of global overproduction (in terms of effective demand, though not necessarily need) when temptations to use the international market to dump surpluses are strong. Lacking adjustment mechanisms or regulatory authorities at the international level, food diplomacy tends to propel issues of competition, market division, penetration and adjustment directly and immediately into domestic political arenas where defensive-minded interest groups encourage protectionist responses from elites too close to avoid such pressures. Trade-restrictive outcomes are frequent; retaliations are normal; costs in terms of economic efficiency, taxpayers' resources and consumers' nutritional well-being are predictable and unfortunate.[7]

Third, to the extent that the global food regime has legitimized the doctrine of national sovereignty over national food and agricultural affairs, it has discouraged international discussion of agricultural practice, food distribution and nutritional well-being within countries. In so doing, it has concealed from international consideration the most telling manifestations of food scarcity in Third World countries, and it has to a large degree rendered nutrition a non-issue. Since food affairs formally are held to be conducted among sovereign states and only elites gain admission to diplomatic forums, representatives are often out of touch with food conditions in their own countries. Even more dramatically, delegates from some poor, Third World states represent governments indifferent to rural modernization, opposed to land reform, and insensitive to food security. Frequently such elites, coming from a background of urban life, high education and little contact with peasants, are fascinated with technical solutions and with solving their domestic production inadequacies through foreign aid.

Fourth, the current global food regime confronts a condition of "diminishing commons" because the regime legitimizes no international authorities or procedures to preserve these domains. Examples of the problem may be seen in unregulated fishing that has led to lower total catches of some species, environmental distortions such as air pollution and cloud seeding, or diversions at the watersheds and upper reaches of international rivers, all of which benefit one country and diminish the availability of benefits to others. In the absence of enforceable regulations concerning their use, "commons" invariably disappear, usually to the benefit of those powerful or wily enough to establish enclosure. Unfortunately, no one involved in the global food system has been charged with caring for the commons.

Finally, by denying authority and withholding legitimacy, the existing regime renders largely ineffective existing bureaucratic services and multilateral mechanisms in international global food organizations. Barred from both consensus-building and regulatory roles at system level, organizations such as the FAO have become

[7]H. B. Malmgren and D. L. Schelchty, "Rationalizing World Agricultural Trade," *Journal of World Trade Law*, #4 (July-August, 1970), pp. 515–537.

bureaucratic labyrinths, political-ideological battlegrounds and technical reporting services. The difficulties experienced by Director-General Saouma in reorienting the FAO bureaucracy toward greater developmental efforts rest only partly upon internal bureaucratic inertia. They also reflect resistence by bureaucrats in member states who prefer the old way of doing things.[8] Yet the World Food Conference set about proliferating new food institutions, as constitutionally impotent as ever, but with the explanation that the older ones "don't work." Needless to say, if some of the institutions could "work" propensities to pathological behavior in the global food system might be controlled. But, then, the pathologies result, after all, precisely from the fact that the current regime is distinctly inhospitable to the notion of "working" international organizations.

Elements for a new regime for food

The critiques of the existing global food regime in this volume lay a foundation for our recommendations for reform. Realistically, any new norms must support a variety of goals; otherwise there could be no hope of their acceptance. We insist, however, that food security, nutritional well-being, enhanced human welfare, economic stability, and global interest be among these goals. To achieve such goals, norms and rules are required that support different outcomes than heretofore, norms that reflect new priorities and changed perspectives.

Encouraging the goal of rural modernization in the Third World should be given top priority as a criterion for the global regime. The most urgent food problem of the next decade is going to be scarcity in poor countries, and rural modernization is a key prerequisite for contending with it. By rural modernization we mean more than enhanced food production via improved technology. It is certainly not simply equivalent to spreading the Green Revolution. Rather, this goal implies the transformation of the countryside in many of the poorer countries in ways such that (1) peasants and farmers receive income incentives and rewards for shifting from less productive to more productive technologies, and production consequently goes up; (2) a rural cash economy exists and rural and urban markets are integrated; (3) information about markets and technology flows freely and rapidly, and producers are trained to use it; (4) infrastructural barriers—economic and political—to production and distribution are overcome; (5) rural wage rates approximate urban ones, and rural underemployment disappears, and (7) social and economic mobility both within and between generations are reasonable expectations for farm families. In most general terms, rural modernization in the Third World means not only that food production is up, but that it is up because effective demand and consumption are up, because income is up, because wages and profits are up, because general economic development is underway and agriculture is an integral part of it.

[8]United States Senate, Select Committee on Nutrition and Human Needs, "The United States, FAO and World Food Politics: U.S. Relations With An International Food Organization," Staff Report (Washington: U.S. Government Printing Office, June, 1976). For a more sympathetic view of international organization in the food area, see, Joseph M. Jones, *The United Nations at Work: Developing Land, Forests, Oceans and People* (Oxford, England: Pergamon Press, 1965).

Setting rural modernization as a primary goal for future food diplomacy does not imply abandoning other purposes. Certainly we would hope that all of the pathologies of the present system discussed above will be treated, and that providing market stability, food relief and assistance, crisis management, and communications and information will remain important criteria for specific norms and rules of food diplomacy. Indeed rural modernization as a goal should enhance rules and practices that promote information flows about production and consumption, and also could undercut norms which permit elite indifference to hunger in international forums.

Moving toward these goals via international relations entails institutionalizing a set of norms that encourage behavior leading to such outcomes or, in other words, instituting a new global food regime. Fundamentally, this requires a change of assumptions, attitudes and perspectives much more than it requires a change of formal institutions. A great deal can be accomplished toward solving world food problems within existing institutions. But behavior within (and without) must be guided by a more comprehensive and instructive set of principles, among which we suggest the following.

1. *Universal rural modernization is imperative.* In contrast to the market-focused global food regime of the postwar era, one for the 1980s must be primarily development-focused. While this does not mean that commercial mechanisms need be repressed, it does imply that international markets be consciously evaluated as vehicles for Third World development, and not simply as sources of First World profits or as factors in balance of payments accounting. This principle further implies that universal agricultural modernization is, as indicated, an international goal of the first priority and that specific regime rules for food trade, concessional food transfers, grain reserves and agricultural assistance must be concerned with encouraging that goal, while behavior discouraging rural change must be widely condemned. Furthermore, modernization must include an attack on the social and institutional barriers to the productivity of the rural poor.[9]

2. *Adequate nutrition is a central human right.* To the extent that the food regime of the past 20 years focused attention upon chronic hunger at all, it did so in a national and quantitative sense only. Hunger meant that a country had too little food to go around. Yet, the international definition of hunger ought to be a qualitative and individual one, and the legitimate focus of international attention ought to be upon dietary enrichment wherever people are debilitated by malnutrition. Clearly, to emphasize nutrition is to revise the international definition of the "world food problem." But malnutrition is a crucial problem precisely because it has been ignored, since it does not show up in national accounts and could be masked in periods when growth was occurring. A more focused monitoring system is needed to change this, one that systematically reports nutrition levels and related health and performance standards, including costs due to malnutrition.

---

[9]These barriers, argues economist Keith Griffin, lead to lower productivity and the large inequalities perpetuated by production patterns that produce "low output and inefficiency," in *Land Concentration and Rural Poverty* (New York: Holmes and Meier, 1976), p. 5.

3. *Internal equity in food distribution is an international concern.* This principle would legitimize norms for international scrutiny of countries' domestic policies concerned with food distribution. It does not necessarily imply redistribution according to any specific formula; it does not legitimize direct intervention. It does, however, stipulate that the international community considers it a violation of basic universal rights and therefore unacceptable that any government should tolerate the conspicuous waste or overconsumption of food by some citizens and the simultaneous starvation of others. Furthermore, because such conditions are wrong, they should be discussed in international forums, and unilateral or multilateral actions may be taken to demonstrate international disapproval of the practices of offending governments.

4. *Investment is a global responsibility.* This principle follows the assumption that rural underdevelopment is a global problem because its impact on most Third World countries produces consequences felt around the world. This may be expected to be even more true in the 1980s and beyond. While national authorities must play pivotal roles in the rural modernization of their countries, the resources for universal modernization must be generated globally. This does not imply such a radical redistribution from rich countries to poor ones that drastic cuts in in western standards of living would be necessary or that monumental contributions from OPEC states would be needed. What it implies is that international capital flows should give rural modernization in the Third World high priority by norms that encourage such investment as legitimate and worth making more attractive in terms of both philosophic and material incentives. As an aside, one important objective in new finance must be to increase the employment of labor, and hence strategies using intermediate labor intensive technology, or involving substantial land redistribution, must be given careful attention and support.[10]

To achieve this, the "returns" on investments must include incentives or rewards for those supplying capital or land beyond the current private returns ("profits") normally allocated by market transactions. Collective benefits and non-monetarized values must be costed, and government policy must be set with respect to programs so as to provide the appropriate incentives for private and public finance. Everyone benefits from fostering rural modernization, and the responsibility for securing these benefits has a price that must be collectively paid.

5. *Food aid should be used as insurance not surplus disposal.* A concessional system of food distribution ought to remain a legitimate element of the global food regime. Yet, food aid should not be usable by donors as a political reward (for good behavior in other issue areas), by recipients as a substitute for efforts at rural modernization, or by traders for marketeering or profiteering. Rather, aid should be held available as insurance for governments and farmers to hedge against risked

[10]The arguments for land reform and for an employment strategy in planning investment are complex, and require adjustment to the specific conditions of each country. The Ethiopian "national" land reform of 1975–76 for instance made sense in one region and was counter-productive elsewhere. Such failures do not vitiate the overall analysis. See International Labor Office, *Employmnet, Growth and Basic Needs: A One-World Problem* (New York: Praeger 1977); Hollis Chenery et al., *Redistribution with Growth* (London: Oxford University Press, 1974), and David Lehman, ed., *Peasants, Landlords and Governments* (New York: Holmes and Meier, 1974).

crop failures, especially those undertaking experiments with new technologies and distribution policies. The insurance scheme proposed by Johnson (Chapter 9) could be an important step in focusing concessionary food flows on this goal. Food aid, when used carefully, can also serve as a disincentive to placing profits ahead of nutrition, as some officials in Ethiopia and Bangladesh did during their shortages in 1974. With lessened risk, the pace of technological and social innovation might be quickened and the pace of rural modernization along with it. There also will be a continuing need for food aid during the course of rural modernization in some countries. Especially in places where neither national self-sufficiency nor commercial purchases seem likely to serve development objectives in the foreseeable future, food aid should be available on a continuing basis. We recognize that food aid can and probably has had subtle, serious and complex disincentive effects with respect to rural modernization. However, with appropriate policies in recipient countries, we see no reason why, on balance, the multiple effects of concessionary food transfers targeted for nutritional and developmental purposes cannot be positive— both for farmers and governments.[11]

6. *Famine relief is an international responsibility.* This principle should be carried over from the present regime. It recognizes that acute hunger anywhere warrants attention from every responsible supplier. In addition, it means that standing organizational means for famine relief should continue as a legitimate international activity, and that new norms, conducive to more timely and efficient relief operations should be established.[12]

7. *Comprehensive information should be widely published.* The current though unevenly supported norms of the presently changing regime should be maintained and strengthened. These call for comprehensive, timely and accurate information flows. Behavior necessary to improve information flows should be encouraged, both on the part of those who have persistently veiled their agriculture and technology in secrecy and those, such as the United States, with extensive intelligence capabilities. Furthermore, to the extent that the goals of rural modernization and nutritional adequacy are elevated under the new food regime, information and research relevant to their attainment and monitoring should be amassed and disseminated on a continuing basis. Moreover, the educational requirements of coping with global food problems must not be underestimated or left underfulfilled. Hundreds of thousands of professionals trained to understand and guide rural development will be needed in coming years, along with millions of literate, technically proficient farmers.

8. *Food markets should be stable.* In accord with what was said in the discussion of the first principle above, the legitimacy of distribution and signals to producers via the international commercial exchanges should remain a central tenet of the global food regime. The pathologies discussed earlier arising from a competitive decentralized system do not apply to the advantages of markets for moving com-

---

[11]See Paul J. Iseman and H. W. Singer, "Food Aid: Disincentive Effects and Their Policy Implications," *Economic Development and Cultural Change,* Vol. 25, #2 (January, 1977), pp. 205–207.

[12]For an analysis and critique of international programs of disaster relief, see, United Nations Association of the United States of America, *Acts of Nature, Acts of Man: The Global Response to Natural Disasters* (UNA, New York, 1977). This report proposes several new rules to expedite relief efforts.

modities smoothly and efficiently from producers to consumers. There is nothing comparable to the economically rationalizing effects and impacts of market behavior. Policies and action geared to overcoming the separation of national and regional markets and to perfecting the international one should continue to be regarded as legitimate and urgent. At the same time, extreme fluctuations of supply and price in the market, as happened between 1972 and 1974, are unacceptable for a host of reasons, not least among these that market instability disrupts development planning and has second-order effects detrimental to rural modernization. One presently finds in the sum of the retrospectives on the 1972–74 "crisis" the argument that the record prices in 1974 which followed the tightening of the market and the drawing down of stocks in 1972 and 1973 were beneficial because they dampened demand at the time and called forth the increased supplies in 1975 and 1976 which averted a prolongation of the crisis. Perhaps so. But we must bear in mind that (1) low prices and monopoly buying manipulations in a poorly monitored market caused the tightening of supplies in the first place, (2) the high prices that ultimately called forth new supplies did so only after wreaking havoc with development plans, squeezing poor people in developed countries, and starving some in less developed countries, and (3) that the high prices did not in fact lead to a new stability of supply and demand, rather they created *oversupplies* which are currently leading export country farmers toward bankruptcy and fostering demands for domestically oriented reserve and price programs. Despite our respect for the efficacy of international grain and other food markets, we would prefer that the global food regime embody the principle of "stable markets" rather than "free markets." By free markets, we mean arenas of unconstrained exchange which permit fluctuations in supply and purchasing policies to result in wide price swings. The main differences between the two market systems in practice are first that the stable market implies the accumulation and release of stocks (i.e., reserves) in countercyclical fashion, while the free market does not, and second, the stable market necessarily operates within price and/or quantity corridors established by public authorities, while the free market does not. Of course, in classical economic theory the free market would be a more efficient allocator of resources, at least of those resources that respond to market incentives. However, many conditions of a free market are simply not obtainable, partly because of strong politically entrenched interests. As a result, the cost of pursuing free market "efficiency" in food production can be exhorbitantly high for human, non-economic values, including the hard to calculate but important economic factor of human capital.

9. *Multilateral capacities must be enhanced.* The postwar global food system flourished in a polyarchic political-economic environment, and the prevailing regime legitimized this decentralized setting while it conversely discouraged attempts at creating central authorities or regulatory processes. Maintaining this setting was most hospitable to the goals of the major participants in food trade, notably the United States. But it was clearly also the case that the decentralized setting yielded pathological behavior, ultimately penalizing to all participants, including the United States. It is our conclusion that the multilateral capacities of food diplomacy must be enhanced in the future, and that more frequent, more intense and more significant

communication, coordination and collaboration at the global level will be required if the earlier stipulated goals are to be realized. Specifically, dependable international consultative and coordinating procedures should be created to synchronize the agricultural policies of major trading countries in order to obviate the penalties and wastes of aggregate over- and underproduction. Mutual guarantees to undertake such multilateral market adjustments such as managing grain reserves should be established. This would buffer extreme price and income fluctuations in ways that spread the costs of maintaining stability. An additional benefit of spreading adjustment responsibilities would be that greater reserve capacity in both idled land and stocks of reserves would be available to back up or provide redundant capability for maintaining the new parameters set by the regime. Internationally regulated market-sharing might be necessary to hedge against trade warfare. Greater international authority should be accorded to bodies such as UNEP and FAO with responsibility for preserving the global "commons" and monitoring and regulating its use. In addition, an international body should be charged with monitoring and publicly reporting upon nutritional well-being within countries. Rural modernization in the Third World requires planning global strategy and mobilizing global resources. In this effort, international development institutions should be the engines and vehicles for these planning and mobilizing tasks. But, prior to all of this, what is urgently required is a global consensus that supports multilateral procedures and permits international authority and regulation. In other words, the principle of mulilateralization must precede the norms and practices it promises to allow, and this principle is fundamental to a new and stable global food regime.

Moving toward the future

Some readers might construe our attempt to promote new priorities and changed norms for the global food regime as largely an exercise in writing clichés. Reformers, of course, have a penchant for clichés. The issues our proposed principles raise, however, are not lofty or unreal considerations; recent events have placed most of them squarely on the international agenda where they are competing for a place in a new regime for managing the international food system.[13]

Increasingly, Third World coalitions, claiming to speak for the "majority of mankind," are deliberately attempting to institutionalize their values and their priorities as global norms. For instance, the urgency of increasing food production has been stressed by FAO Director-General Saouma, while UNCTAD has pressed the need to get more earnings from poor country agricultural exports. This latter aim would benefit unfortunately only a limited number of countries.[14] Issues of rural

---

[13]See, for instance, Roger Hansen, "Major U.S. Options on North-South Relations: A Letter to President Carter," in John W. Sewell, ed., *The United Nations and World Development* (New York: Praeger, 1977), pp. 21–84. Debate and reformulation of United States food policy in the Carter administration has been explicitly addressed to many of the issues we have raised in the summary.

[14]See International Food Policy Research Institute, *Potentials of Agricultural Exports to Finance Increased Food Imports in Selected Developing Countries,* Occasional Paper #2 (Washington: IFPRI, August, 1977).

modernization are embodied in both the Third World spokesmen's calls for a New International Economic Order and in some industrialized countries' diplomats' call for a "basic human needs" strategy. A growing priority to rural modernization may be evidenced by the funding shifts of aid institutions, suggesting that this principle may be becoming institutionalized in the global food regime.[15]

In addition, some of the other principles we have urged such as the food aid for insurance (security) and greater investment are hardly new. They were the unanimous recommendation of the 1974 World Food Conference. Food aid remains eminently legitimate in contemporary affairs, and both bilateral and multilateral flows have increased since the nadir of 1973–74. Developments since 1975 suggest that international financing of agricultural modernization has been elevated in priority. Evidence includes the formal operations of the International Fund for Agricultural Development in 1977, the redirecting of World Bank programs and the research efforts of international food research centers toward aiding small farmers in Third World countries; and the newly conceived U.S. Title XII program for international agricultural education and research. The direction of a number of USAID and FAO field programs, as in the Sahel and the Senegal River Basin, also supports this conclusion.[16]

Such principles as international famine relief and the free flow of information are already accepted by most as desirable norms of the global food regime. Attempts to establish formal rules to secure market stability are at the heart of ongoing discussions concerning food reserves. In preparation for renewing the International Wheat Agreement in 1978, American unilateral grain reserves have been increasing with over eight million tons in place by the end of 1977 and 30 million tons forecast to be held privately by the summer of 1978. The principle of an international reserve is largely accepted. Multilateralization of resources, however, is not yet supported by norms of the global food regime, for most countries are reluctant to accept international regulation of their international grain trade, and are even less willing to allow external decisions to penetrate into their domestic farm policies. Still, the necessity of increased multilateral communication, coordination and collaboration in food affairs is more widely recognized, at least as evidenced by the agreement on many issues displayed at the World Food Council meetings in June 1977, where even the Soviet Union supported Council recommendations, as long as no new costs to the Soviets were entailed.[17] Whether any of the new agencies, such as the WFC, can or will evolve into effective international authorities remains to be seen.

Of course other elements of our preferred global food regime are not in place. International attention to questions of nutrition remains slim, and, when raised,

---

[15]According to CGFPI figures, however, international public investment in agriculture hit a plateau in 1976, after rapid rises after 1973.

[16]Martin Kriesberg, *International Organization and Agricultural Development,* U.S. Department of Agriculture, Economic Research Service, Foreign Agricultural Economic Report #131 (Washington: USDA, May, 1977).

[17]See United Nations, World Food Council, *Report of the World Food Council on the Work of the Third Session,* WFC/5-, June 28, 1977, supplement No. 19 to *Official Records of the General Assembly,* 33rd Session, A/32/19.

these questions tend to be pushed aside by assertions either that quantitative scarcities must be treated first or that these are income problems, not food problems. Equity in internal food distribution has not yet reached the serious diplomatic agenda, mainly, we suspect, because the total costs of malnutrition are seldom calculated, and malnutrition is seldom directly detrimental to elites of Third World governments. Not surprisingly, they seldom want it discussed. Aid as insurance has not yet found its time, not least because of internal debates in the United States surrounding the aims and utility of programs under Public Law 480. The older principle of aid priorities established on the basis of recipients' strategic importance has been partially de-emphasized in the American system, though there remains a connection between United States concerns for certain countries' political stability and food aid allocations (and this connection remains primary in the programs of some other donor countries). Still, there is currently emerging in both American and Canadian policy-making a recognition that food aid and Third World economic development must be more firmly linked. But, there are now no generally accepted priorities among the norms guiding concessional food transfers, so that building a consensus around the principle of food aid as insurance presents an immediate and urgent task for diplomacy.

Clearly, much remains to be done before the changes in the global food regime we propose could be fully institutionalized. Food problems are persistent and steps taken now may be decisive five or ten years hence. However, thanks to the return to market surpluses in the mid-1970s trends toward longer-run global scarcity again seem academic in the thinking of policy-makers. Selective memory has already begun to set in, and some are even saying that the food system actually performed rather well during the crisis years at the beginning of the decade, and that reform of market norms and priorities for nutrition and development are unnecessary or even undesirable. In other words, the urgency in reforming the food regime has diminished with the shift in attention to other problems. Most of the steps toward reform noted here were initiated in the immediate aftermath of the 1972–74 crisis. Steps toward translating general principles into working rules and norms progressed markedly at first. But more recently, with both physical urgency and public pressures diminished, movement has slowed, and perhaps stopped.

In light of these observations, our recommendation to participants in food diplomacy is that they support those new regime principles tentatively in place, and help to institute those that have not yet been established. We believe that catastrophe can be avoided through the development of the rural areas of the Third World, in the context of a stabilized international market in foodstuffs, and in an ethical environment that emphasizes collective international action to enhance mankind's nutritional well-being. Action consistent with the principles presented here, and backed by the initiative and support of United States elites (still the most powerful force in food affairs), can bring solutions to the complex and interconnected problems of world agriculture, can further Third World Development, and can hedge against hunger.

Reference Matter

International Food Organizations:
A Glossary *

ABD   Asian Development Bank (1966). Promotes investment of public and private capital in Asia; $1,545 million in loans as of 1976.

AFDB   African Development Bank (1964). Promotes investment of public and private capital in its 41 member states; $217 million committed as of 1976.

CAP   Common Agriculture Policy (1962). Common policy which joins the separate national farm policies of the EEC.

CARE   Cooperative for American Relief Everywhere Inc. (1945). Provides food and self-help assistance, and through MEDICO, medical attention to the needy of developing countries.

CCC   Commodity Credit Corporation (1933). Part of USDA, provides loans for purchase of agricultural commodities on the U.S. market; provides funding for AID Food for Peace Program.

CFNI   Caribbean Food and Nutrition Institute (1967). Works with existing organizations to improve the food and nutrition situation in the Caribbean.

CGFPI   Consultative Group on Food Production and Investment (1975). Coordinates donor countries and organizations with recipient countries.

CGIAR   Consultative Group for International Agricultural Research (1971). Sponsors research and training programs. $78 million in expenditures in 1977.

CIAP   Inter-American Committee on the Alliance for Progress (1963). Coordinates the administration of the Alliance for Progress (also ICAP).

CIAT   International Center of Tropical Agriculture (1967). Identifies and seeks solution for tropical crop, livestock and distribution problems and runs training programs.

CIEC   Conference on International Economic Cooperation (1975–77). OPEC, industrialized, and developing nations participated in four commissions dealing with development, energy, raw materials, and financing.

CIMMYT   Centro Internacional para el Mejoramento de Maiz y Trigo (1967). Serves as the hub of international, multi-disciplinary wheat research network; located in Mexico.

CRS   Catholic Relief Services. Provides food and self-help assistance in developing countries.

DAC   Development Advisory Committee (1963). Coordinates aid efforts of OECD countries.

*For most organizations, the date of its founding and some budget figures have been included.

ECA	Economic Commission for Africa.
ECLA	Economic Commission for Latin America.
ECOSOC	United Nations Economic and Social Council (1949). Studies, reports and recommends action on international economic, social, cultural, educational, health, and human rights issues to the General Assembly.
EEC	European Economic Community (1958). Promotes harmonious development of economic activities, balanced expansion, and stability within the community.
ERS	Economic Research Service, United States Department of Agriculture.
FAO	Food and Agriculture Organization of the United Nations (1945). Works for improvement of nutrition levels, of food production and distribution, and of rural living conditions, on a worldwide basis. Annual regular budget for 1978 of $106 million, about one-third of its total budget (including UNDP funds).
FAS	Foreign Agriculture Service, United States Department of Agriculture. 1976 budget: $37 million.
GATT	General Agreement of Trade and Tariffs (1947). Regulates trade and mediates in international trade disputes.
IBRD	International Bank for Reconstruction and Development (World Bank) (1945). Provides loans and technical assistance to governments for economic development; $6,937 million committed as of 1972.
IDA	International Development Association (1960). Supplements the World Bank by soft loan activities; $4,815 million extended as of 1973.
IDB	Inter-American Development Bank (1959). Promotes investment of public and private capital in member states.
IFAD	International Fund for Agricultural Development (1977). Established to channel special contributions from industrialized and OPEC countries of over $1 billion into the financing of agricultural projects in poor countries; it is associated with the UN.
IFDC	International Fertilizer Development Center (1974). Founded to increase and improve the quality of fertilizer at lower costs and to apply such technology to developing countries.
IFPRI	International Food Policy Research Institute (1975). Information systems and economic analysis.
IMF	International Monetary Fund (1945). Promotes international monetary cooperation through management of exchange policies.
INCAP	Institute of Nutrition for Central America and Panama (1946). Promotes the development of nutritional science among its member countries.
IRRI	International Rice Research Institute (1960). Conducts research on the rice plant, its production, management, distribution, and improvement.
IWC	International Wheat Council (1949). Concerned with expanding and stabilizing the world wheat market; provides the framework for negotiating provisions relating to the price of wheat.
OAS	Organization of American States (1890). Established to promote security and stability in Latin American countries.

OECD	Organization for Economic Cooperation and Development (1961). Promotes policies to achieve maximum economic growth with stability of its member countries.
OPEC	Organization of the Petroleum Exporting Countries (1960). Promotes unified petroleum policies for the member countries.
OXFAM	(1942). Private education and relief organization with an emphasis on long term developing projects.
PAG	Protein-Calorie Advisory Group (United Nations). Disbanded in 1977, its work was taken over by the FAO.
UNCTAD	United Nations Conference on Trade and Development (1964). Aim is to accelerate economic development and trade among developing countries.
UNDP	United Nations Development Programme (1965). Aims to help low-income nations develop using "voluntary" contributions.
UNDRO	United Nations Disaster Relief Office (1971). Directs and coordinates the relief efforts of the UN.
UNICEF	United Nations Children's Fund (1946). Aids governments in their efforts to undertake long term programs benefiting children and youths.
UNIDO	United Nations Industrial Development Organization (1967). Responsible for furthering industrialization in developing countries.
USAID	U.S. Agency for International Development (1961). $2,505 million in obligations and loans in 1975. (Food for Peace: $1,328 million in obligations in 1975).
WFC	World Food Council. Policy-making body for UN food network, created by World Food Conference (Nov. 1974).
WFP	World Food Program (1961). Promotes economic and social development; helps alleviate emergency situations through food aid.
WHO	World Health Organization (1948). Coordinates and assists FAO efforts to improve health and agriculture.

Selected Bibliography

I. Annotated Items

Abelson, Philip H., ed. *Food: Politics, Economics, Nutrition, Research*. Washington: American Association for the Advancement of Science, 1975. 202 pp.

>A collection of *Science* articles on the roles of economics, politics, and social structure in food production; nutrition and nutrition policy; agricultural research; and basic biology's relationships to food production.

Berg, Alan. *The Nutrition Factor: Its Role In National Development*. Washington: The Brookings Institution, 1973. 290 pp.

>A comprehensive introduction: topics covered include the economic costs of malnutrition, the relationship of adequate nutrition to population stability, the nutritional potential of the Green Revolution and new fortified or synthesized foods, and the roles of private industry and public policy in providing for adequate nutrition.

Borgstrom, Georg. *The Food and People Dilemma*. North Scituate, Mass.: Duxbury Press, 1973. 140 pp.

>Borgstrom's outlook in this popularly-written book is frankly Malthusian. Taking an ecological perspective, he recommends an integrated strategy to attack the world's food problems, encompassing food production, population control, better storage and utilization, nutrition, disease control, and resource appraisal.

Brown, Lester R., with Erik P. Eckholm. *By Bread Alone*. New York: Praeger Publishers, 1974. 272 pp.

>A discussion of the world's food problems in the 1970s. The crisis is seen as the result of continuing population growth and increasing affluence which clash with supply constraints, particularly ecological deterioration of food systems.

Eckholm, Erik, P. *Losing Ground: Environmental Stress and World Food Prospects*. New York: W.W. Norton, 1976. 223 pp.

>A popularly-written survey of how food production systems are undermined through ecological deterioration. Eckholm maintains this is more severe in poor countries than in industrialized ones, and he proposes to ameliorate it through population restraint, the use of new, low-cost energy sources, tree planting, and more attention to the environment in development planning.

George, Susan. *How the Other Half Dies—The Real Reasons for World Hunger*. New York, Penguin Books, 1976. 349 pp.

>George argues that world hunger is a result of control of the world's food supplies by the rich. Multinational agribusiness corporations, Western Governments' aid policies and multilateral development organizations are all indicted, particularly U.S. "agripower."

Griffin, Keith. *The Political Economy of Agrarian Change: An Essay on the Green Revolution*. Cambridge, Mass.: Harvard University Press, 1974. 264 pp.

>An analysis of the economic, social, and political changes brought about by the introduction of high-yielding varieties of wheat and rice into countries of Asia and Latin America. Griffin argues that the 'Green Revolution' has not increased per capita agricultural production or

reduced malnutrition. Instead, the benefits accrue largely to the more prosperous regions and the more prosperous landowners, intensifying rural class conflict.

Hayami, Jujiro, and Vernon W. Ruttan. *Agricultural Development: An International Perspective*. Baltimore: Johns Hopkins Press, 1971. 367 pp.

A statement of the late 1960s consensus that agricultural growth is critical to industrialization and overall development. American and Japanese historical patterns of agricultural development are reviewed, followed by discussions of technology transfer, land reform, improved marketing and credit institutions, extension services, and land and water resource development.

Huddleston, Barbara. *Commodity Trade Issues in International Negotiations*. Occasional Paper No. 1, January 1977, International Food Policy Research Institute. 47 pp.

Concise analysis of the issues involved in the integrated commodities program outlined by UNCTAD IV, followed by a brief description of several specific commodities trade issues and of the possibilities for export earnings to aid food-deficit developing countries.

International Food Policy Research Institute. *Food Needs of Developing Countries*. Research Report No. 3. Washington: I.F.P.R.I., 1977. 157 pp.

This third report of a new food research group projects trends in population, food production, and food deficits for developing market economies. Country-by-country breakdown.

Isenman, Paul J., and H. W. Singer. "Food Aid: Disincentive Effects and Their Policy Implications," *Economic Development and Cultural Change*. 25, No. 2 (January, 1977) 205–237. C347.8

A review of research and arguments concerning the disincentive effects of food aid on agricultural production. The article concludes that food aid can make positive contributions to development of LDCs and emphasizes positive aid consequences.

Johnson, D. Gale. *World Agriculture in Disarray*. London, Macmillan Press, Ltd., 1973. 304 pp.

Johnson argues that the protectionist agricultural policies of industrial nations have had numerous ill-effects, both at home and in developing nations. A multilateral liberalization of trade policies is advocated, as well as education programs that will assist the migration of rural labor to other economic sectors.

Johnson, D. Gale. *World Food Problems and Prospects*. Washington: American Enterprise Institute of Public Policy Research, 1975. 83 pp.

A discussion of the causes of the large increase in food prices in 1973–1974 and of the problems of food production in less developed countries. More agricultural research, more fertilizer, expanding the cultivated area, and using free market incentives to motivate farmers are cited as some of the requirements for increasing food production in less developed countries.

Johnston, Bruce F., and Peter Kilby. *Agriculture and Structural Transformation: Economic Strategies in Late Developing Countries*. New York: Oxford University Press, 1975. 474 pp.

Focus is on "the reciprocal interaction between agricultural development and the expansion of manufacturing and other non-farm sectors." The authors argue for a "unimodal" pattern of agricultural development, characterized by modernization of a large and increasing fraction of a country's farms, with relatively equal distribution of farm units.

Lehmann, David, ed. *Peasants, Landlords and Governments: Agrarian Reform in the Third World*. New York: Holmes & Meier, 1974. 320 pp.

Nine essays which attempt to "lay the way for a reappraisal" of land reform in developing countries by taking into consideration both political and economic factors. The contributions deal with India, Peru, Chile, and China.

Mellor, John W. *The Economics of Growth: A Strategy for India and the Developing World*. Ithaca: Cornell University Press, 1976. 335 pp.

Using the example of India, Mellor argues for development based on measures intended to increase food supply as part of an integrated strategy involving broad changes in other sectors. A strategy of increased employment and greater participation of the poor in economic growth is argued to be preferable to redistribution of existing output, and the creation of a modern, technologically dynamic agriculture is shown to be essential.

National Academy of Sciences. *World Food and Nutrition Study: The Potential Contribution of Research.* Washington: NAS, 1977. 192 pp.

> This report by the NAS Commission on International Relations results from a two-year survey commissioned by President Ford into ways that American research efforts could alleviate world food problems. A five volume set of very useful *Supporting Papers* is also available from the Academy's Printing and Publishing Office.

Ross, Douglas N. *Partners in Agroeconomic Development.* Conference Board, 1977 (report no. 711). 50 pp.

> Ross reviews the role of international agribusiness corporations in LDCs. Innovative efforts now under way to address the food problem are particularly emphasized.

Rothschild, Emma. "Food Politics," *Foreign Affairs,* vol. 54, no. 2 (January, 1976). pp. 285–308.

> Argues against the "deceptive" doctrine that the U.S. can exert "food power" to increase its profits on sales or influence other countries' agricultural policies. Rothschild calls on the U.S. Government to turn back from the market-oriented food policy of the 1970s and strengthen its commitment to development goals and government-held grain reserves.

Scientific American. "Food and Agriculture," vol. 235, no. 3, September, 1976. 222 pp.

> In this issue are twelve articles that survey hunger and nutrition, food chains and agricultural systems, agriculture in the U.S., Mexico, and India, and increasing agricultural production. Includes, maps, charts, and satellite photographs.

Scott, James C. *The Moral Economy of the Peasant; Rebellion and Subsistence in Southeast Asia.* New Haven: Yale University Press, 1976. 246 pp.

> A discussion of relationships among economic circumstances, cultural features and political developments. Scott argues that the fear of food shortages explains many features of peasant society, and has even led to peasant insurrections.

Sinha, Radha, *Food and Poverty: The Political Economy of Confrontation.* New York: Holmes & Meier, 1976. 196 pp.

> Radha argues that hunger, malnutrition, and poverty increase the danger of confrontation between rich and poor countries. By implementing an ideology of "solidarity" developing nations will be enabled to obtain meaningful aid and trade concessions.

Srivastava, Uma K., Earl O. Heady, Keith D. Rogers, and Leo V. Mayer. *Food Aid and International Economic Growth.* Ames, Iowa: Iowa State University Press, 1975. 160 pp.

> An economic study of the role of PL 480 in development, with particular reference to India. The authors agree that food aid can be an effective tool for economic development under certain conditions.

Trager, James. *The Great Grain Robbery.* New York: Ballantine Books, 1975. 233 pp.

> A popularly-written account of the massive 1972 sales of grain and soybeans to the Soviet Union, and their impact on food prices and on politics in the United States.

United States Department of Agriculture. *The World Food Situation and Prospects to 1985.* Foreign Agricultural Economic Report No. 98. Washington: Government Printing Office, 1974. 90 pp.

> A sourcebook of data and projections of food prices, supply and demand conditions, grain stocks and food security, nutritional levels, and food aid. Concludes that more food can be produced per person, but, "substantial malnutrition will probably persist among low-income groups in the less prosperous developing countries."

United States General Accounting Office. *Disincentives to Agricultural Production in Developing Countries.* Washington: General Accounting Office, ID-76-2, 1975. 117 pp.

> Documents the numerous policies pursued by less developed countries which inhibit greater agricultural production. Appendices report on Indonesia, Sri Lanka, India, Pakistan, Kenya, Tanzania, Peru, and Uruguay, and list specific disincentives in some forty other countries.

United States House of Representatives. *Food Problems of Developing Countries: Implications for U.S. Policy.* Hearings before the Subcommittee on International Resources, Food, and Energy of the Committee on International Relations, Ninety-fourth Congress, First Session, May 21, June 3 and 5, 1975. Washington: Government Printing Office, 1975. 355 pp.

> Testimony from AID, State Department, and Agriculture Department officials, representatives

of private organizations concerned with development and food policy, and spokesmen for overseas voluntary aid agencies.

Wallerstein, Immanuel. *The Modern World-System: Capitalist Agriculture and the Origins of the European World Economy in the 16th Century.* New York: Academic Press, 1974. 410 pp.

An important analysis of the relationship between food production, norms governing economic relationships, and political patterns. The impact of capitalist practices on European society and Europe's subsequent imperialist expansion raises questions for the prospects and consequences of efforts to change peasant agriculture in contemporary third world countries. The book is particularly useful in providing an historical perspective to analyses by Migdal, Paige and Scott of modern-day peasant political economy.

II. General issues—world hunger and food supplies.

Borgstrom, Georg, "The Dual Challenge of Health and Hunger: A Global Crisis," *Bulletin of the Atomic Scientists,* vol. XXVI, no. 8 (October, 1970), pp. 42–46.

Brown, Lester, *Increasing World Food Output.* New York: Arno Press, 1976.

Campbell, Keith, "Constraints on Future World Food Supply—Real or Imaginary?," *Australian Quarterly.* vol. 48, no. 3 (September, 1976). pp. 4–12.

Dumont, Rene, and Bernard Rosier. *The Hungry Future,* New York: Praeger Publishers, 1969.

Dunn, James E., et al., *Endangered Species,* Broadman, 1977.

Ehrlich, Paul R., and Anne H. Ehrlich, "The World Food Problem: No Room for Complacency," *Social Science Quarterly,* vol. 57, no. 2 (September, 1976), pp. 375–82.

Freeman, W. H. *Food and Agriculture.* Scientific American Books, 1976.

Goulet, Denis, "World Hunger: Putting Development Ethics to the Test," *Sociological Inquiry,* 1975, vol. 45, no. 4, pp. 3–11.

International Food Policy Research Institute, *Recent Prospective Developments in Food Consumption: Some Policy Issues,* Draft Report prepared for the 24th session of the Protein Advisory Group (PAG) of the U.N., January 31–February 4, 1977.

Iowa State University, *Proceedings, World Food Conference of 1976.* Ames, Iowa: Iowa State University Press, 1977.

Jacobsen, Michael, and Catherine Lerza, eds. *Food for People, Not for Profit.* New York: Ballantine, 1975.

Johnson, D. Gale, ed. *World Food Supply,* 33 vols. New York: Arno Press, 1976.

Marei, Sayed, *The World Food Crisis.* New York: Longman, 1976.

Mesarovic, Mihajilo, and Edward Pestel, *Mankind at the Turning Point.* New York: Dutton, 1974.

Omvet, Gail, "The Political Economy of Starvation," *Race and Class,* vol. 17, no. 2, (Autumn, 1975), pp. 111–30.

Paddock, William and Paul, *Time of Famines.* Boston: Little, Brown, 1976.

Schertz, Lyle P., "World Food: Prices and the Poor," *Foreign Affairs,* vol. 52, April, 1974, pp. 511–537.

Schultz, T. W., ed. *Food for the World.* New York: Arno Press, 1976.

Shepherd, Jack, *The Politics of Starvation.* New York: Carnegie Endowment for International Peace, 1975.

Taylor, L., "The Misconstrued Crisis: Lester Brown and World Food," *World Development,* vol. 3, no. 11/12, pp. 827–38.

The Transnational Institute. *World Hunger: Causes and Remedies.* Amsterdam: A Transnational Institute Report, 1974.

United Nations World Food Conference. *Assessment of the World Food Situation: Present and Future.* Rome, 1974.

University of California, *A Hungry World: The Challenge to Agriculture.* Division of Agricultural Sciences, University of California, 1974.

Utrecht, Ernst, "An Alternative Report on World Hunger," *Cultures et Développement,* 1976, vol. VIII, no. 1, pp. 145–50.

Wallensteen, Peter, "Scarce Goods as Political Weapons: The Case of Food," *Journal of Peace Research,* vol. 13, no. 4, 1976, pp. 277–298.

Walters, Harry, "Difficult Issues Underlying Food Problems," *Science,* vol. 188, no. 4188, May 9, 1975, pp. 524–530.

III. Population and food

Brown, Lester, *Man, Land, and Food*. New York: Arno Press, 1976.

FAO, *FAO Studies in Food and Population*, M. Bekele, et al., FAO Economic and Social Development Series, 1 (Rome: 1976).

Kumar, Joginder, *Population and Land in World Agriculture: Recent Trends and Relationships*. Berkeley: Institute of International Studies, 1973.

Revelle, Roger, "Food and Population," *Scientific American,* vol. 231, (September, 1974), pp. 160–70.

Ross, Douglas N., ed., *The Challenge of Overpopulation and Food Shortages*. New York: Conference Board, Report Series No. 684, 1976.

Russel, J., *World Population and World Food Supplies*. Westport, Conn.: Greenwood Press, 1976.

Smith, T. Lynn, *The Race Between Population and Food Supply in Latin America*. Albuquerque: U. of New Mexico Press, 1976.

Tuve, G. L. *Energy, Environment, Populations, and Food*. New York: Wiley, 1976.

United States Central Intelligence Agency, *Potential Implications of Trends in World Population, Food Production and Climate*. Washington: Office of Political Research, August, 1974.

IV. Nutrition

Berg, A., N. N. Scrimshaw, and D. L. Call, eds. *Nutrition, National Development and Planning: Proceedings of an International Conference*. Cambridge, Mass.: MIT Nutrition Program, 1971.

Mayer, Jean, "Coping with Famine," *Foreign Affairs,* vol. 53, no. 1 (October, 1974), pp. 98–120.

Reutlinger, Shlomo, and Marcelo Selowsky, *Malnutrition and Poverty: Magnitude and Policy Options*. Washington: World Bank Staff Occasional Papers #23, 1976.

Reutlinger, Shlomo, and Marcelo Selowsky. *The Anatomy of Hunger*. Baltimore: Johns Hopkins University Press, 1976.

V. Economic forces affecting the international food system: trade policies and multinational corporations

Austin, James E., *Agribusiness in Latin America*. New York: Praeger, 1974.

Blau, G. *International Commodity Arrangements and Policies*. Rome: FAO Commodity Policy Studies No. 16, 1964.

The Brookings Institution, *Toward the Integration of World Agriculture*. Washington: Brookings, 1973.

Connelly, P., and R. Perlman, *The Politics of Scarcity: Resource Conflicts in International Relations*. London: Oxford University Press, 1975.

Food and Agriculture Organization, *National Grain Policies, 1975*. Rome: FAO, 1975.

Food and Agriculture Organization, *The World Food Problem: Proposals for National and International Action*. Document E/CONF. 65/4, World Food Conference, Rome: FAO, 1974.

Goldberg, Ray A., *International Agribusiness Coordination*. Ballinger Cambridge, Mass.:, 1975.

Henrichsmeyer, W., et al., *Trade Negotiations and World Food Problems*. London: Trade Policy Research Center, 1974.

Jones, David, *Food and Interdependence: The Effect of Food and Agricultural Policies of Developed Countries on the Food Problems of Developing Countries*. London: Overseas Development Institute, Research Publications Services, 1976.

Nagle, J. C., *Agricultural Trade Policies*. Lexington, Mass.: Lexington Books, 1976.

United States Comptroller General, "Exporters' Profits on Sales of U.S. Wheat to Russia." GPO, Washington, D.C., February 12, 1974.

United States Senate, *World Food Situation, Trade Patterns and Markets*. Committee on Agriculture and Forestry, Sub-committee on Foreign Agricultural Policy, Washington: GPO, 1976.

VI. Agricultural development

Aziz, Sartaj, "The Chinese Approach to Rural Development," *International Development Review,* vol. 15, no. 4 (1973–74), pp. 2–7.

Aziz, Sartaj, ed., *Hunger, Politics and Markets: The Real Issues in The Food Crisis*. New York: New York University Press, 1975.

Bates, Robert H. *The Rural Factor: Rural Responses to Industrialization in Zambia*. New Haven: Yale University Press, 1977.

Beckford, George L., *Persistent Poverty, Underdevelopment in Plantation Economies of the Third World*. London: Oxford University Press, 1972.

Brown, Lester, *Seeds of Change: The Green Revolution and Development in the 1970s*. New York: Praeger, 1970.

Chenery, H., M. S. Ahluwalia, D. L. G. Bell, J. H. Duloy and R. Jolly. *Redistribution with Growth*. London: Oxford University Press, 1974.

Cochrane, Willard W. *Agricultural Development Planning: Economic Concepts, Administrative Procedures, and Political Process*. New York: Praeger, 1974.

Frankel, Francine R., *India's Green Revolution: Political Costs of Economic Growth*. Princeton University Press, 1971.

Griffin, Keith, *Land Concentration and Rural Poverty*. New York: Holmes & Meier, 1976.

Hayami, Yujiro, et. al., eds., *Agricultural Growth in Japan, Taiwan, Korea, and the Phillipines*. Honolulu: University of Hawaii Press, 1976.

Hunter, Guy, *Administration of Agricultural Development: Lessons from India*. London: Oxford University Press, 1970.

International Labour Office, *Employment, Growth, and Basic Needs*. New York: Praeger, 1977.

Keith, Robert G., *Conquest and Agrarian Change*. Cambridge, Mass.: Harvard University Press, 1976.

Lehmann, D., ed., *Agrarian Reform and Agrarian Reformism*. London: Faber and Faber, 1974.

Lele, Uma. *The Design of Rural Development*. Baltimore: Johns Hopkins University Press, 1975.

Leonard, David K., *Reaching the Peasant Farmer, Organization Theory and Practice in Kenya*. Chicago: University of Chicago Press, 1977.

Makhijani, Arjun with Alan Poole, *Energy and Agriculture in the Third World*. Cambridge, Mass.: Ballinger Publishers, 1975.

Mellor, John W., *The Economics of Agricultural Development*. Ithaca: Cornell University Press, 1966.

Paige, Jeffrey M., *Agrarian Revolution: Social Movements and Export Agriculture in the Underdeveloped World*. New York: The Free Press, 1975.

Priebe, Hermann, "Tasks and Objectives of Agricultural Development Aid," *Economics* (Tübingen), no. 14, 1976, pp. 107–122.

Prosterman, Roy L., "Land Reform as Foreign Aid," *Foreign Policy*, no. 6 (Spring, 1972), pp. 128–42.

Schultz, T. W., *Transforming Traditional Agriculture*. New York: Arno Press, 1976.

Sen, Sudhir, *Reaping the Green Revolution—Food and Jobs for All*. New York: Orbis Books, 1975.

Shaw, R., "Strategies for Employment-Creating Agriculture," in Karl Wohlmuth, ed., *Employment Creating in Developing Societies*. New York: Praeger Publishers, 1973, pp. 156–183.

Stevens, Robert D., "Three Rural Development Models for Small Farm Agricultural Areas in Low-Income Nations," *Journal of Developing Areas*, vol. 8, April 1974, pp. 409–420.

Stewart, F., "Technology and Employment in LDCs" *World Development*, vol. 2., no. 3 (March 1974).

Southworth, Herman M., and Bruce F. Johnston, eds., *Agricultural Development and Economic Growth*. Ithaca: Cornell University Press, 1967.

Szczepanik, Edward F., *Agricultural Policies at Different Levels of Development*. Rome: FAO, 1976.

Thorbecke, Erik, ed., *The Role of Agriculture in Economic Development*. New York: National Bureau of Economic Research, 1969.

Valliantos, E. G., *Fear in the Countryside: The Control of Agricultural Resources in the Poor Countries by Non-Peasant Elites*. Cambridge, Mass.: Ballinger Pub., 1976.

VII. International agricultural organizations

"Aftermath of the World Food Conference," *Ceres*, vol. 8, no. 1 (Jan.–Feb. 1975).

Belshaw, H., "The Food and Agriculture Organization of the United Nations," *International Organization*, vol. I, no. 2 (June 1947), pp. 291–306.

CGIAR, *Consultative Group on International Agricultural Research*. New York: CGIAR, 1976. Copies available from United Nations Development Programme, 1 U.N. Plaza, New York 10017.

Cottman, Grant, "The World Food Conference," *Fieldstaff Reports*, West Europe Series, vol. 9, no. 5, (December, 1974).

FAO, *Agricultural Development: A Review of FAO's Field Activities*. Basic Study no. 23, Rome: FAO, 1970.

Gardner, Richard N., ed., *The World Food and Energy Crises: The Role of International Organizations*. Rensselaerville, N.Y.: Institute on Science and Man, 1974.

Gosovic, B., *UNCTAD, Conflict and Compromise: The Third World's Quest for an Equitable World Order through the United Nations*. Leiden: Sijthoff, 1975.

Revelle, Roger, "Ghost at the Feast: World Food Conference," *Science*, March 21, 1975, 1026.

Revelle, Roger, "International Cooperation in Food and Population," *International Organization*, vol. XXII, no. 1 (Winter 1968), pp. 362–91.

United States Senate, *The United States, FAO, and World Food Politics: U.S. Relations with an International Food Organization*. A Staff Report Prepared for the Select Committee on Nutrition and Human Needs, Washington: U.S. Government Printing Office, 1976.

United States Department of Agriculture, *International Organizations and Agricultural Development,* Prepared by Martin Kriesberg. Foreign Agriculture Economic Report No. 131, Washington: ERS, 1977.

United States General Accounting Office, *U.S. Participation in International Food Organizations: Problems and Issues.* August 6, 1976, ID-76-66.

Weiss, Thomas G., and Robert S. Jordan, "Bureaucratic Politics and the World Food Conference," *World Politics,* vol. XXVIII, No. 3, pp. 422–439 (April 1976).

Weiss, Thomas G., and Jordan, Robert S., *The World Food Conference and Global Problem Solving.* New York: Praeger, 1976.

VIII. The United States and international food questions

Brown, Lester, *The Politics and Responsibility of the North American Breadbasket.* Washington: Worldwatch Institute, Worldwatch paper #2, October 1975.

Brown, Peter G., and Henry Shue, eds., *Food Policy: The Responsibility of the United States in the Life and Death Choices.* New York: The Free Press, 1977.

Cochrane, Willard W., *Feast or Famine: The Uncertain World of Food and Agriculture and the Policy Implications to the United States.* Washington: National Planning Assoc., 1974.

Cochrane, Willard W., and Ryan, Mary E., *American Farm Policy, 1948–1973,* University of Minnesota Press, 1976.

Committee for Economic Development, "A New U.S. Farm Policy for Changing World Food Needs," New York, 1974.

Gelb, Leslie, and Anthony Lake, "Washington Dateline: Less Food, More Politics," *Foreign Policy,* no. 17 (Winter, 1974), pp. 176–189.

Hopkins, Raymond F., "How to Make Food Work," *Foreign Policy,* no. 27 (Summer, 1977), pp. 89–108.

Johnson, D. Gale and John A. Schnittker, *U.S. Agriculture in a World Context: Policies and Approaches for the Next Decade.* New York: Praeger, 1974.

McCune, W., *Who's Behind Our Farm Policy?* Westport, Conn.: Greenwood Press, 1975.

Overseas Development Council, *The United States and World Development, Agenda 1977.* New York: Praeger Publishers, 1977.

Paddock, William and Paul, *Famine—1975! America's Decision: Who Will Survive?* Boston, Little, Brown and Co., 1967.

Robbins, William, *The American Food Scandal.* New York: William Morrow and Company, 1974.

Rosenfeld, Stephen S., "The Politics of Food," *Foreign Policy,* no. 14, pp. 17–29 (Spring, 1974).

Schneider, William, *Food, Foreign Policy, and Raw Materials Cartels.* New York: Crane Russak, 1976.

Simon, Paul and Arthur, *The Politics of World Hunger: Grass-Roots Politics and World Poverty.* New York: Harper's Magazine Press, 1973.

Symposium: Food and Agricultural Policy, *Public Administration Review,* vol. 36, no. 2 (Mar.–Apr.), 1976.

Talbot, R. B., *The World Food Problem and U.S. Food Politics and Policies: 1972–76.* Ames, Iowa: Iowa State University Press, 1977.

United States Senate, Committee on Agriculture and Forestry, *U.S. Agricultural Outlook.* Washington: Government Printing Office, 1977.

United States General Accounting Office, *Issues Surrounding the Management of Agricultural Exports.* Report to the Congress, May 2, 1977.

United States House Committee on International Relations, *Implementation of Recommendations of the World Food Conference.* A report submitted by the Agency for International Development. Ninety-fourth Congress; second session, 1976.

United States House of Representatives, *The Right-to-Food Resolution.* Subcommittee on International Resources, Food, and Energy of the Committee on International Relations, June 22, 23, 24, and 29, 1976. Washington: GPO, 1976.

United States Congress, Office of Technology Assessment, *Food Information Systems.* Washington: Office of Technology Assessment, 1976.

United States Senate, *Multinational Corporations and United States Foreign Policy: International Grain Companies.* Hearing Before the Subcommittee on Multinational Corporations of the Committee on Foreign Relations, Ninety-fourth Congress; second session; June 18, 23, and 24, 1976 (Part 16); Washington: GPO, 1977.

United States Congressional Budget Office, *U.S. Food and Agricultural Policy in the World Economy*, Apr. 26, 1976.

United States Senate, *Who's Making Foreign Agricultural Policy?* Hearings before the Subcommittee on Foreign Agricultural Policy of the Committee on Agriculture and Forestry; Ninety-fourth Congress; second session; January 22 and 23, 1976. Washington: GPO, 1976.

Warley, T. K., *Agriculture in an Interdependent World: U.S. and Canadian Perspectives*. Canadian-American Commission, May 1977.

IX. Agricultural policy in industrialized countries

Andrews, Stanley, *Agriculture and the Common Market*. Ames, Iowa: Iowa State University Press, 1973.

Dirks, Harlan J., "Japan's Strategy to Stabilize Food Supplies." Washington: U.S. Department of State Sixteenth Session Seminar in Foreign Policy, 1973–74.

European Community Committee, *The Agricultural Policy of the European Community* (Eur. documentation 1976/S), European Community's official publication office, Luxembourg, 1976.

Hahn, Werner G. *The Politics of Soviet Agriculture: 1969–1970*. Baltimore: Johns Hopkins University Press, 1972.

Harris, Simon, "The World Commodity Scene and the Common Agricultural Policy." Occasional Paper No. 1, Centre for European Agricultural Studies, Wyde College, Ashford, Kent, England, 1975.

Hayami, Yujiro, *A Century of Agricultural Growth in Japan: Its Relevance to Asian Development*. Minneapolis: University of Minnesota Press, 1976.

Macaluso, Emanuele, "The Agricultural Policy of the EEC," *World Marxist Review* 20, March 1977, pp. 110–118.

Organization for Economic Cooperation and Development, Agricultural Policy Reports Series, *Agricultural Policy in Australia*. Paris: OECD, 1973. Other volumes are: Denmark (1974), European Economic Community (1974), Belgium (1973), Luxembourg (1975), Norway (1975), Spain (1974), Sweden (1975), Switzerland (1973), Finland (1975), France (1974), Germany (1975), United Kingdom (1974), Greece (1973), Ireland (1974), Italy (1974), Japan (1974), Netherlands (1974), Turkey (1974), Yugoslavia (1973), United States (1974), New Zealand (1974).

Tracy, Michael, *Agriculture in Western Europe: Crisis and Adaptation*. New York: Praeger, 1964.

Trant, Gerald I., et al., eds. *Trade Liberalization and Canadian Agriculture*. University of Toronto Press, 1968.

United States General Accounting Office, *Grain Marketing Systems in Argentina, Australia, Canada, and the European Community; Soybean Marketing System in Brazil*. May 28, 1976, LD-76-61.

United States Senate, *Russian Grain Transactions*. Report of the Permanent Subcommittee on Investigations, Committee on Government Operations, Washington: GPO, July 29, 1974.

Wädekin, Karl-Eugen, "The Place of Agriculture in the European Community Economies," *Soviet Studies* 29 (April, 1977), pp. 238–254.

Wagstaff, H. R., "EEC Food Imports from the Third World and International Responsibility in Agricultural Policy," *European Review of Agricultural Economics*, 1974/75, Vol. 211, pp. 7–23.

X. Food aid

Balz, Daniel J., "Politics of Food Aid Presents U.S. with Policy Dilemma," *National Journal Reports*, November 30, 1974, pp. 1787–92.

Bard, Robert L., *Food Aid and Agricultural Trade: A Study in Legal and Administrative Control*. Lexington, Mass.: D.C. Heath, 1972.

Brandow, J. E., "The Place of U.S. Food in Eliminating World Hunger," *Annals of the American Academy*, no. 429 (Jan. 1977), pp. 1–11.

Costa, E., "The World Food Programme and Employment: Ten Years of Multilateral Food Aid for Development," *International Labour Review* 107(3) (March, 1973), pp. 209–221.

Ladejinsky, W., "Wheat Procurement in India in 1974 and Related Matters," *World Development*, vol. 3 (Feb.–Mar., 1974), pp. 91–111.

deLattre, Anne, "Food Aid," *OECD Observer*, no. 81, May–June, 1976, pp. 14–16.

Lewis, John P., and Kapun, Ishan, *The World Bank Group, Multilateral Aid, and the 1970s*. Lexington, Mass.: Lexington Books, 1973.

McHenry, Donald F., and Kai Bird, "Food Bungle in Bangladesh," *Foreign Policy*, no. 27 (Summer, 1977), pp. 72–88.

Mettrick, Hal, *Food Aid and Britain.* London: Overseas Development Institute, 1969.

Morgan, Dan, "The Food Aid Business," *The Washington Post,* March 9–14, 1975.

Pinstrup-Andersen, Tweeten, "The Value, Cost, and Efficiency of American Food Aid," *American Journal of Agricultural Economics,* vol. 53, no. 3 (August, 1971), pp. 431–440.

Srivastava, Uma K., et al., *Food Aid and International Economic Growth.* Ames: Iowa State University Press, 1975.

Schneider, H., *The Effects of Food Aid on Agricultural Production in Recipient Countries.* Paris: OECD Development Centre, 1975.

Shefrin, F., "Multilateral Food Aid Development: A Decade of WFP Operations," *Agriculture Abroad,* vol. 281, 1973, pp. 37–57.

Stanley, Robert G., *Food for Peace: Hope and Reality of U.S. Food Aid.* London: Gordon and Breach, 1972.

Toma, Peter A., *The Politics of Food for Peace.* Tucson: University of Arizona Press, 1967.

United States Department of Agriculture. *PL 480 Concessional Sales: History, Procedures, Negotiating and Implementing.* By Amalia Vellianitis-Fidas and Eileen Manfredi, Washington: Foreign Agricultural Economic Report no. 142, December, 1977.

United States General Accounting Office, *Disincentives to Agricultural Production in Developing Countries.* ID-76-2 November 26, 1975.

United States General Accounting Office, *Impact of U.S. Development and Food Aid in Selected Developing Countries.* ID-76-53 April 22, 1976.

United States Senate Subcommittee on Foreign Agricultural Policy of the Committee on Agriculture and Forestry, *Hearings on Foreign Food Assistance,* April 4, 1974.

Vicker, Ray. *This Hungry World.* New York: Scribner, 1975.

XI. Grain reserves

Hillman, Jimmye, D. Gale Johnson, and Roger Gray, "Food Reserve Policies for World Food Security: A Consultant Study on Alternative Approaches," Rome: FAO, ESC:CSP/75/2. Jan., 1975.

Josling, Timothy, *An International Grain Reserve Policy.* Washington: National Planning Association, 1973.

Reutlinger, Shlomo, "Simulation of World-Wide Buffer Stocks of Wheat," *American Journal of Agricultural Economics,* vol. 58, no. 1 (February, 1976), pp. 1–12.

Reutlinger, Shlomo, David Eaton, David Bigman, and David Blum, "Stabilization, Economic Efficiency and Income Distribution Implications of Grain Reserve Investments by Developing Countries: A Simulation Approach," Washington: World Bank working paper, 1976.

Sarris, Alexander H., Philip C. Abbott, and Lance Taylor, "International Grain Reserves and Food Aid" (paper prepared for the Overseas Development Council. October 1976).

Schnittker, John A., "Grain Reserves—Now," *Foreign Policy,* No. 20, (Fall, 1975), pp. 225–231.

Trezise, Philip H., *Rebuilding Grain Reserves.* Washington: Brookings Institution, 1976.

United States Congress, House of Representatives, Committee on Foreign Affairs, Subcommittee on International Organization and Movements, *International Food Reserves: Background and Current Proposals.* Washington: U.S. Government Printing Office, 1974.

United States General Accounting Office, *Grain Reserves: A Potential U.S. Food Policy Tool.* March 26, 1976, OSP-76-16.

XII. Government publications

Ceres. Rome: FAO, bimonthly.

Food Aid Bulletin. Rome: FAO, quarterly.

Food and Nutrition. Rome: FAO, quarterly.

Foreign Agricultural Trade of the United States (FATUS). Washington: USDA, monthly; it contains extensive US and world statistics.

Foreign Agriculture. Washington: USDA, weekly.

The State of Food and Agriculture. Rome: FAO, bi-annual.

World Agricultural Situation. Washington: USDA, June, September, December.

Index

Accountability: in global food system, 231–32; of grain companies, 232–33; in distribution, 234

Acquisition policy, 197

Acreage: limitation, 43–44, 217, 218; diversion, 45, 45n–46n; allocation of, 133n; allotments, 152; tradeoff, 185; wheat, 231, 271; feedgrain, 271

Administrative Committee on Coordination (ACC), 243, 254

Advisory Council on Agricultural Policy (of Japan), 90

Affluence: and food system, 22; and diet, 89, 91, 98; and equity, 148

AFL-CIO, 69

Africa, 15, 105, 109–10, 142, 143, 162, 206, 208, 225, 274; grain trade in, 8; sub-Saharan, 9, 106, 108, 112; demand for food in, 10; production in, 16; calorie intakes in, 18, 173, 173n; peasantry of, 37; EEC trade concessions to, 87; politics of distribution in, 117–22; reserve stocks in, 118, 119, 120, 121; droughts in, 118, 119–22; consumption in, 118, 181–82, 210n; low priority of agriculture in, 119; fair price shops in, 120–21; farmers of, 121; problems of poor in, 121; urban workers of, 121, 122; food aid to, 121–22; military coups in, 122; agricultural expenditures in, 122–24; land redistribution in, 139; malnutrition in, 169, 169n, 238–39; leaders of, 253; grain insurance program for, 278–82

African Development Bank (AFDB), 30

African Rural Development Study (ARDS), 130n

Agency for International Development (AID), 43, 245–46, 247

Agribusiness, 28, 72, 283; and global food regime, 35–36; multinational corporations in, 35–36; USDA bias toward, 76–77; American, 188, 192–95

Agricultural Act of 1970, 45

Agricultural assistance, 290

Agricultural commodities, 84, 184, 184n, 204; trade barrier to, 266; capital-intensive, 270; labor-intensive, 270; land-intensive, 270

Agricultural development, 24, 26, 34, 35, 103, 111, 214, 223n, 234, 243; of Communist countries, 24; and IFAD, 31; Third World, 91, 97, 98, 127–36, 224–25; international, 91, 290; management of, 143; in OPEC, 226

Agricultural economists, 178

Agricultural education, 295

Agricultural inputs, 174, 175, 185, 265; allocation of, in Third World, 189–90; access to, 191; socially optimal, 191; investment in, 198; price of, 275

Agricultural modernization, 16–17, 231; in Japan, 87; finance of, 295

Agricultural planning, 130

Agricultural policy. See Farm policy

Agricultural Policy Committee, 73

Agricultural Prices Commission, 133n

Agricultural sector: intervention in, 211

Agriculture: expenditures on, 114, 122–24, 125, 128, 234, 245, 259n; in Africa, 117; communalization of, 132; subsidization of, 184n; intensive, 192; extensive, 192, 195; labor-inten-

DATE DUE
